INUYASHIKI 3

HIROYA OKU

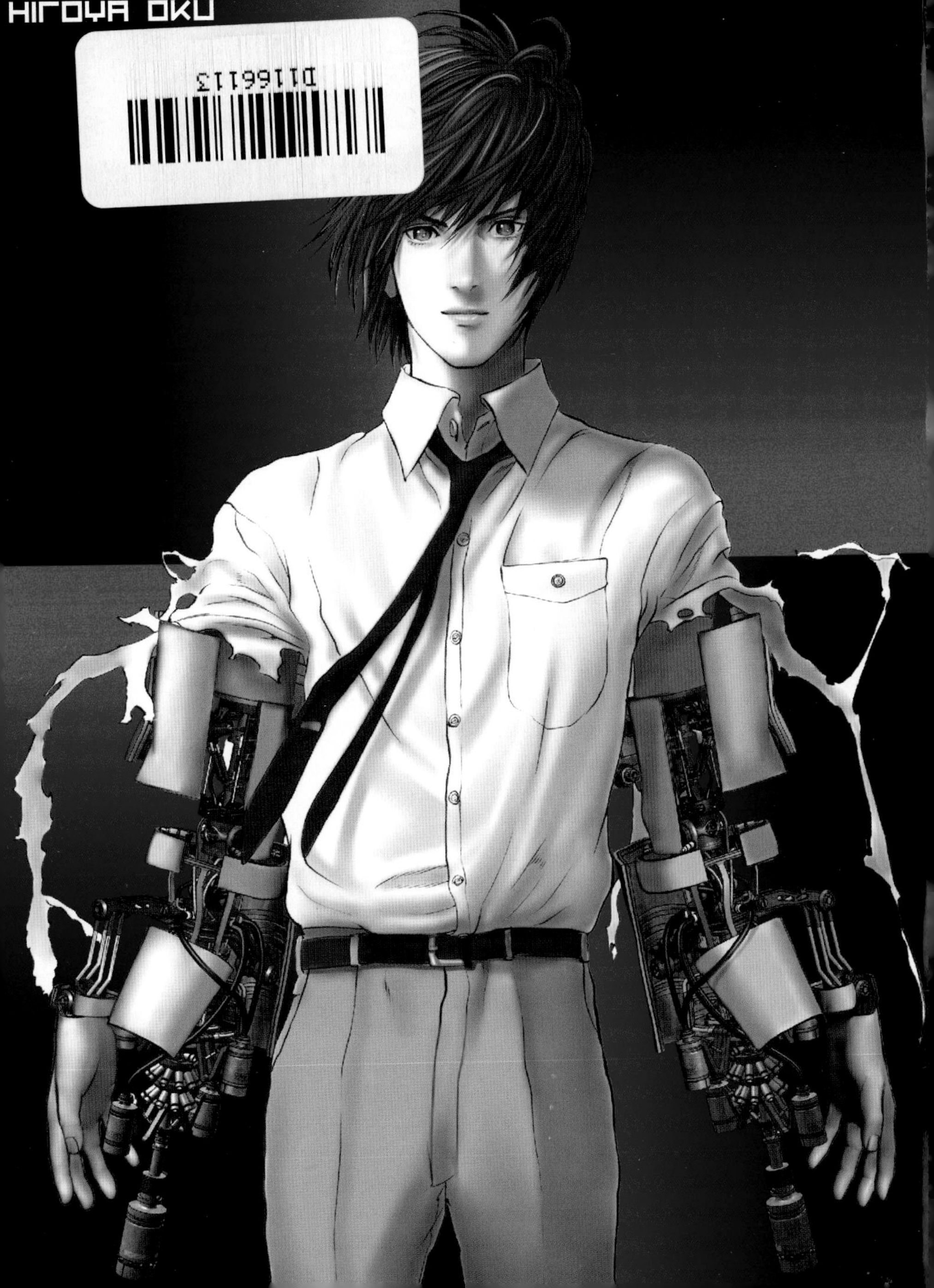

INUYASHIKI 3 CONTENTS

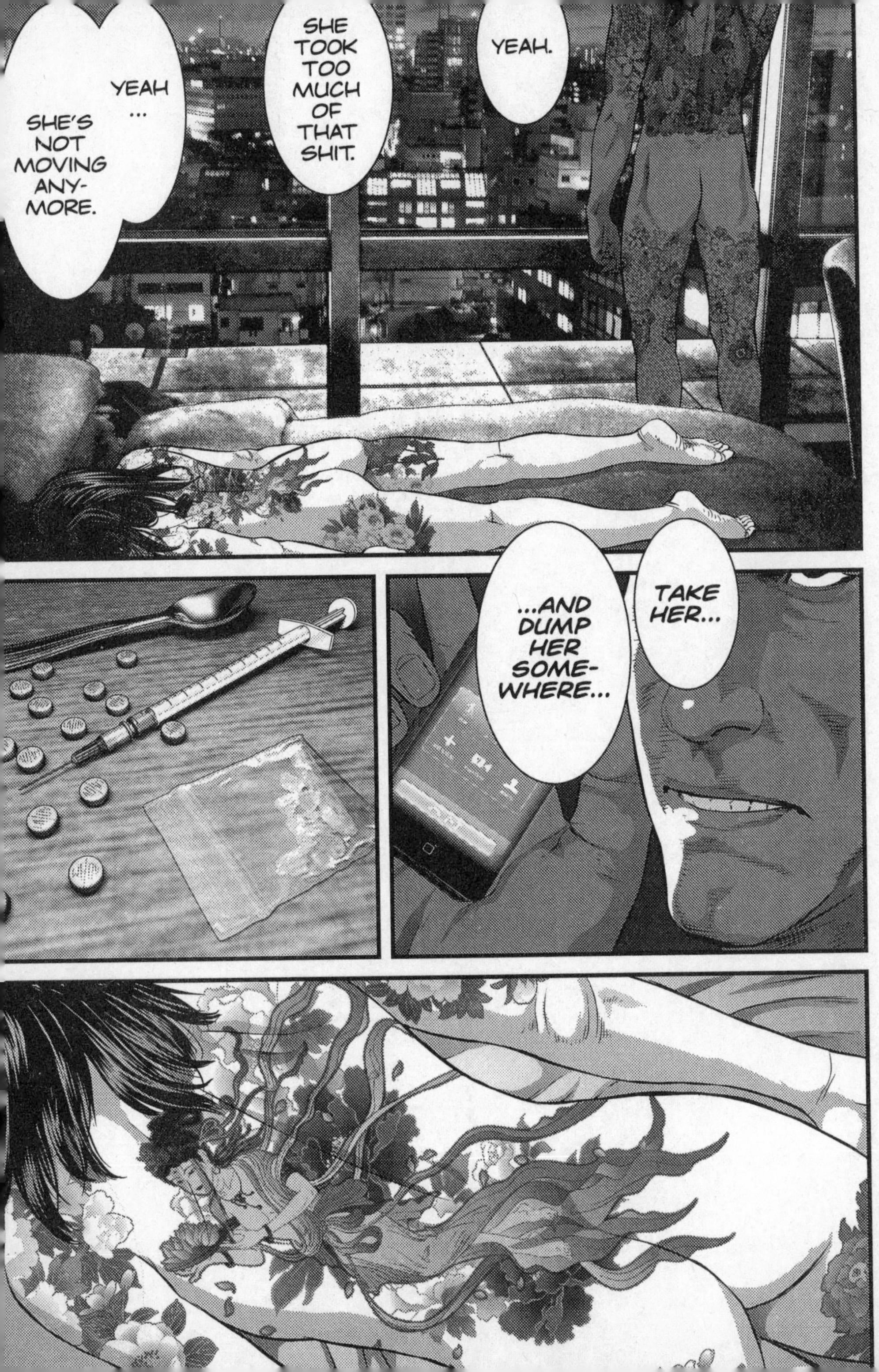
YEAH.
SHE TOOK TOO MUCH OF THAT SHIT.
YEAH ... SHE'S NOT MOVING ANY-MORE.
TAKE HER...
...AND DUMP HER SOME-WHERE...

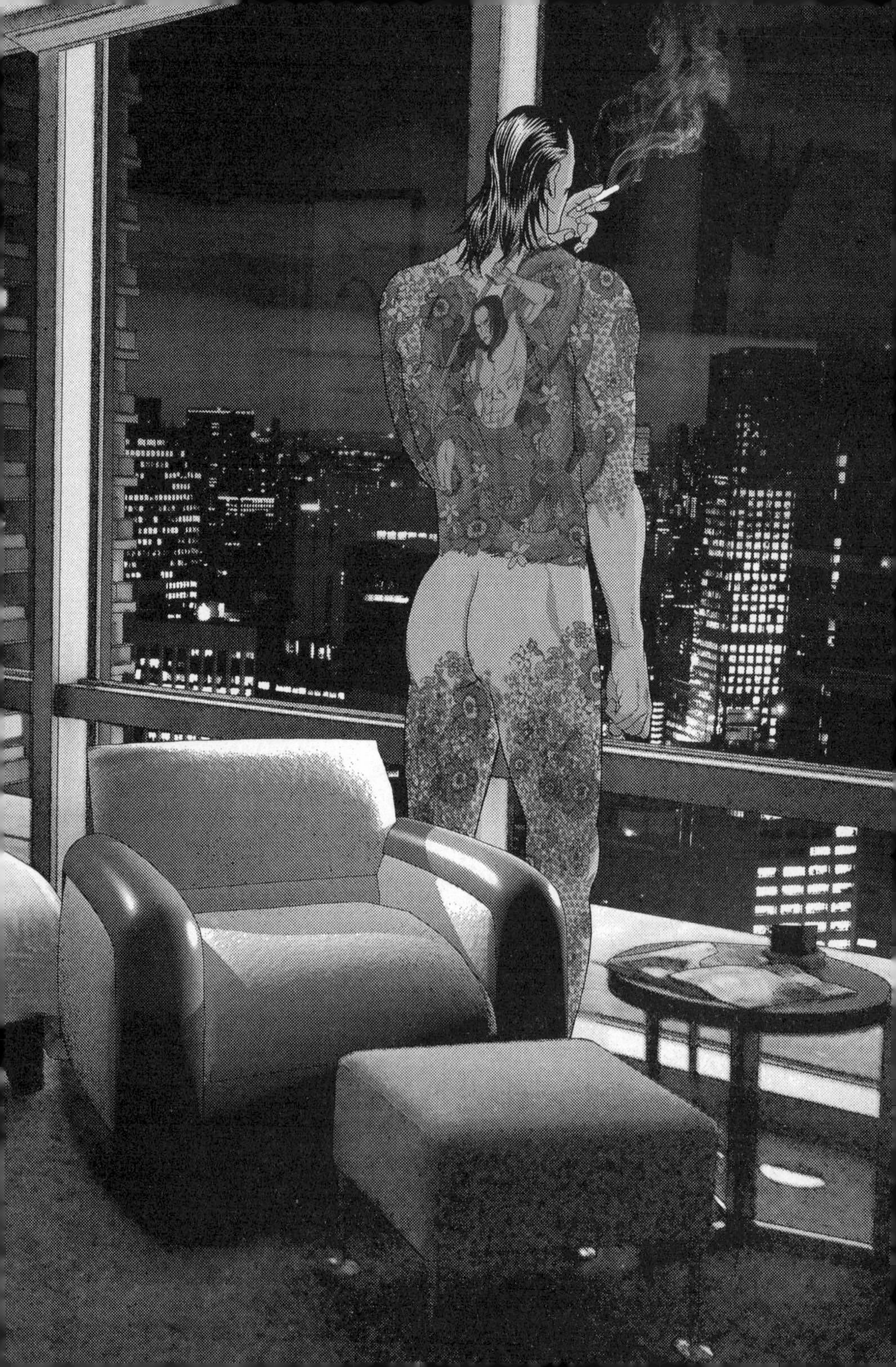

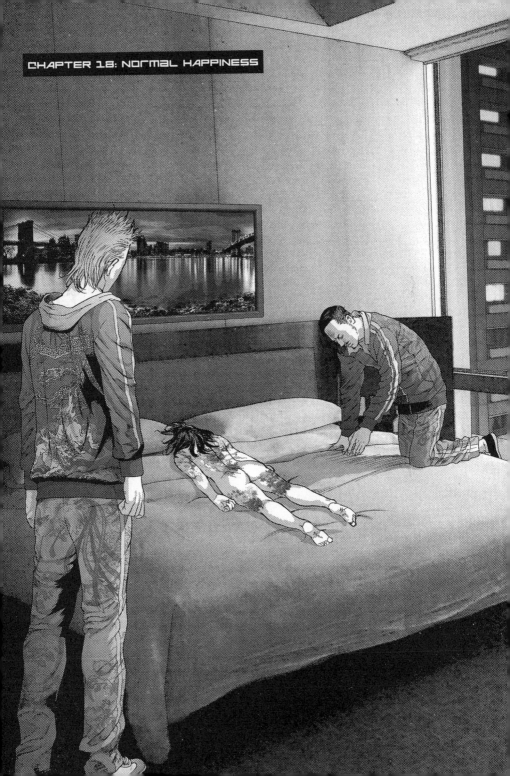

CHAPTER 18: NORMAL HAPPINESS

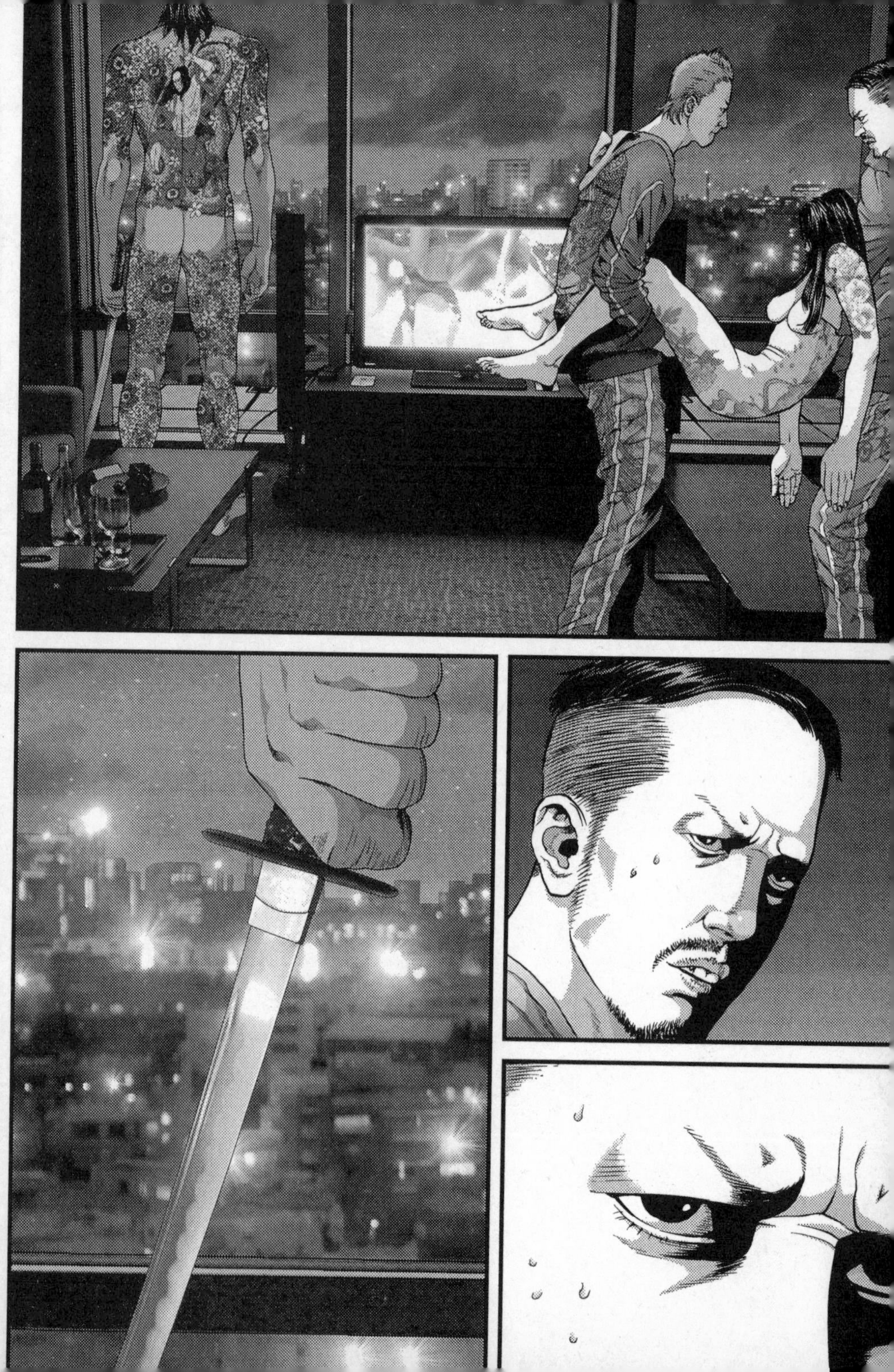

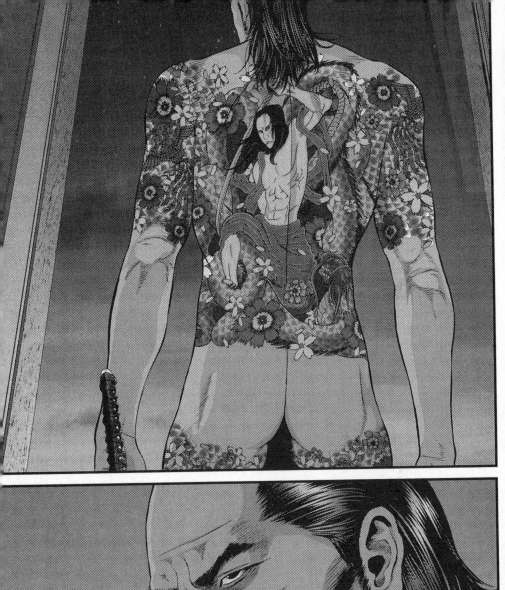

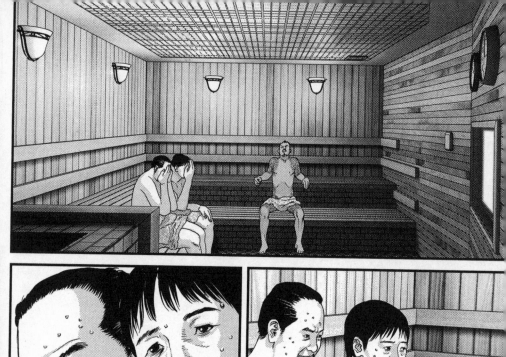

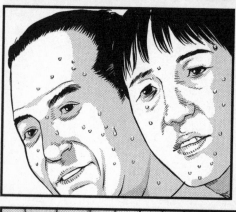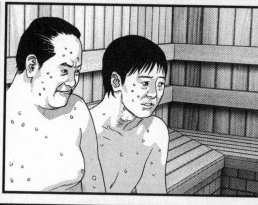

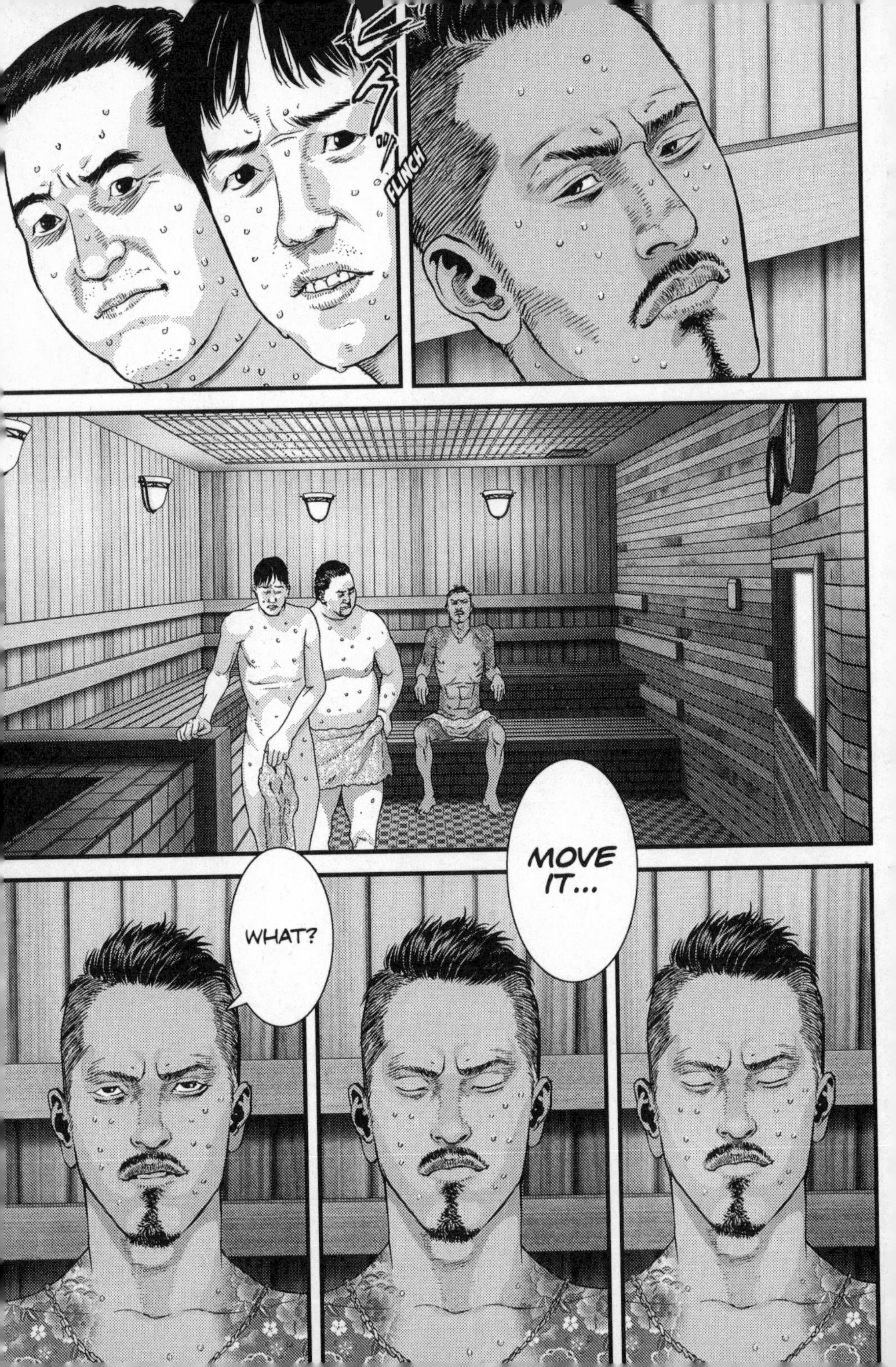
FLINCH
MOVE IT...
WHAT?

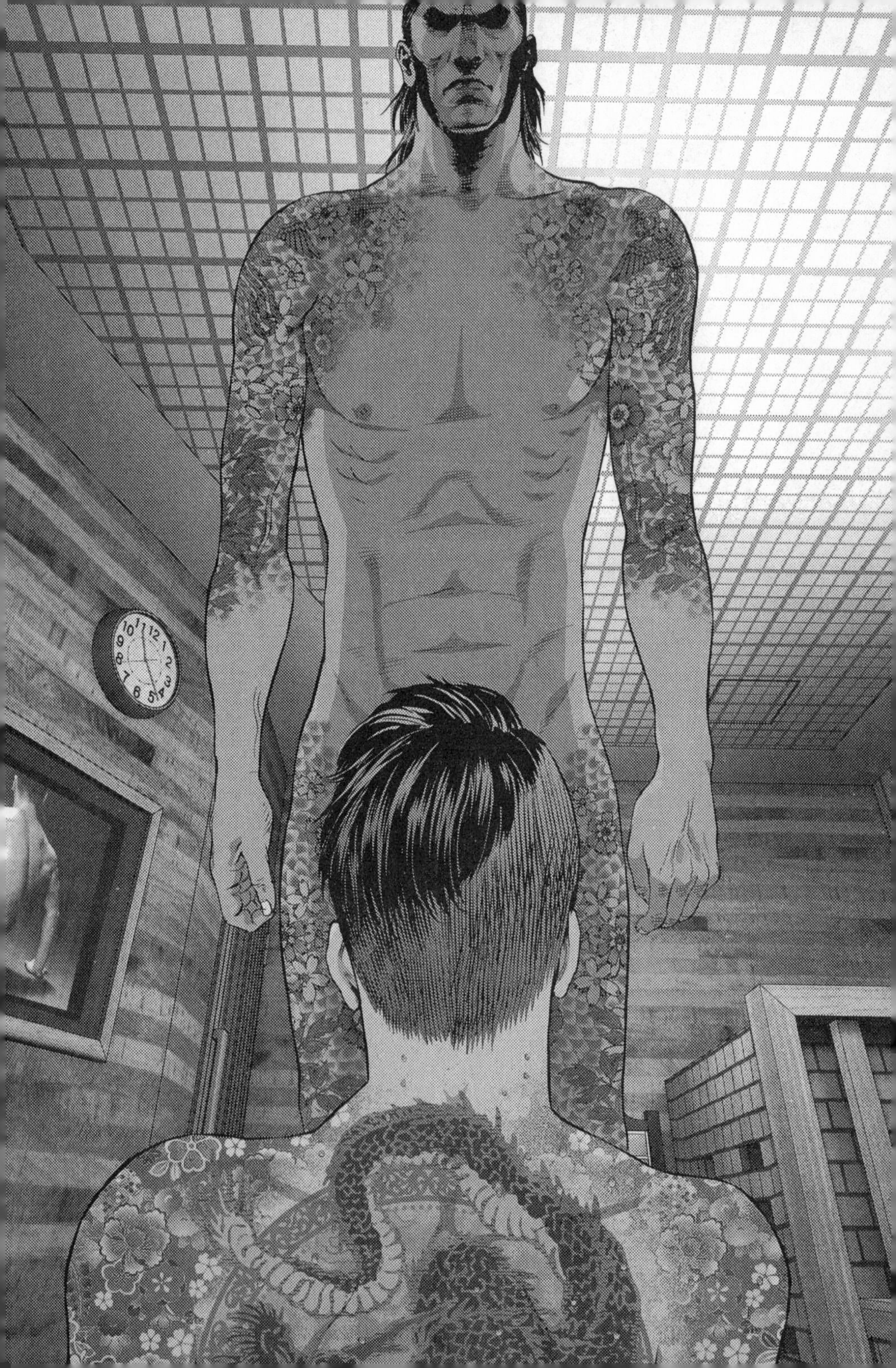

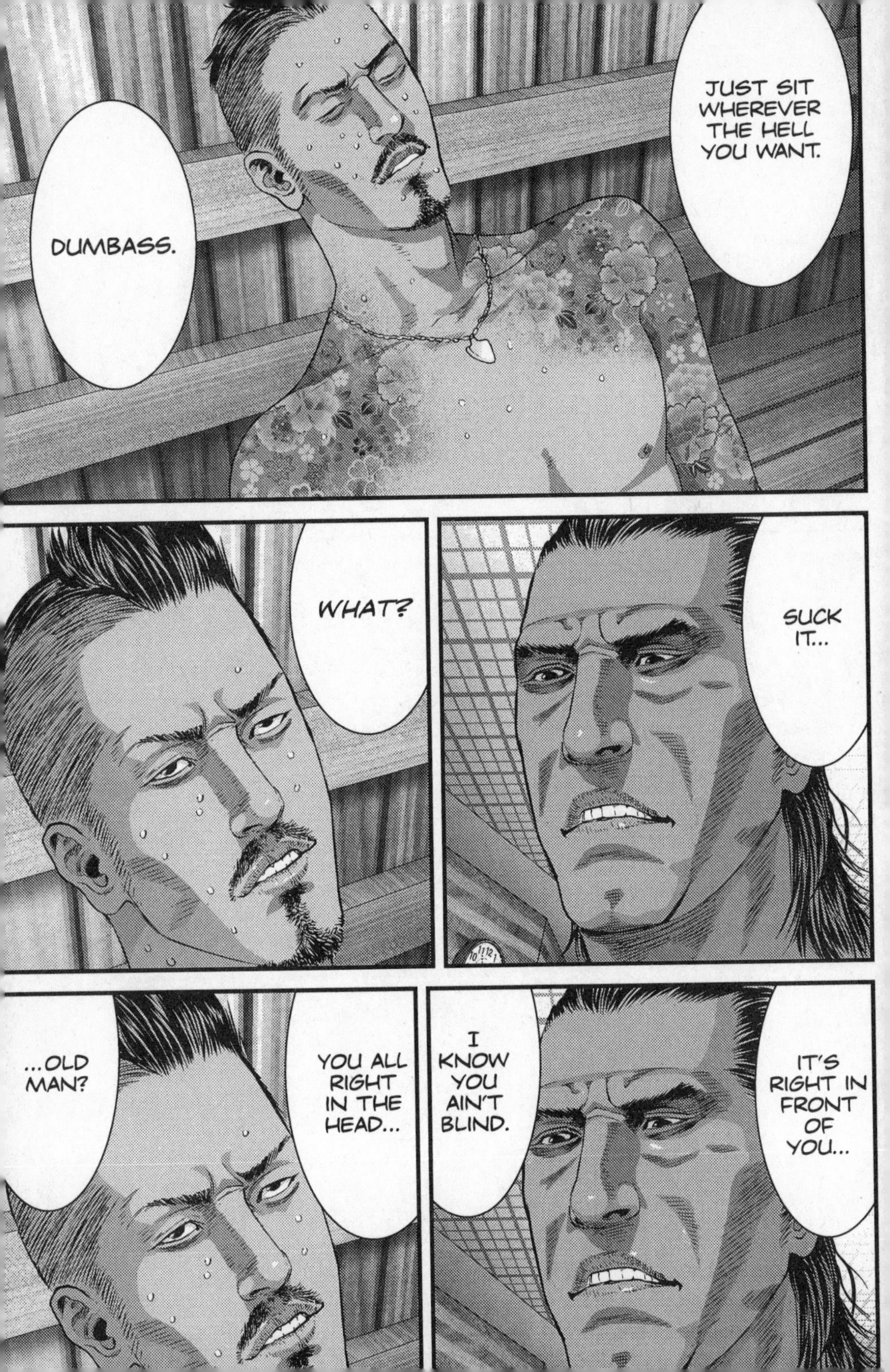
JUST SIT WHEREVER THE HELL YOU WANT.
DUMBASS.
SUCK IT...
WHAT?
IT'S RIGHT IN FRONT OF YOU...
I KNOW YOU AIN'T BLIND.
YOU ALL RIGHT IN THE HEAD...
...OLD MAN?

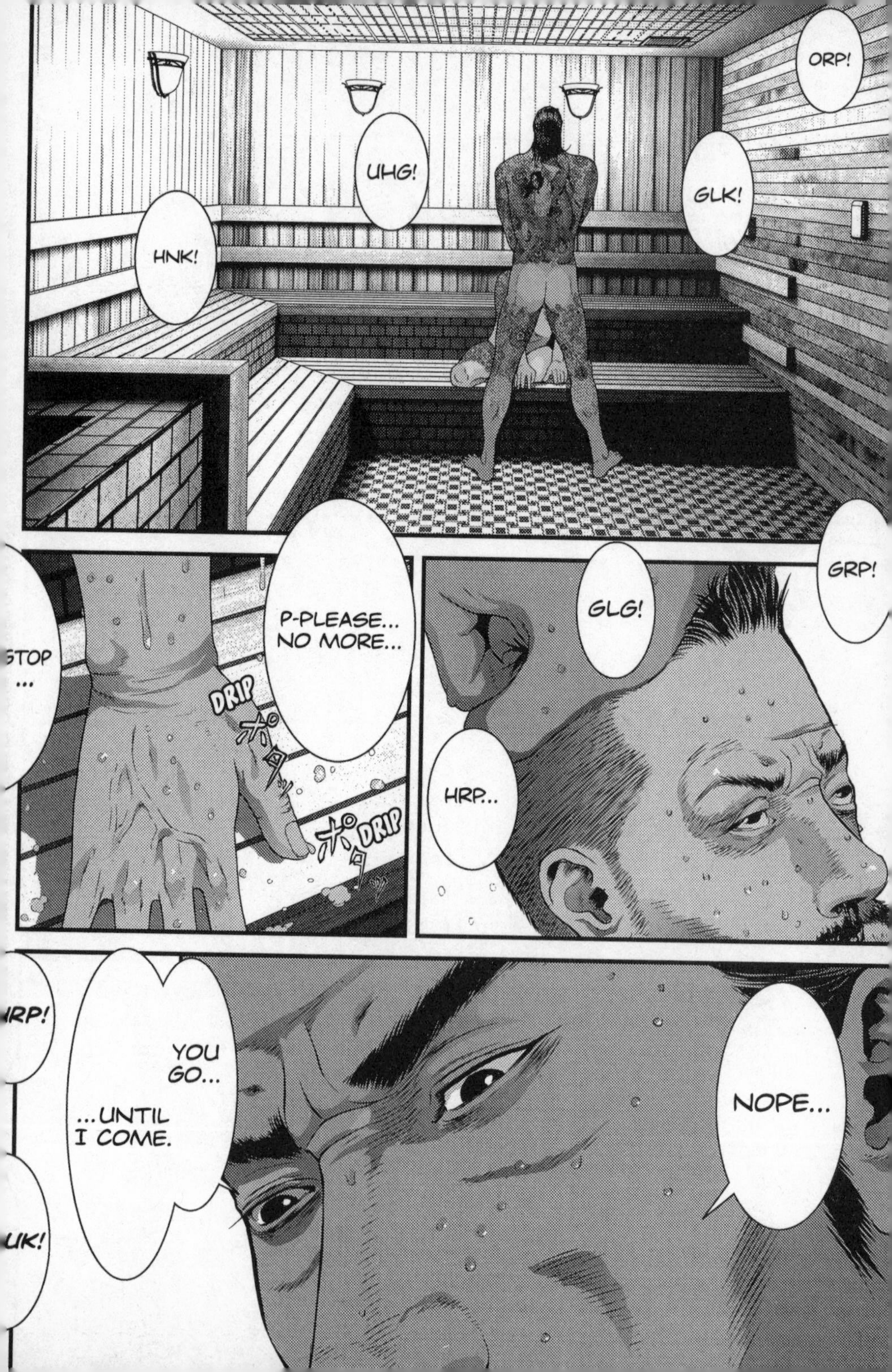
ORP!
GLK!
UHG!
HNK!
GRP!
GLG!
HRP...
P-PLEASE... NO MORE...
DRIP
ポタッ
ポタ
DRIP
STOP ...
NOPE...
YOU GO...
...UNTIL I COME.
RP!
UK!

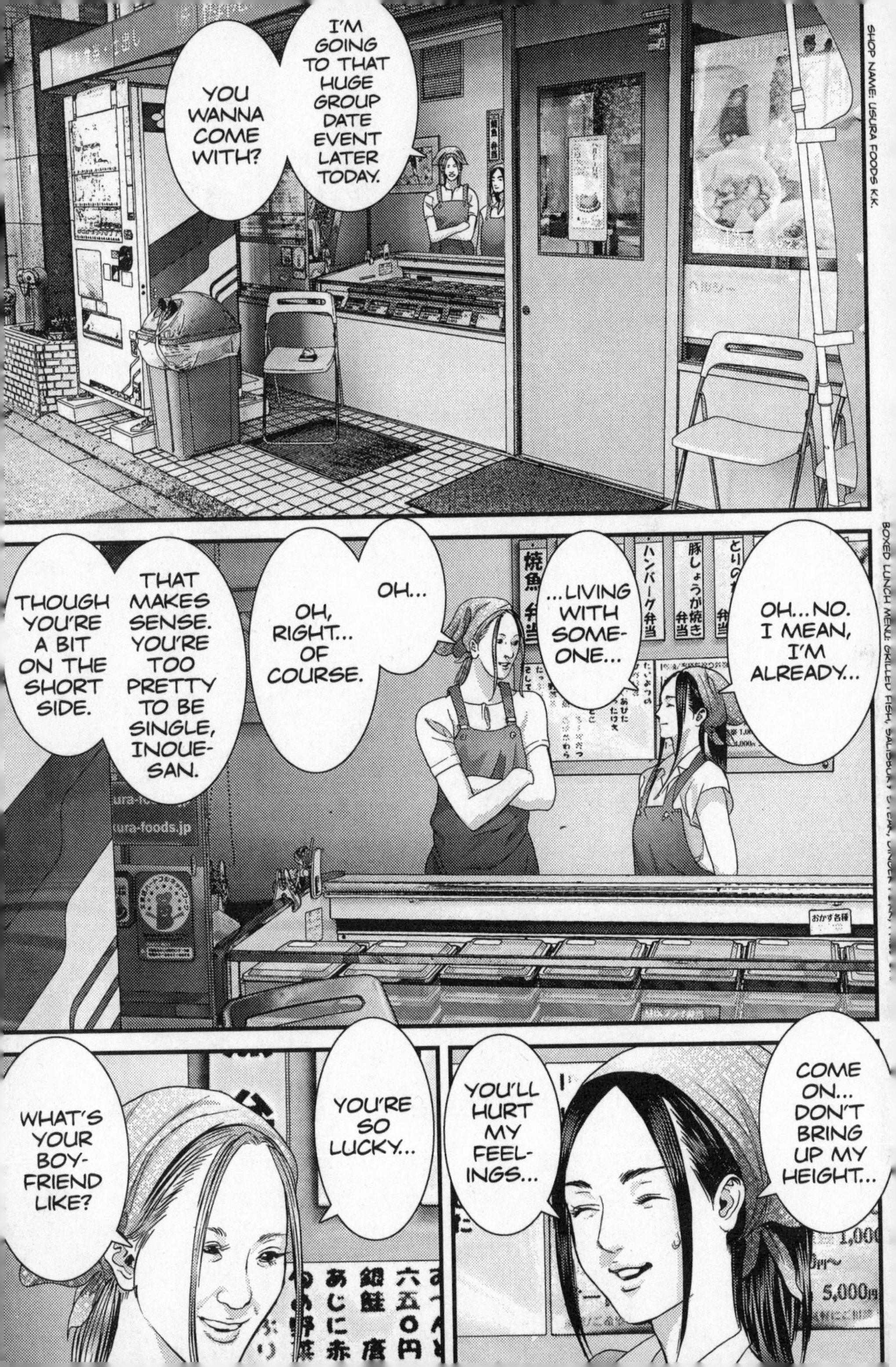
SHOP NAME: USURA FOODS K.K.
I'M GOING TO THAT HUGE GROUP DATE EVENT LATER TODAY.
YOU WANNA COME WITH?
BOXED LUNCH MENU: GRILLED FISH, SALISBURY STEAK, GINGER
OH...NO. I MEAN, I'M ALREADY...
...LIVING WITH SOME-ONE...
OH...
OH, RIGHT... OF COURSE.
THAT MAKES SENSE. YOU'RE TOO PRETTY TO BE SINGLE, INOUE-SAN.
THOUGH YOU'RE A BIT ON THE SHORT SIDE.
COME ON... DON'T BRING UP MY HEIGHT...
YOU'LL HURT MY FEEL-INGS...
YOU'RE SO LUCKY...
WHAT'S YOUR BOY-FRIEND LIKE?

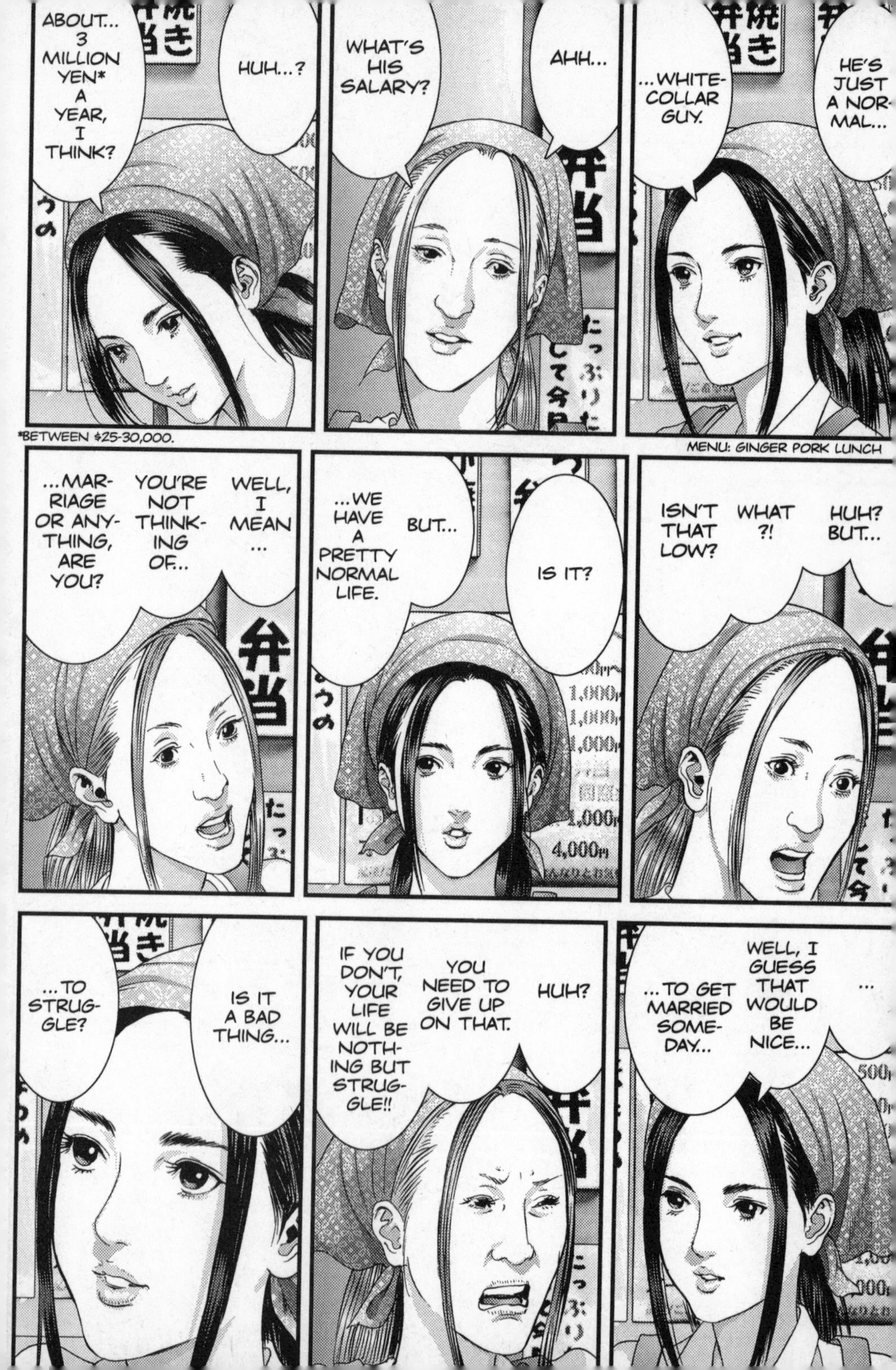
HE'S JUST A NORMAL...
...WHITE-COLLAR GUY.
AHH...
WHAT'S HIS SALARY?
HUH...?
ABOUT... 3 MILLION YEN* A YEAR, I THINK?
MENU: GINGER PORK LUNCH
HUH? BUT...
WHAT?!
ISN'T THAT LOW?
IS IT?
BUT...
...WE HAVE A PRETTY NORMAL LIFE.
WELL, I MEAN...
YOU'RE NOT THINKING OF...
...MARRIAGE OR ANYTHING, ARE YOU?
...
WELL, I GUESS THAT WOULD BE NICE...
...TO GET MARRIED SOMEDAY...
HUH?
YOU NEED TO GIVE UP ON THAT.
IF YOU DON'T, YOUR LIFE WILL BE NOTHING BUT STRUGGLE!!
IS IT A BAD THING...
...TO STRUGGLE?

*BETWEEN $25-30,000.

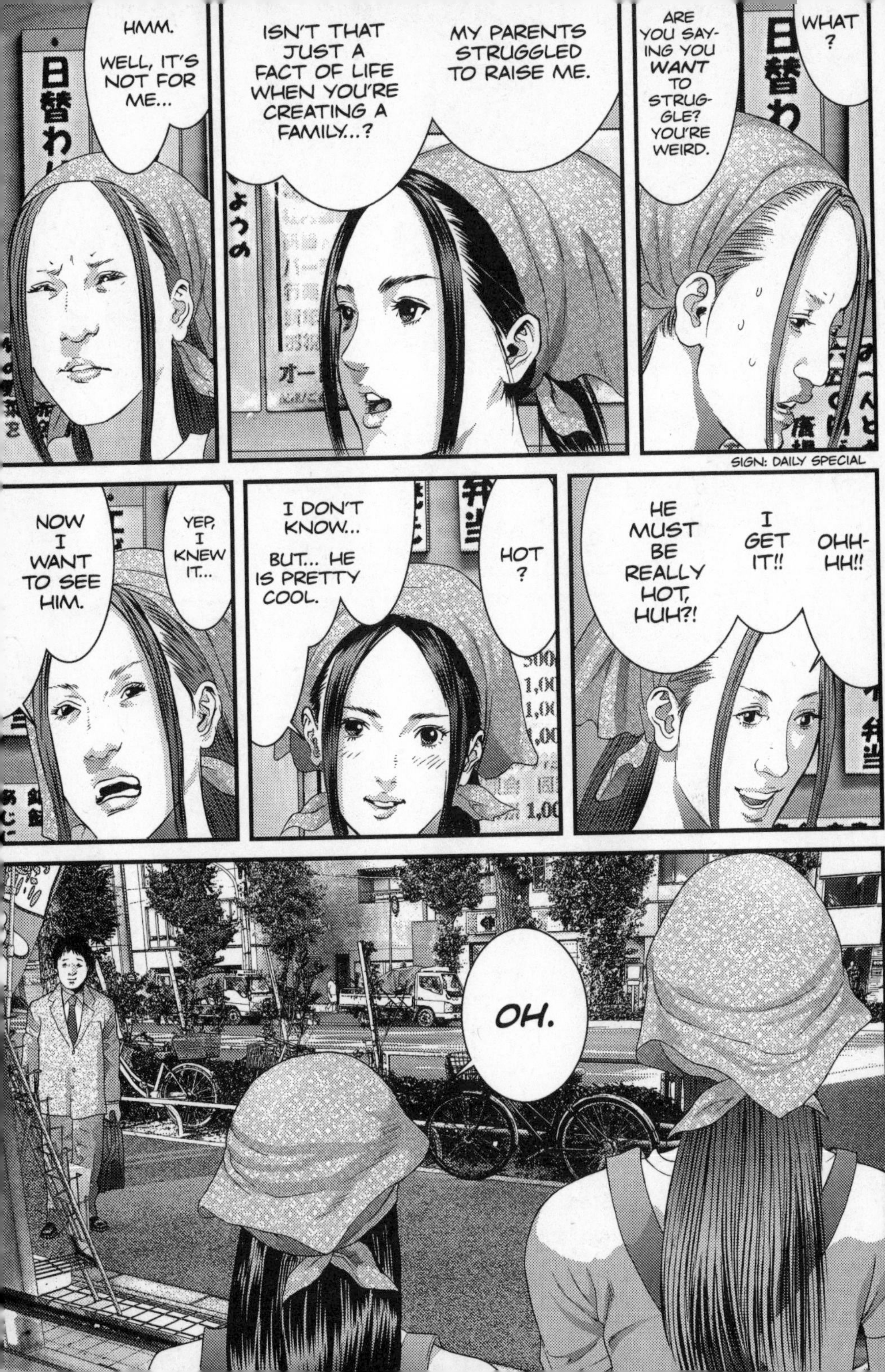
WHAT?
ARE YOU SAYING YOU WANT TO STRUGGLE? YOU'RE WEIRD.
MY PARENTS STRUGGLED TO RAISE ME.
ISN'T THAT JUST A FACT OF LIFE WHEN YOU'RE CREATING A FAMILY...?
HMM. WELL, IT'S NOT FOR ME...
SIGN: DAILY SPECIAL
OHH-HH!!
I GET IT!!
HE MUST BE REALLY HOT, HUH?!
HOT?
I DON'T KNOW... BUT... HE IS PRETTY COOL.
YEP, I KNEW IT...
NOW I WANT TO SEE HIM.
OH.

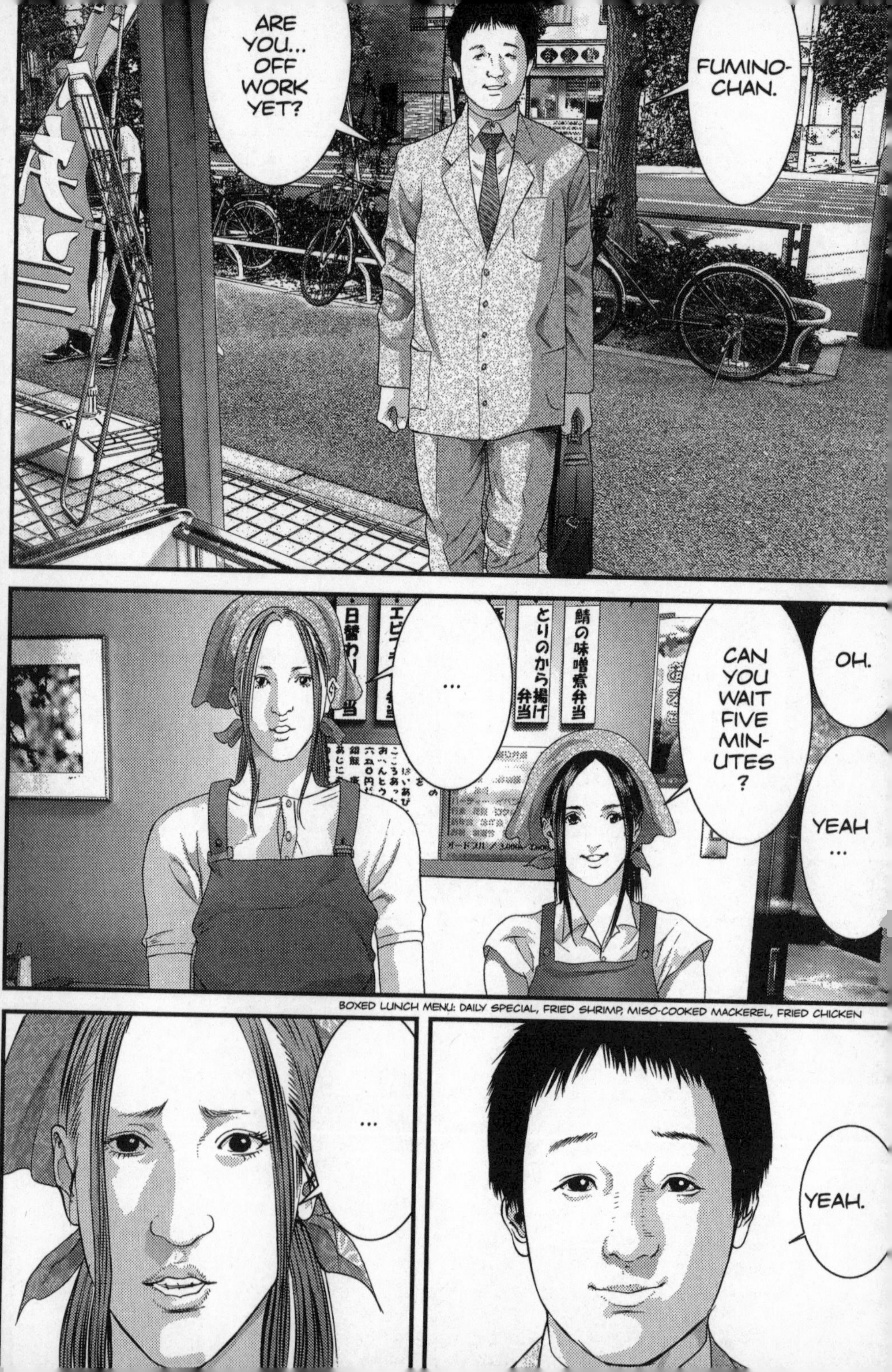
FUMINO-CHAN.
ARE YOU... OFF WORK YET?
鯖の味噌煮弁当
とりのから揚げ弁当
OH.
CAN YOU WAIT FIVE MIN-UTES?
YEAH ...
...
BOXED LUNCH MENU: DAILY SPECIAL, FRIED SHRIMP, MISO-COOKED MACKEREL, FRIED CHICKEN
YEAH.
...

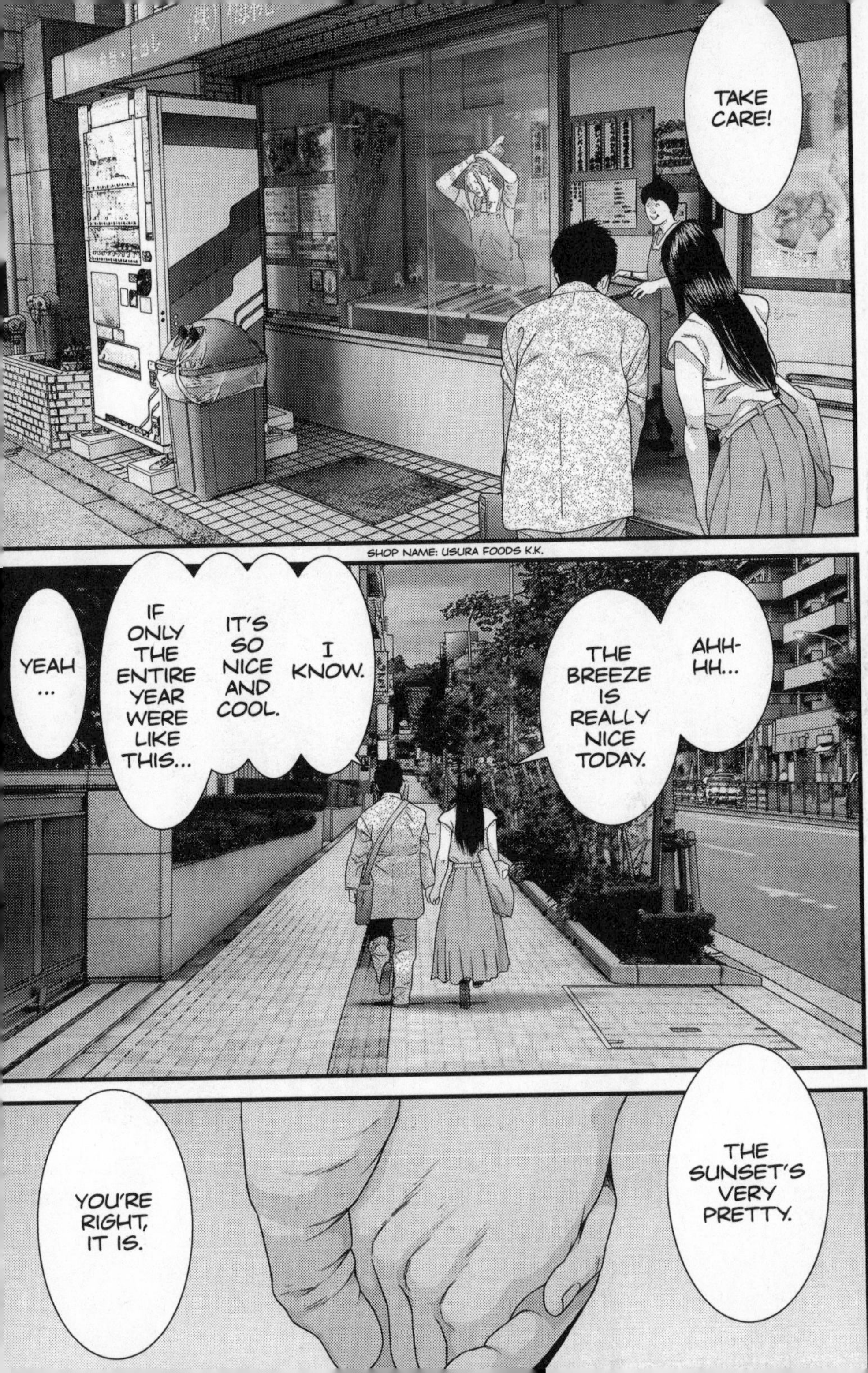
TAKE CARE!
SHOP NAME: USURA FOODS K.K.
AHH-HH...
THE BREEZE IS REALLY NICE TODAY.
I KNOW.
IT'S SO NICE AND COOL.
IF ONLY THE ENTIRE YEAR WERE LIKE THIS...
YEAH ...
THE SUNSET'S VERY PRETTY.
YOU'RE RIGHT, IT IS.

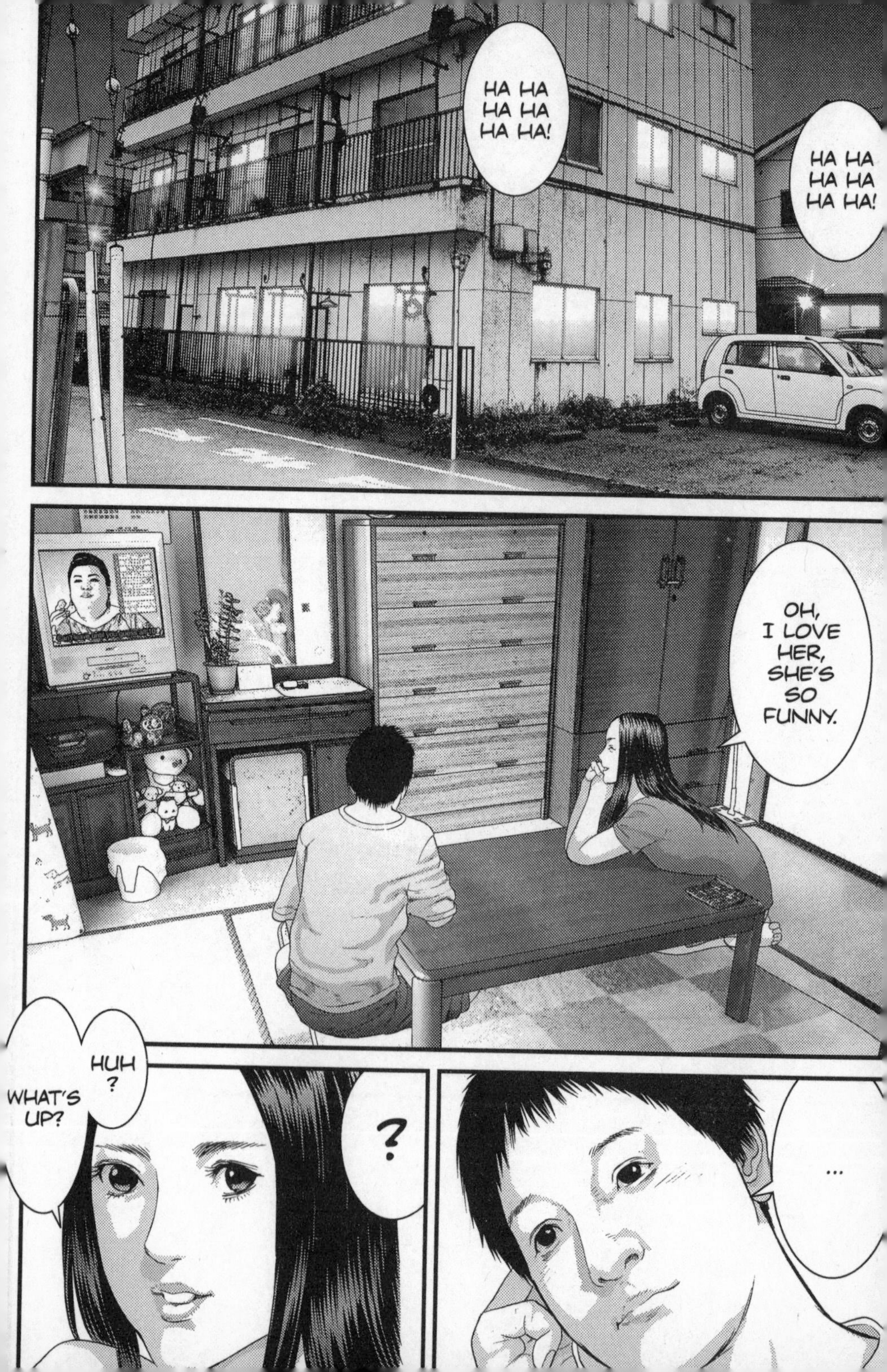
HA HA HA HA HA HA!
HA HA HA HA HA HA!
OH, I LOVE HER, SHE'S SO FUNNY.
...
?
HUH ?
WHAT'S UP?

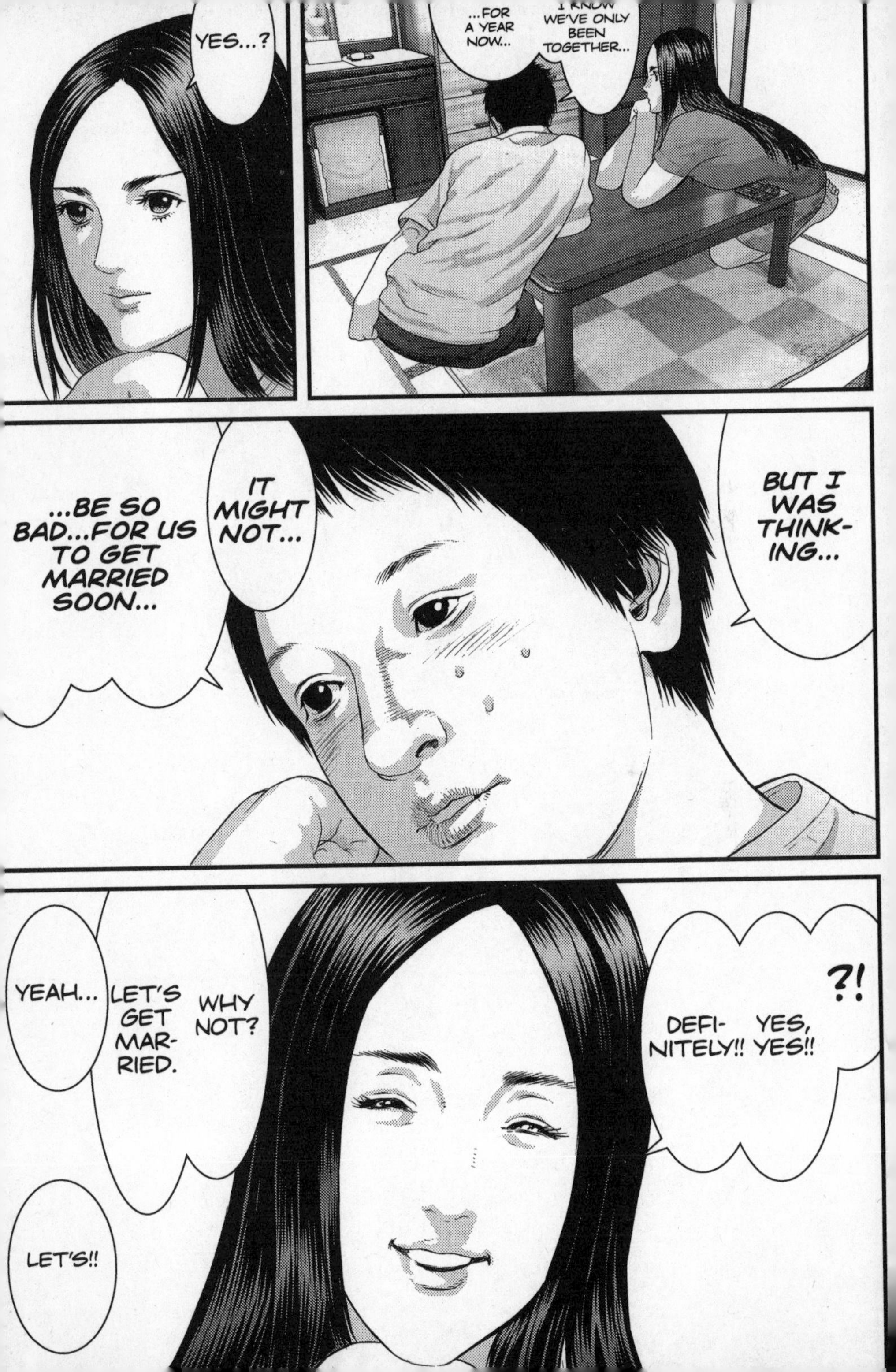
I KNOW WE'VE ONLY BEEN TOGETHER...
...FOR A YEAR NOW...
YES...?
BUT I WAS THINKING-ING...
IT MIGHT NOT...
...BE SO BAD...FOR US TO GET MARRIED SOON...
?!
YES, YES!!
DEFINITELY!!
WHY NOT?
LET'S GET MARRIED.
YEAH...
LET'S!!

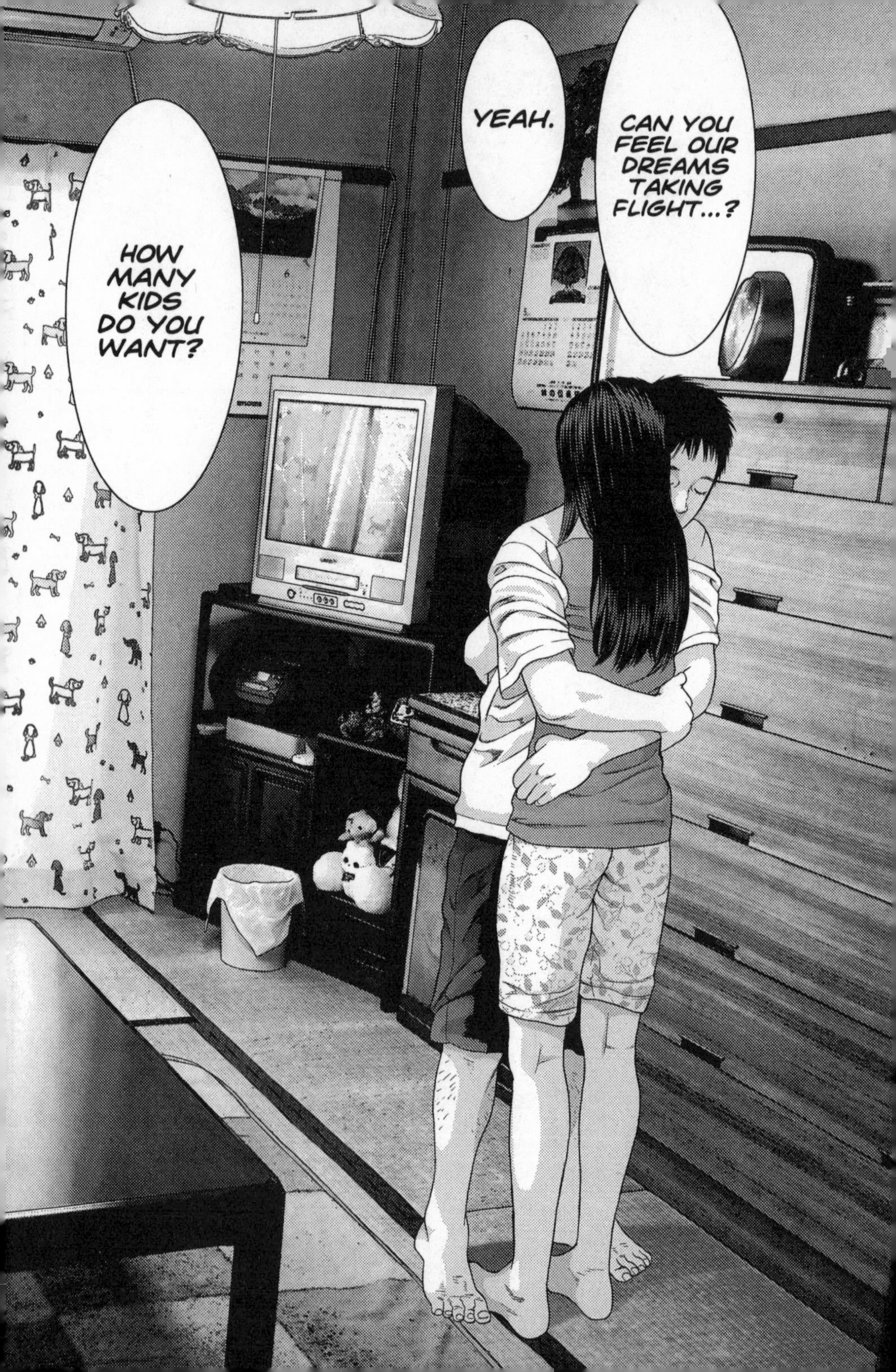
CAN YOU FEEL OUR DREAMS TAKING FLIGHT...?
YEAH.
HOW MANY KIDS DO YOU WANT?

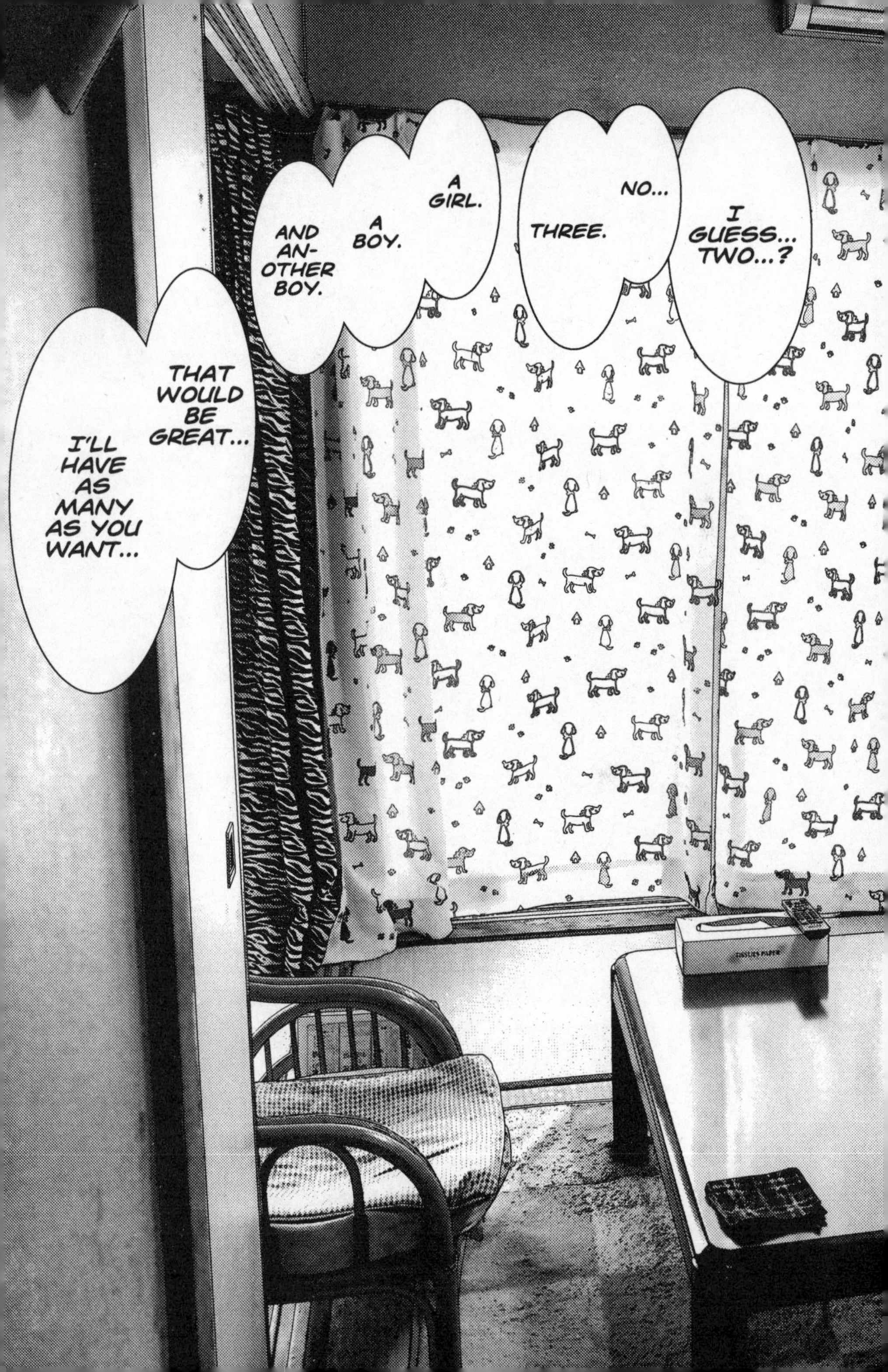
I GUESS... TWO...?
NO... THREE.
A GIRL.
A BOY.
AND AN-OTHER BOY.
THAT WOULD BE GREAT...
I'LL HAVE AS MANY AS YOU WANT...

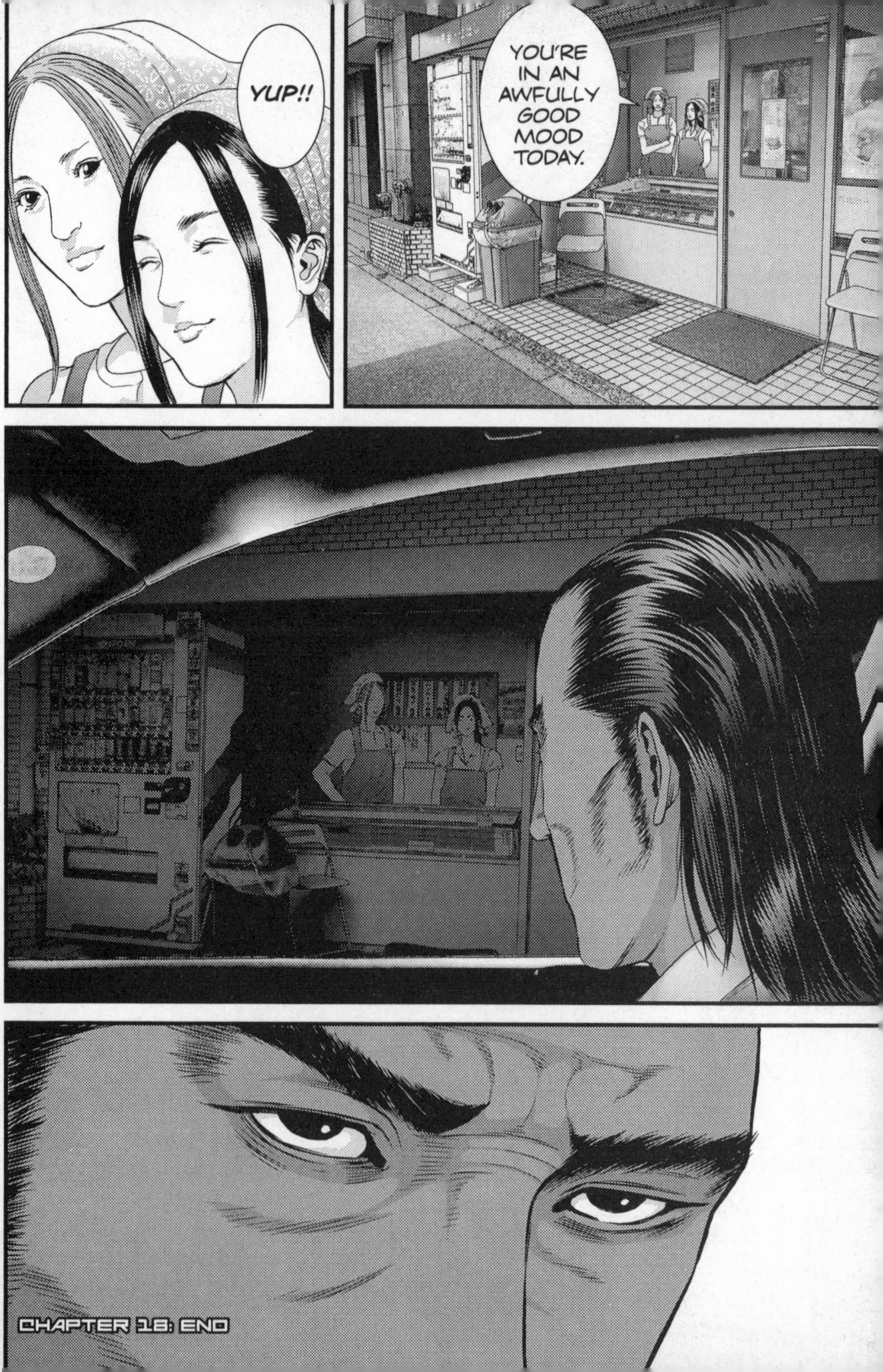
YOU'RE IN AN AWFULLY GOOD MOOD TODAY.
YUP!!
CHAPTER 18: END

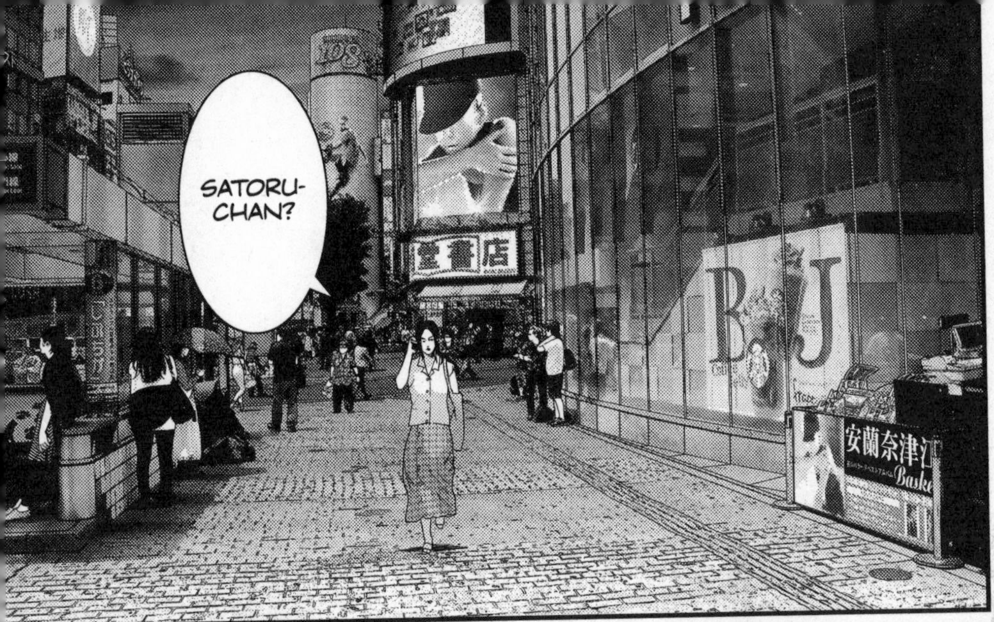
SATORU-CHAN?
安蘭奈津江
Basket

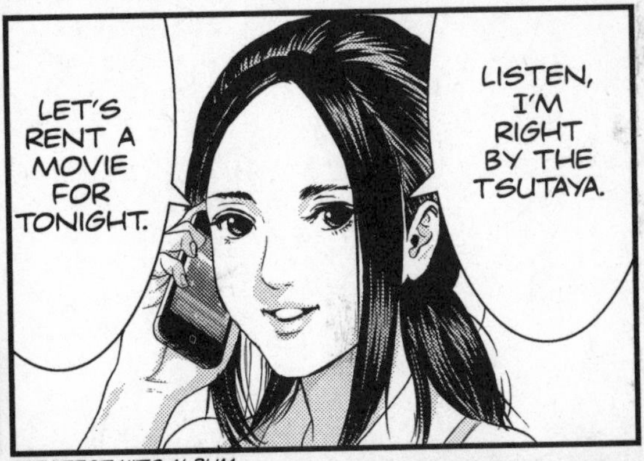
LISTEN, I'M RIGHT BY THE TSUTAYA.
LET'S RENT A MOVIE FOR TONIGHT.

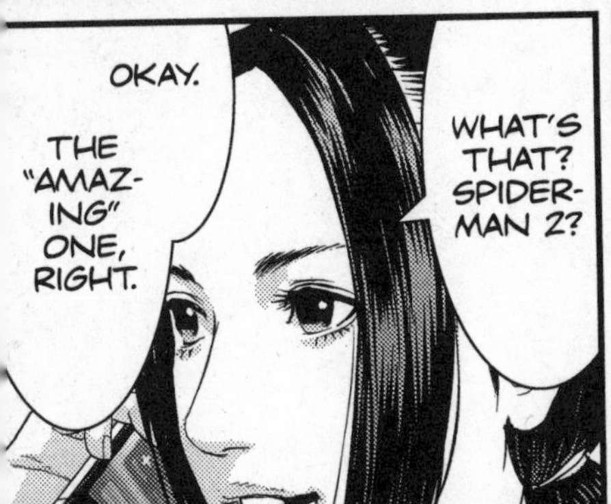
WHAT'S THAT? SPIDER-MAN 2?
OKAY.
THE "AMAZING" ONE, RIGHT.

POSTER: NATSUE ARAN, HER FIRST ALL-BALLAD GREATEST HITS ALBUM

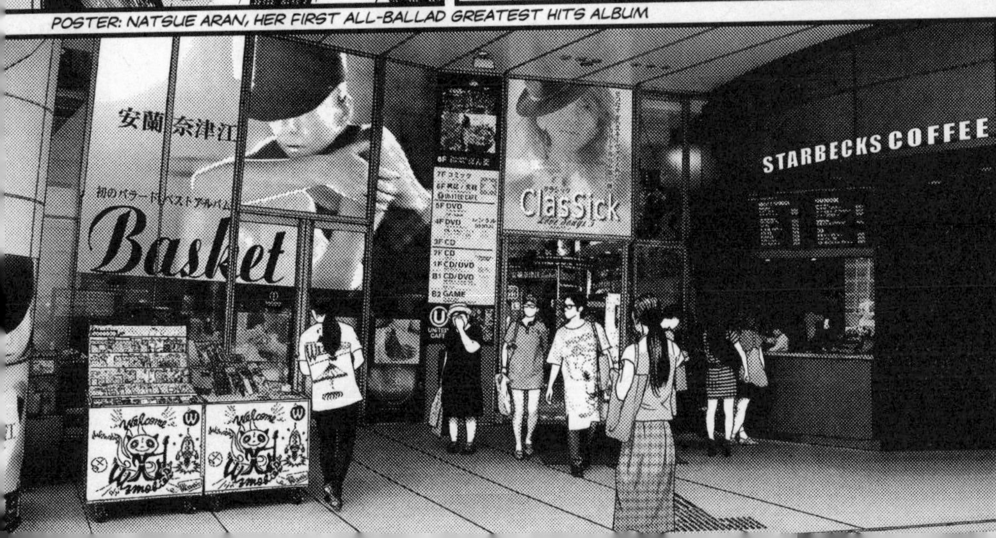
安蘭 奈津江
初のバラードベストアルバム
Basket
ClasSick
STARBECKS COFFEE

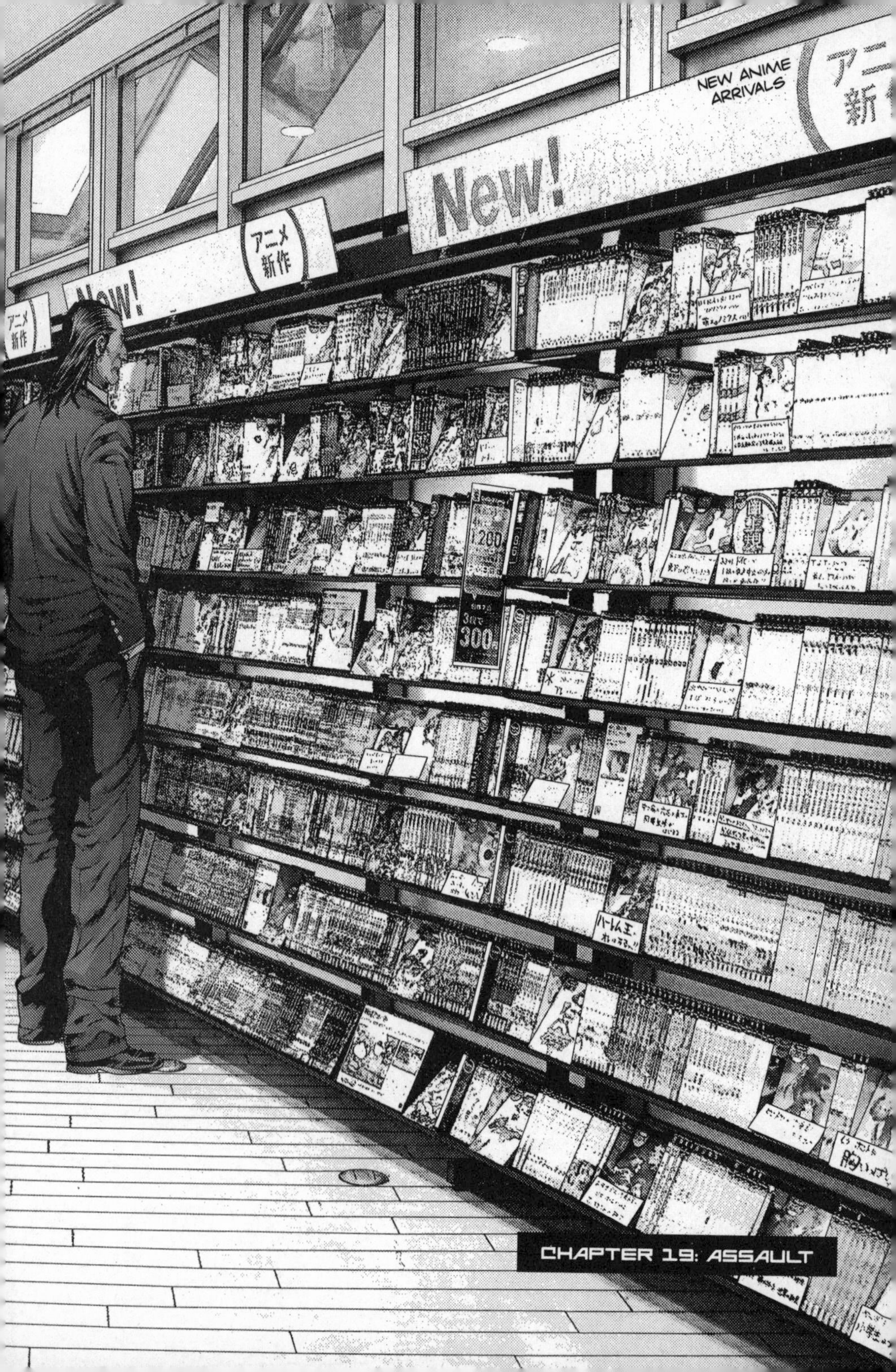
NEW ANIME ARRIVALS
アニ
新
New!
アニメ
新作
New!
アニメ
新作
1200
300
CHAPTER 19: ASSAULT

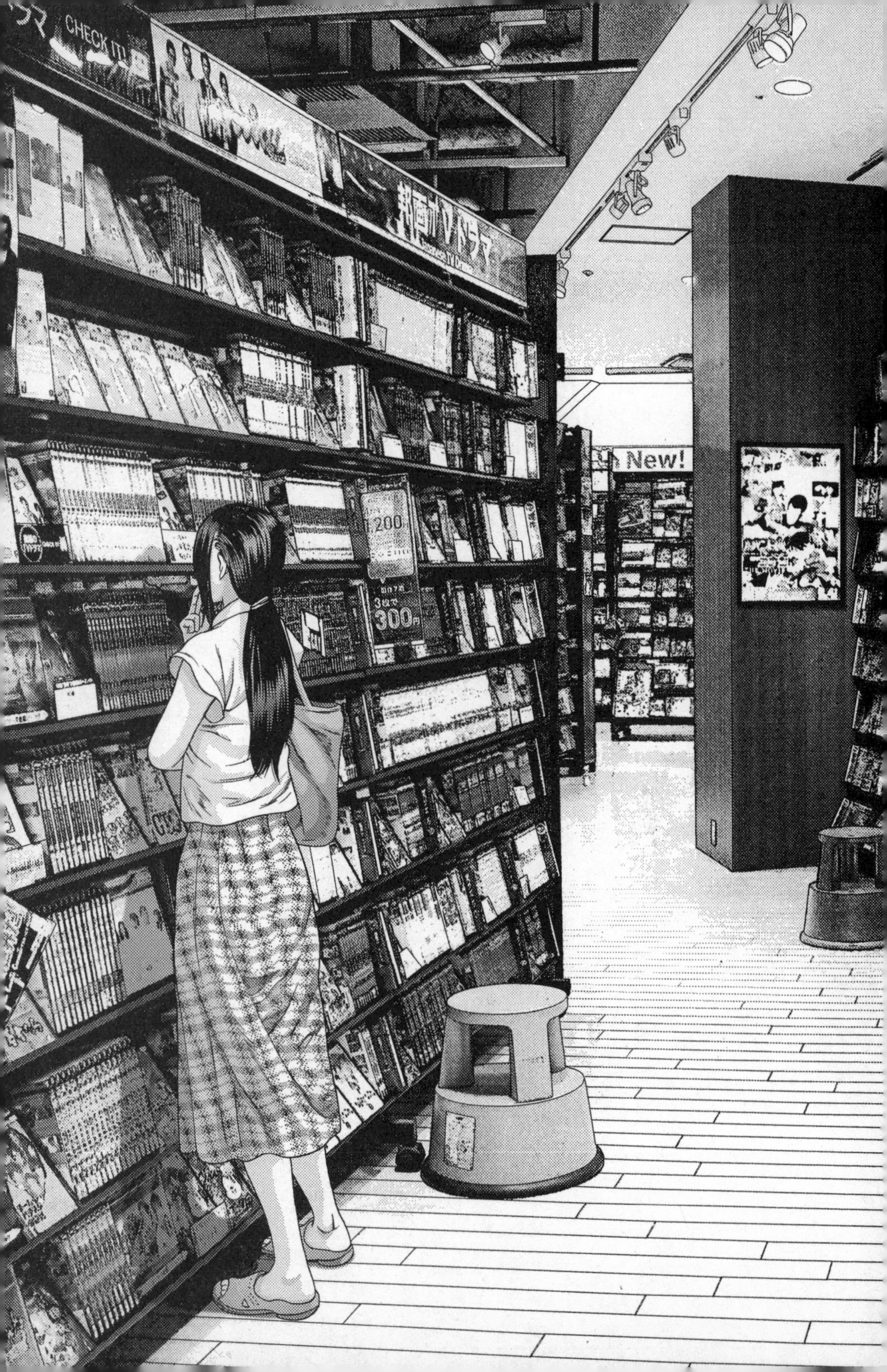
CHECK IT!
邦画&TVドラマ
200
3枚で
300円
New!

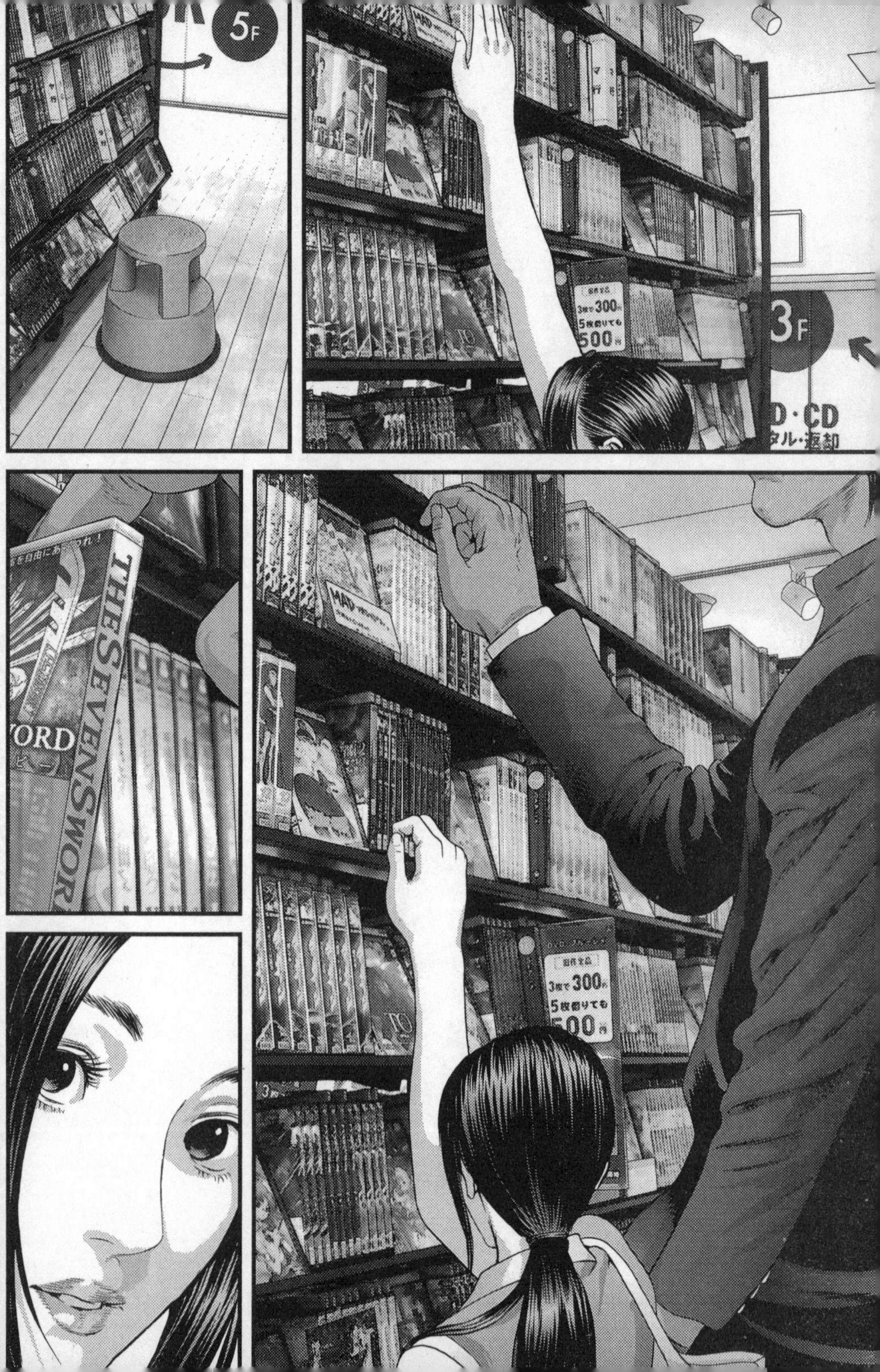
3枚で300円
5枚借りても
500円
3F
D・CD
タル・返却
5F
3枚で300円
5枚借りても
500円
THE SEVEN SWOR
WORD

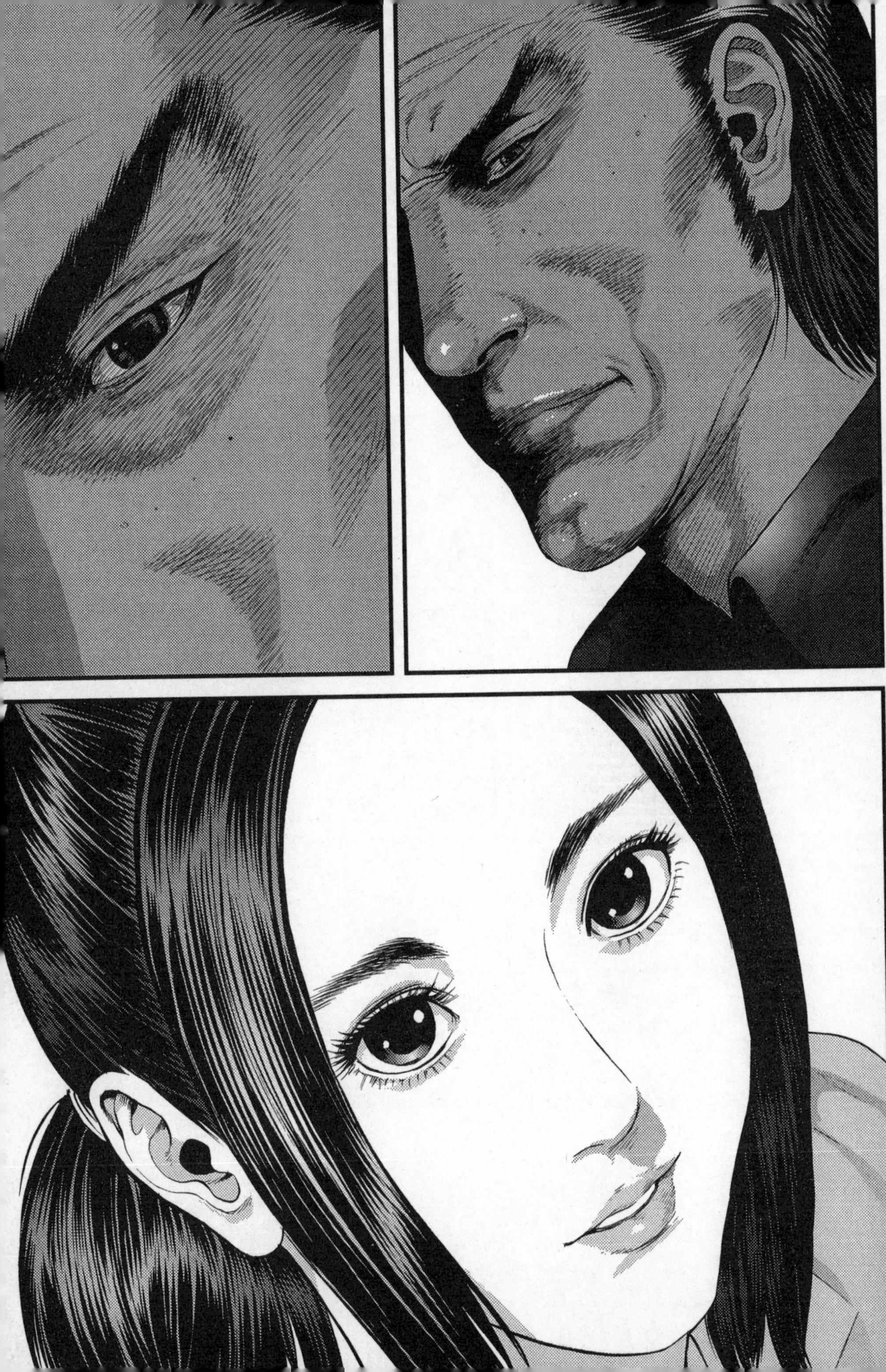

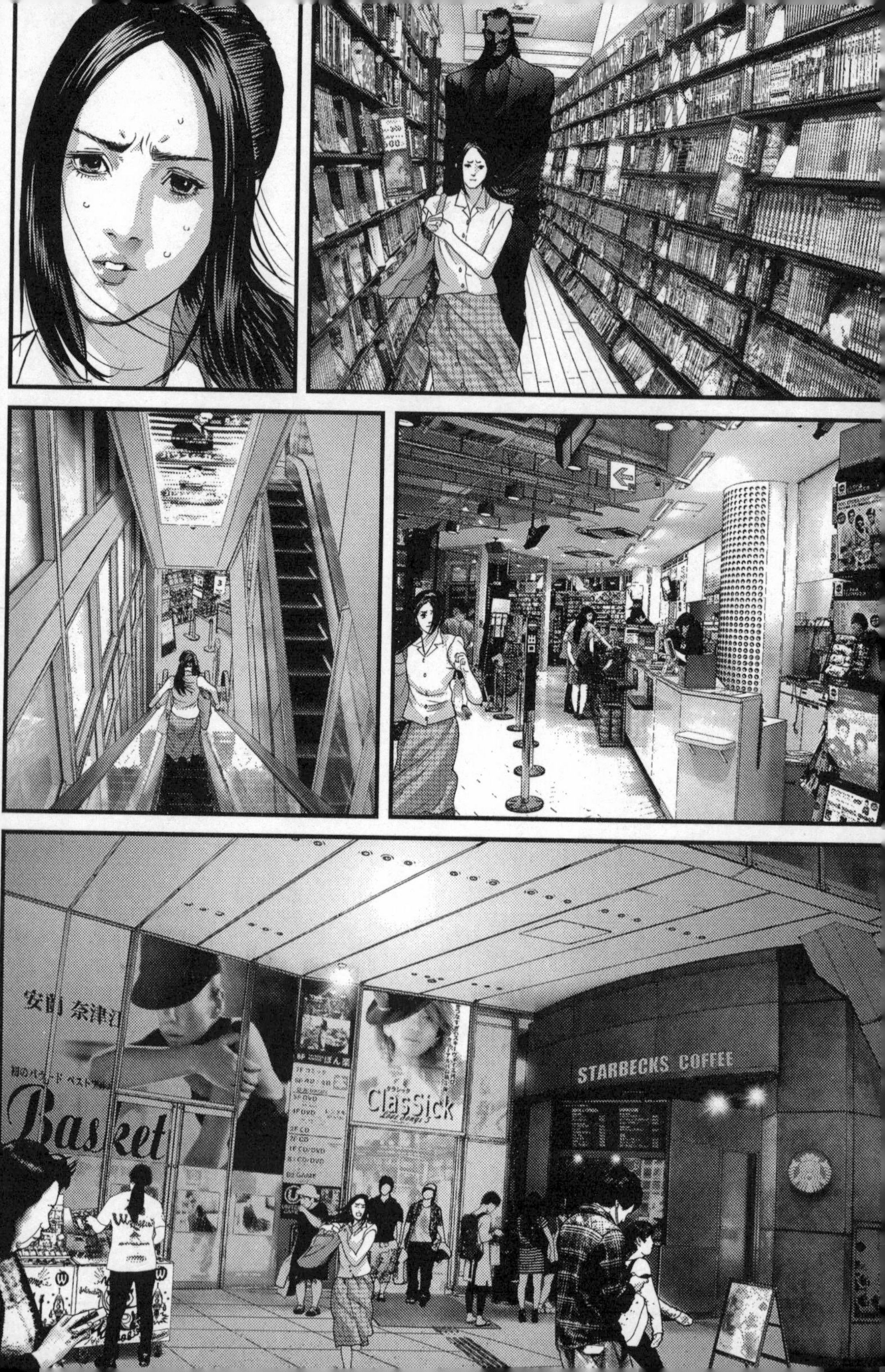
Basket
ClasSick
STARBECKS COFFEE

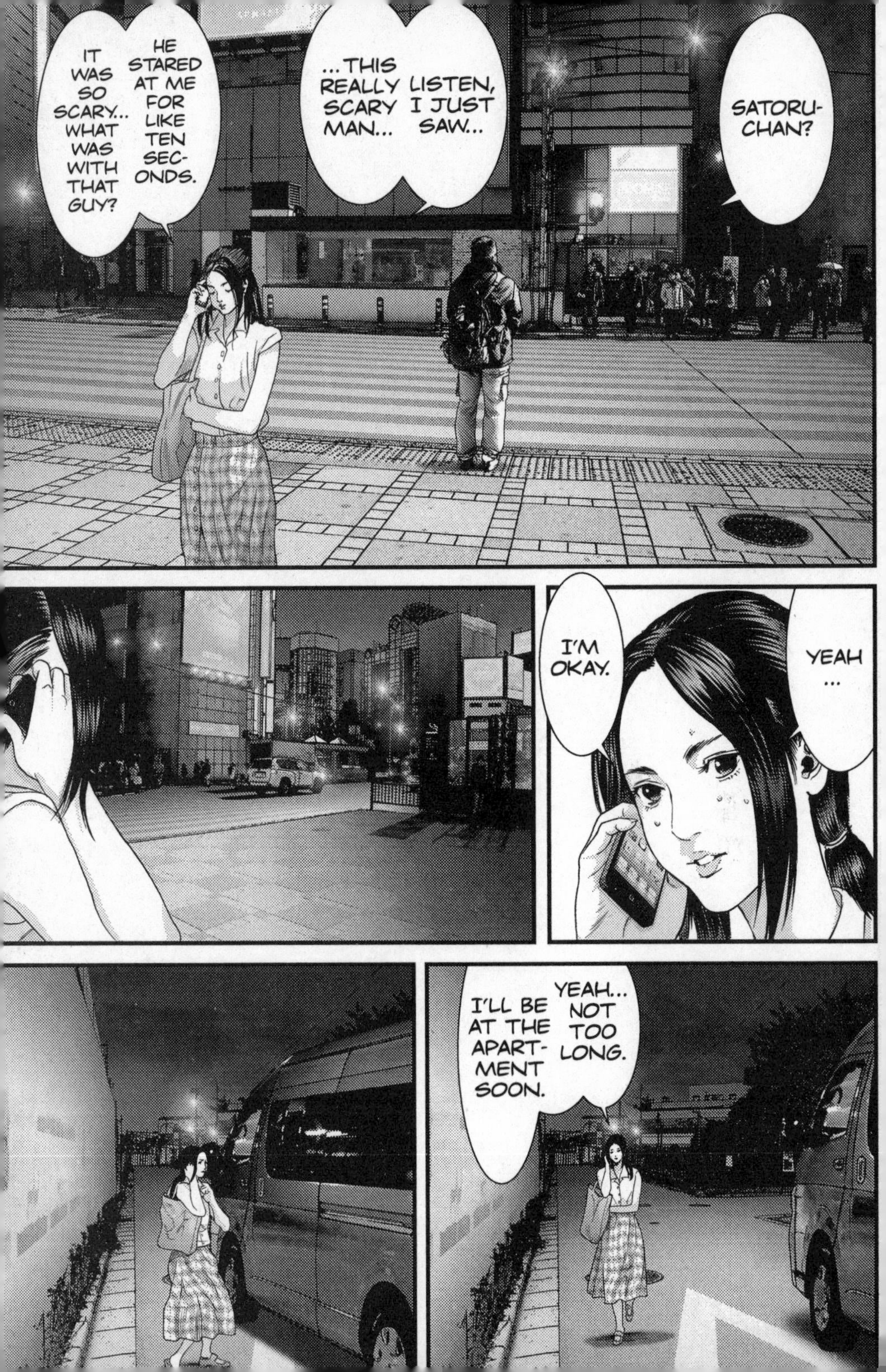
SATORU-CHAN?
LISTEN, I JUST SAW...
...THIS REALLY SCARY MAN...
HE STARED AT ME FOR LIKE TEN SECONDS.
IT WAS SO SCARY... WHAT WAS WITH THAT GUY?
YEAH ...
I'M OKAY.
YEAH... NOT TOO LONG.
I'LL BE AT THE APARTMENT SOON.

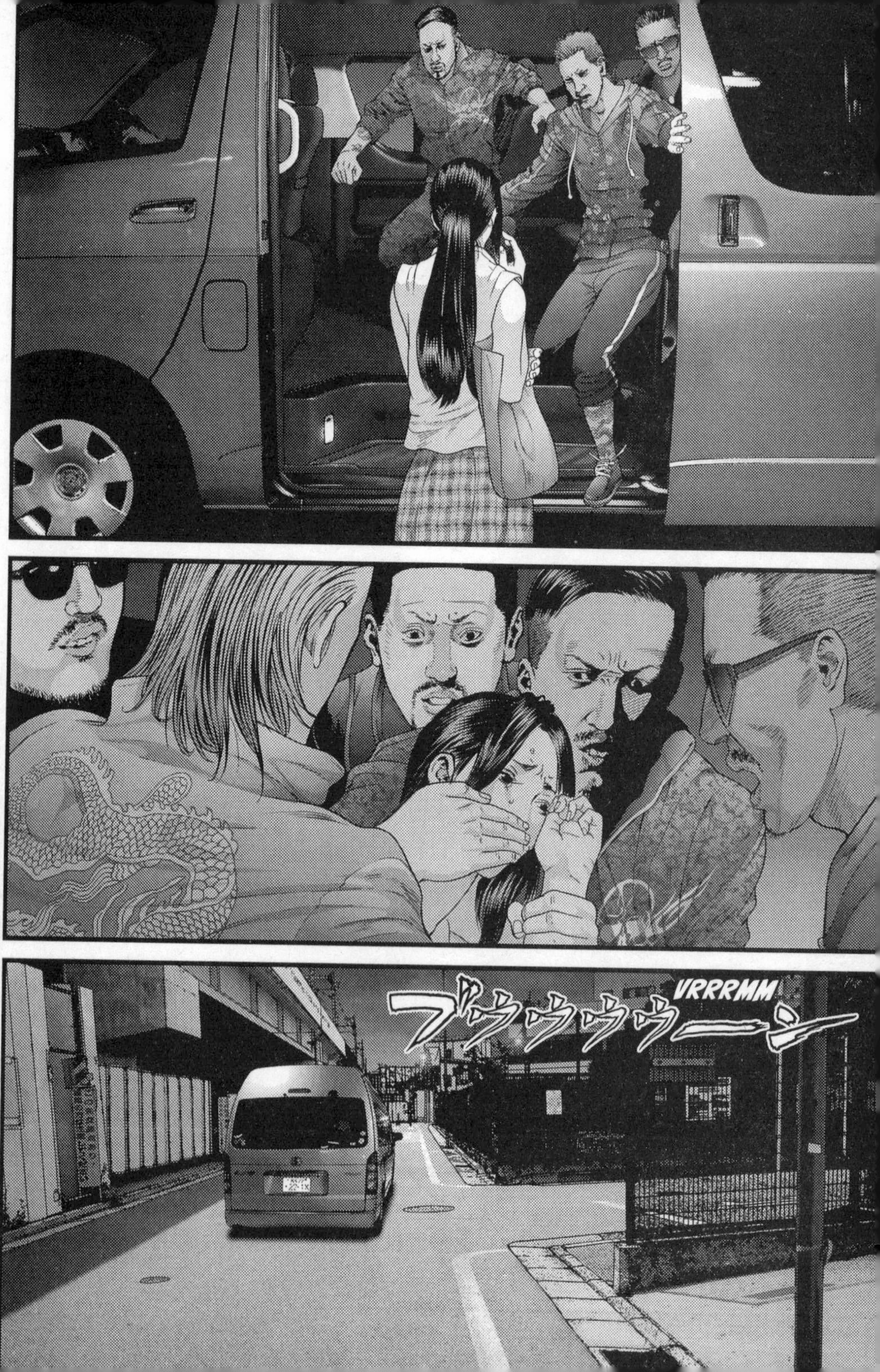
VRRRMM
ブウウウウーン

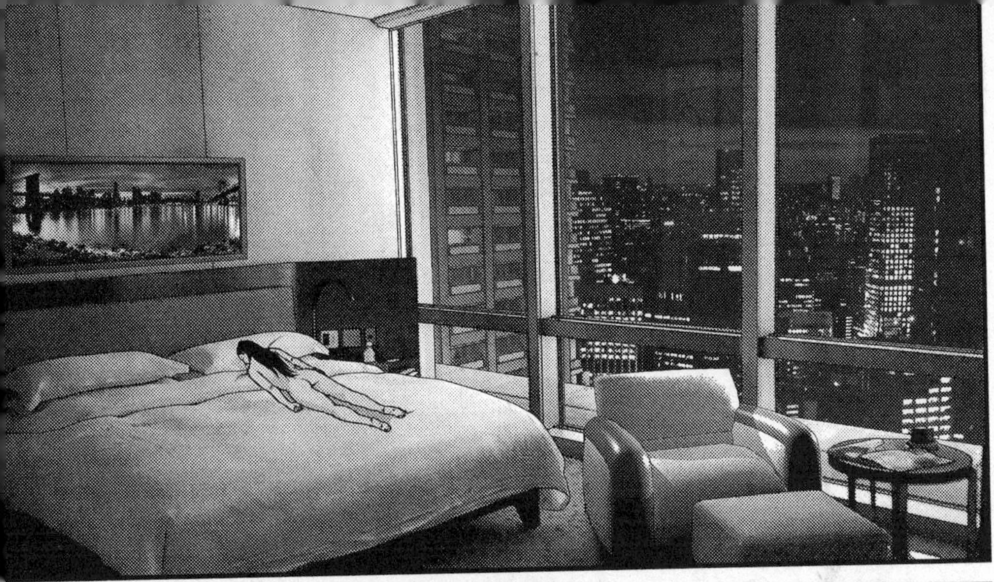
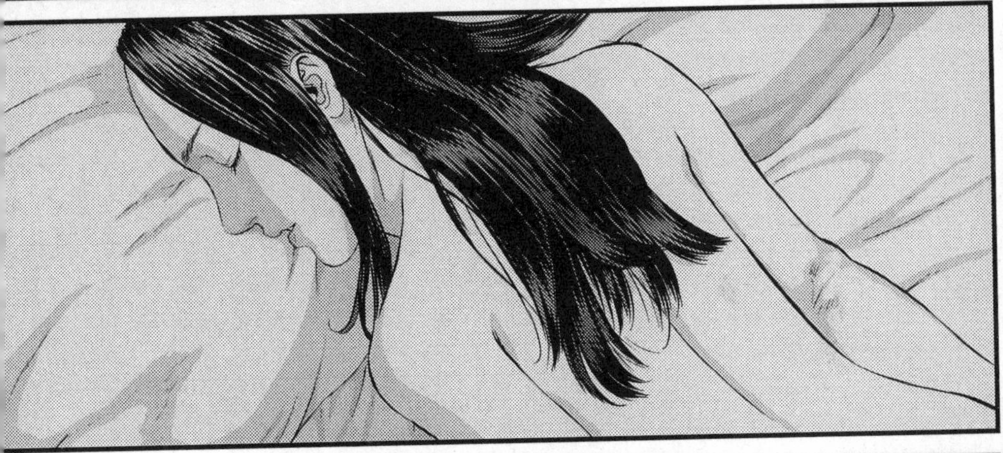
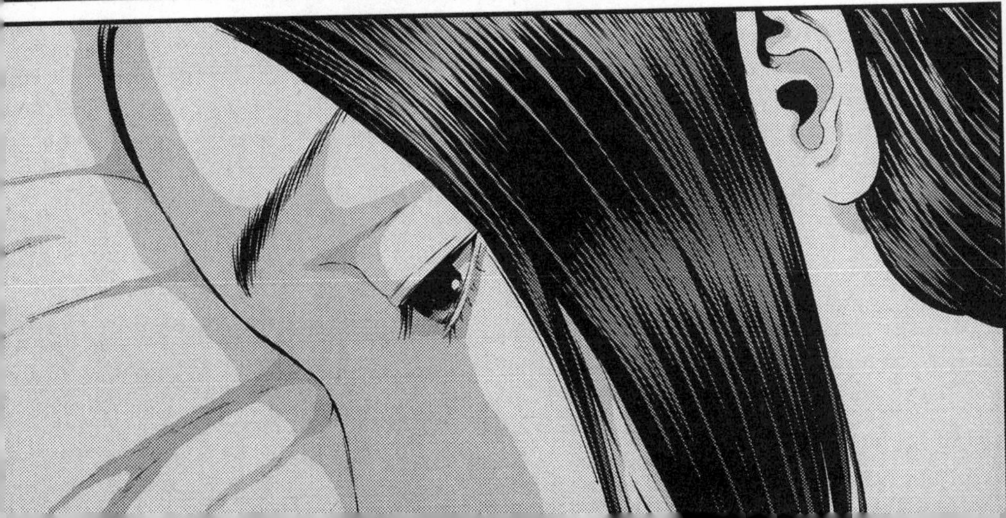

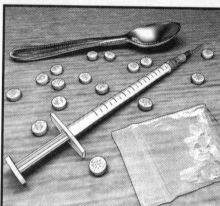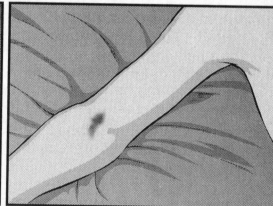

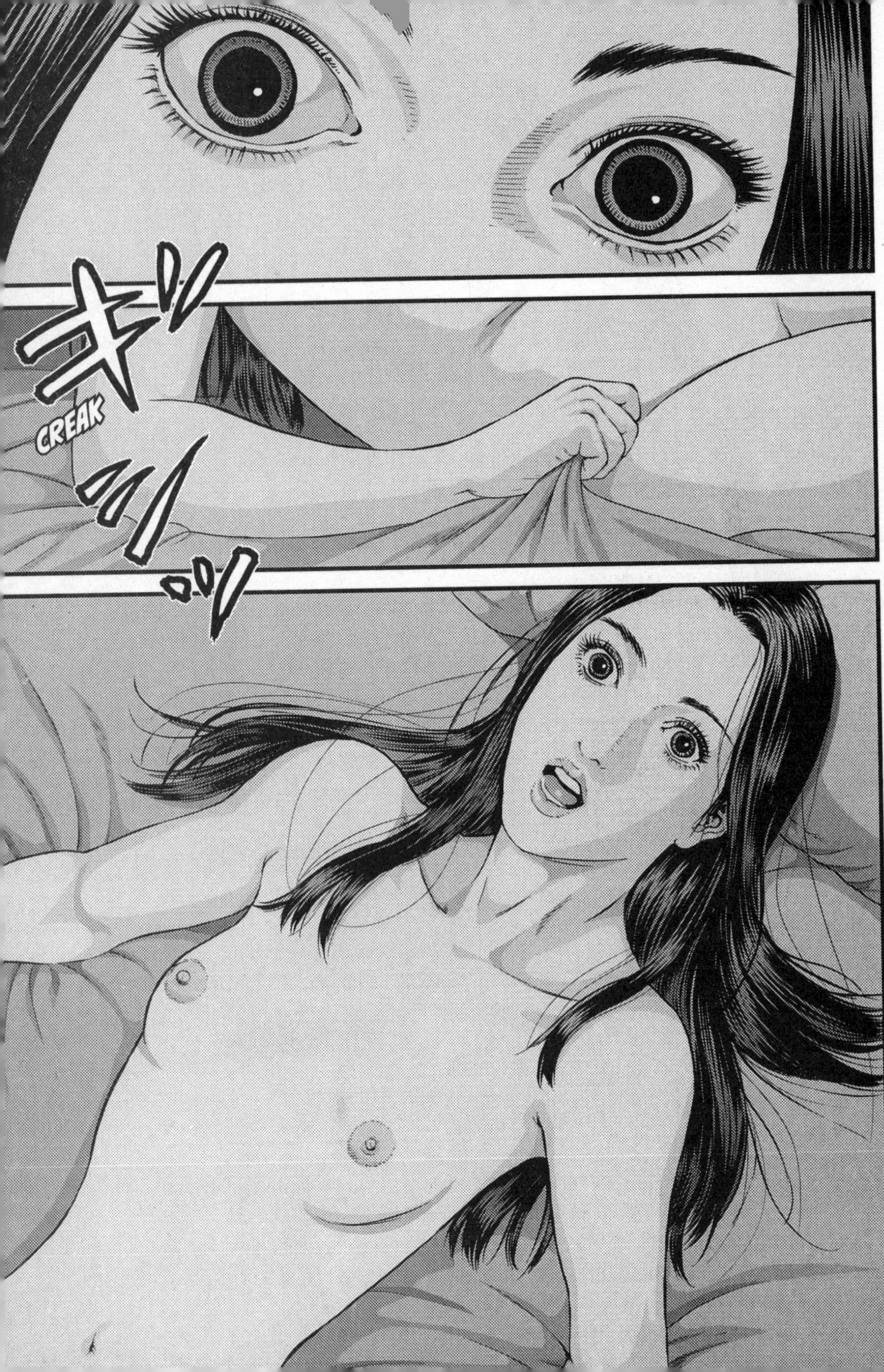
ギシッ
CREAK

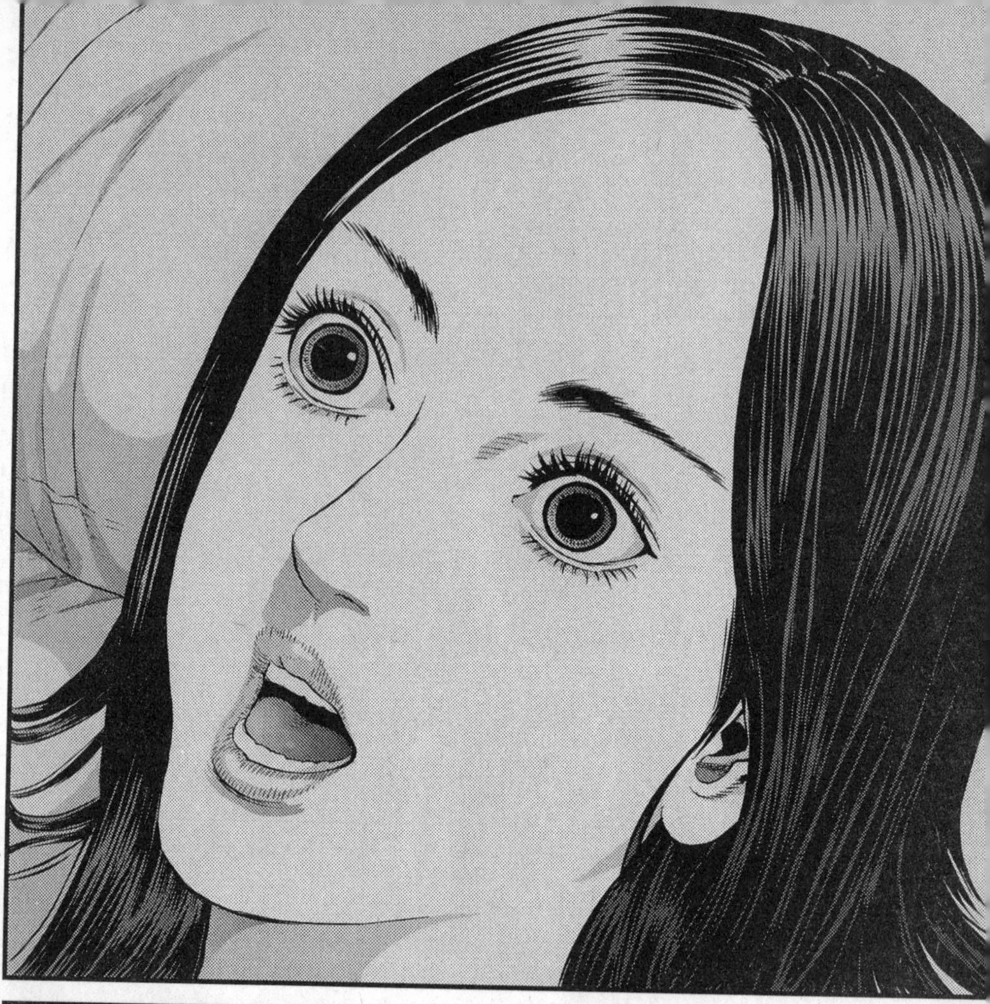

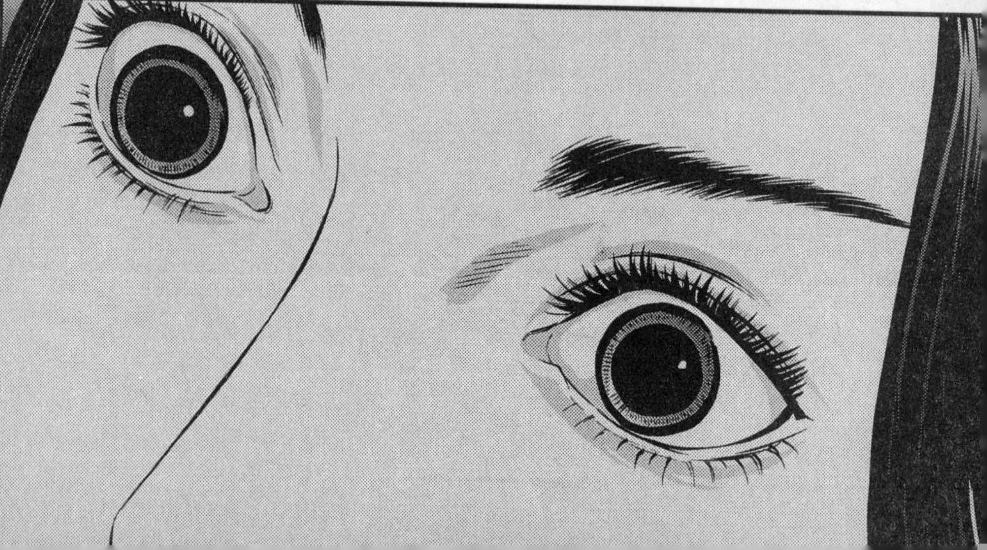

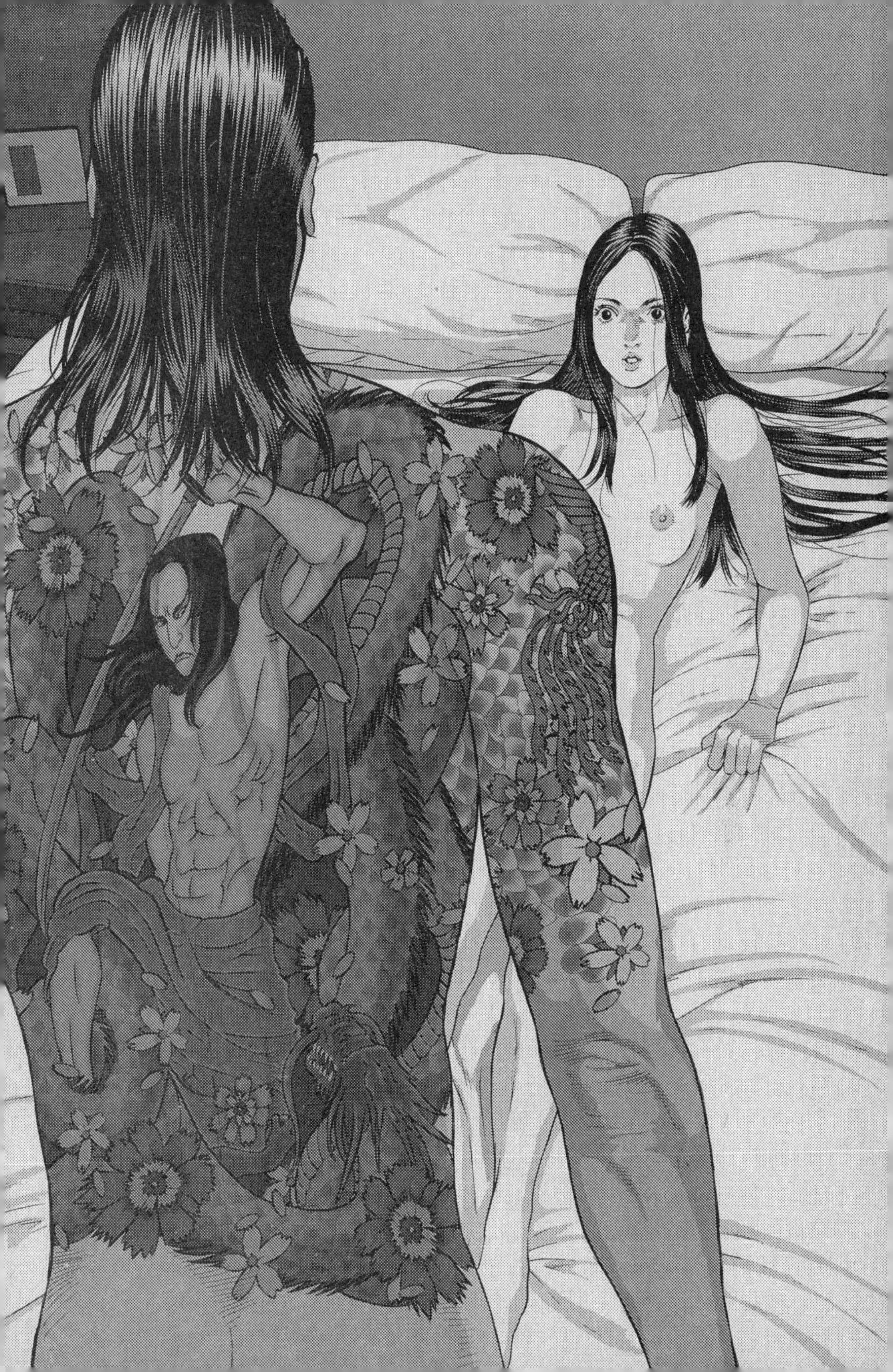

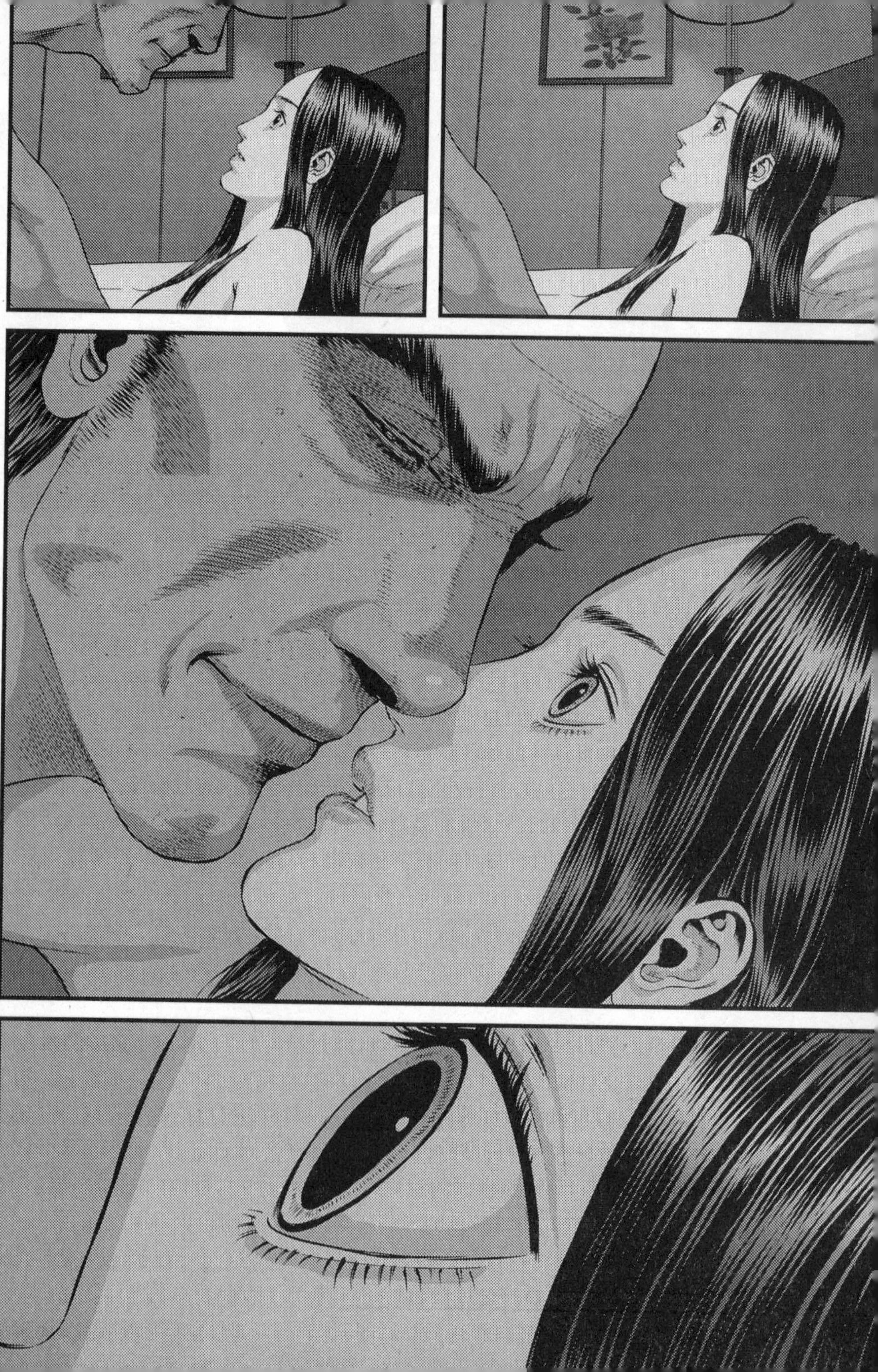

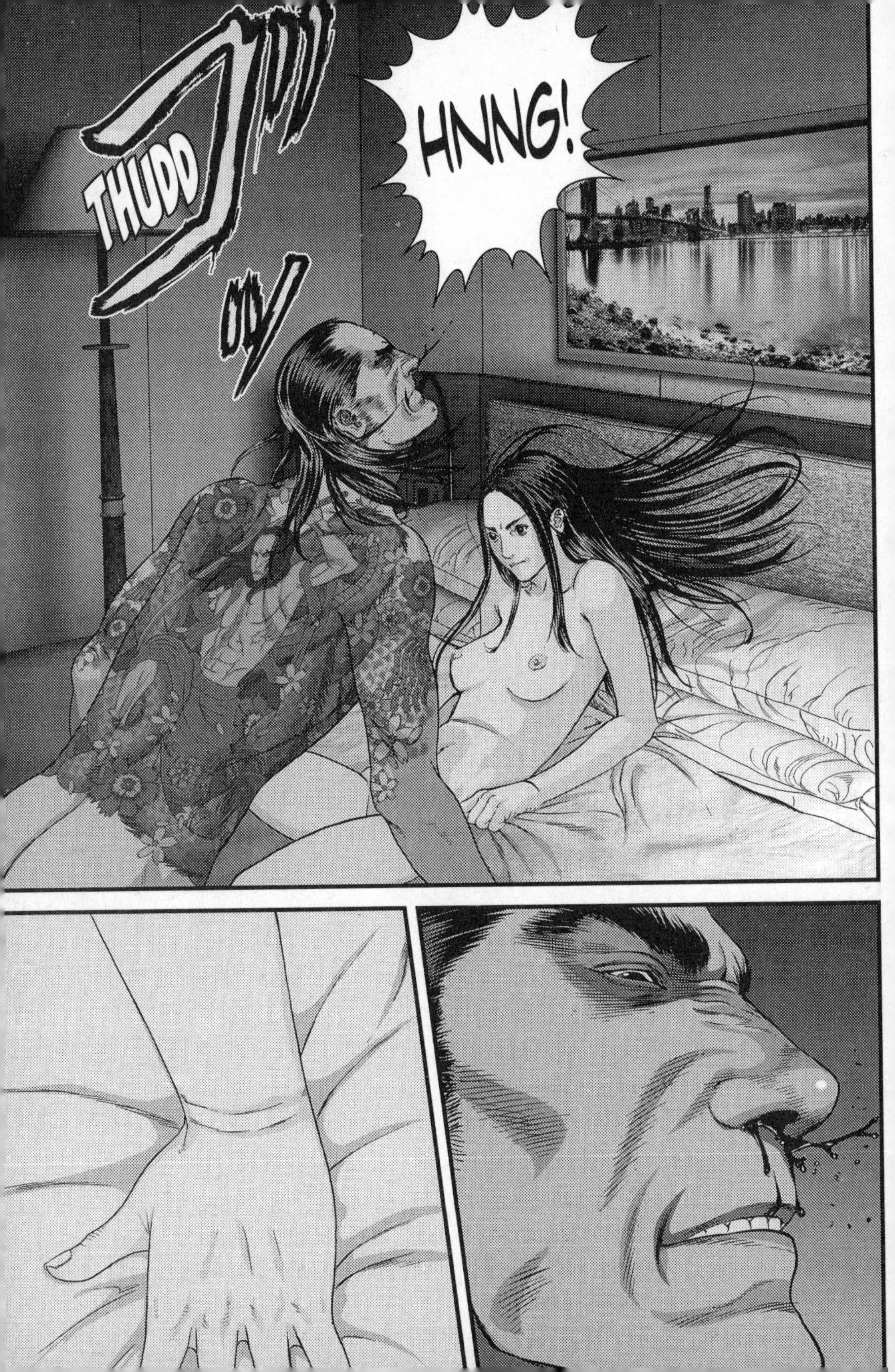
HNNG!
THUDD

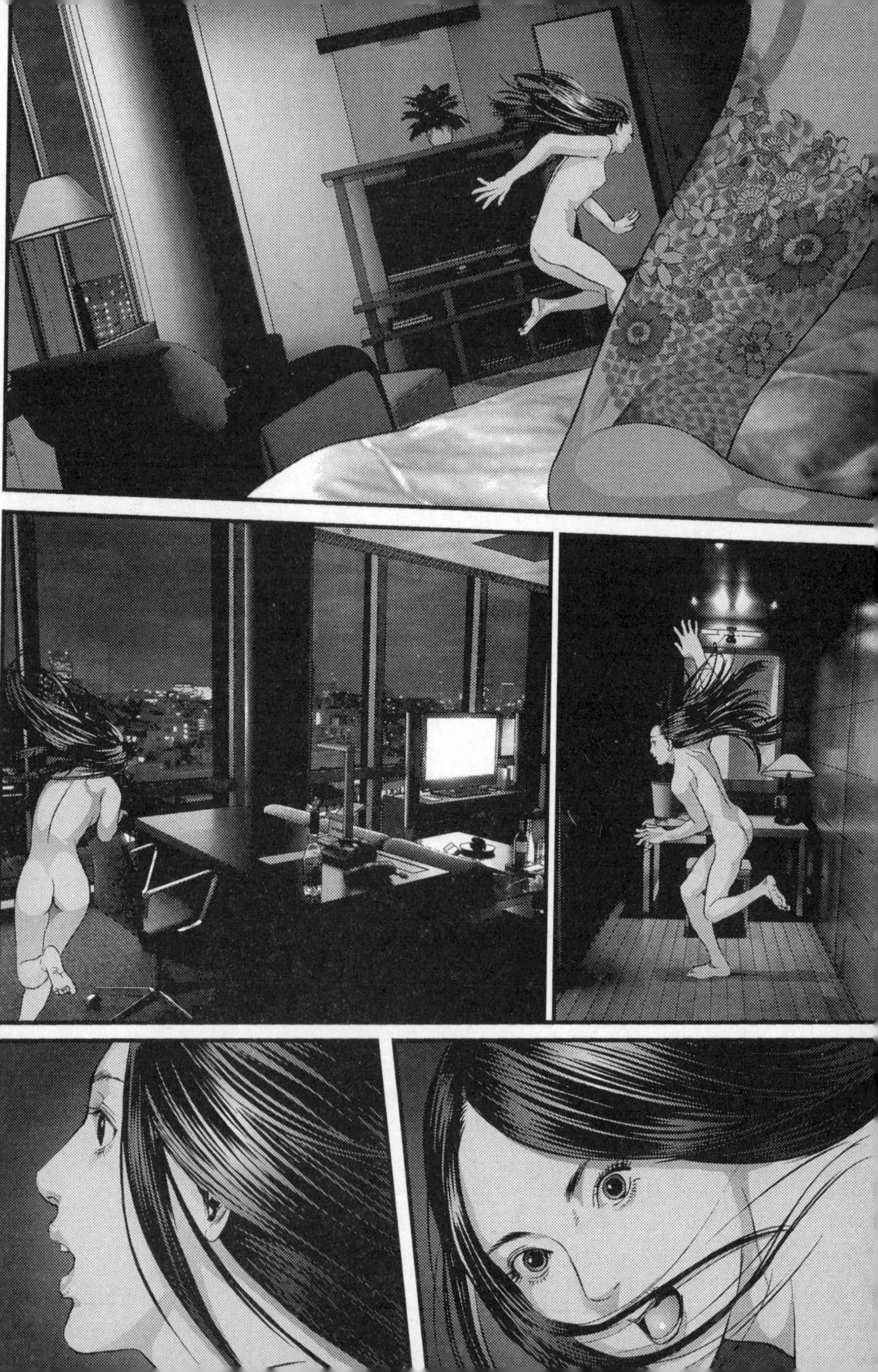

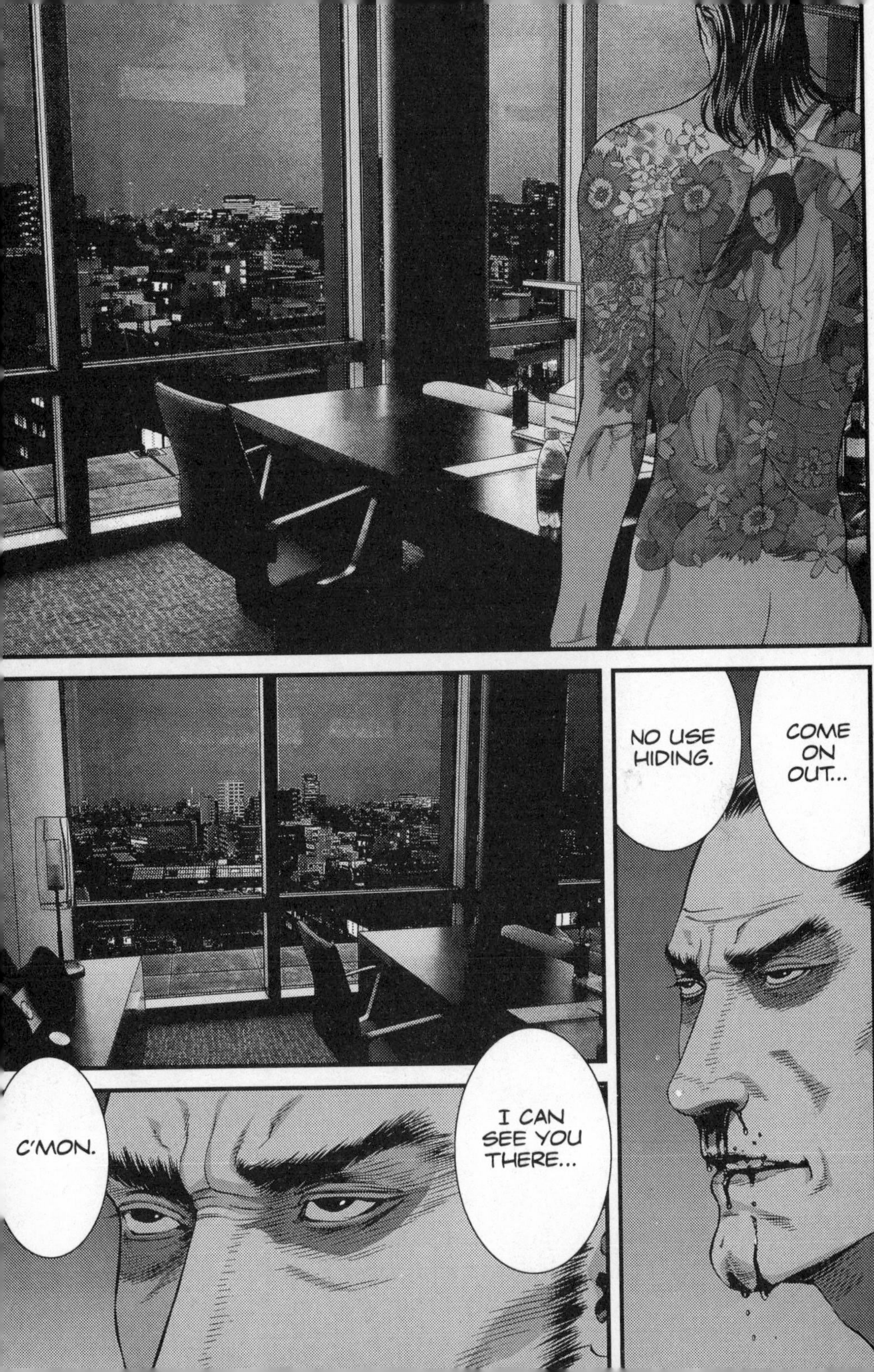
COME ON OUT...
NO USE HIDING.
I CAN SEE YOU THERE...
C'MON.

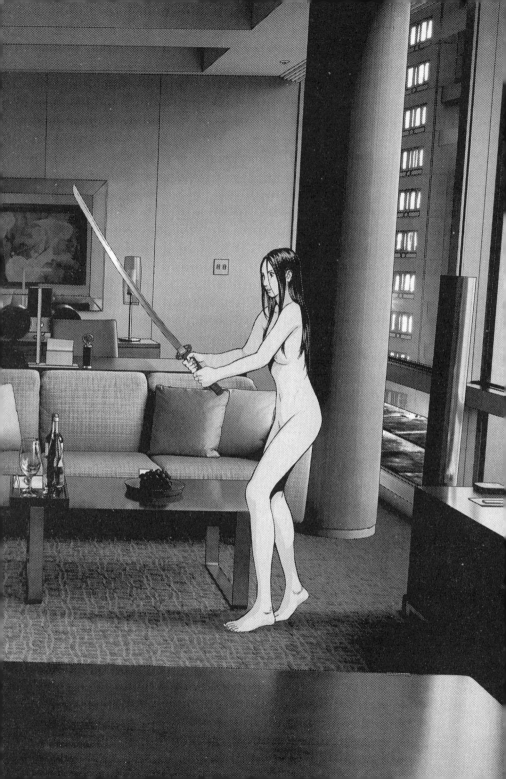

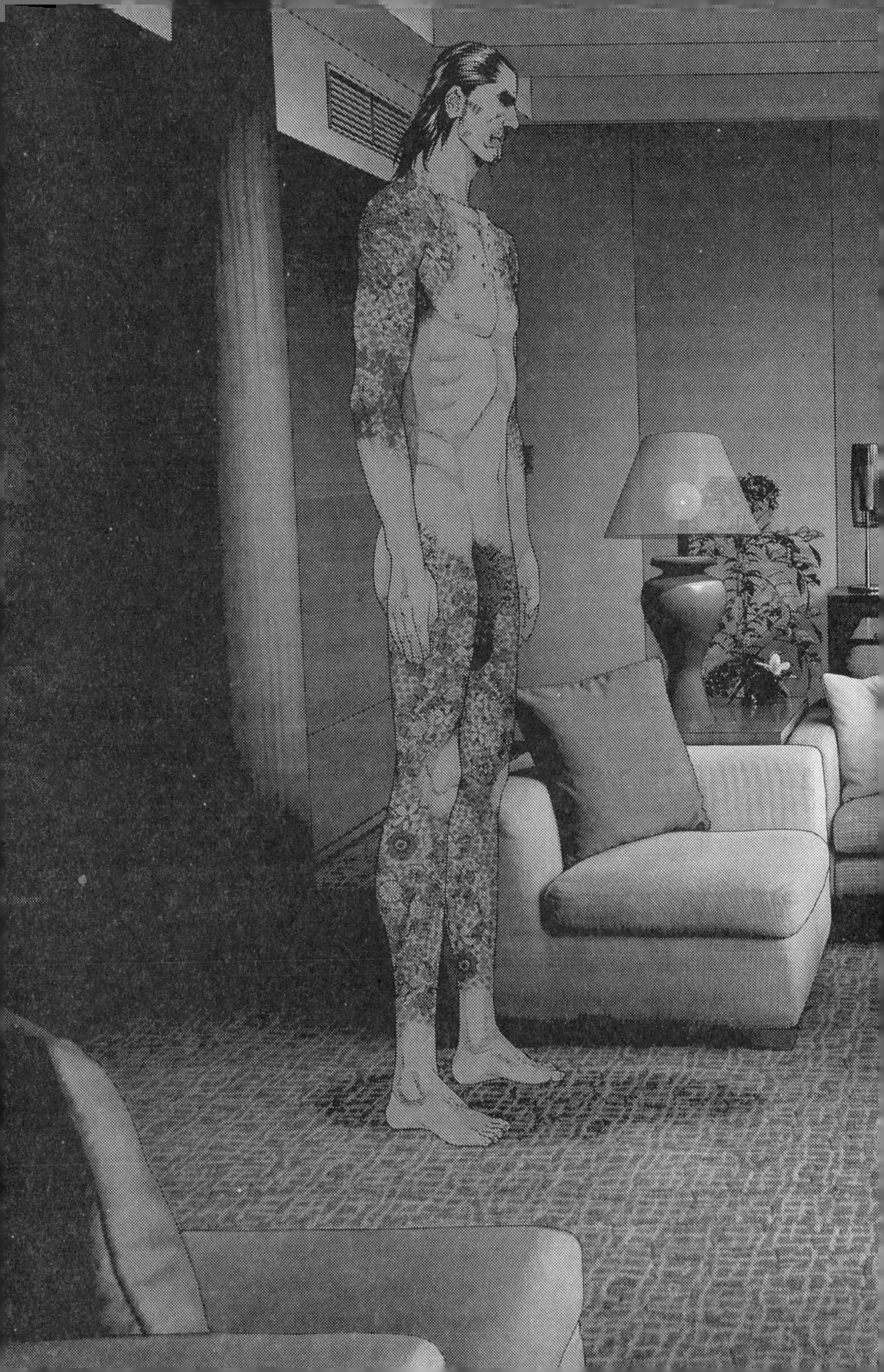

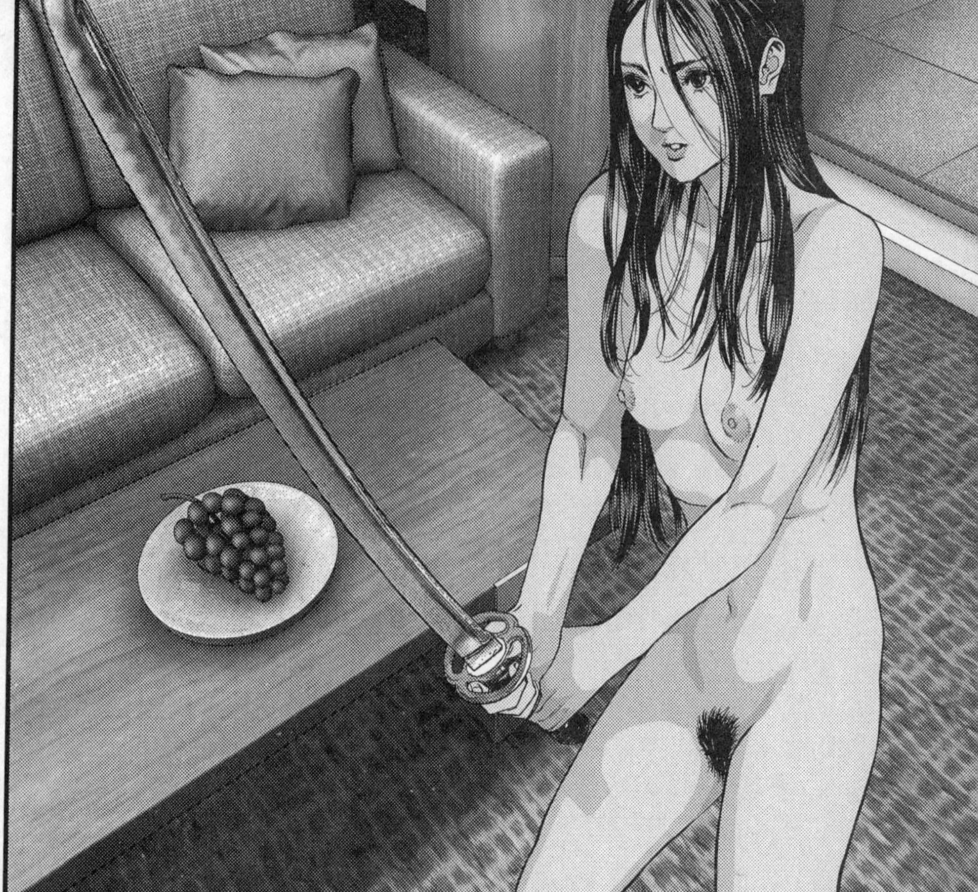

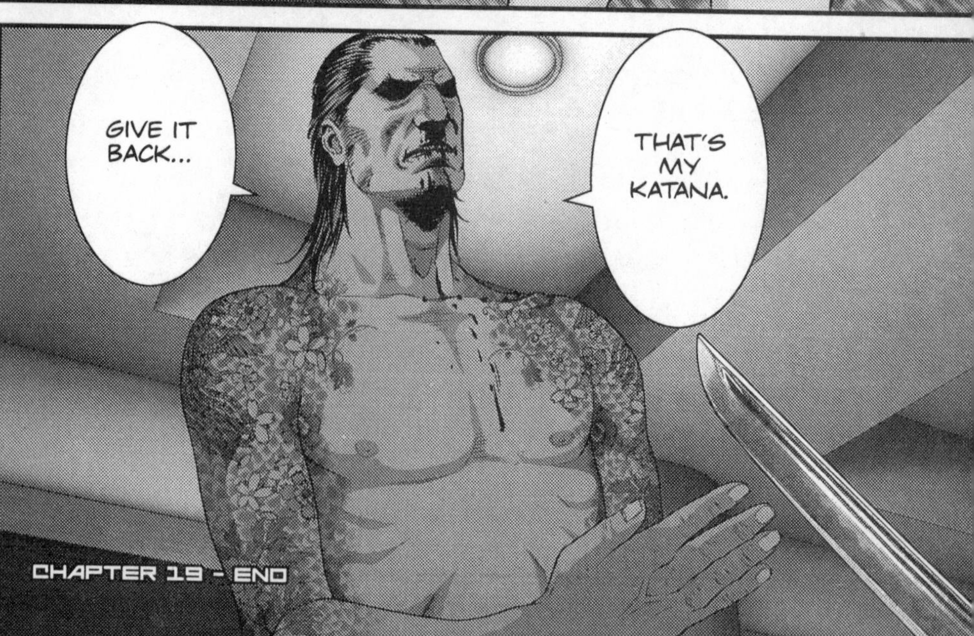
THAT'S MY KATANA.
GIVE IT BACK...
CHAPTER 19 - END

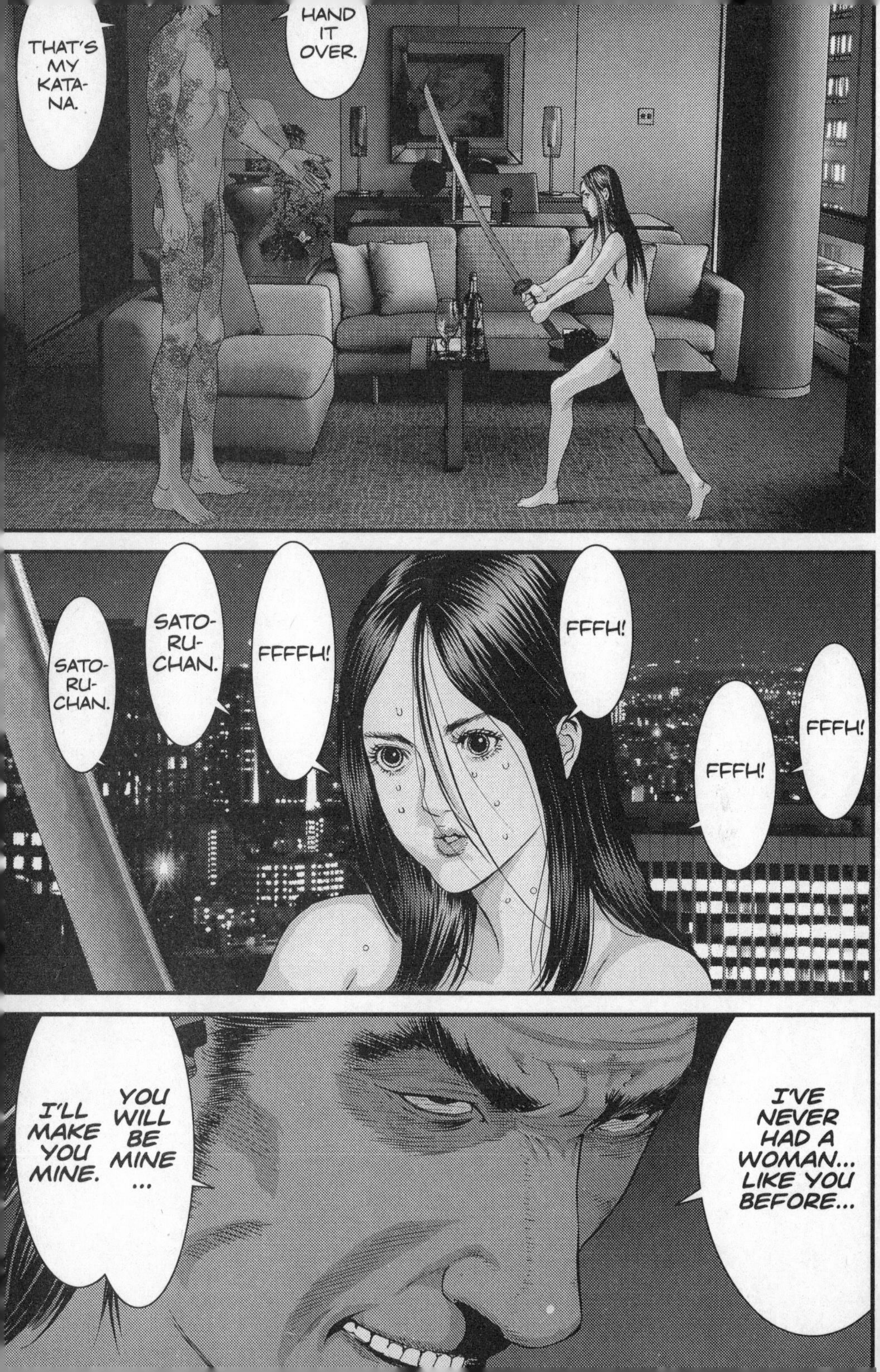
HAND IT OVER.
THAT'S MY KATA-NA.
FFFH!
FFFH!
FFFH!
FFFFH!
SATO-RU-CHAN.
SATO-RU-CHAN.
I'VE NEVER HAD A WOMAN... LIKE YOU BEFORE...
YOU WILL BE MINE ...
I'LL MAKE YOU MINE.

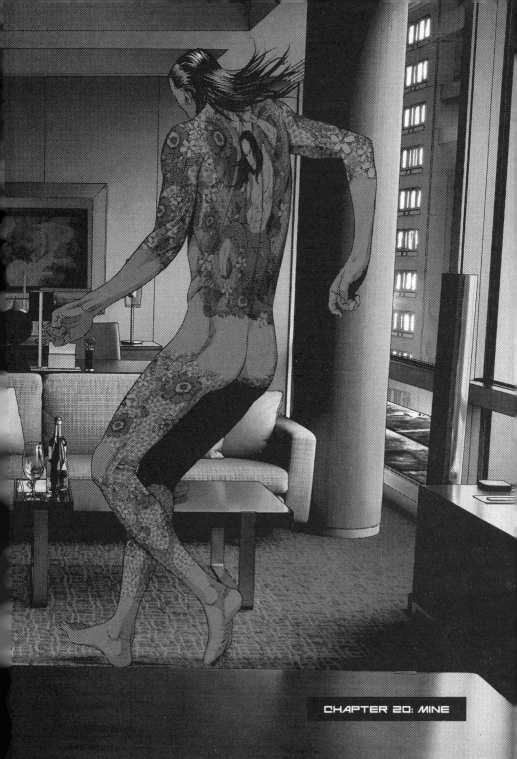

CHAPTER 20: MINE

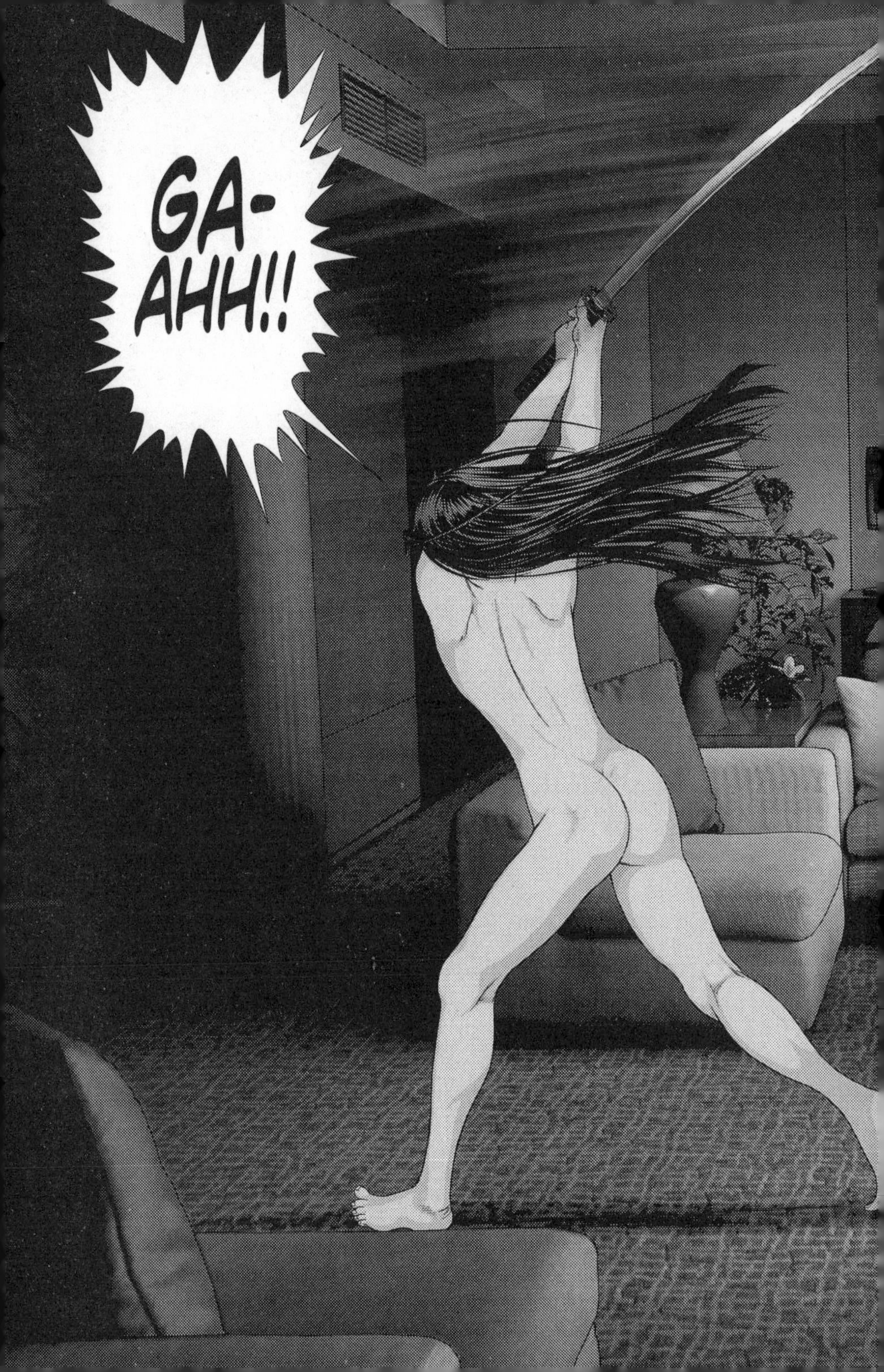
GA-
AHH!!

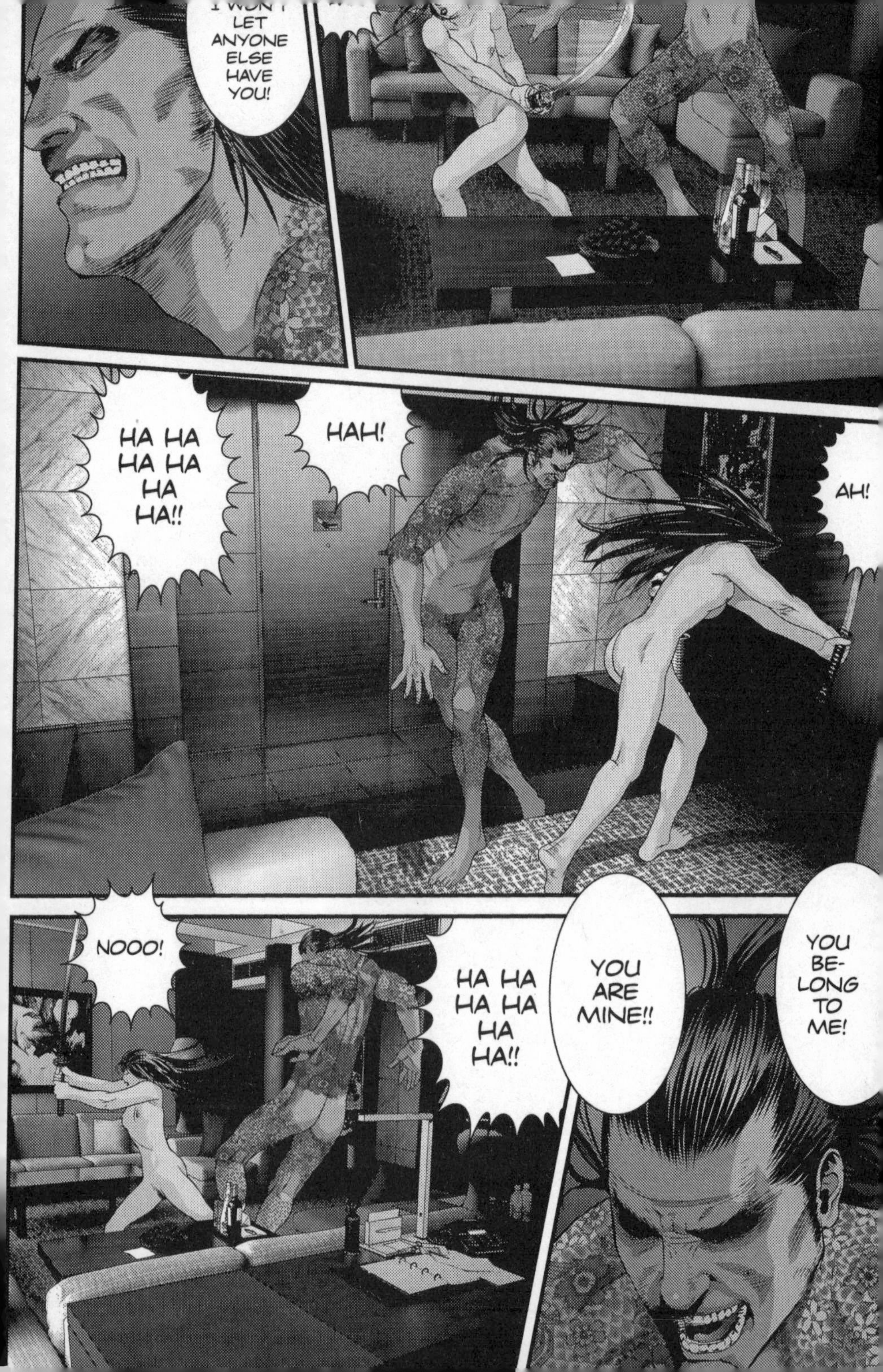
I WON'T LET ANYONE ELSE HAVE YOU!
AH!
HAH!
HA HA HA HA HA HA!!
YOU BE-LONG TO ME!
YOU ARE MINE!!
HA HA HA HA HA HA!!
NOOO!

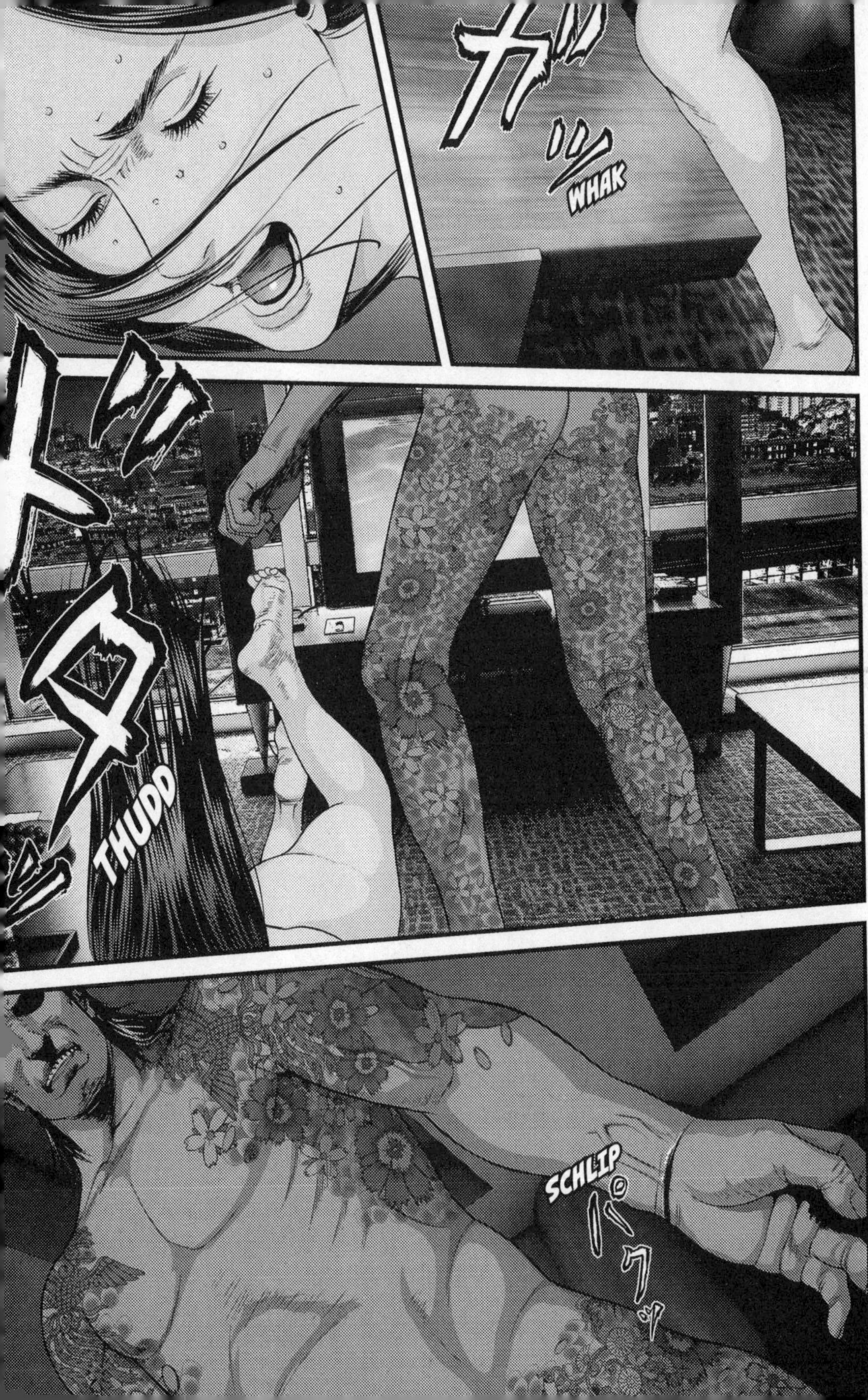
WHAK
THUDD
SCHLIP

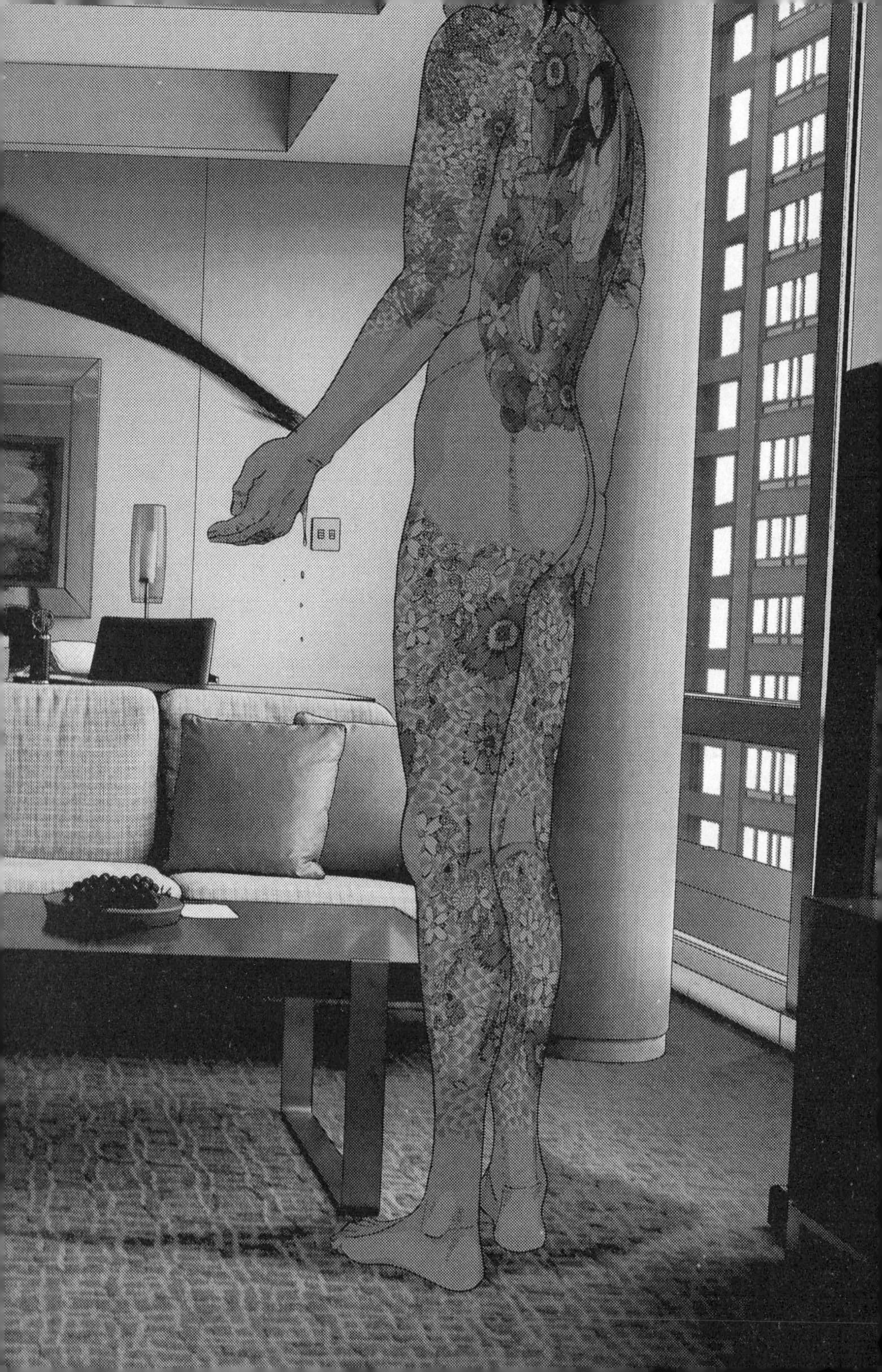

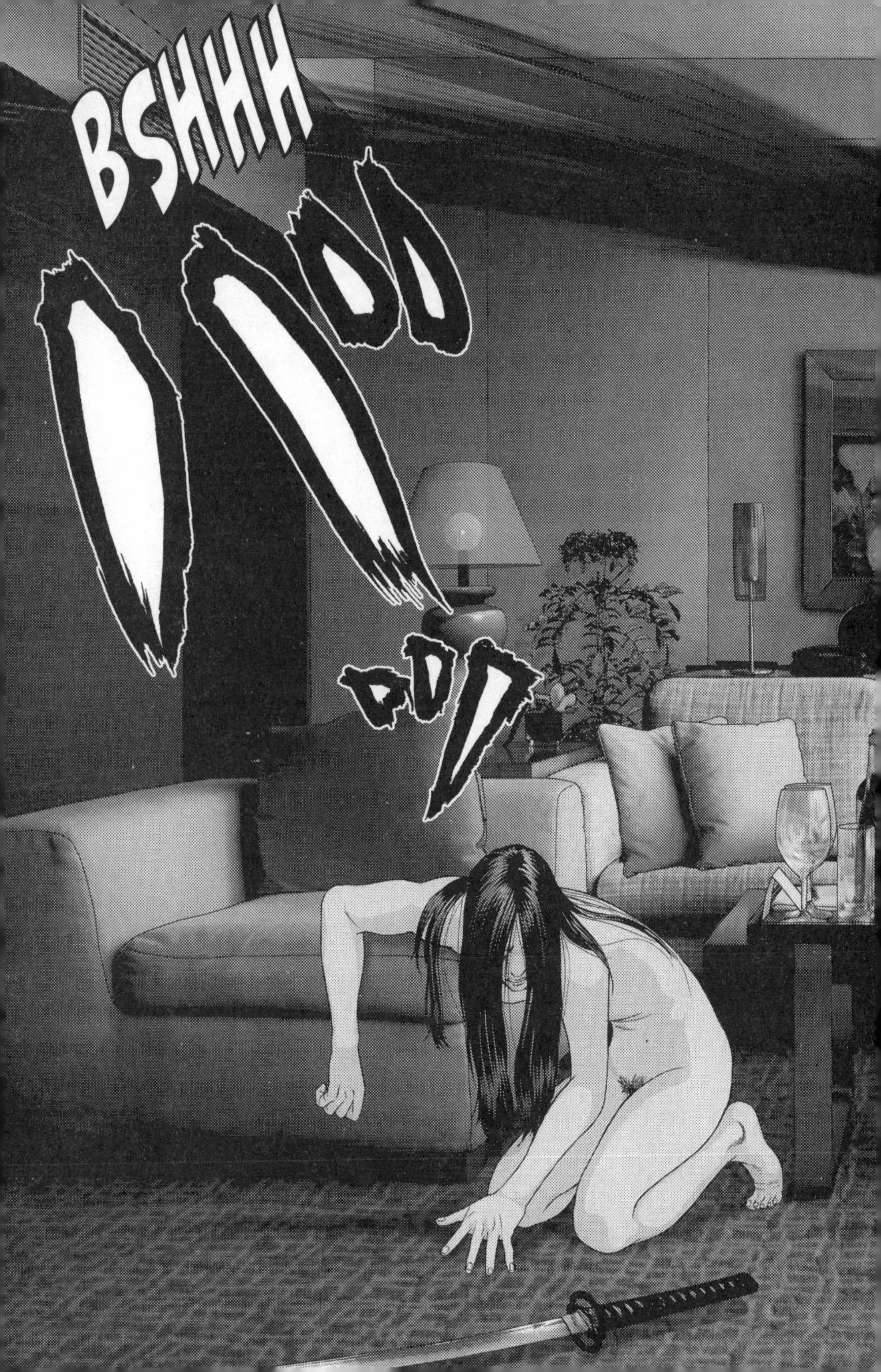
BSHHH

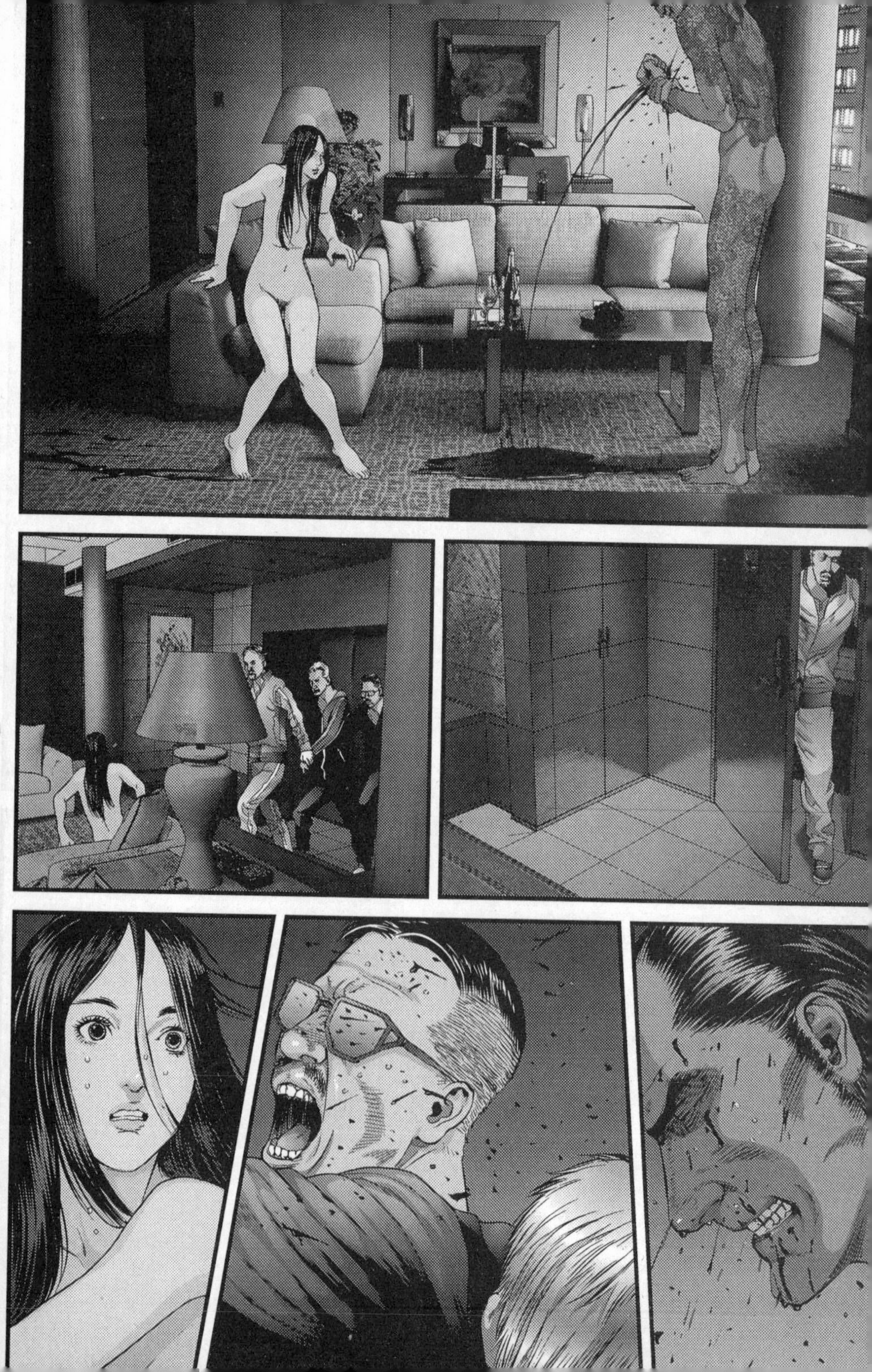

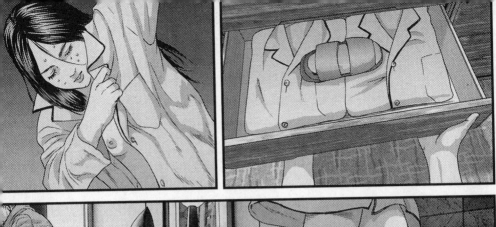

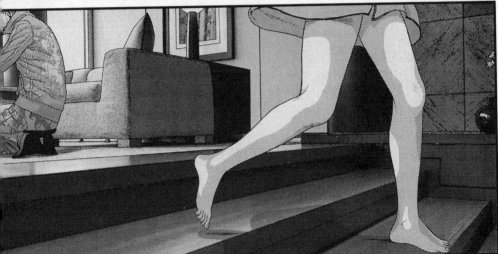

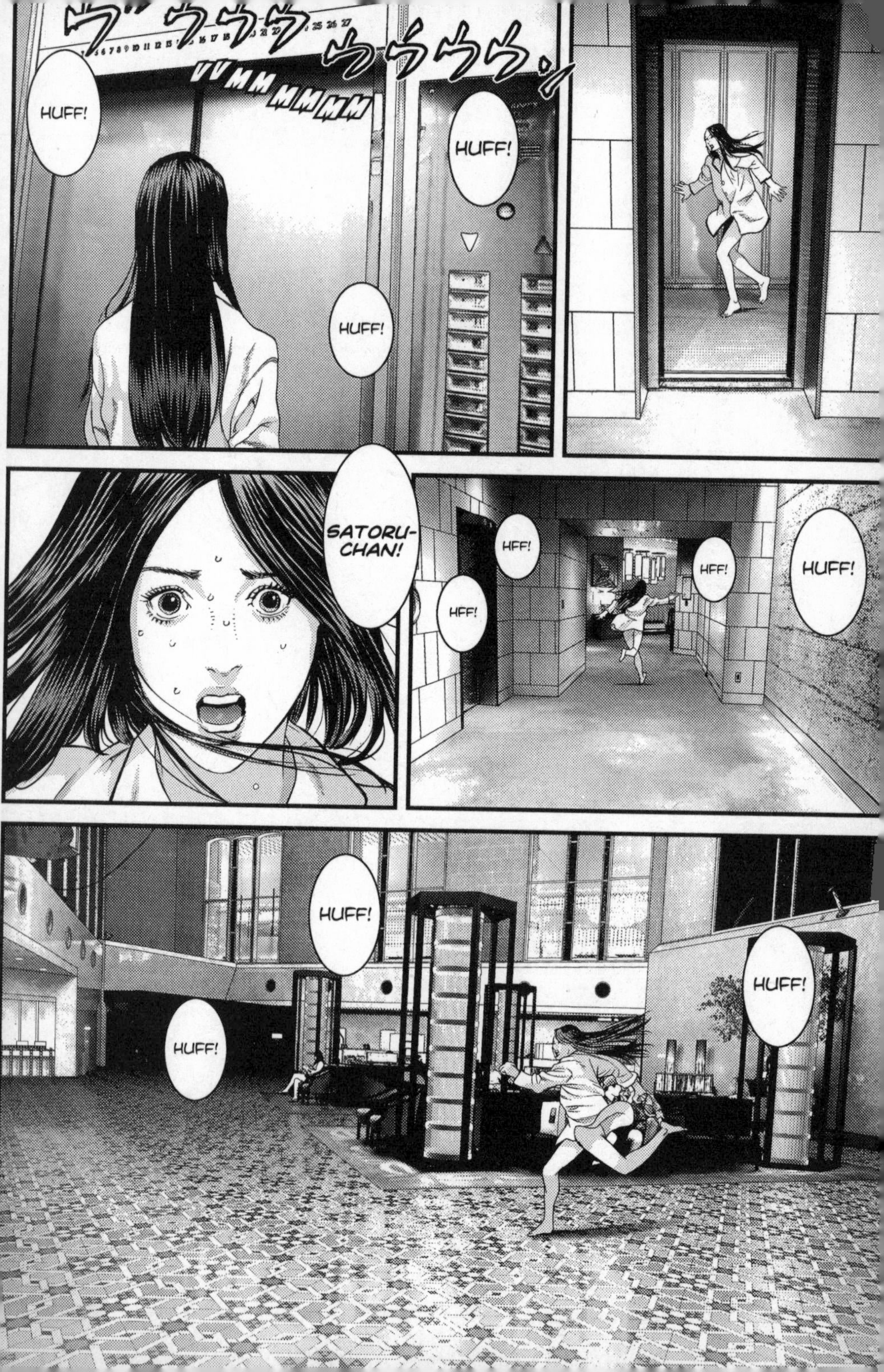
VVMMMMMMM
HUFF!
HUFF!
HUFF!
HUFF!
HFF!
HFF!
HFF!
SATORU-CHAN!
HUFF!
HUFF!
HUFF!

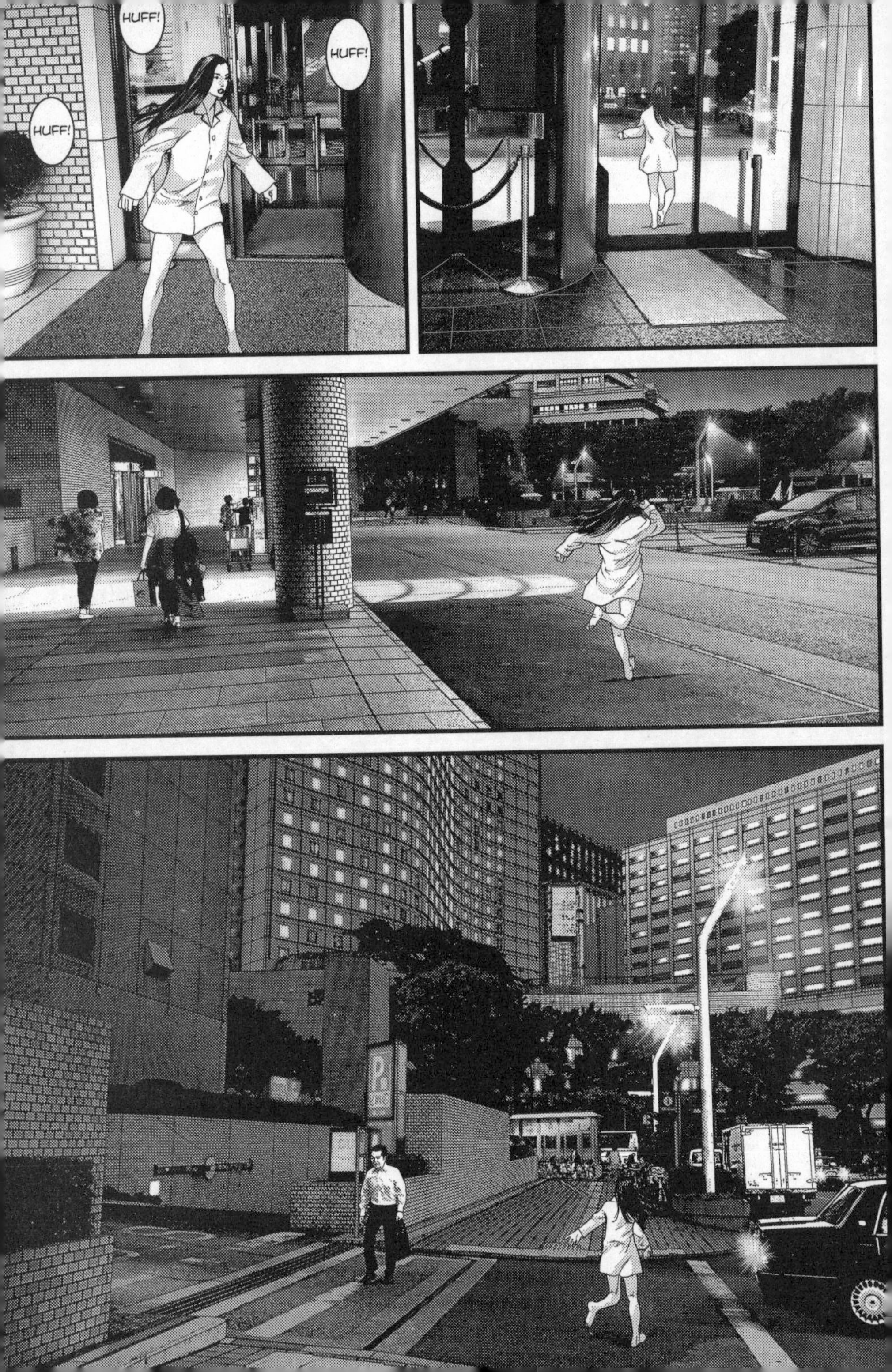
HUFF!
HUFF!
HUFF!

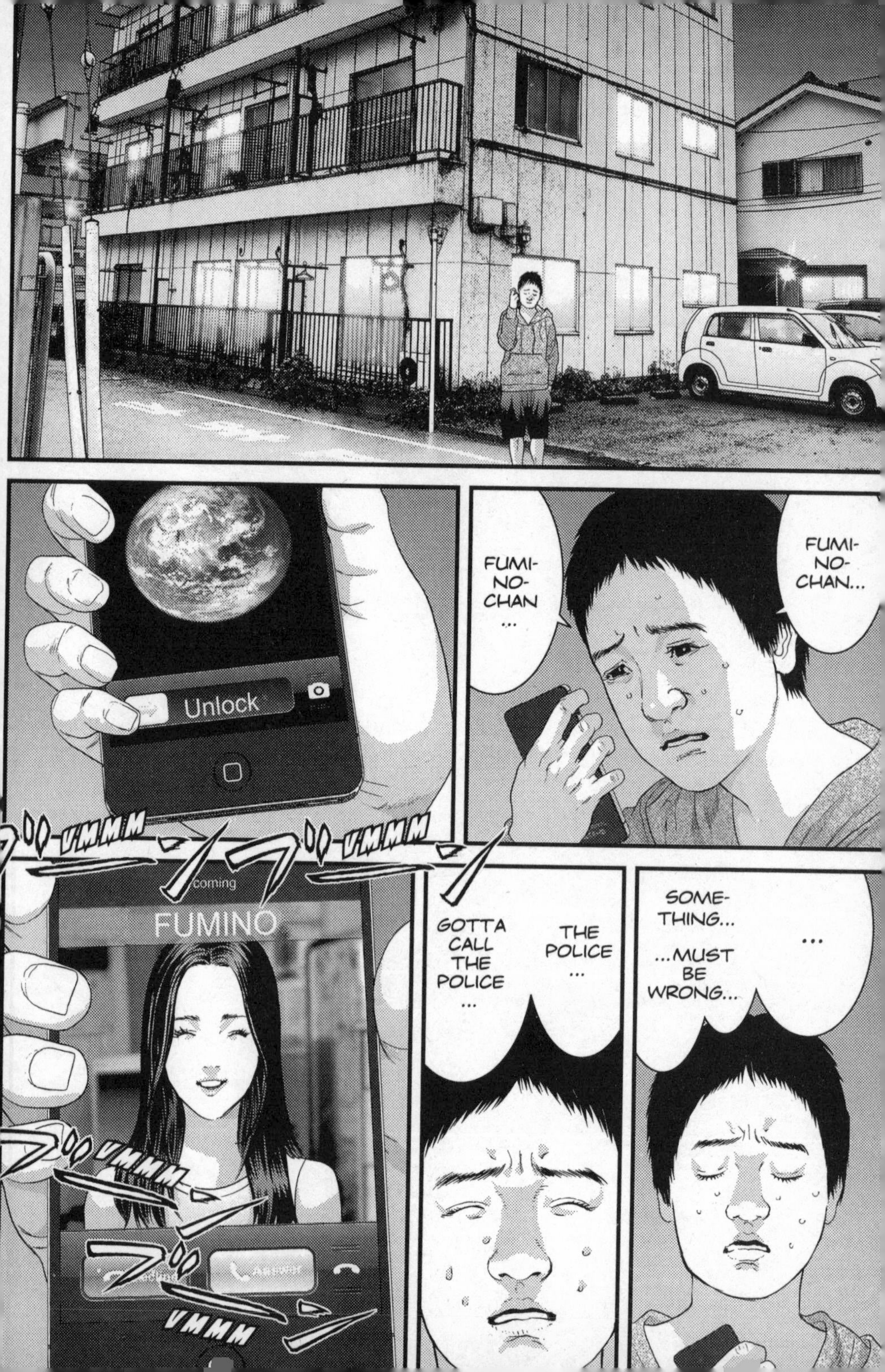
FUMI-NO-CHAN...
FUMI-NO-CHAN ...
Unlock
VMMM
VMMM
...
SOME-THING... ...MUST BE WRONG...
THE POLICE ...
GOTTA CALL THE POLICE ...
coming
FUMINO
VMMM
VMMM

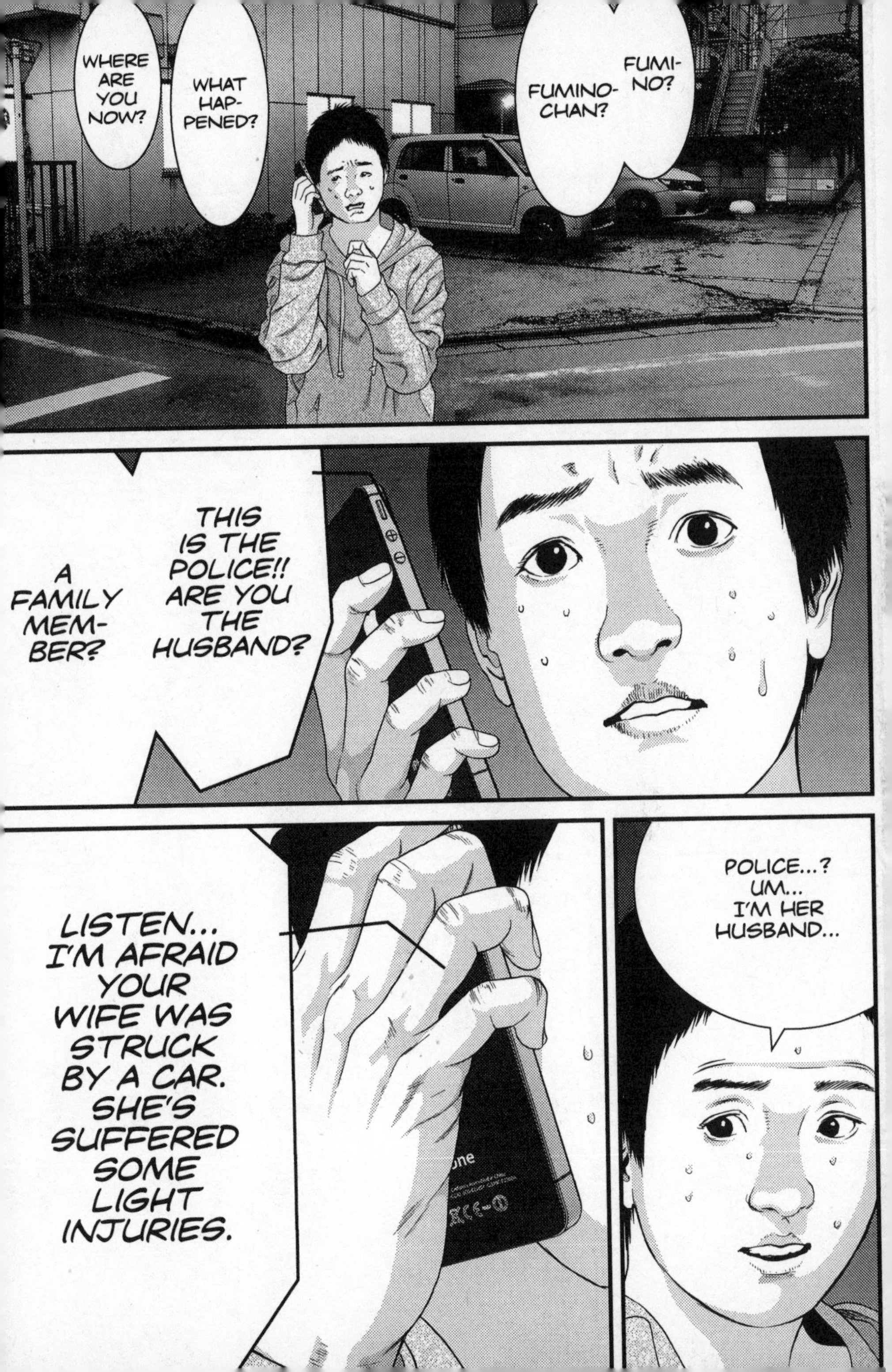
FUMI-NO?
FUMINO-CHAN?
WHAT HAP-PENED?
WHERE ARE YOU NOW?
THIS IS THE POLICE!! ARE YOU THE HUSBAND?
A FAMILY MEM-BER?
POLICE...? UM... I'M HER HUSBAND...
LISTEN... I'M AFRAID YOUR WIFE WAS STRUCK BY A CAR. SHE'S SUFFERED SOME LIGHT INJURIES.

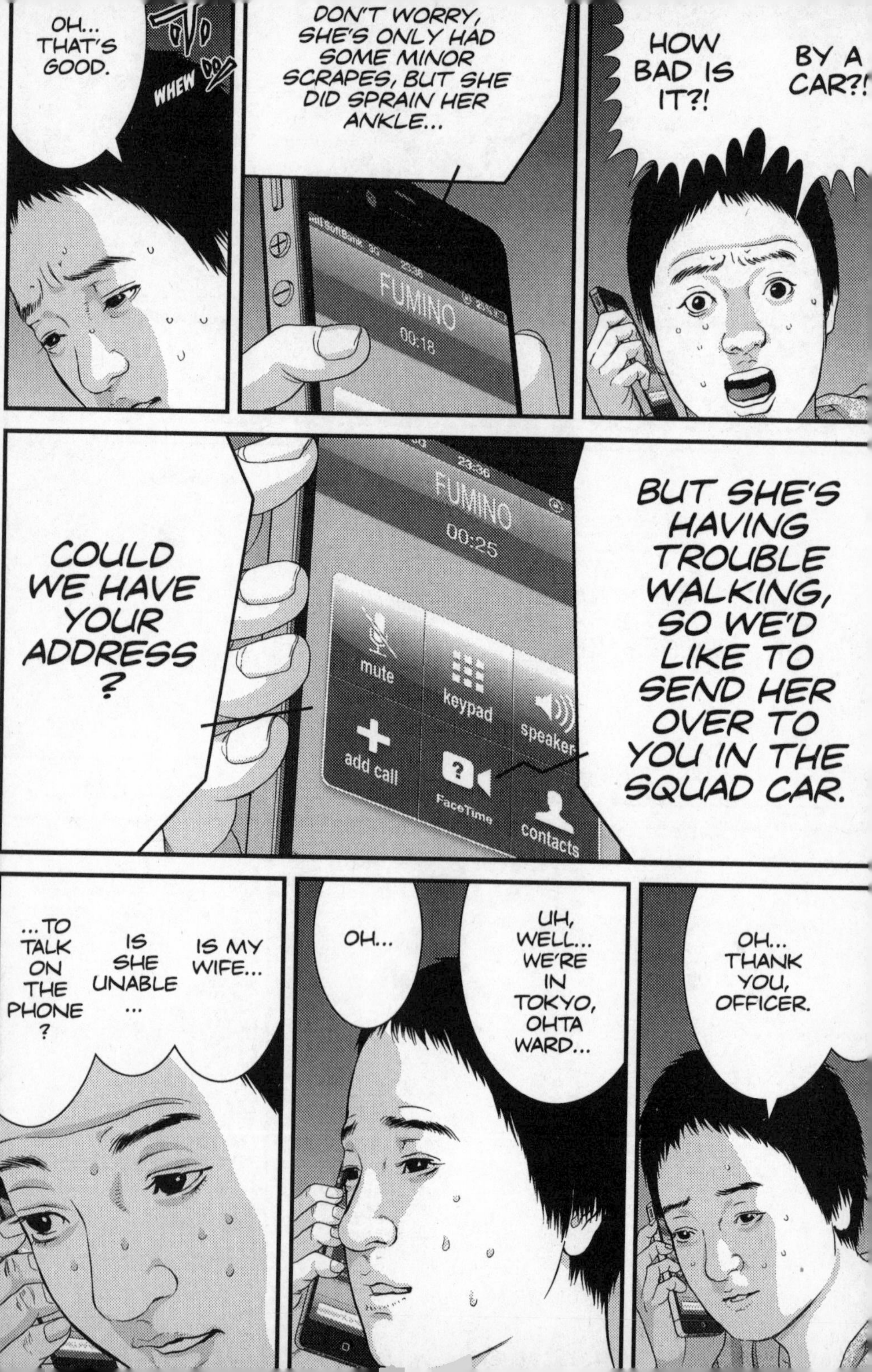
BY A CAR?!
HOW BAD IS IT?!
DON'T WORRY, SHE'S ONLY HAD SOME MINOR SCRAPES, BUT SHE DID SPRAIN HER ANKLE...
FUMINO
00:18
OH... THAT'S GOOD.
WHEW
BUT SHE'S HAVING TROUBLE WALKING, SO WE'D LIKE TO SEND HER OVER TO YOU IN THE SQUAD CAR.
FUMINO
00:25
mute
keypad
speaker
add call
FaceTime
contacts
COULD WE HAVE YOUR ADDRESS?
OH... THANK YOU, OFFICER.
UH, WELL... WE'RE IN TOKYO, OHTA WARD...
OH...
IS MY WIFE...
IS SHE UNABLE...
...TO TALK ON THE PHONE?

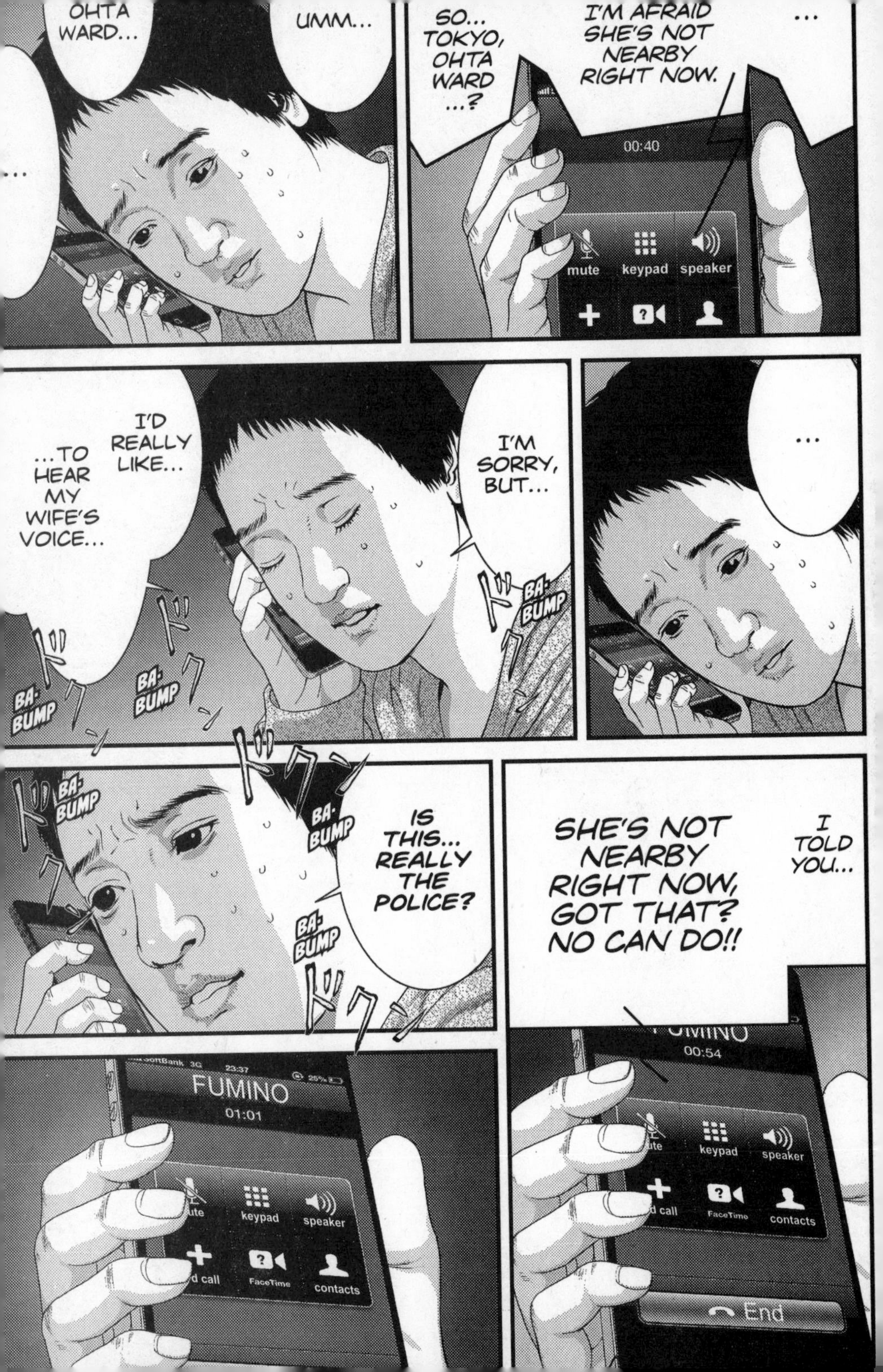
...
I'M AFRAID SHE'S NOT NEARBY RIGHT NOW.
SO... TOKYO, OHTA WARD ...?
00:40
mute
keypad
speaker
UMM...
OHTA WARD...
...
...
I'M SORRY, BUT...
BA-BUMP
I'D REALLY LIKE...
...TO HEAR MY WIFE'S VOICE...
BA-BUMP
BA-BUMP
I TOLD YOU...
SHE'S NOT NEARBY RIGHT NOW, GOT THAT? NO CAN DO!!
00:54
keypad
speaker
FaceTime
contacts
End
BA-BUMP
IS THIS... REALLY THE POLICE?
BA-BUMP
BA-BUMP
BA-BUMP
SoftBank 3G
23:37
25%
FUMINO
01:01
keypad
speaker
FaceTime
contacts

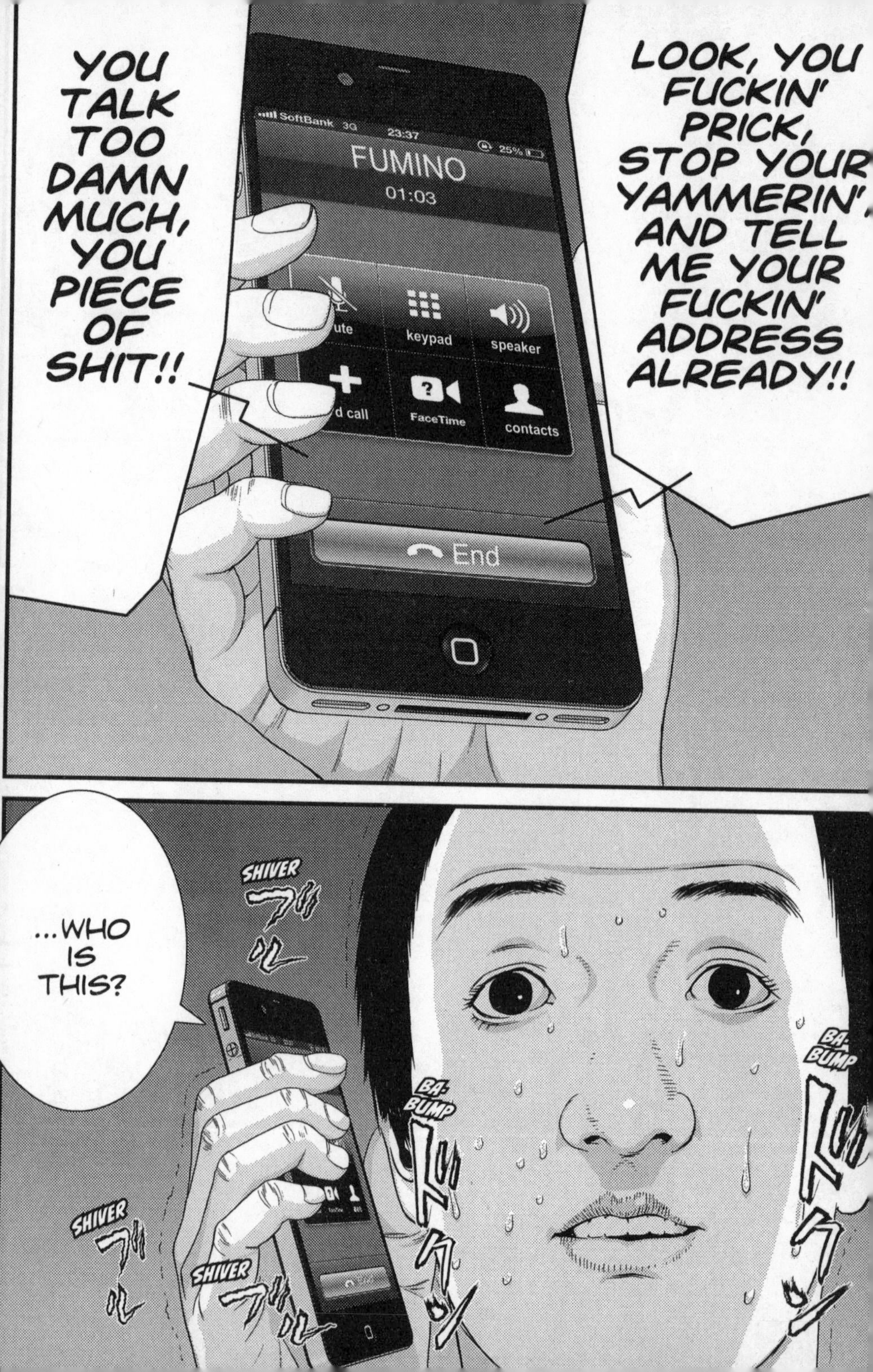
LOOK, YOU FUCKIN' PRICK, STOP YOUR YAMMERIN', AND TELL ME YOUR FUCKIN' ADDRESS ALREADY!!
SoftBank 3G
23:37
25%
FUMINO
01:03
keypad
speaker
FaceTime
contacts
End
YOU TALK TOO DAMN MUCH, YOU PIECE OF SHIT!!
BA-BUMP
BA-BUMP
SHIVER
...WHO IS THIS?
SHIVER
SHIVER

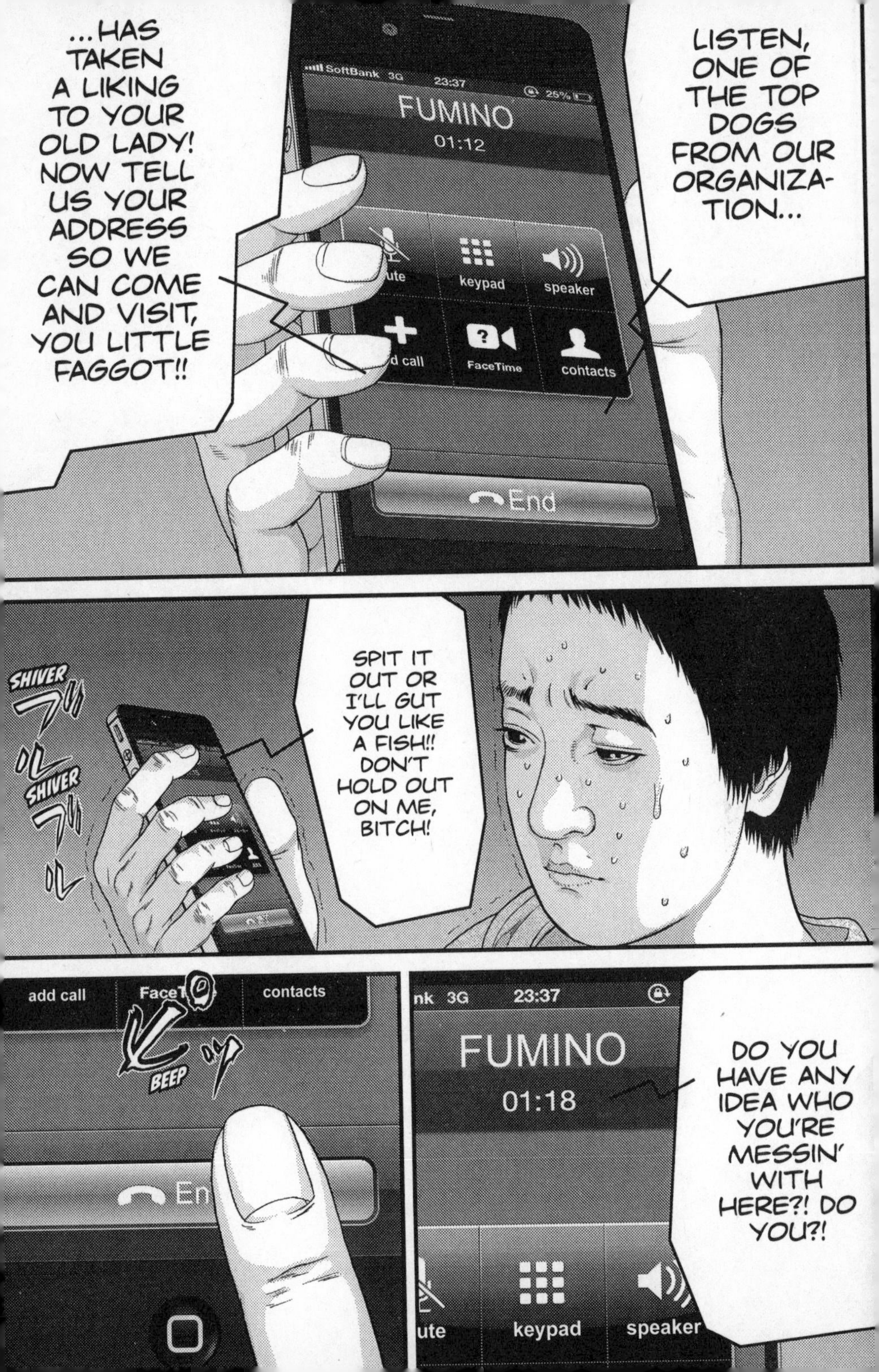
SoftBank 3G
23:37
25%
FUMINO
01:12
keypad
speaker
FaceTime
contacts
End
LISTEN, ONE OF THE TOP DOGS FROM OUR ORGANIZATION...
...HAS TAKEN A LIKING TO YOUR OLD LADY! NOW TELL US YOUR ADDRESS SO WE CAN COME AND VISIT, YOU LITTLE FAGGOT!!
SPIT IT OUT OR I'LL GUT YOU LIKE A FISH!! DON'T HOLD OUT ON ME, BITCH!
SHIVER
SHIVER
3G
23:37
FUMINO
01:18
DO YOU HAVE ANY IDEA WHO YOU'RE MESSIN' WITH HERE?! DO YOU?!
keypad
speaker
add call
contacts
BEEP

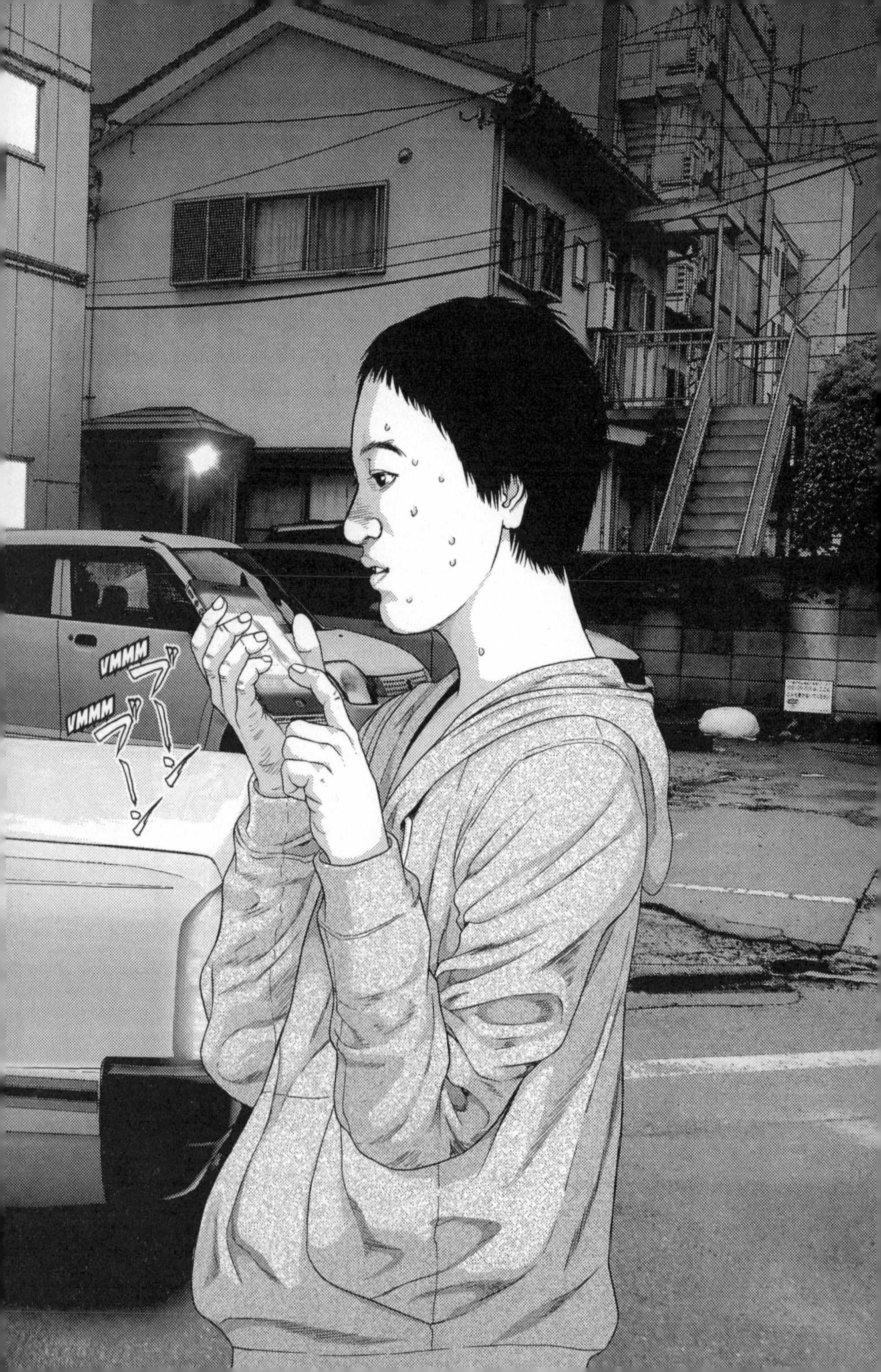
VMMM
VMMM

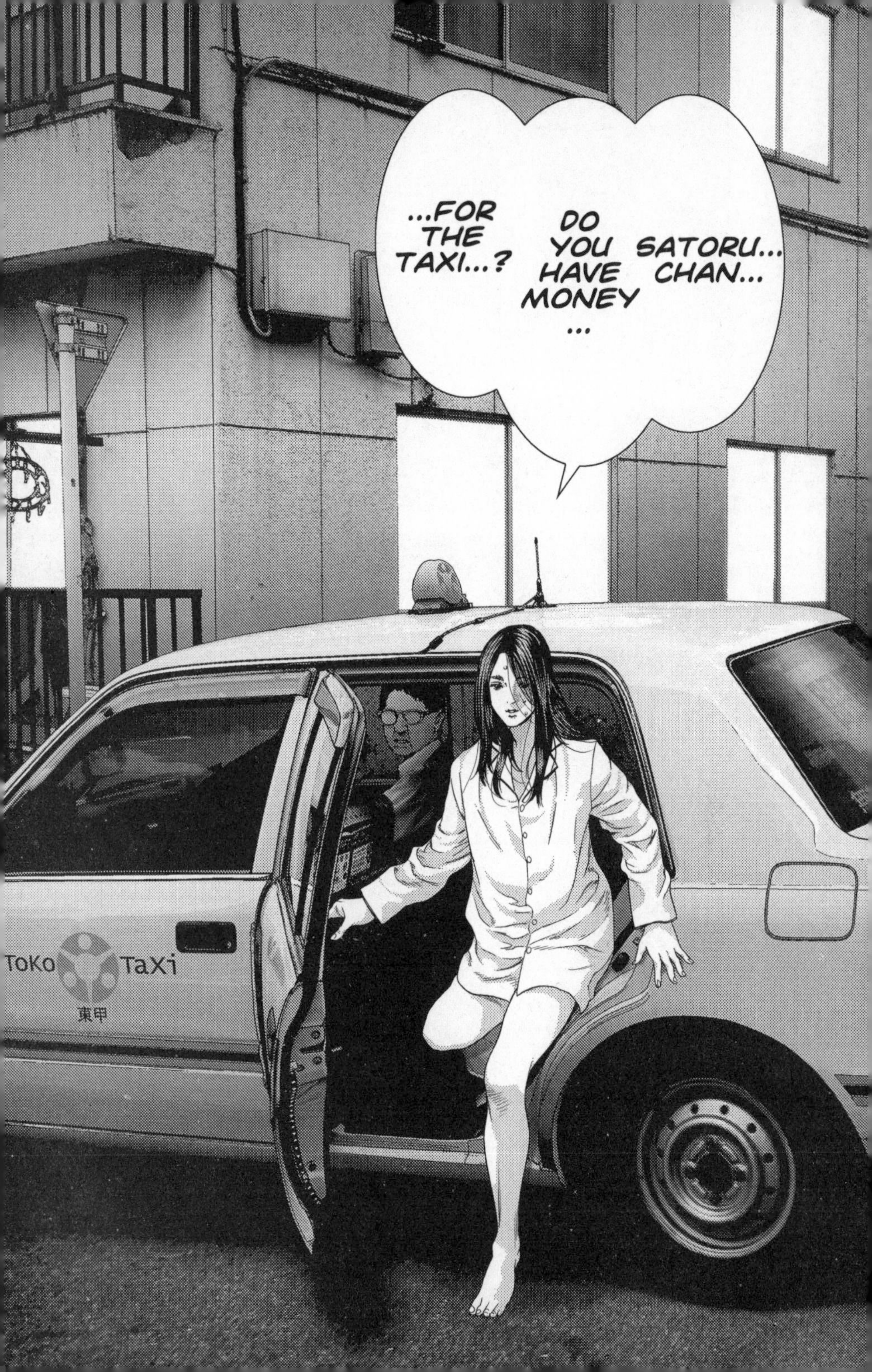
SATORU... CHAN... DO YOU HAVE MONEY ... ...FOR THE TAXI...?
ToKo TaXi
東甲

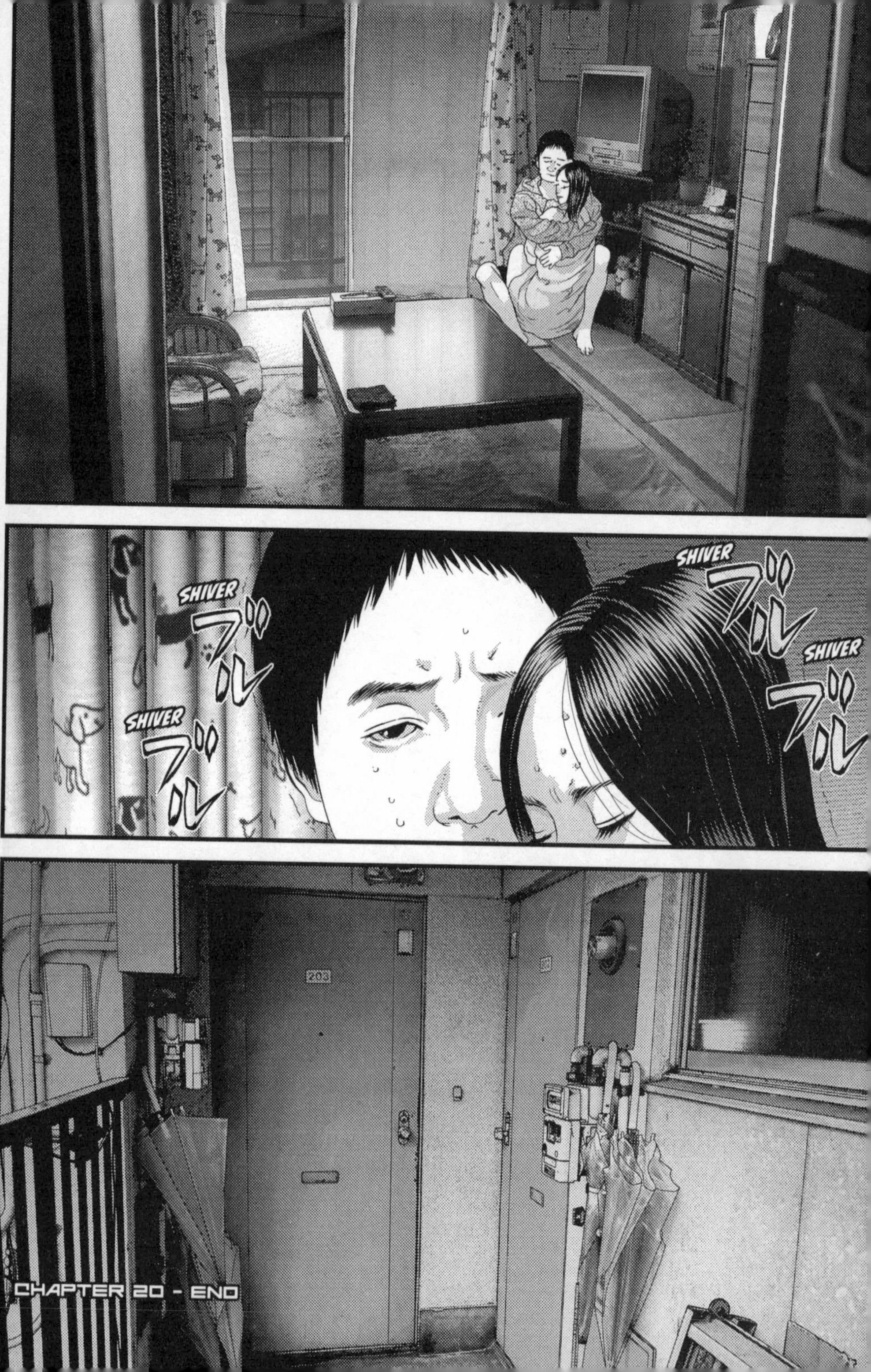
SHIVER
ブル
SHIVER
ブル
SHIVER
ブル
SHIVER
ブル
CHAPTER 20 - END

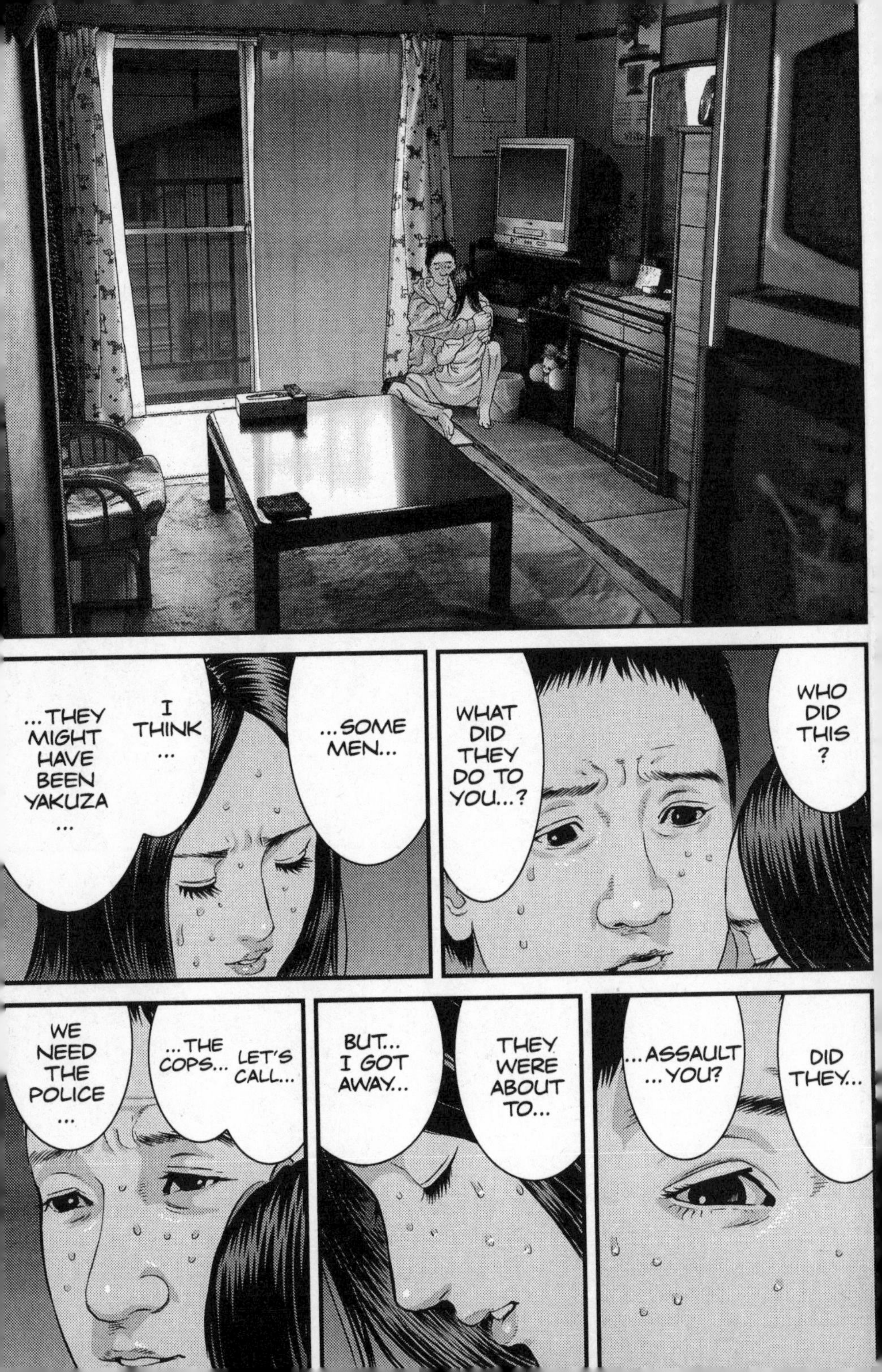
WHO DID THIS?
WHAT DID THEY DO TO YOU...?
...SOME MEN...
I THINK...
...THEY MIGHT HAVE BEEN YAKUZA...
DID THEY...
...ASSAULT ...YOU?
THEY WERE ABOUT TO...
BUT... I GOT AWAY...
LET'S CALL...
...THE COPS...
WE NEED THE POLICE...

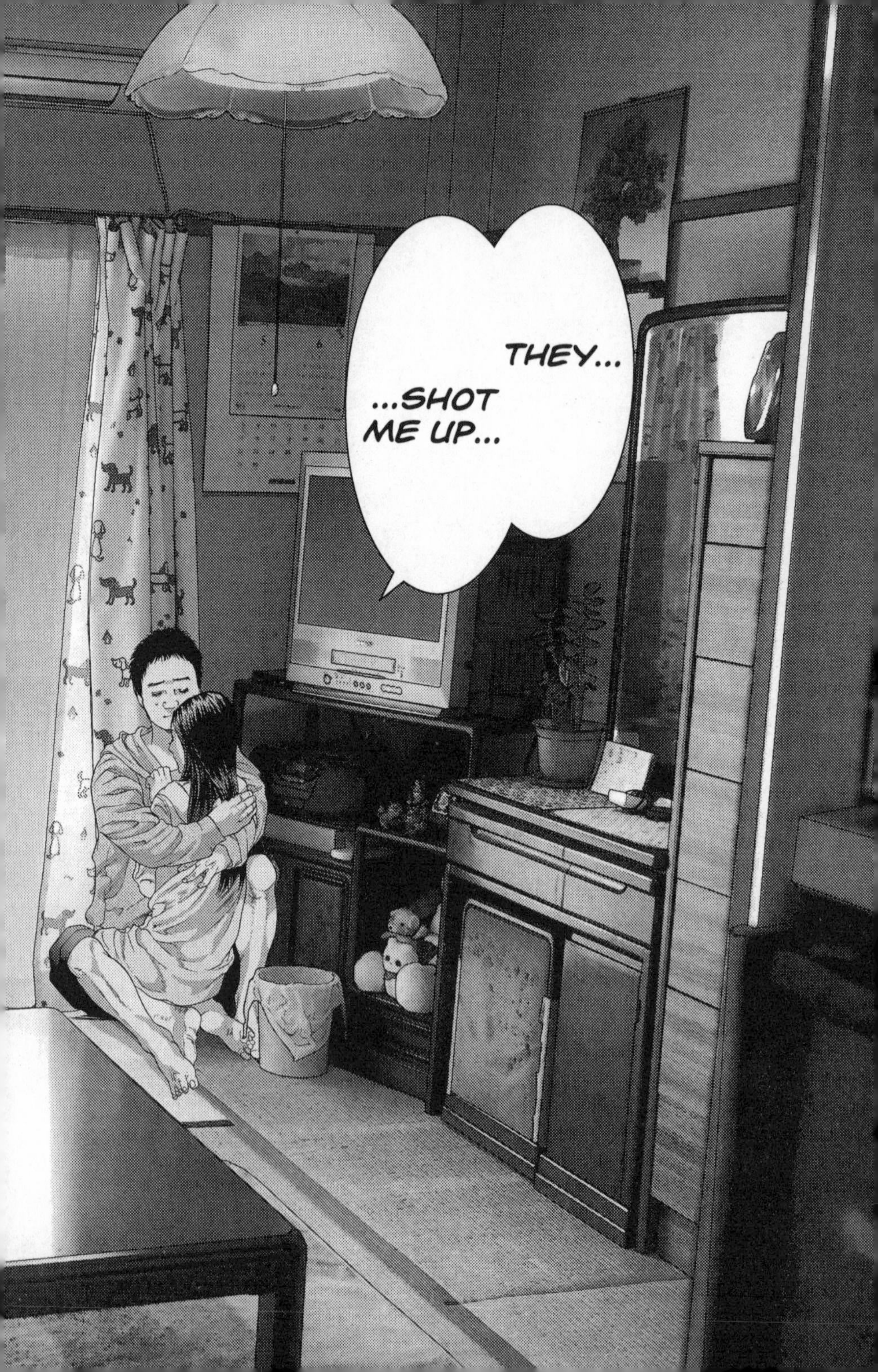
THEY...
...SHOT ME UP...

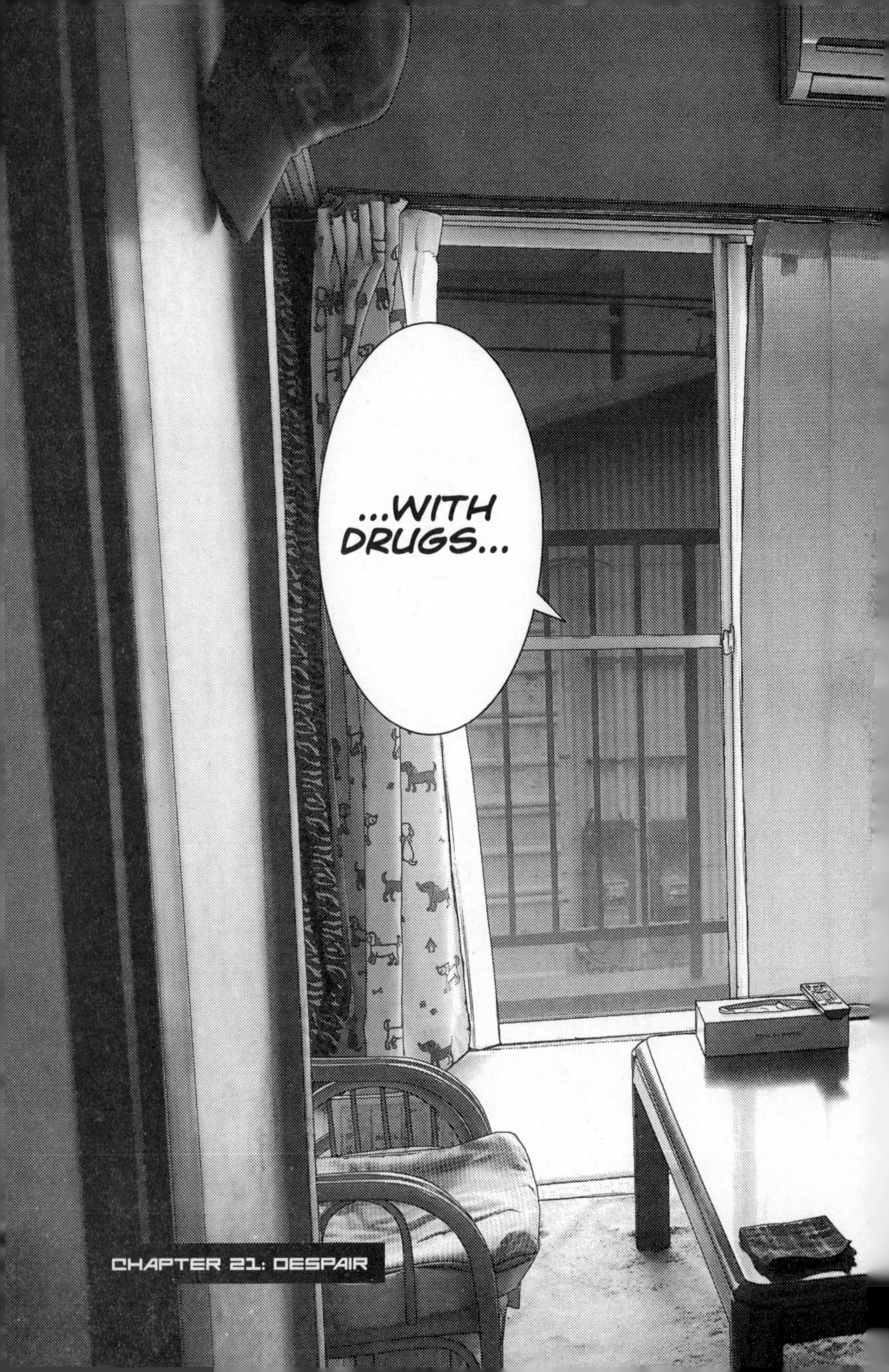
...WITH DRUGS...
CHAPTER 21: DESPAIR

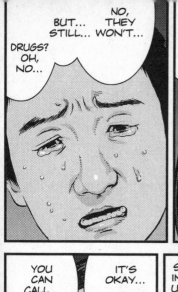

...?!
DRUGS...?
I THINK ...
...THE POLICE... MIGHT ARREST ME...
NO, THEY WON'T...
BUT... STILL...
DRUGS? OH, NO...
THEY'LL TEST MY PEE...
...AND GET A POSITIVE RESULT.
WHY WOULD THEY DO THIS TO YOU...?
SHOOTING YOU UP WITH DRUGS? IT MAKES NO SENSE ...
IT'S OKAY... MAKE THE CALL...
YOU CAN CALL... ...THE POLICE...
SoftBank 3G
0:22
9/24 (Wed)
24%
If you tell the cops we'll kill your entire family
Read
JING-A-LING

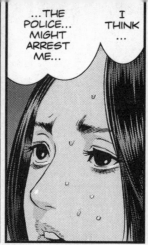

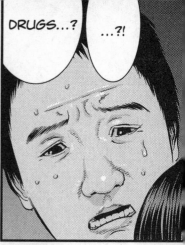

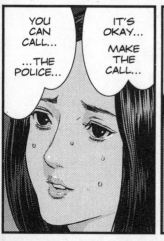

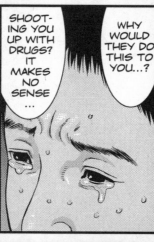

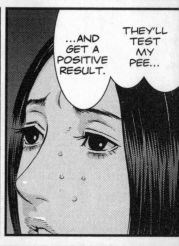

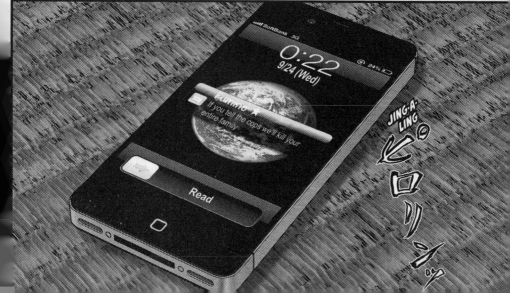

Fumino ★
If you tell the cops we'll kill your entire family
SHIVER
SHIVER
SHIVER
SHIVER
SHIVER
SHIVER
BUT THIS... THIS MAKES NO SENSE.
WHY WOULD ANY-ONE DO THIS ...?
WE DIDN'T DO ANY-THING WRONG...
WHY... WOULD THIS HAPPEN ...?

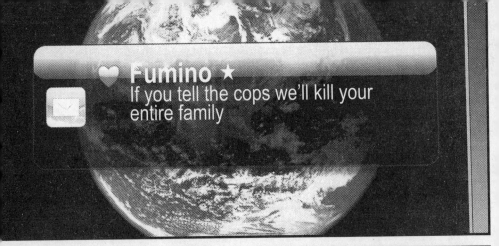

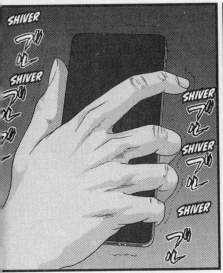

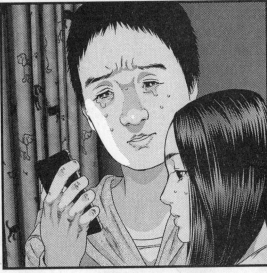

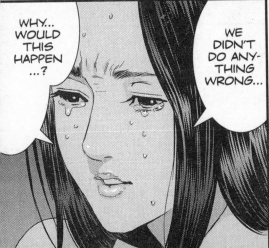

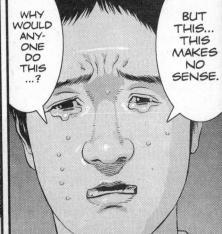

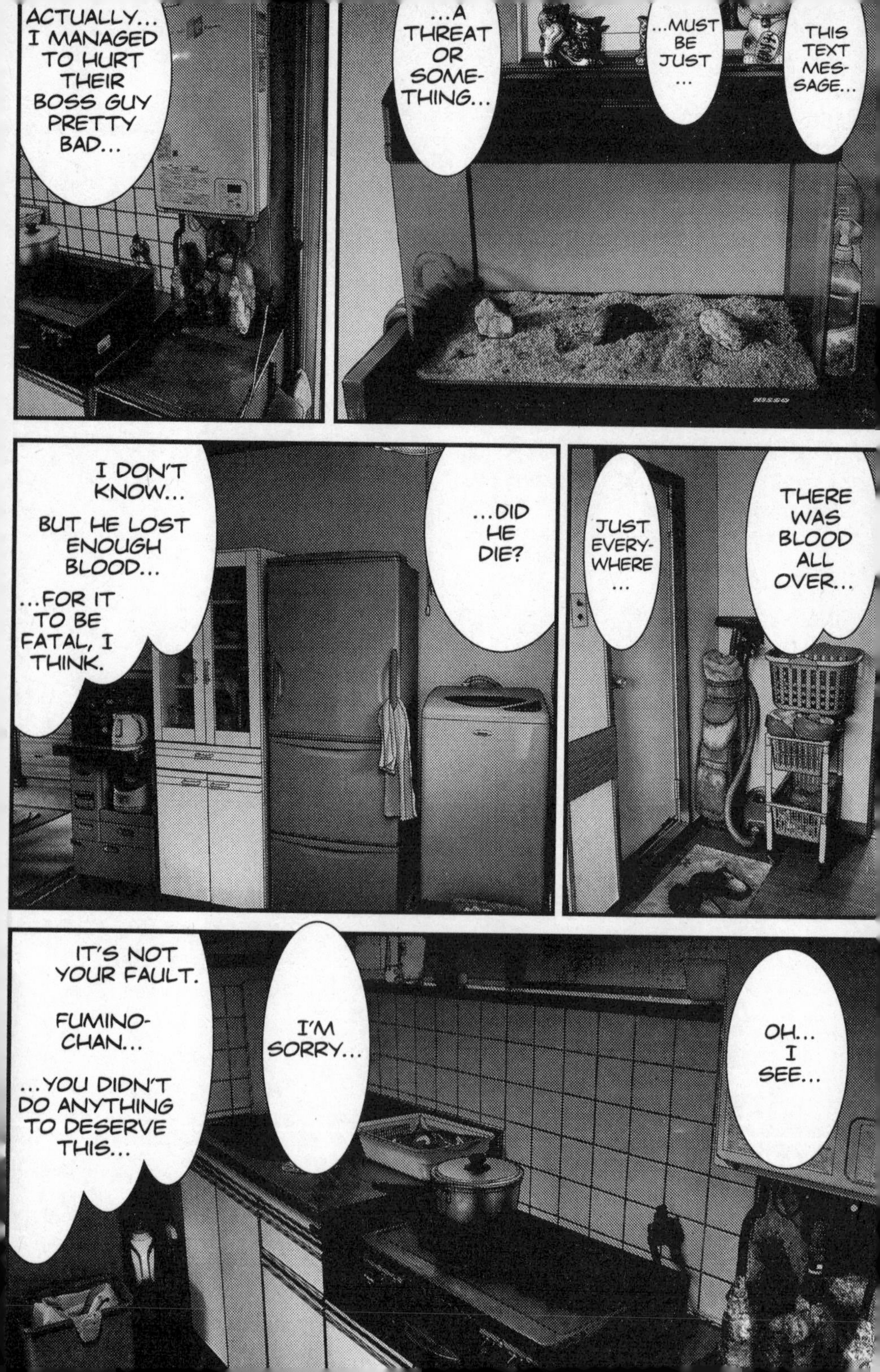
THIS TEXT MESSAGE...
...MUST BE JUST...
...A THREAT OR SOMETHING...
ACTUALLY... I MANAGED TO HURT THEIR BOSS GUY PRETTY BAD...
THERE WAS BLOOD ALL OVER...
JUST EVERYWHERE...
...DID HE DIE?
I DON'T KNOW...
BUT HE LOST ENOUGH BLOOD...
...FOR IT TO BE FATAL, I THINK.
OH... I SEE...
I'M SORRY...
IT'S NOT YOUR FAULT.
FUMINO-CHAN...
...YOU DIDN'T DO ANYTHING TO DESERVE THIS...

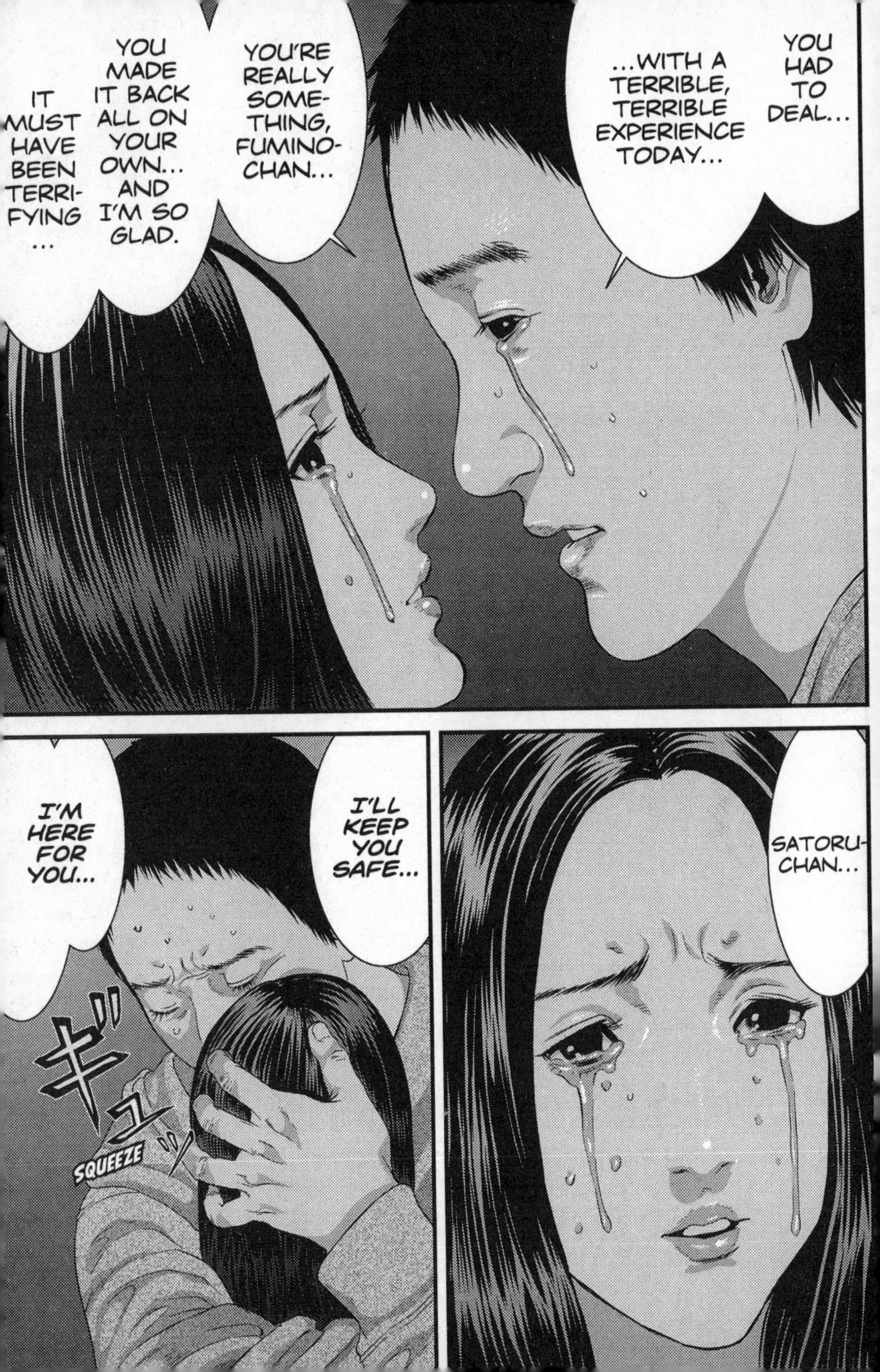
YOU HAD TO DEAL...
...WITH A TERRIBLE, TERRIBLE EXPERIENCE TODAY...
YOU'RE REALLY SOME-THING, FUMINO-CHAN...
YOU MADE IT BACK ALL ON YOUR OWN... AND I'M SO GLAD.
IT MUST HAVE BEEN TERRI-FYING...
SATORU-CHAN...
I'LL KEEP YOU SAFE...
I'M HERE FOR YOU...
SQUEEZE

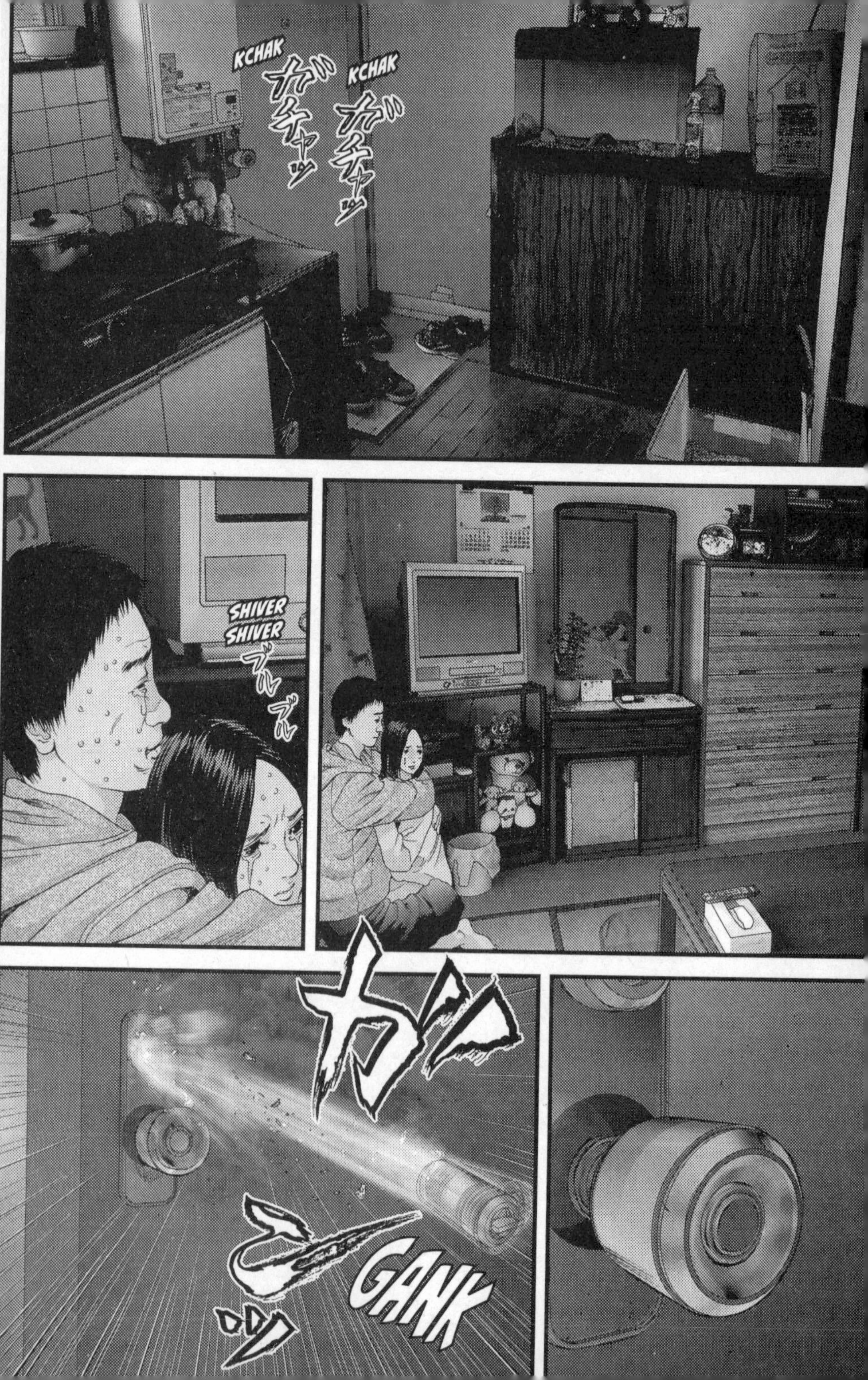
KCHAK
ガチャッ
KCHAK
ガチャッ
SHIVER
SHIVER
ブルブル
ガン
GANK

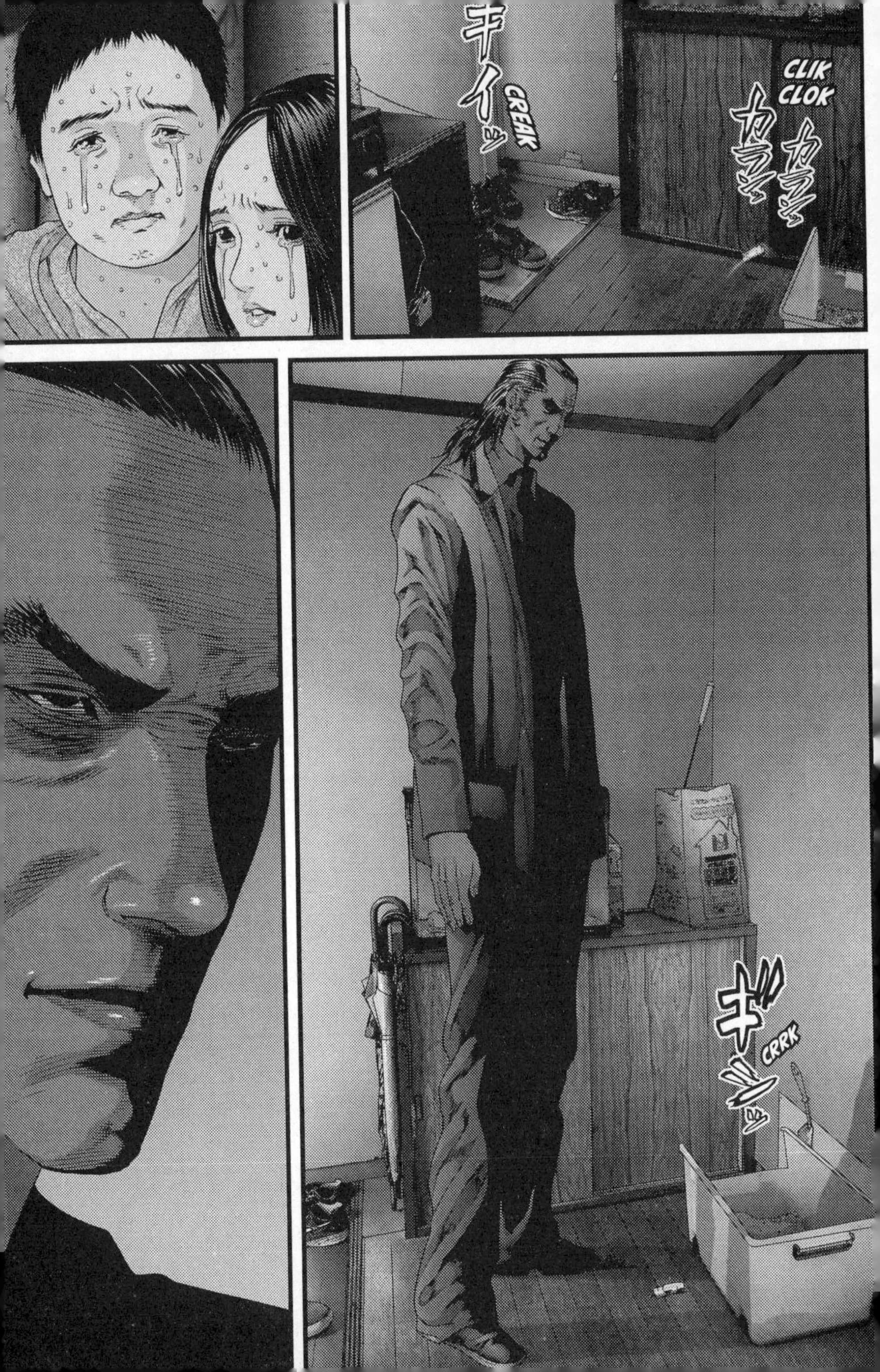
CLIK CLOK
カランカラン
キイッ
CREAK
ギシッ
CRRK

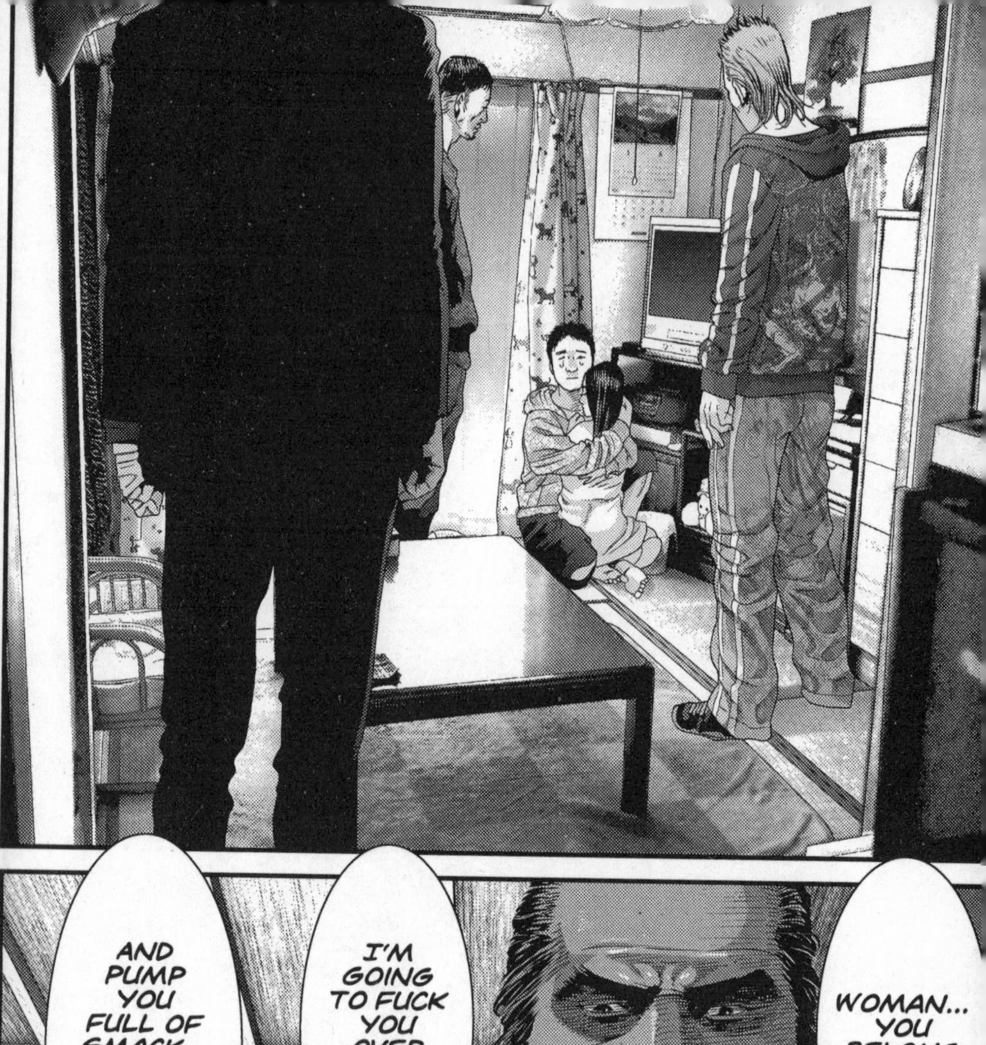
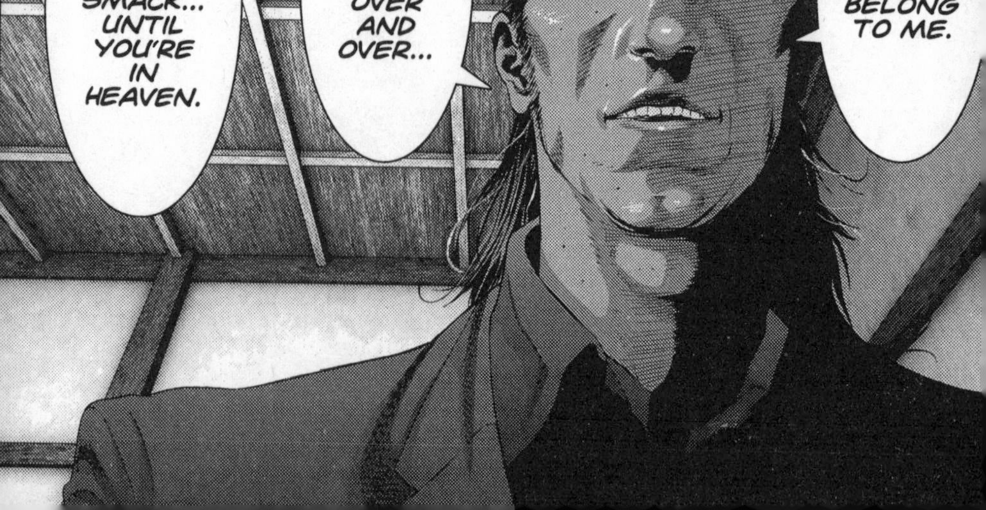
WOMAN... YOU BELONG TO ME.
I'M GOING TO FUCK YOU OVER AND OVER...
AND PUMP YOU FULL OF SMACK... UNTIL YOU'RE IN HEAVEN.

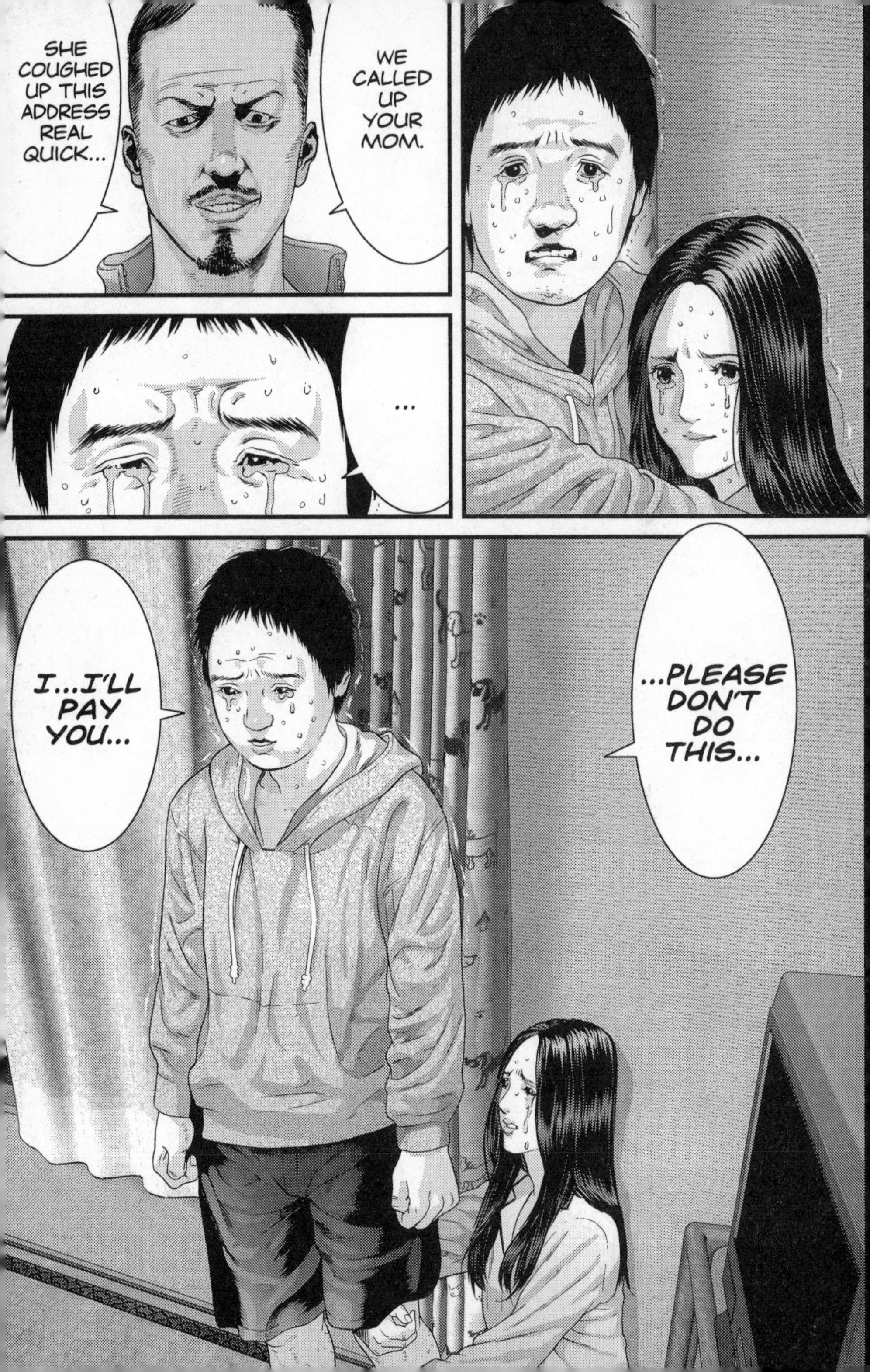
WE CALLED UP YOUR MOM.
SHE COUGHED UP THIS ADDRESS REAL QUICK...
...
...PLEASE DON'T DO THIS...
I...I'LL PAY YOU...

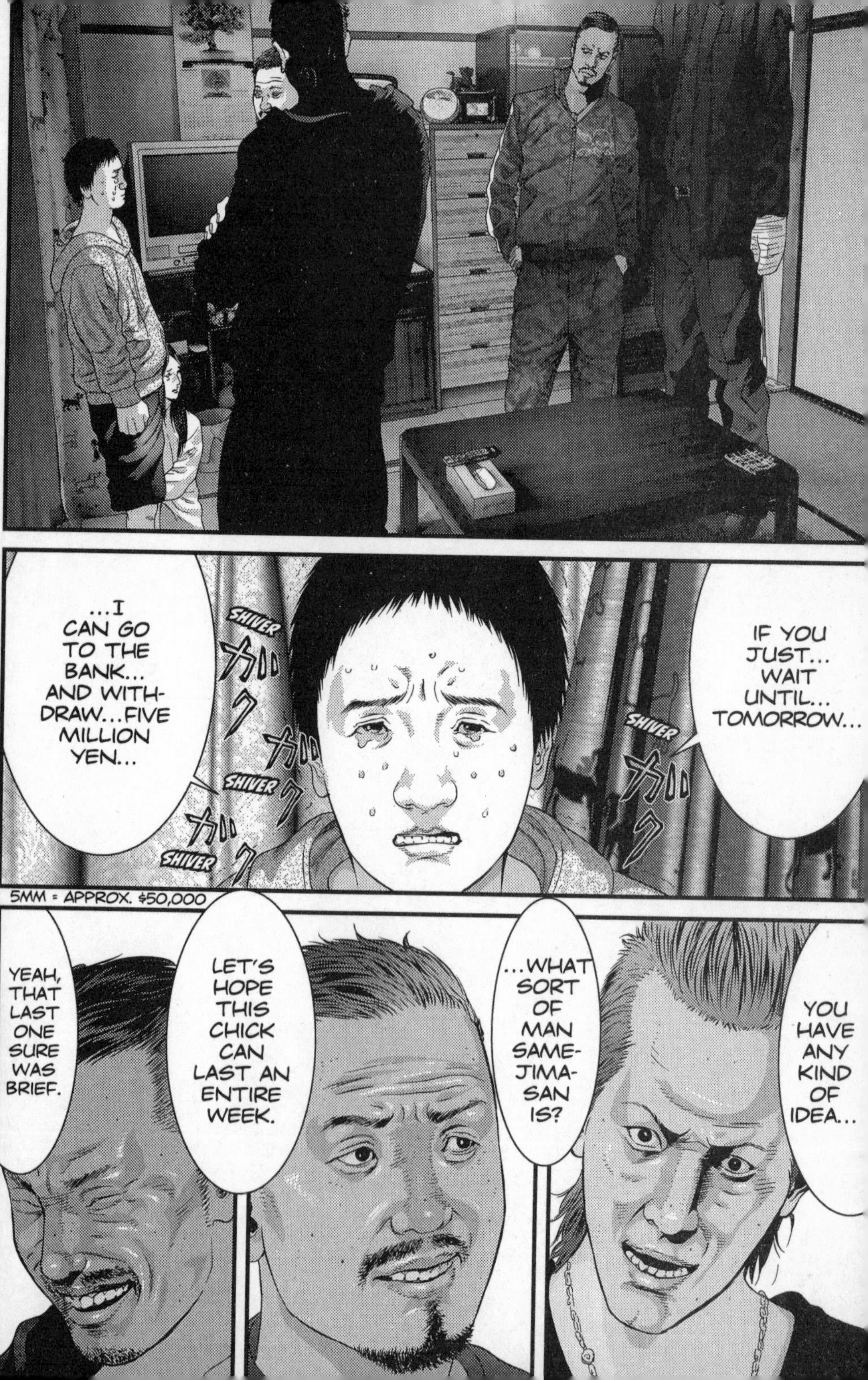

IF YOU JUST... WAIT UNTIL... TOMORROW...
SHIVER
カク
...I CAN GO TO THE BANK... AND WITH-DRAW...FIVE MILLION YEN...
SHIVER
カク
SHIVER
カク
SHIVER
カク
5MM = APPROX. $50,000
YOU HAVE ANY KIND OF IDEA...
...WHAT SORT OF MAN SAME-JIMA-SAN IS?
LET'S HOPE THIS CHICK CAN LAST AN ENTIRE WEEK.
YEAH, THAT LAST ONE SURE WAS BRIEF.

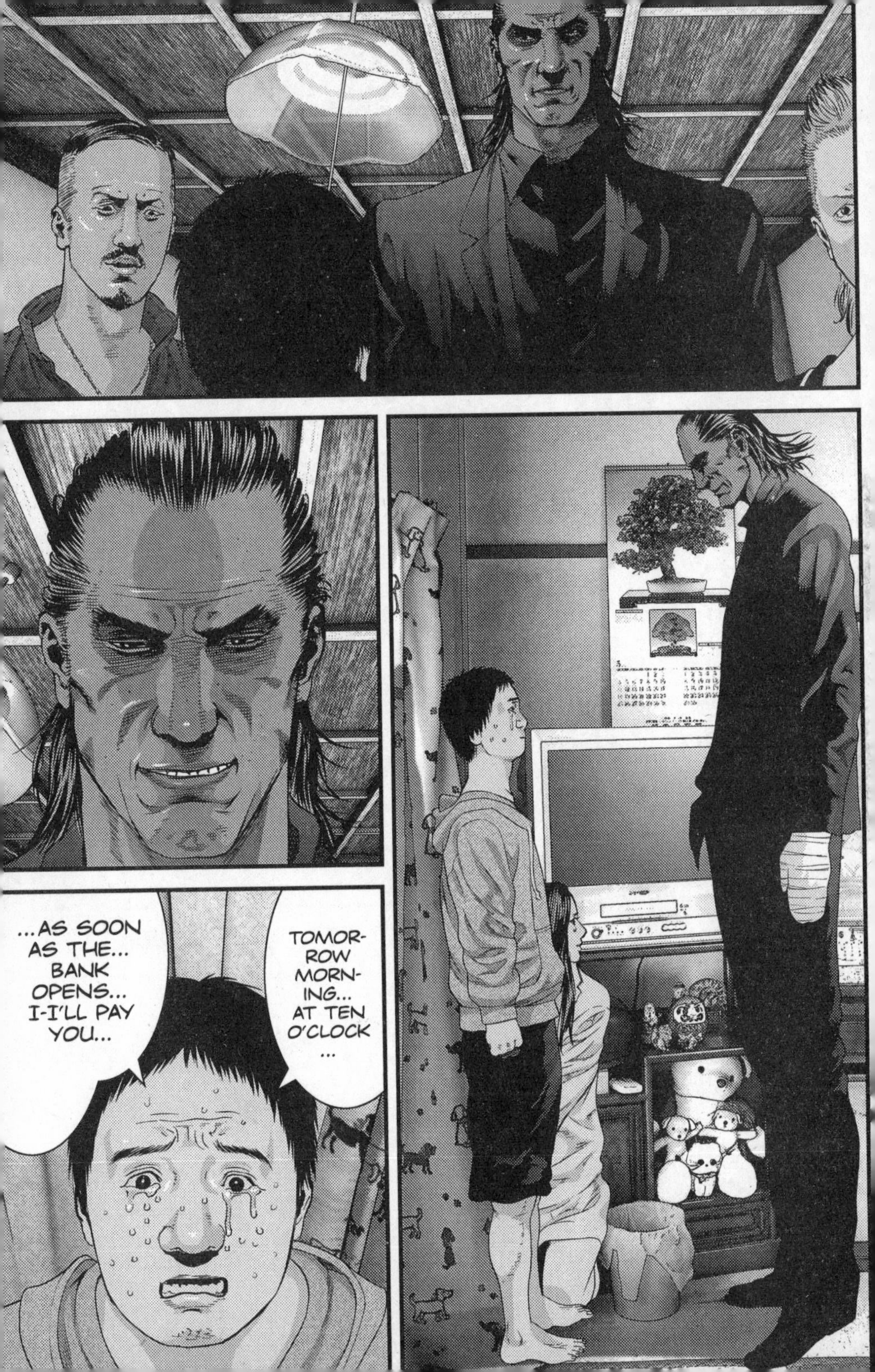
TOMOR-ROW MORN-ING... AT TEN O'CLOCK ...
...AS SOON AS THE... BANK OPENS... I-I'LL PAY YOU...

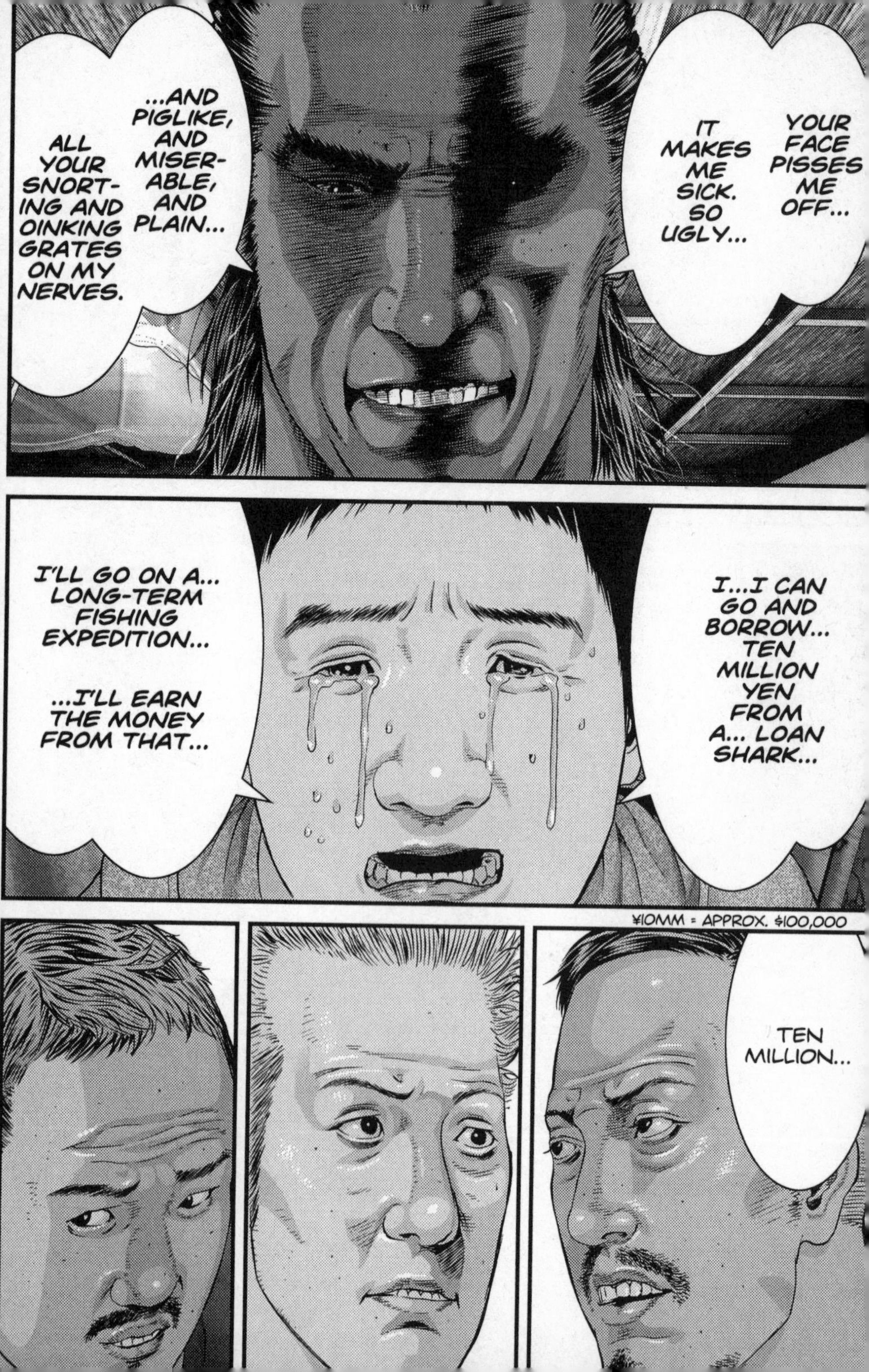
YOUR FACE PISSES ME OFF...
IT MAKES ME SICK. SO UGLY...
...AND PIGLIKE, AND MISERABLE, AND PLAIN...
ALL YOUR SNORTING AND OINKING GRATES ON MY NERVES.
I...I CAN GO AND BORROW... TEN MILLION YEN FROM A... LOAN SHARK...
I'LL GO ON A... LONG-TERM FISHING EXPEDITION...
...I'LL EARN THE MONEY FROM THAT...
¥10MM = APPROX. $100,000
TEN MILLION...

YOU? TEN MILLION YEN?

TEN MILLION YEN...

PAT

PAT

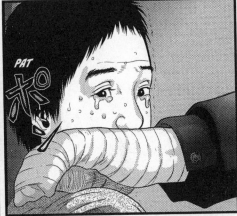

PAT

SATO-RU-CHAN...

NO... YOU CAN'T...

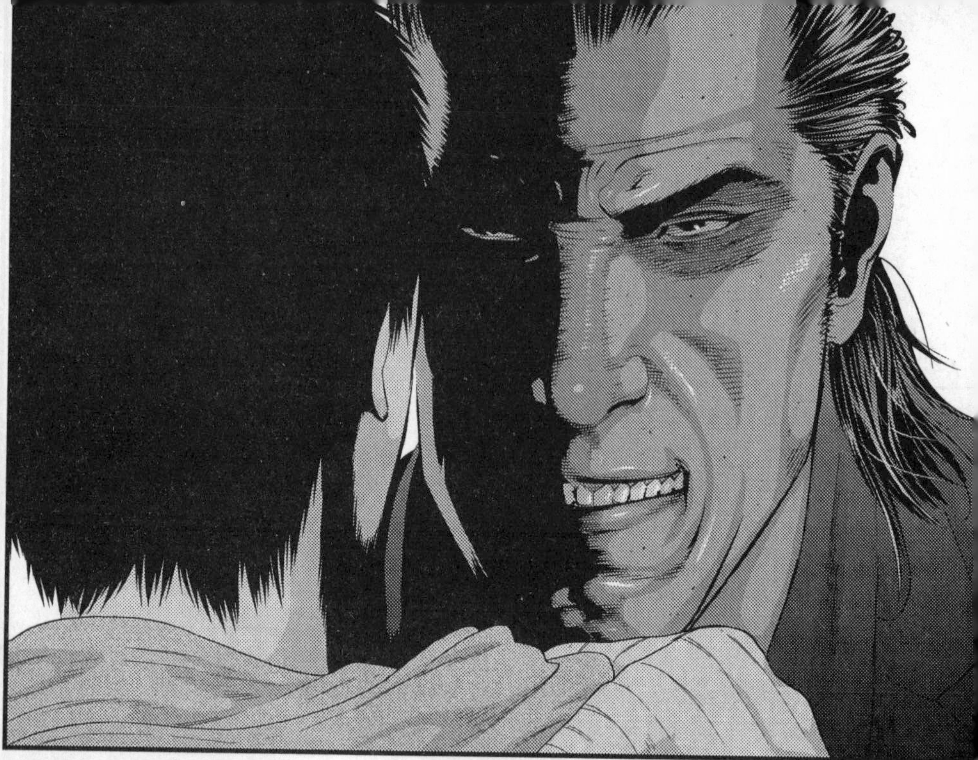

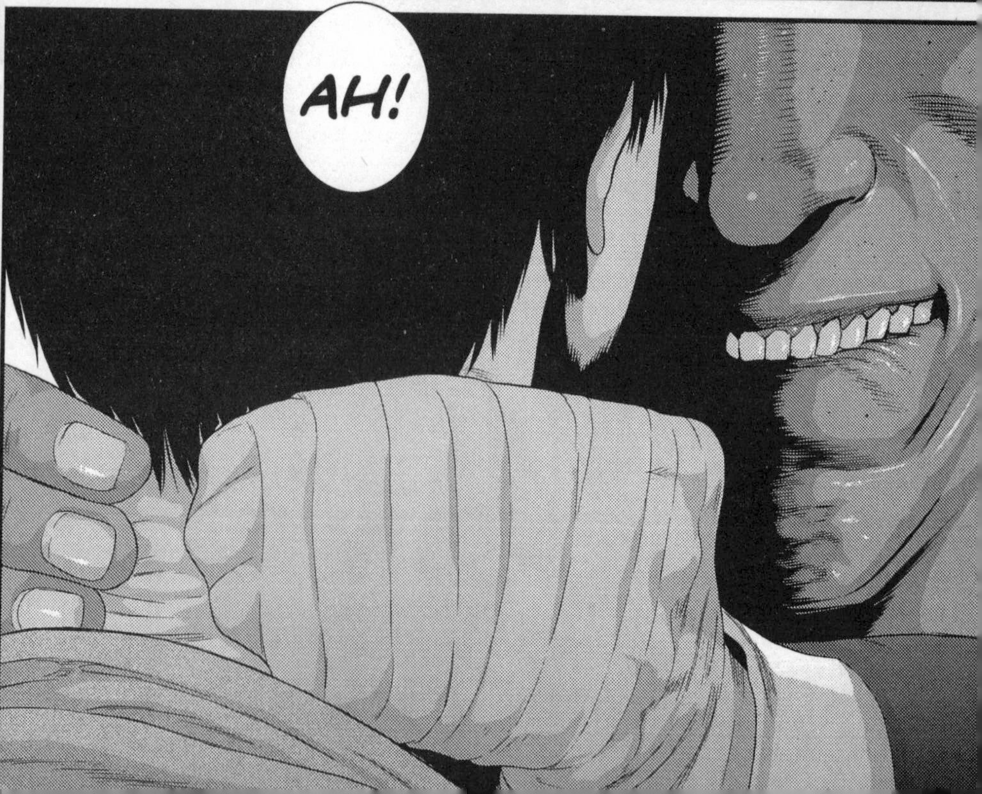
AH!

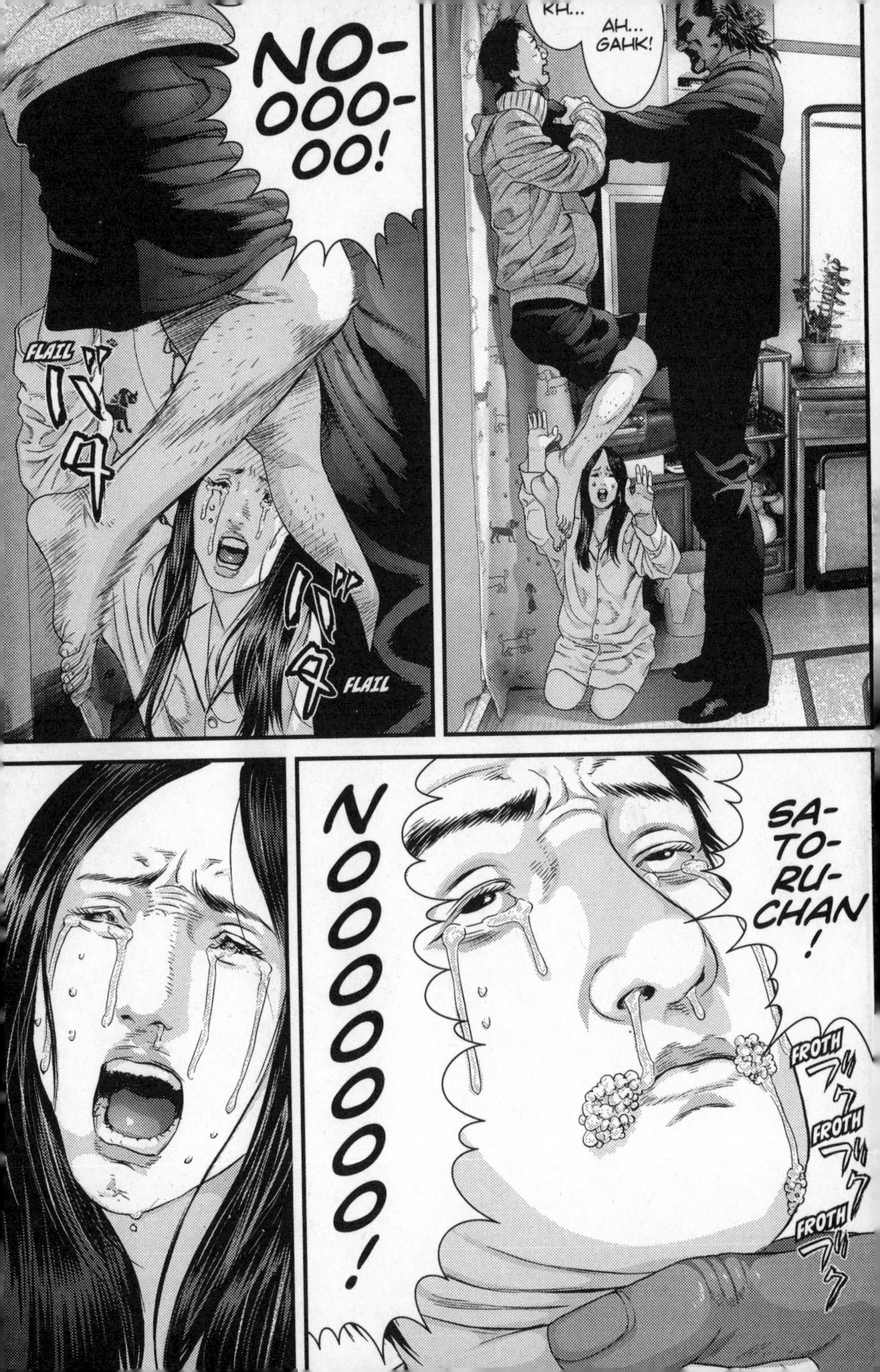
KH...
AH... GAHK!
NO-OOO-OO!
FLAIL
FLAIL
SA-TO-RU-CHAN!
FROTH
FROTH
FROTH
NOOOOOOO!

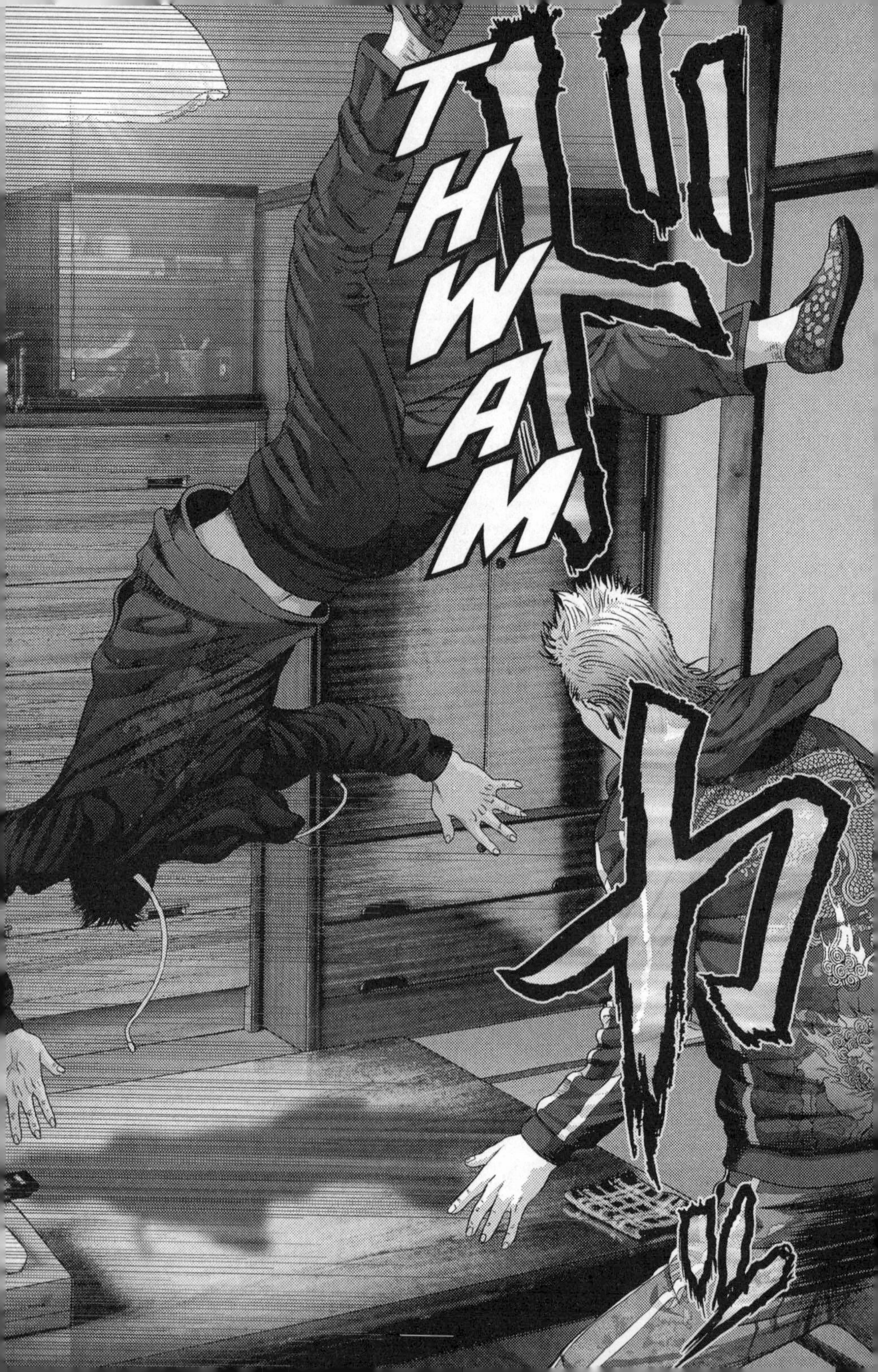
THWAM

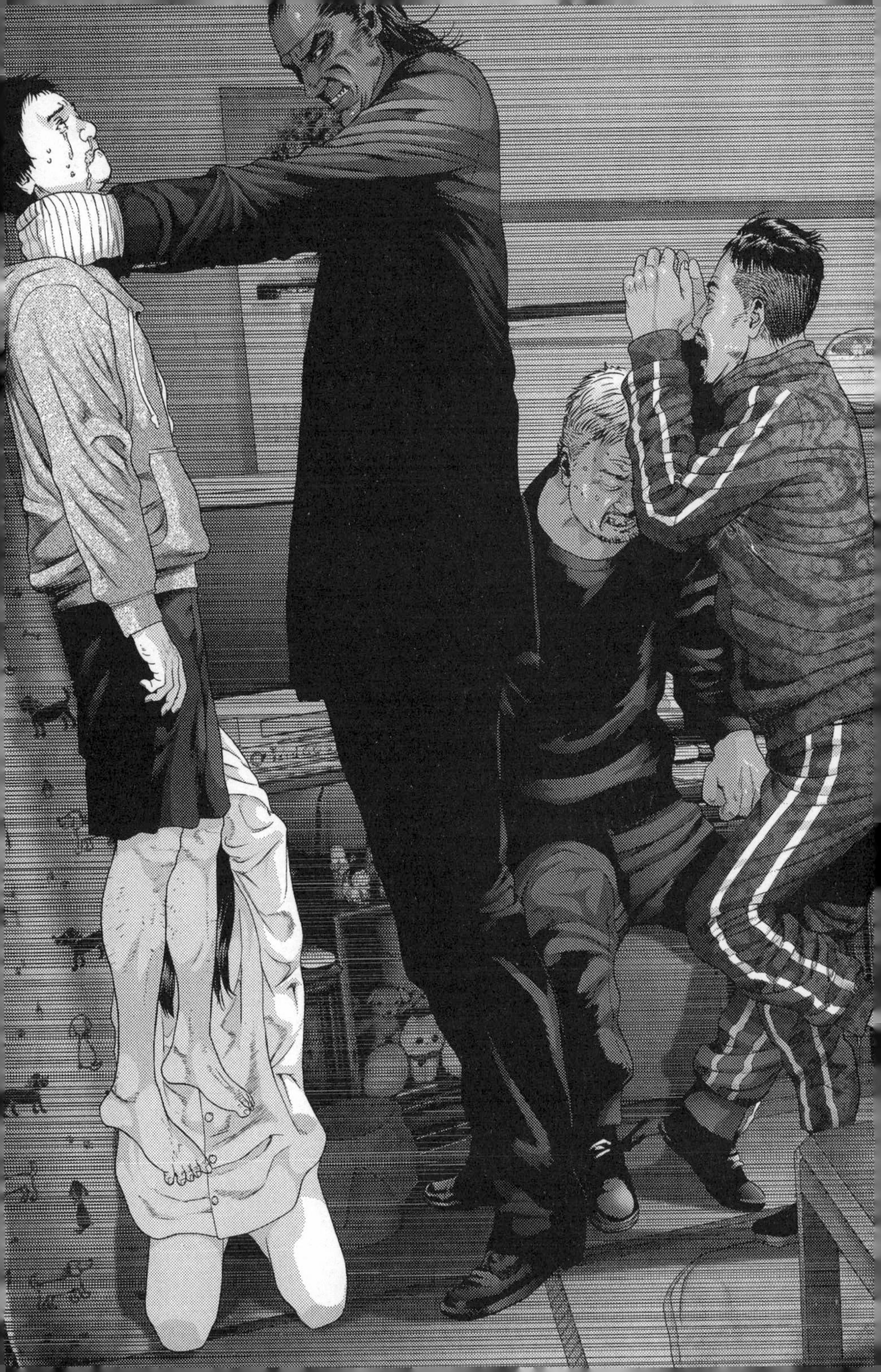

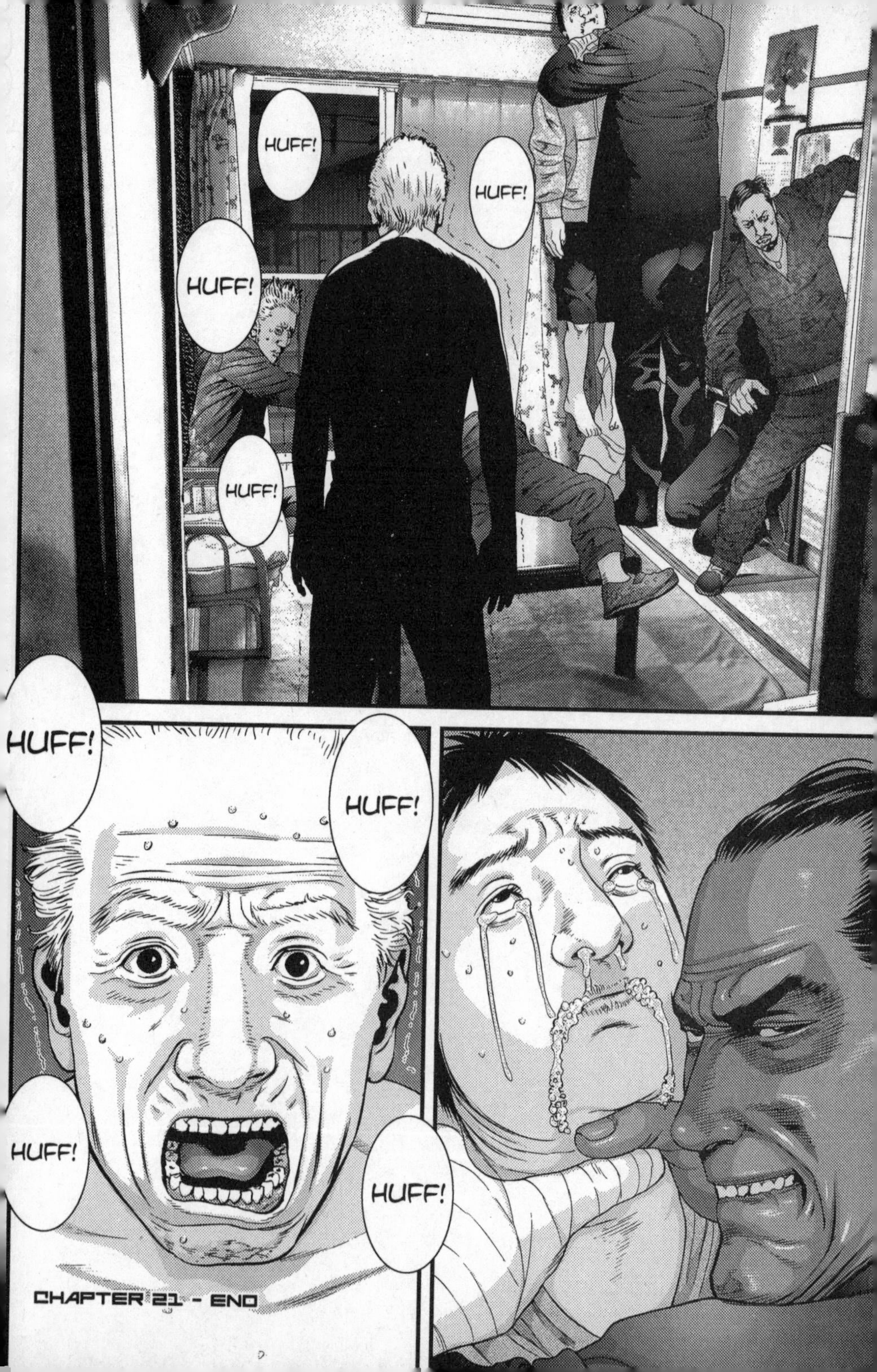
HUFF!
HUFF!
HUFF!
HUFF!
HUFF!
HUFF!
HUFF!
HUFF!
HUFF!
CHAPTER 21 - END

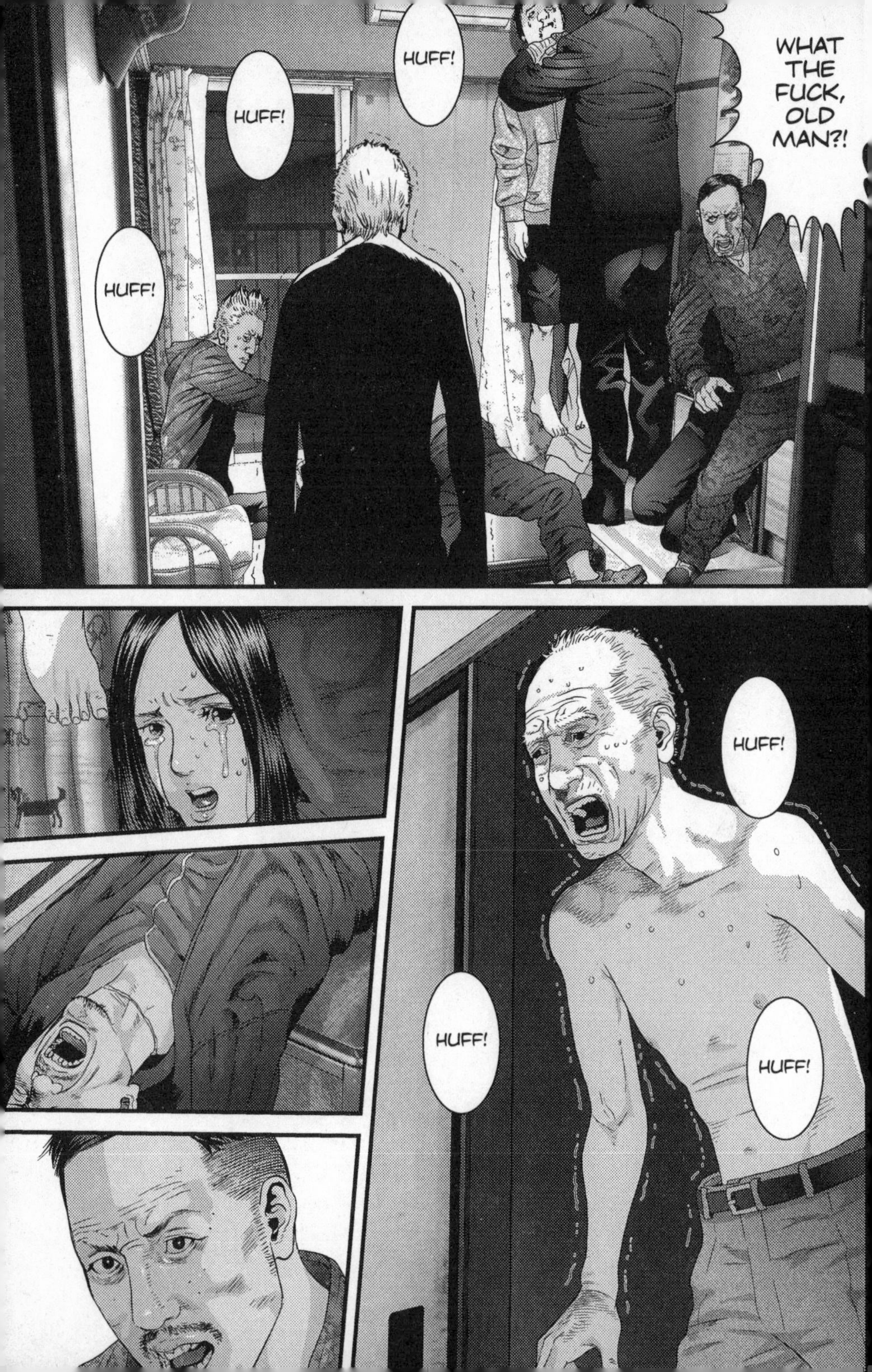
WHAT THE FUCK, OLD MAN?!
HUFF!
HUFF!
HUFF!
HUFF!
HUFF!
HUFF!

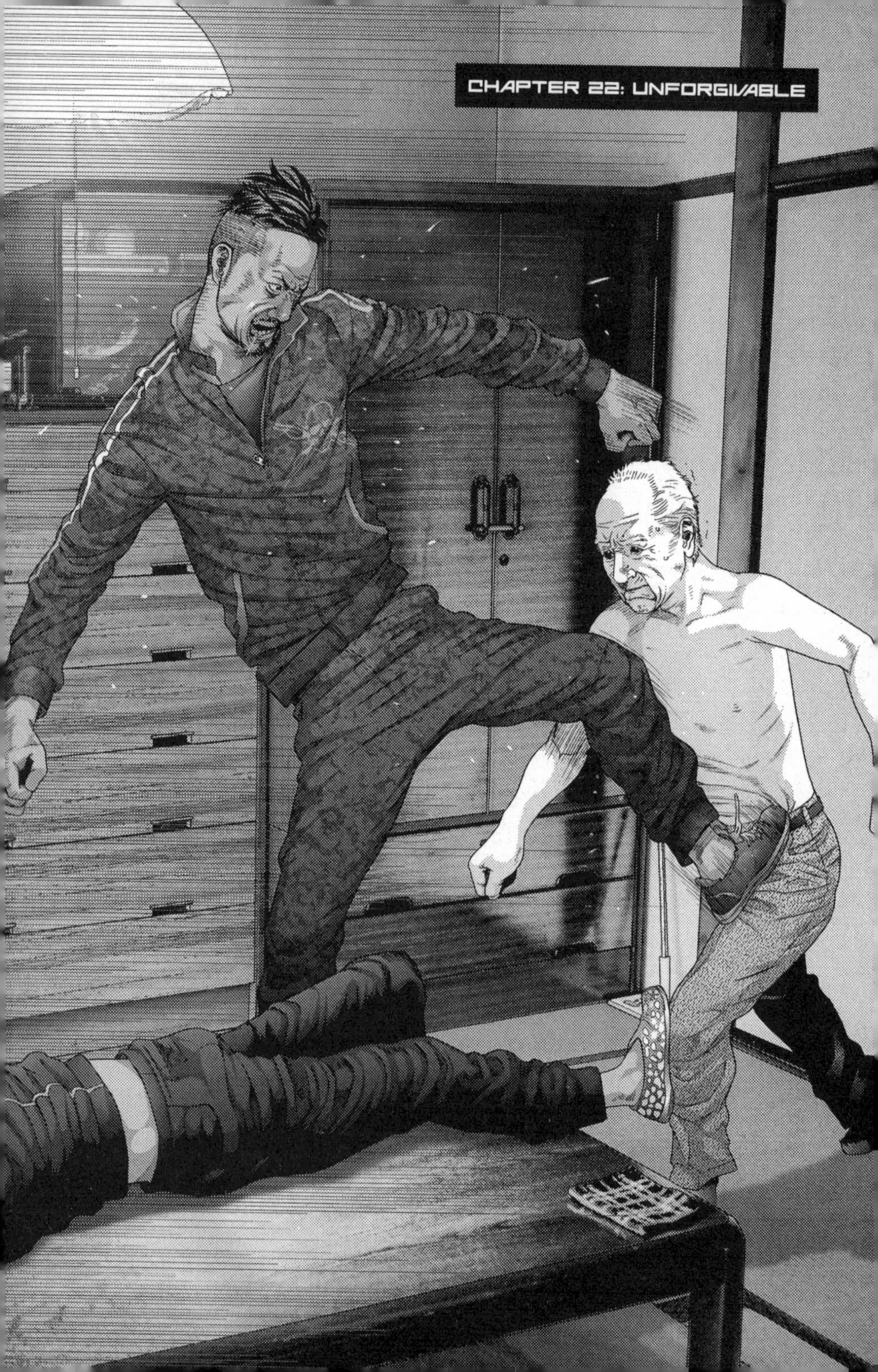
CHAPTER 22: UNFORGIVABLE

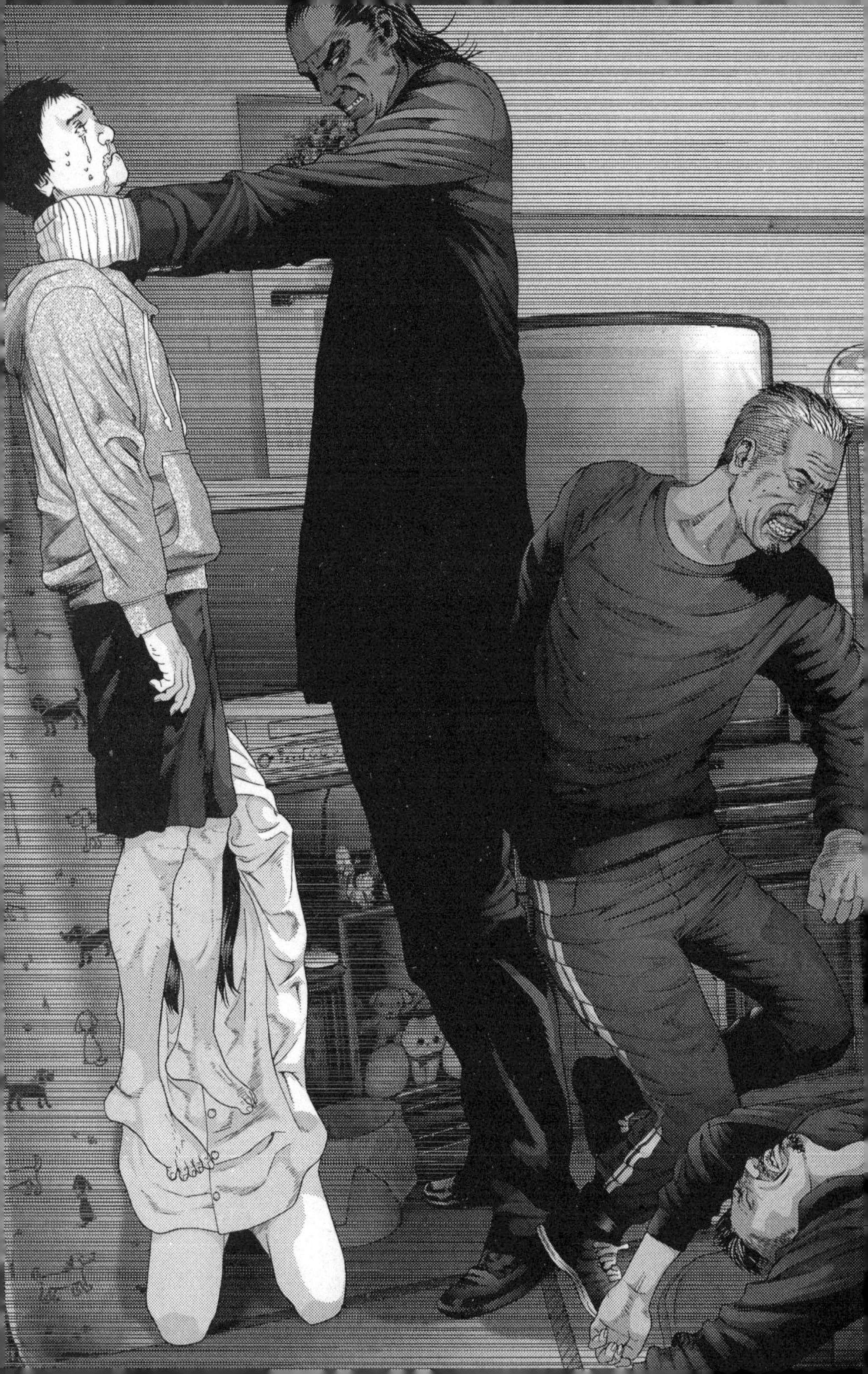

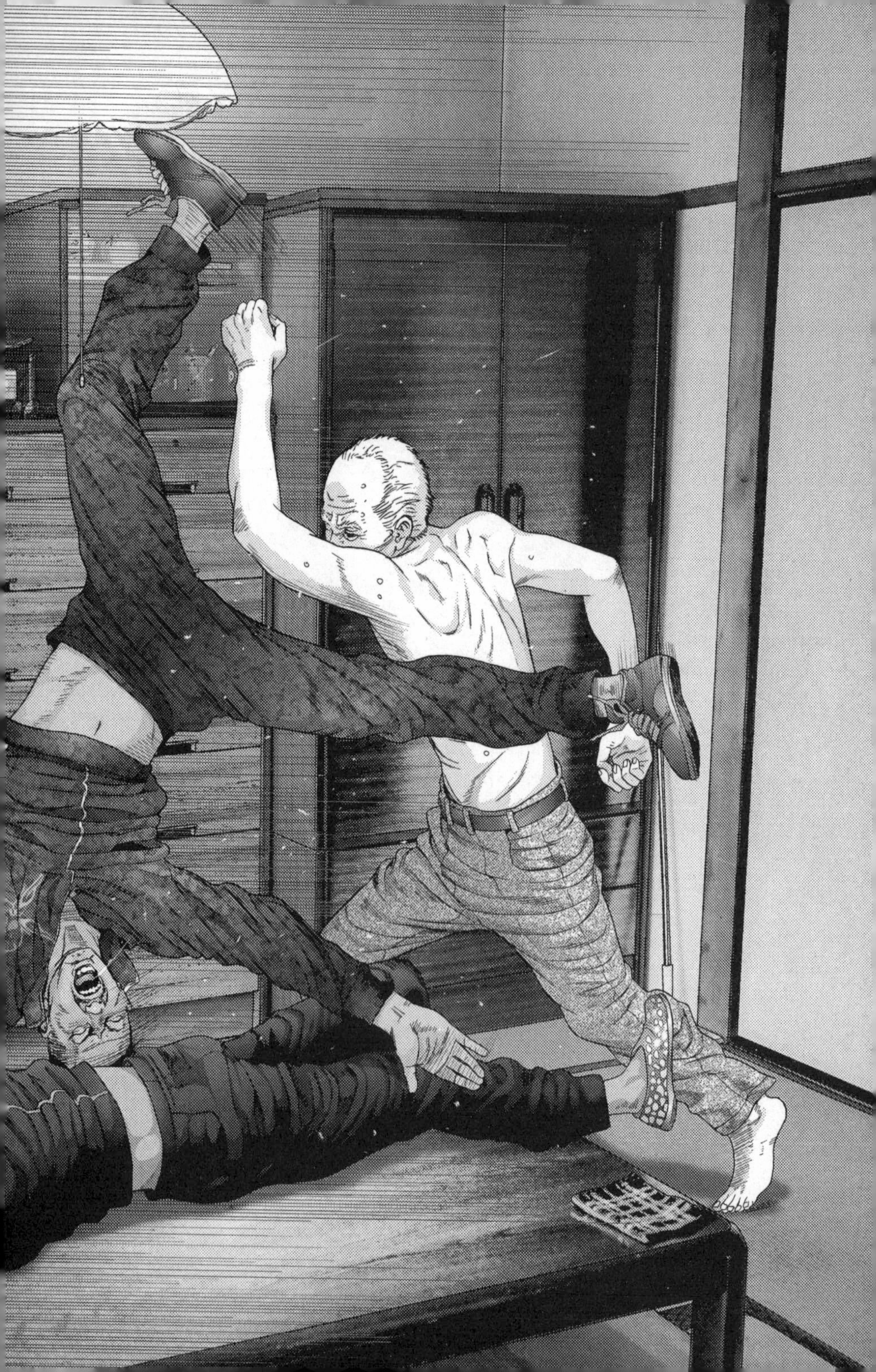

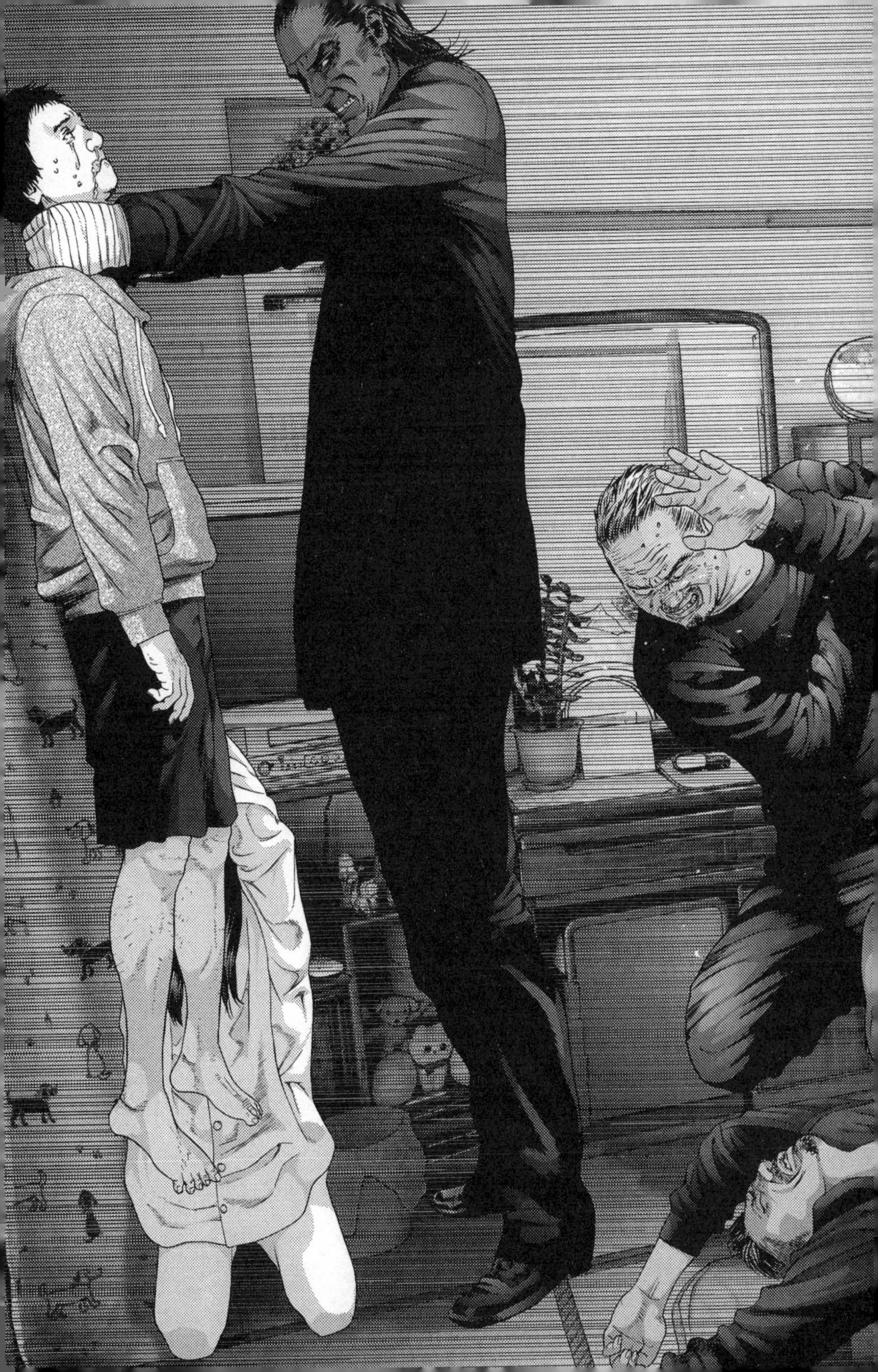

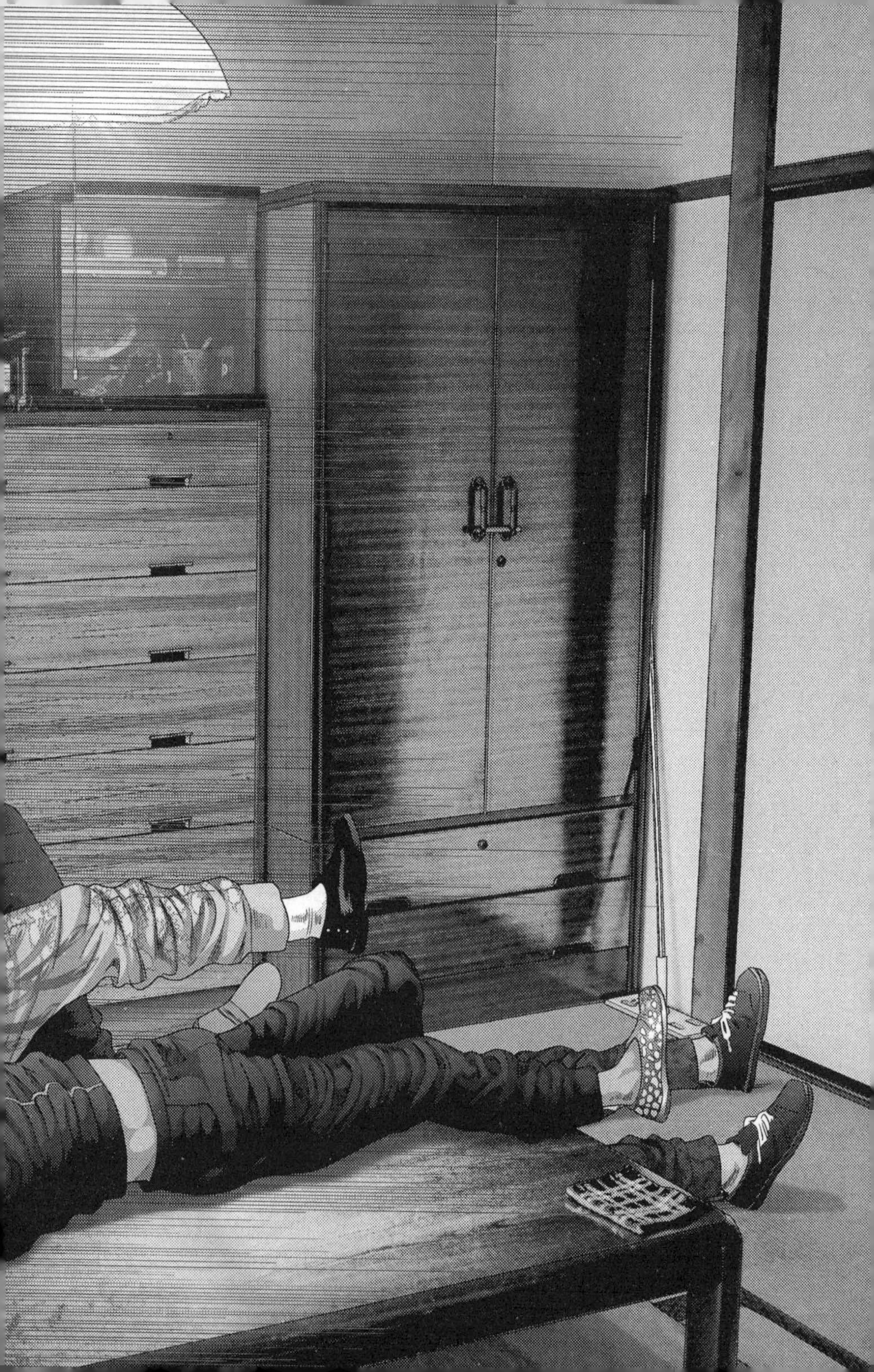

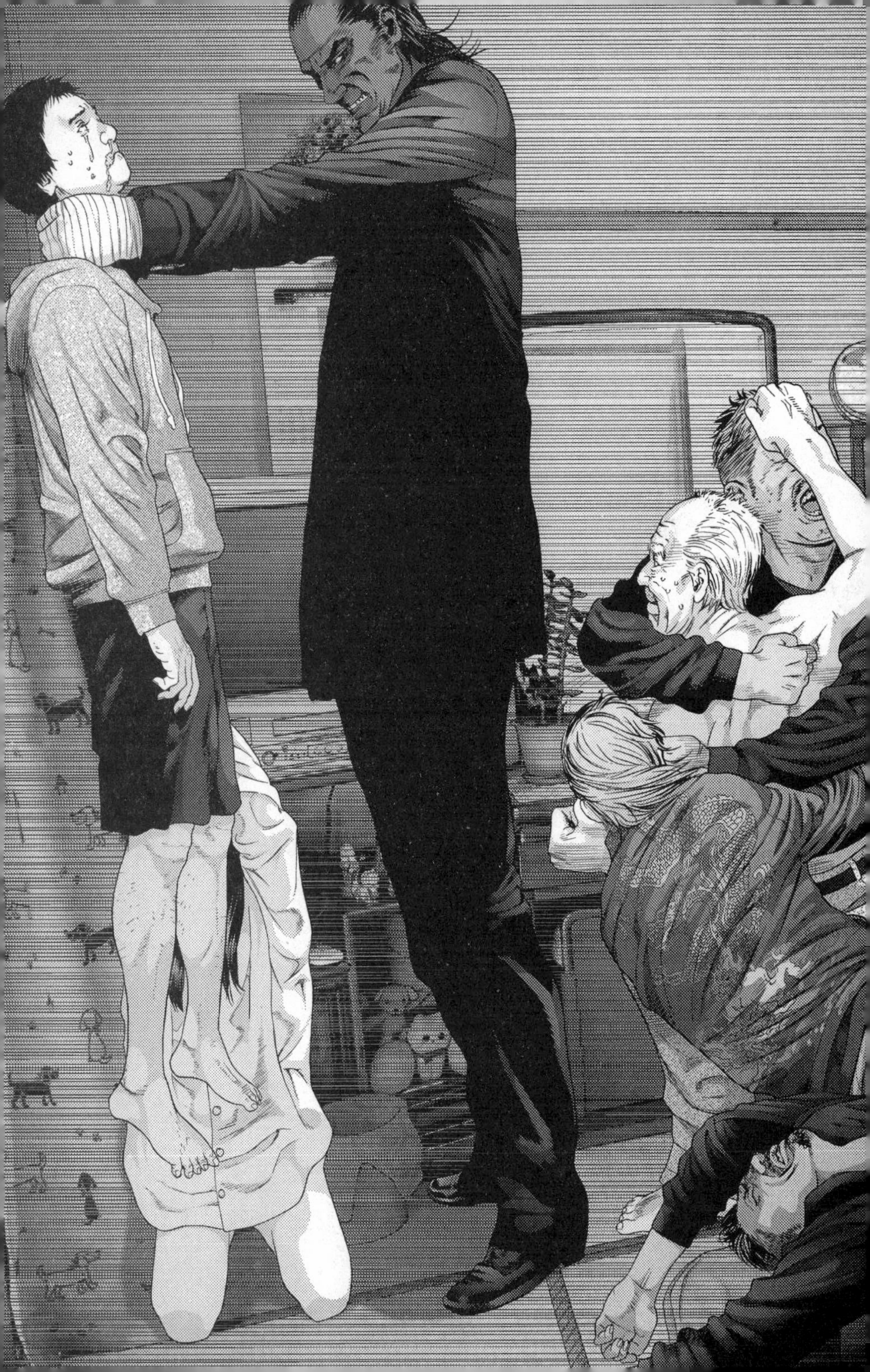

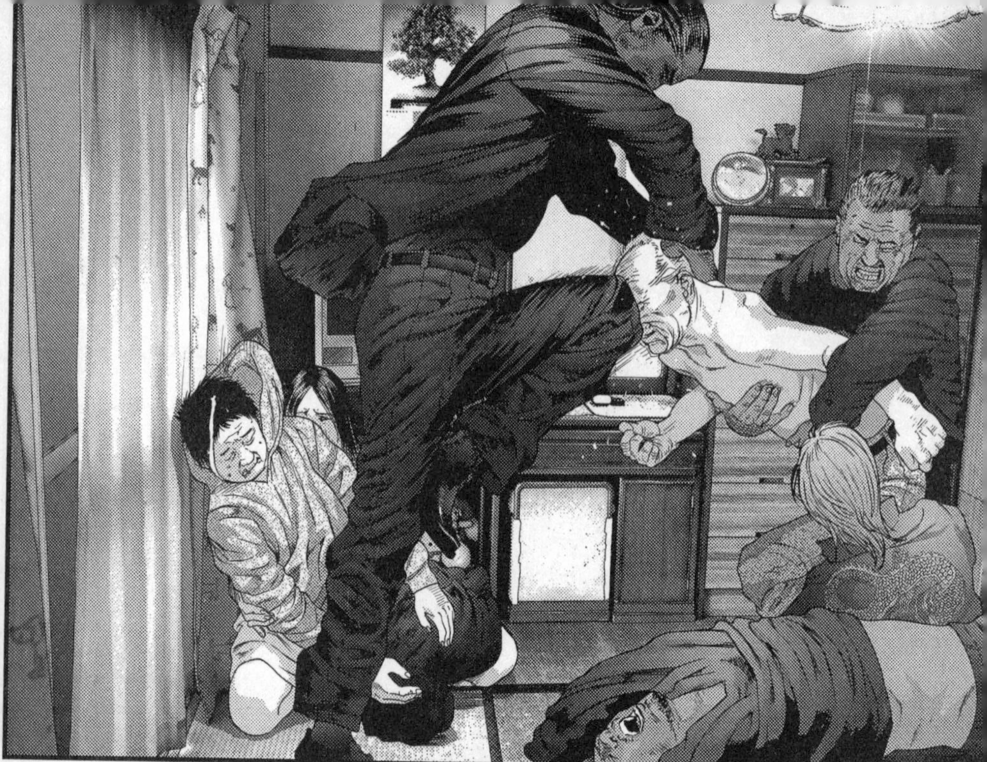
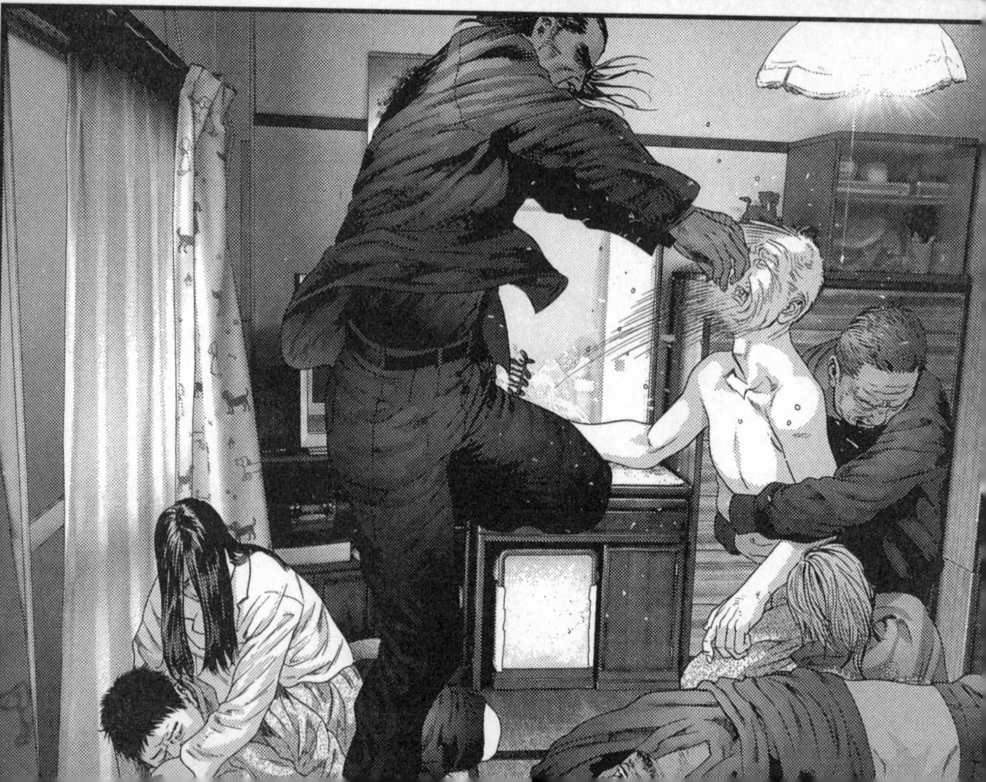

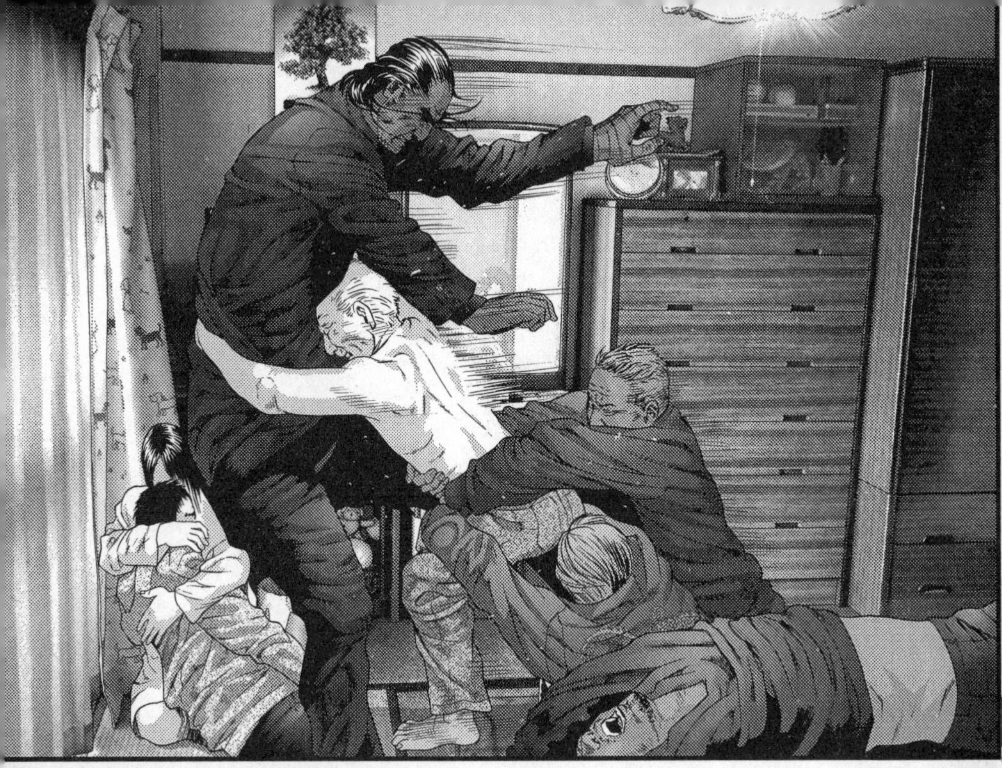
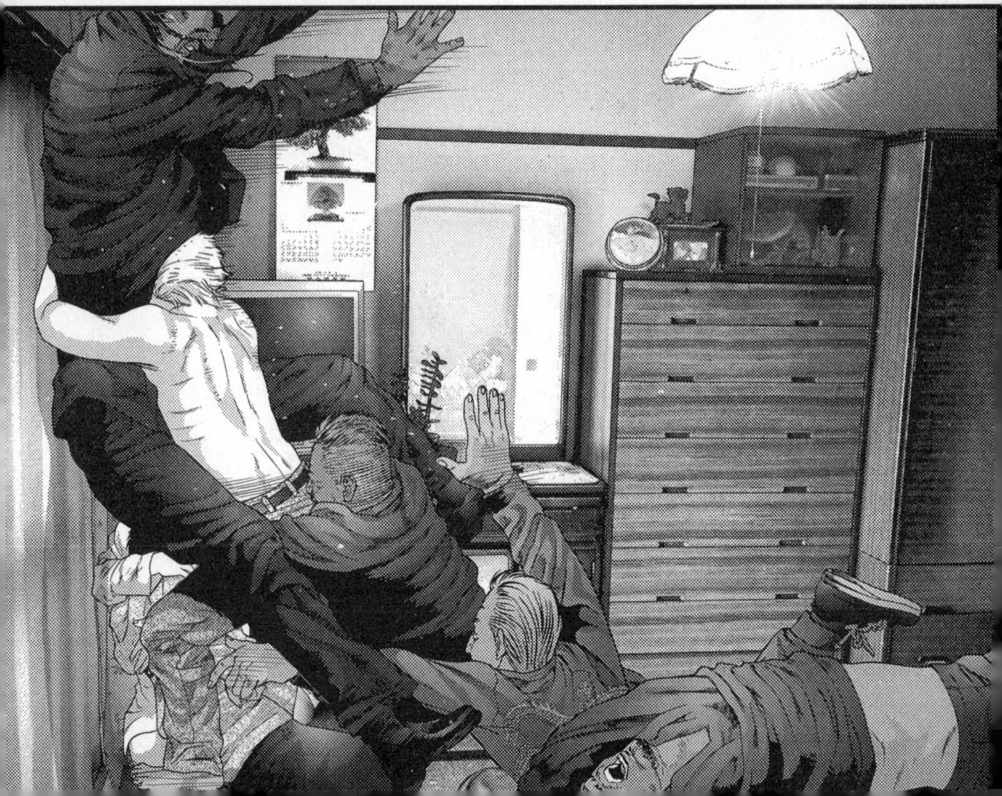

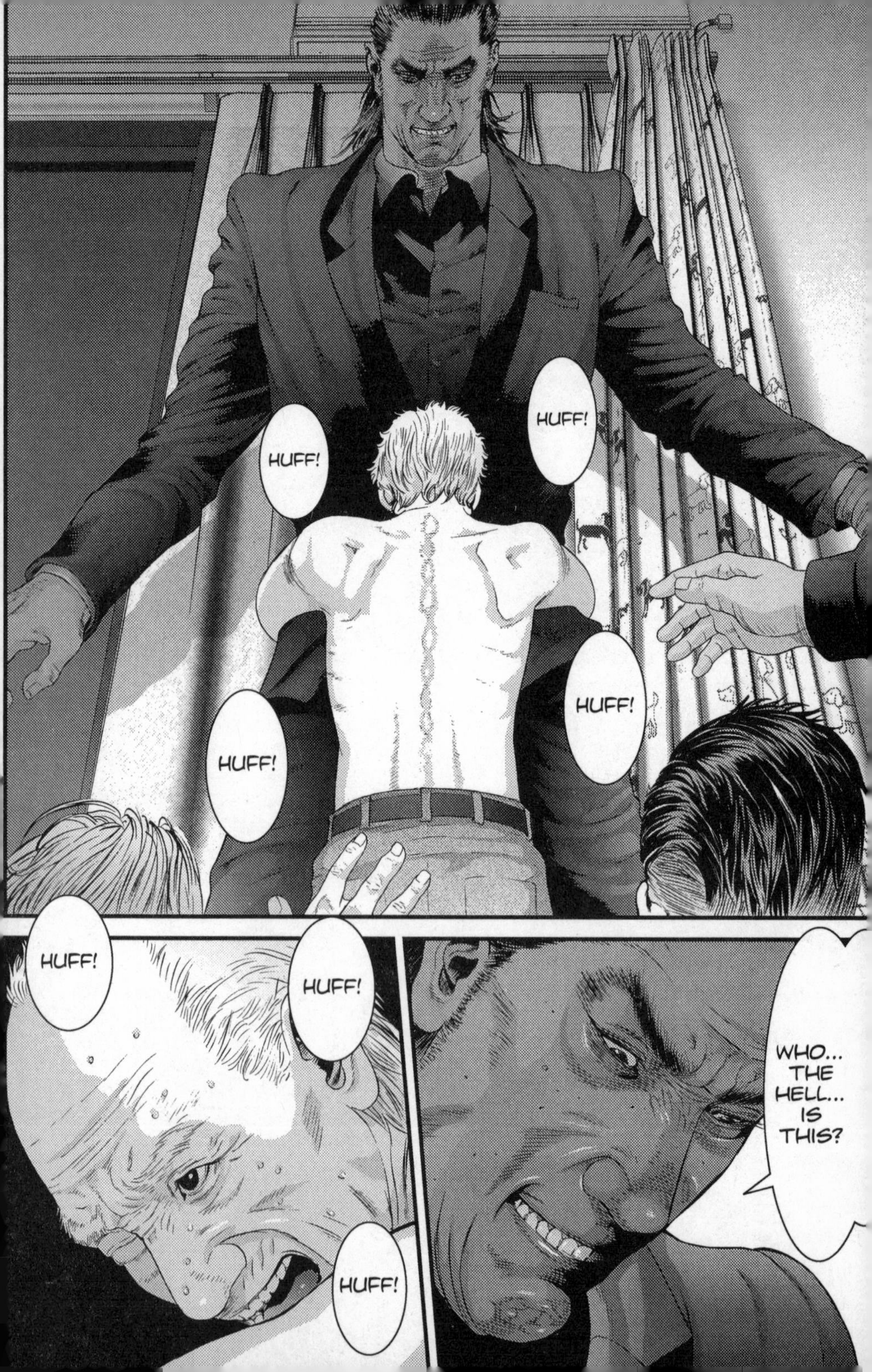
HUFF!
HUFF!
HUFF!
HUFF!
WHO... THE HELL... IS THIS?
HUFF!
HUFF!
HUFF!

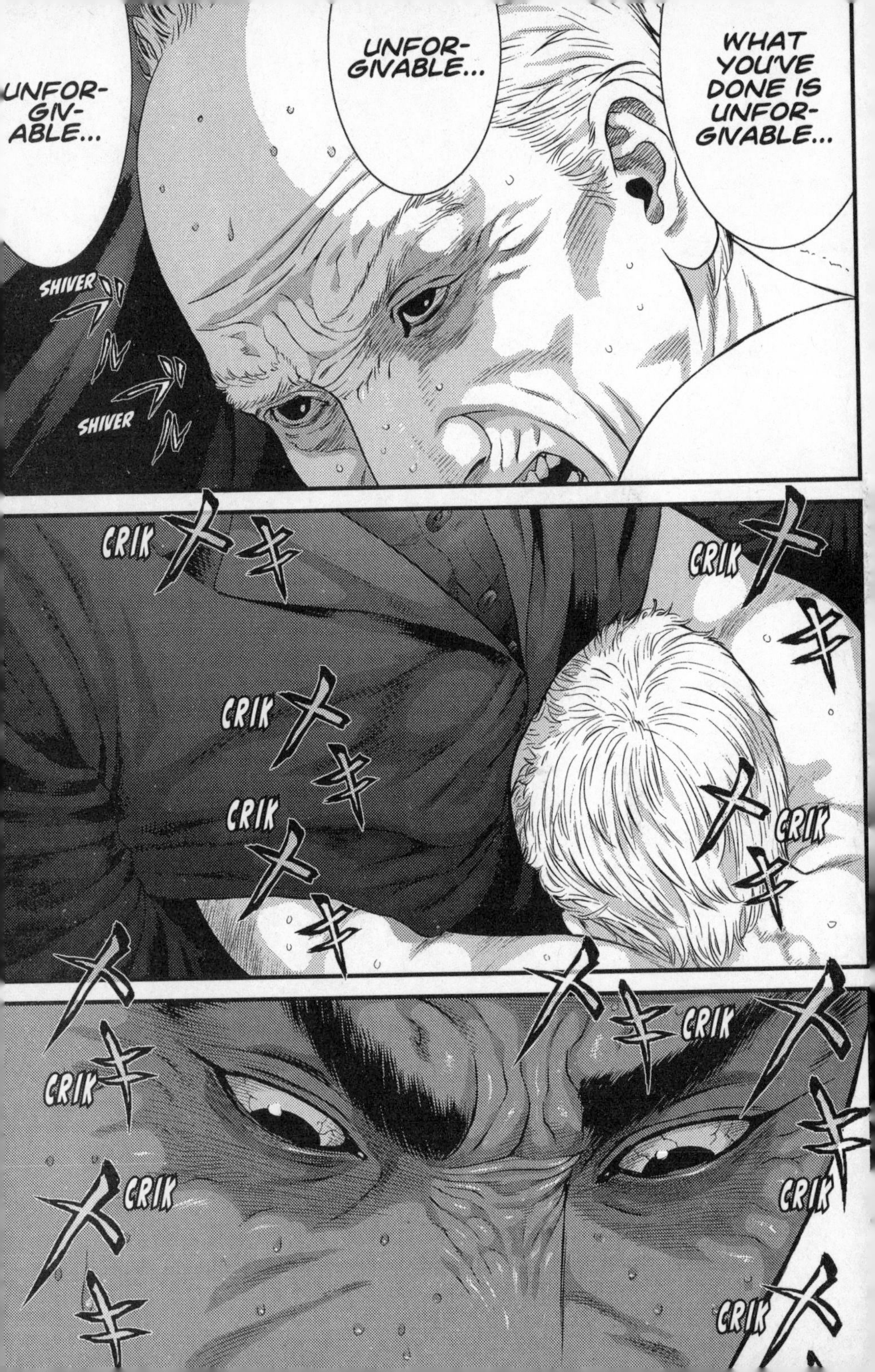
WHAT YOU'VE DONE IS UNFORGIVABLE...
UNFORGIVABLE...
UNFORGIVABLE...
SHIVER
SHIVER
CRIK
CRIK
CRIK
CRIK
CRIK
CRIK
CRIK
CRIK
CRIK
CRIK

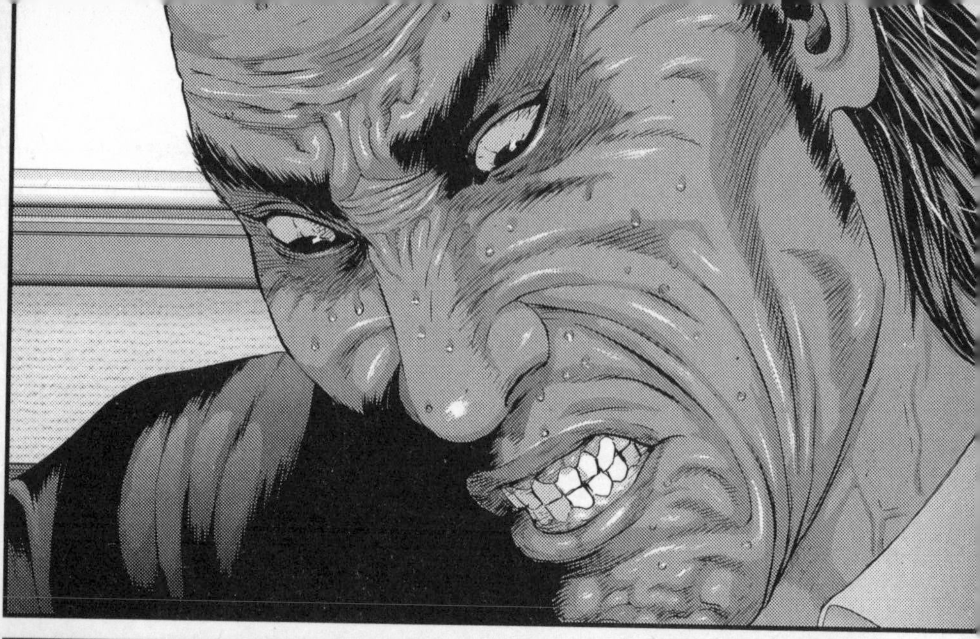
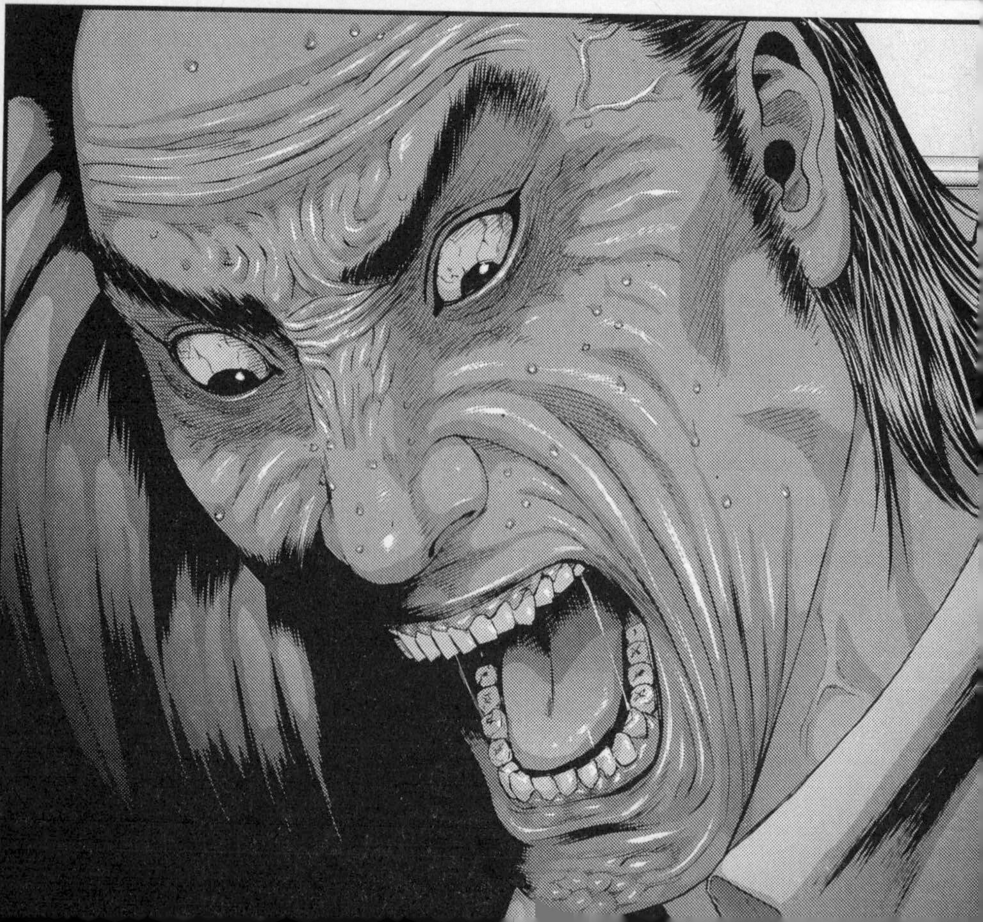

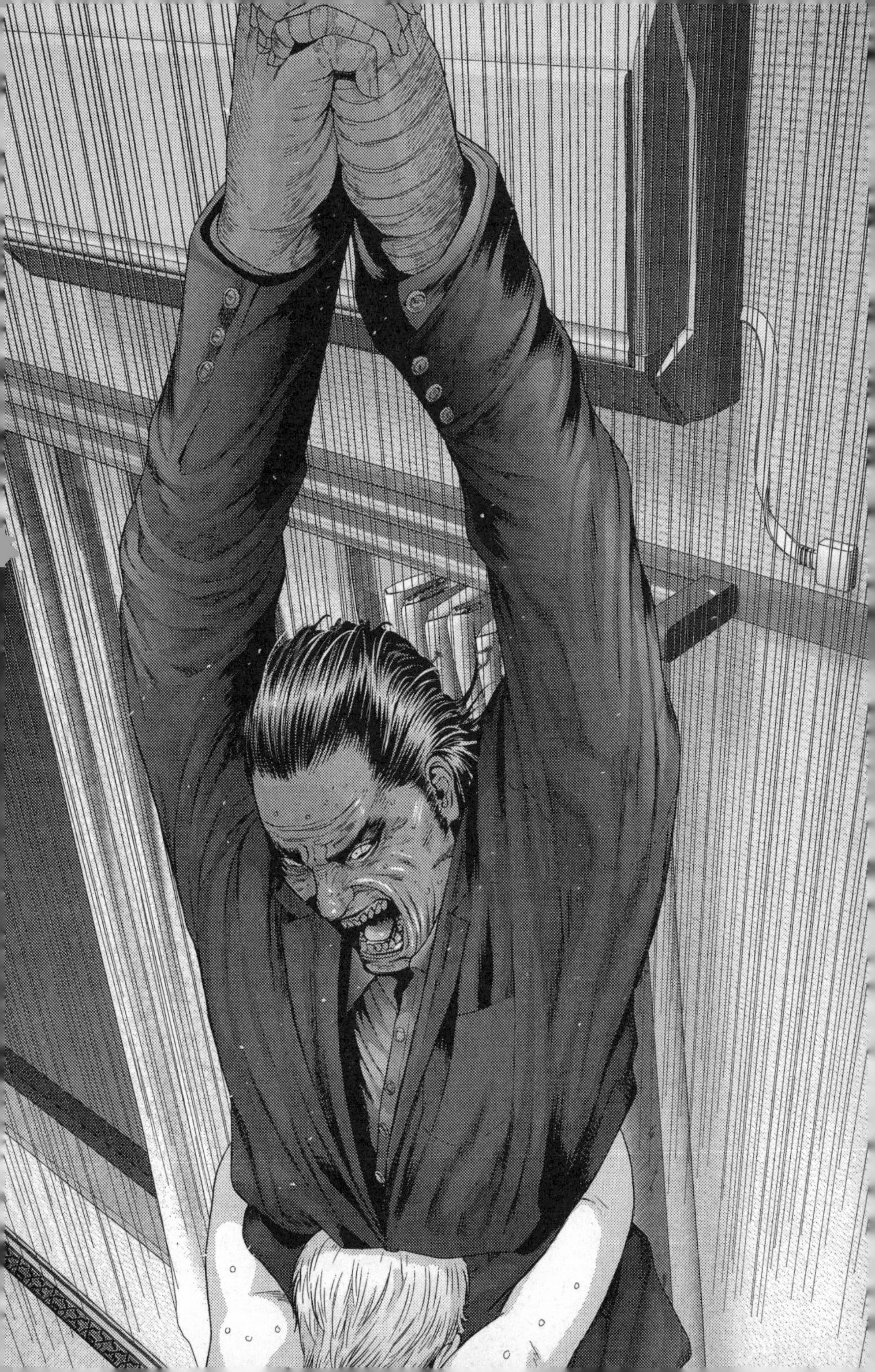

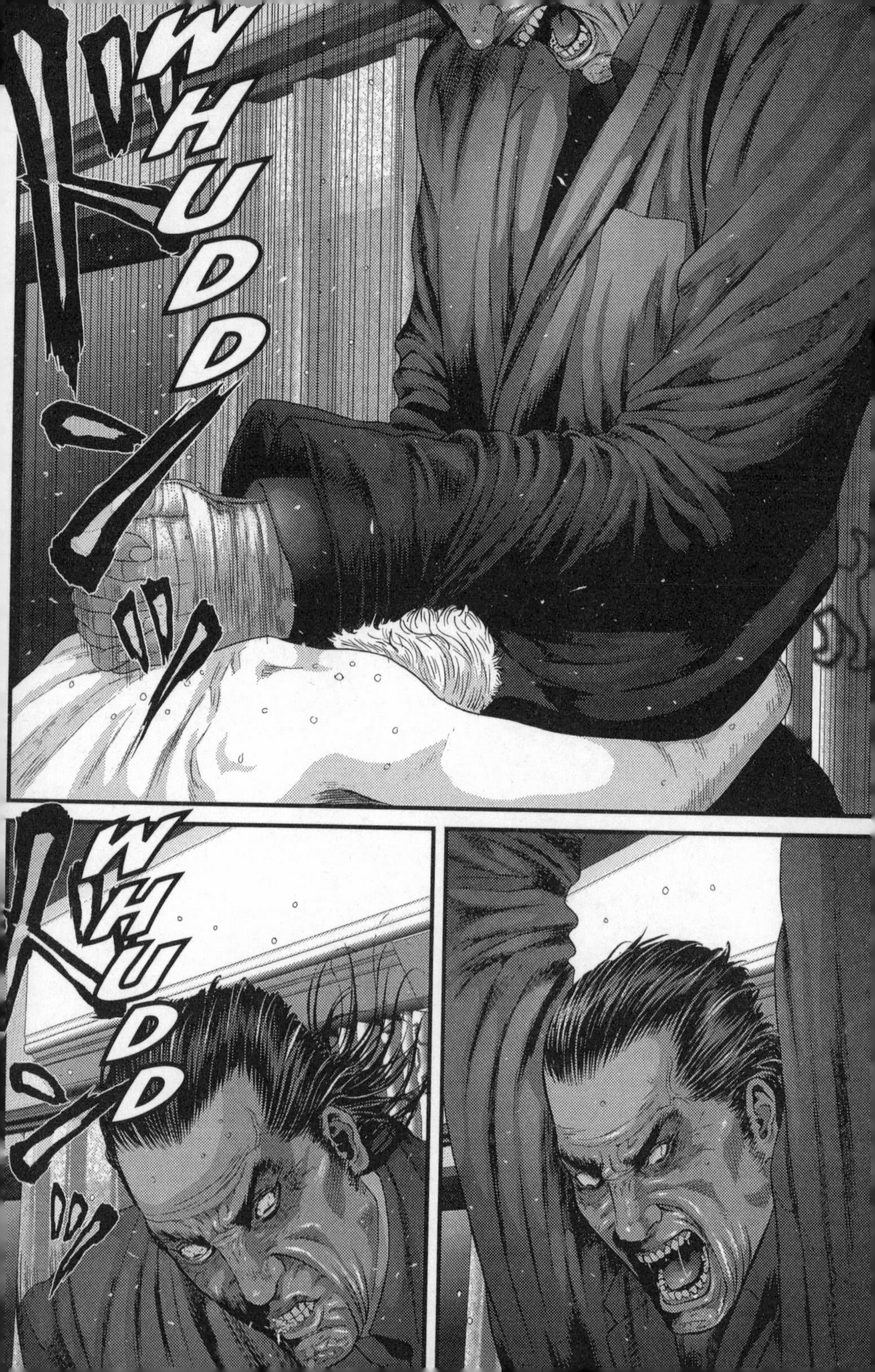
WHUDD
WHUDD

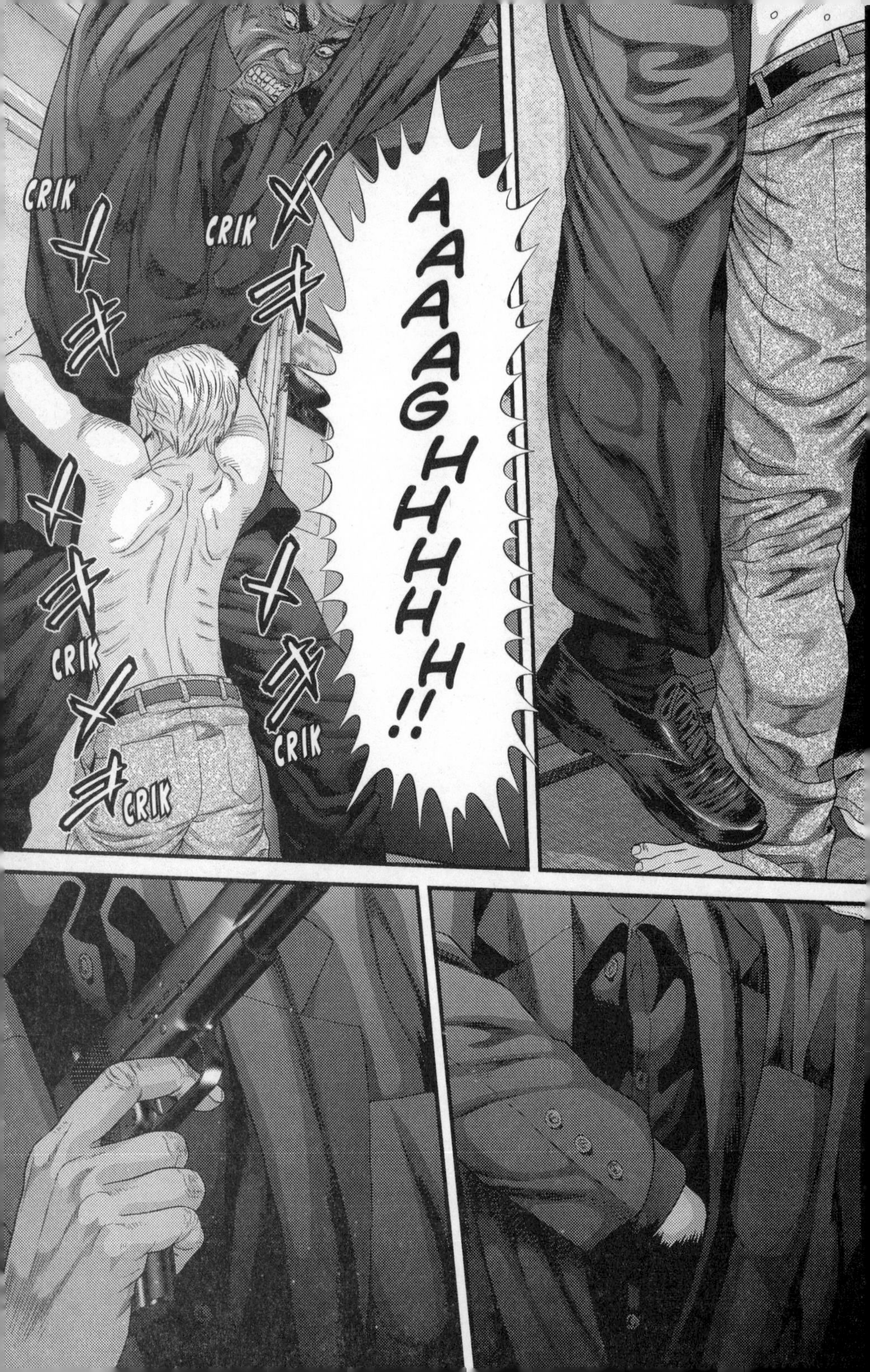
AAAAGHHHHH!!
CRIK
CRIK
CRIK
CRIK
CRIK

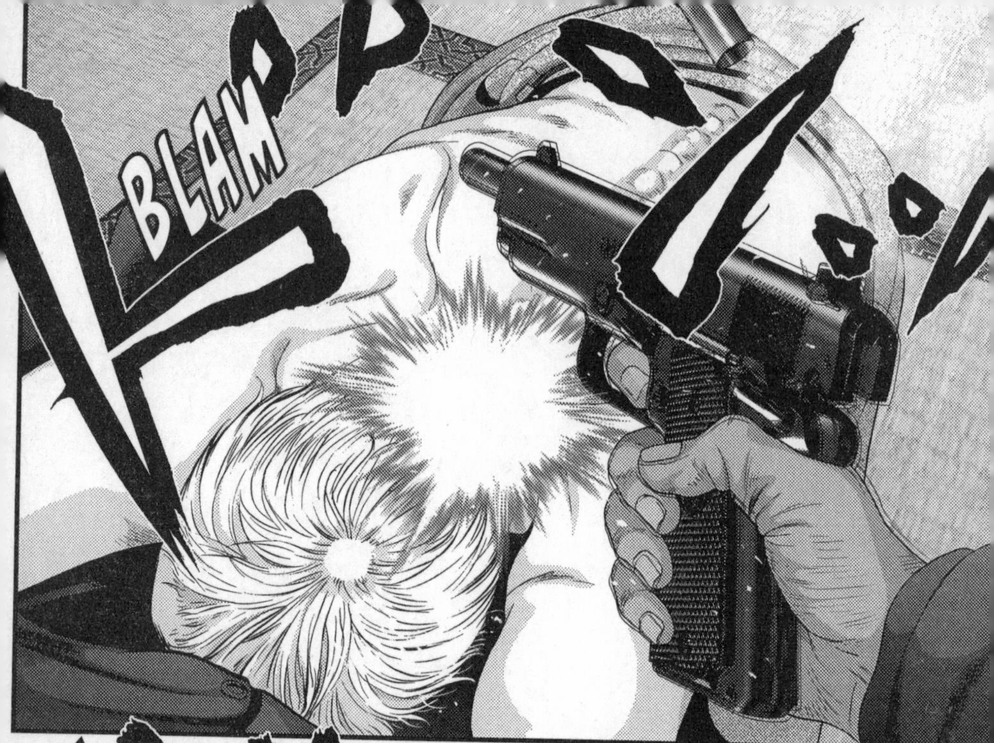
BLAM
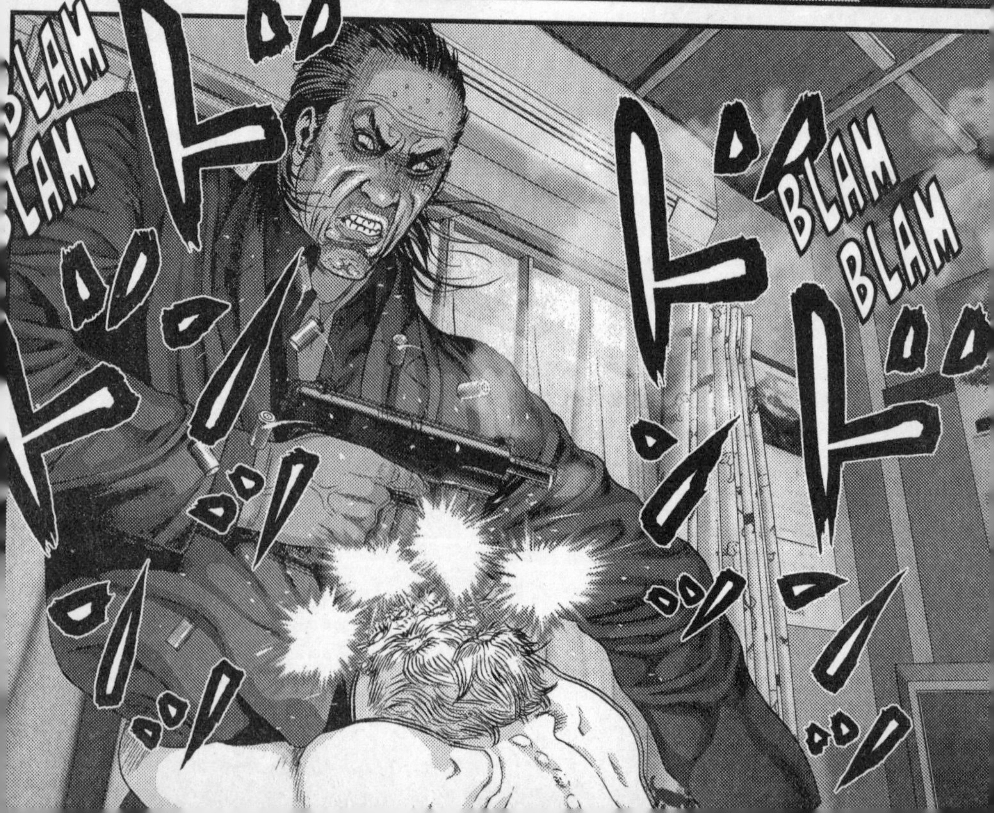
BLAM
BLAM
BLAM
BLAM

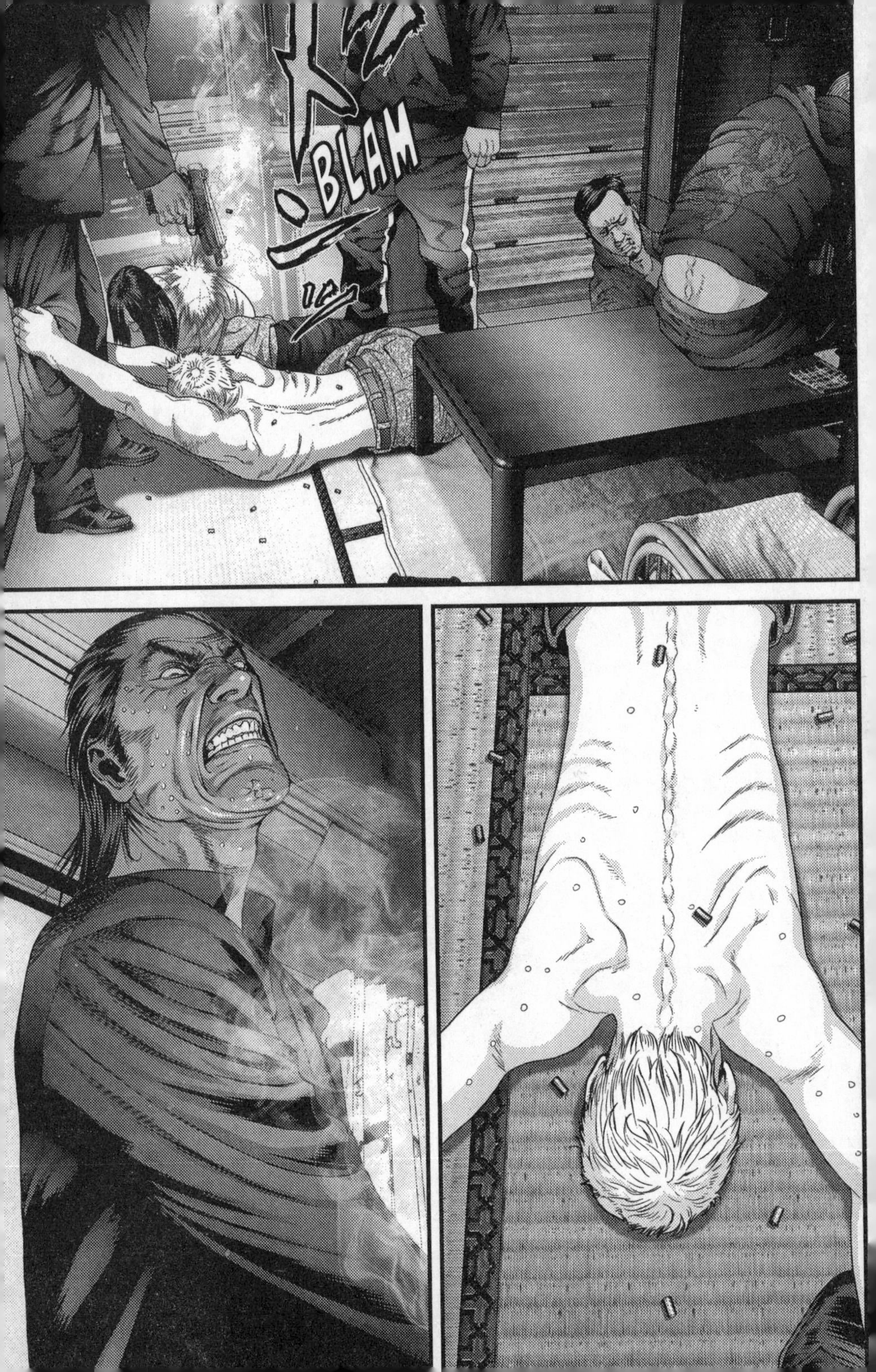
BLAM

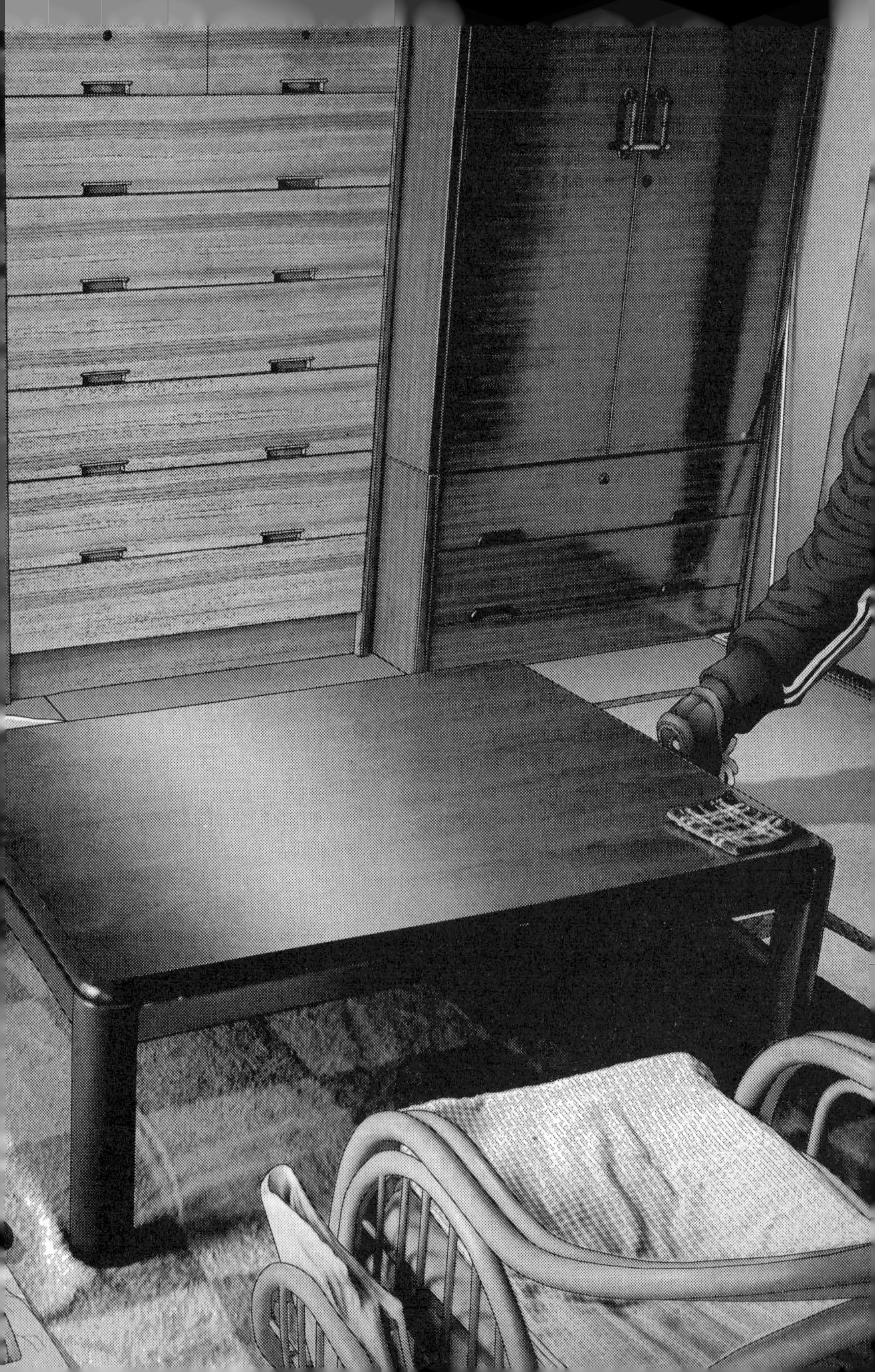

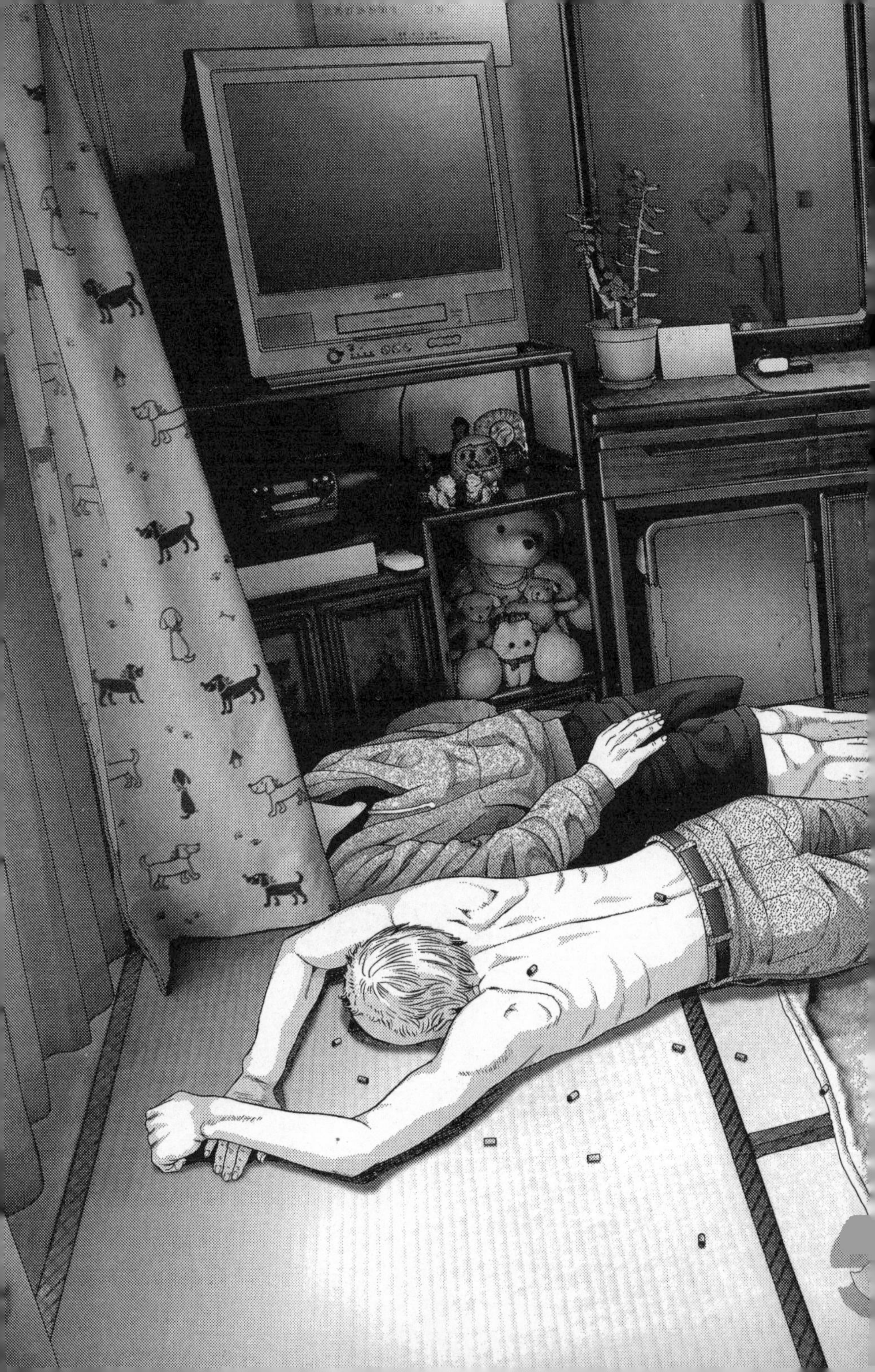

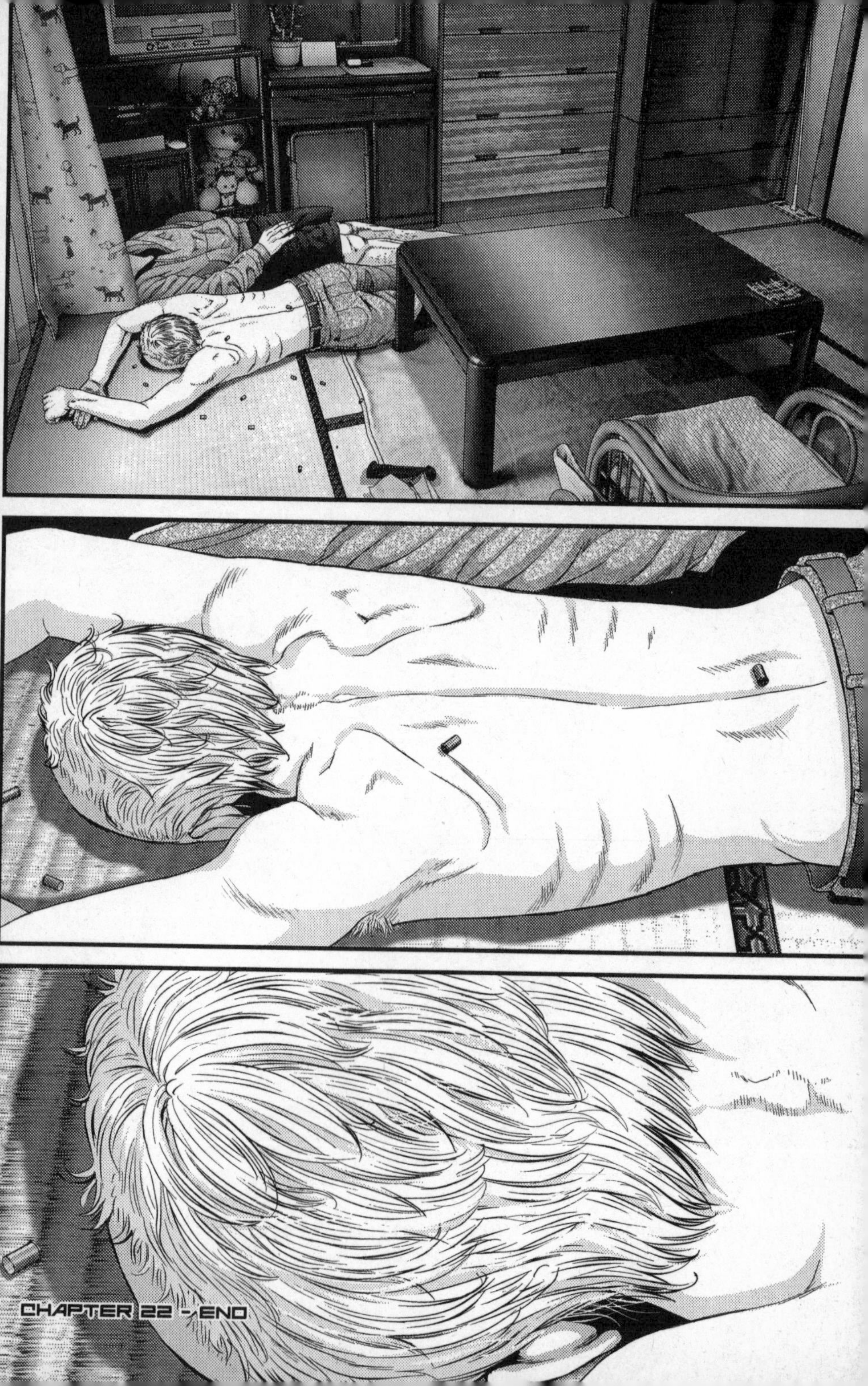
CHAPTER 22 - END

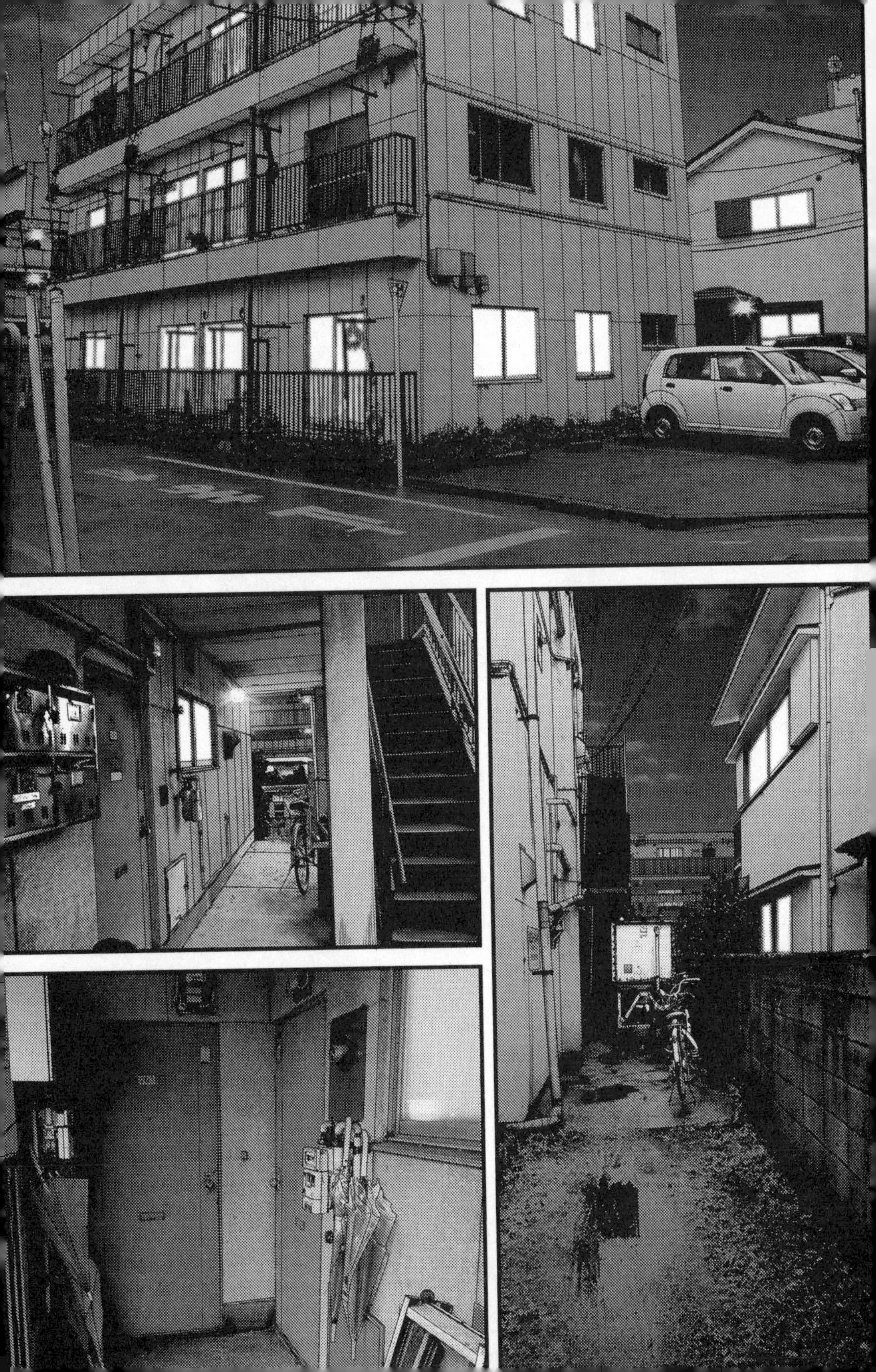

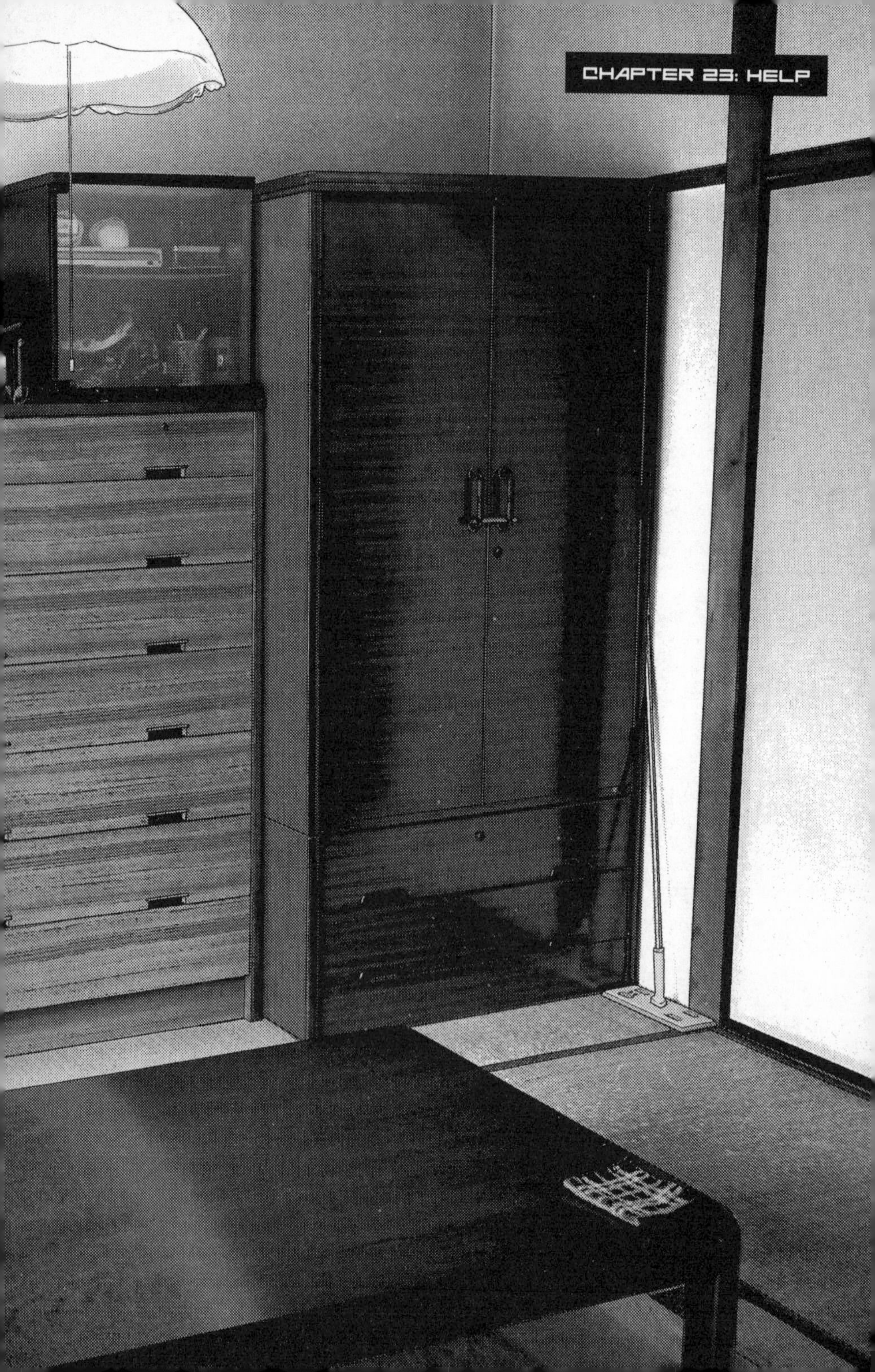
CHAPTER 23: HELP

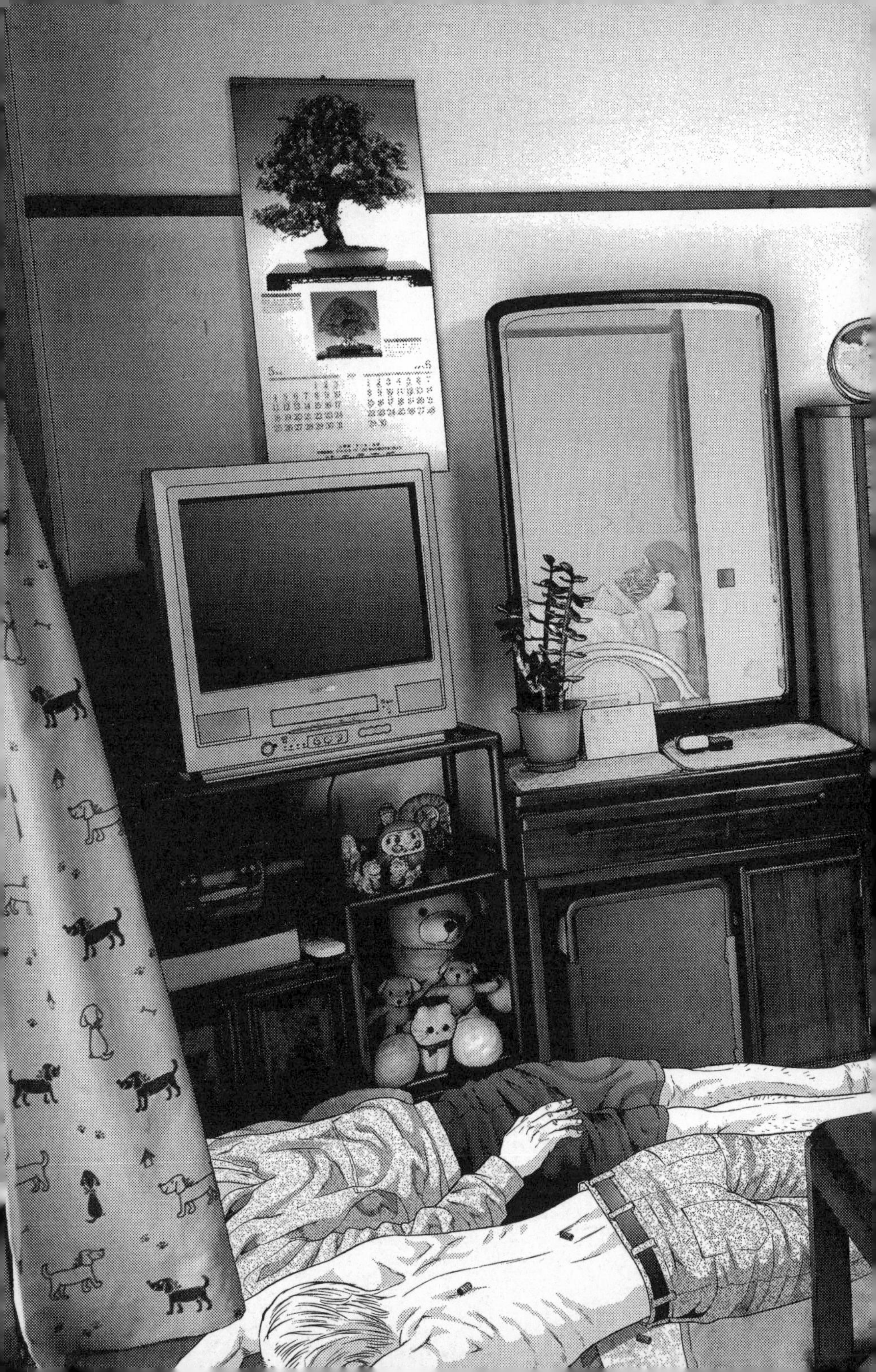

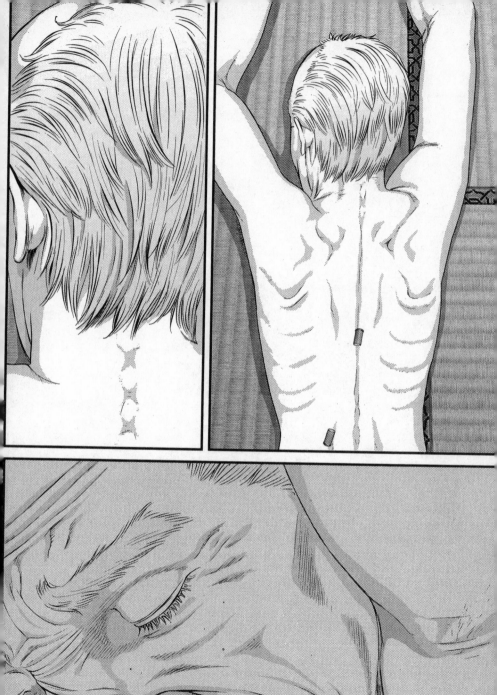

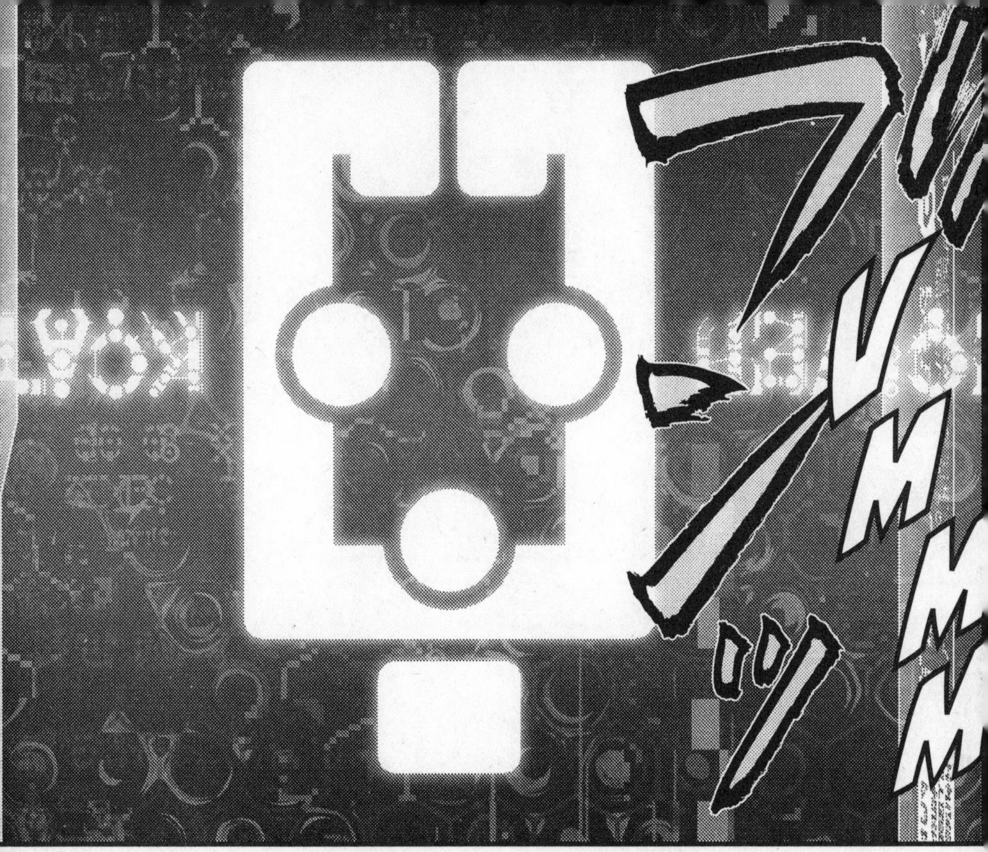
VUMMMMM
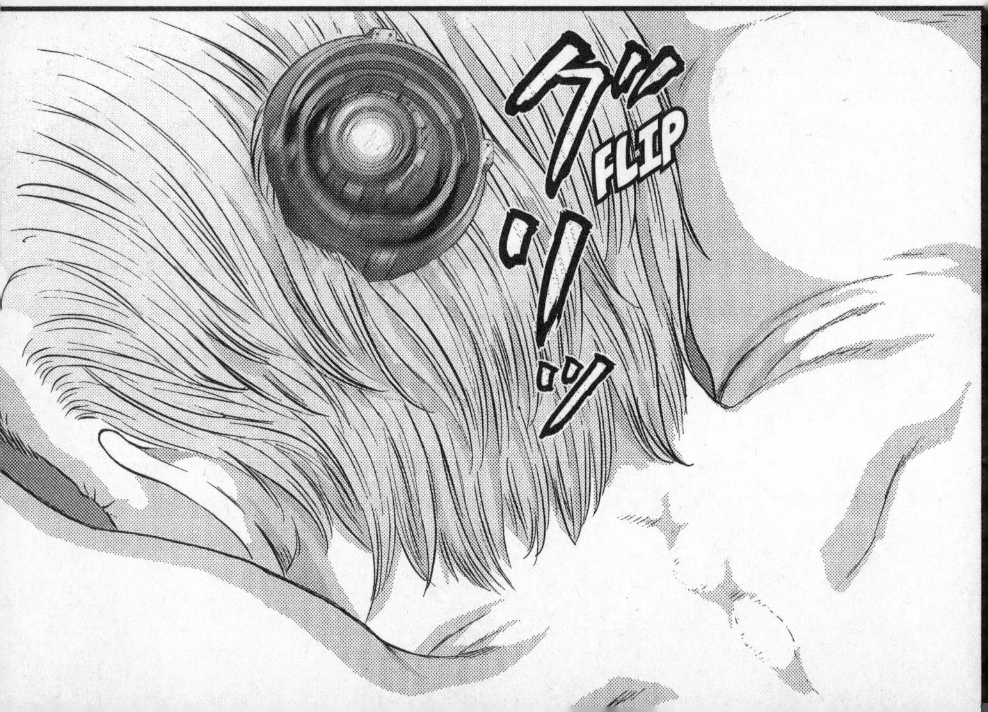
FLIP

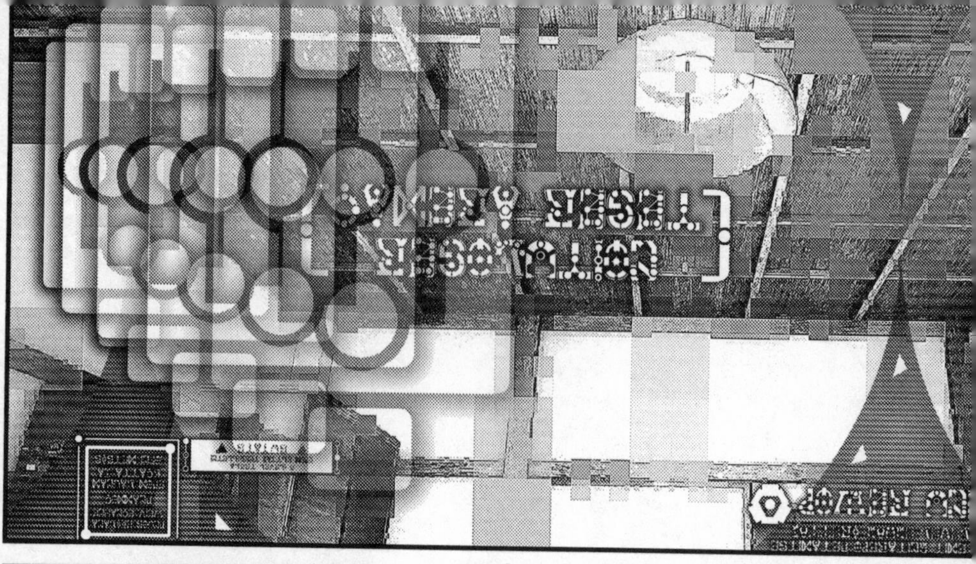

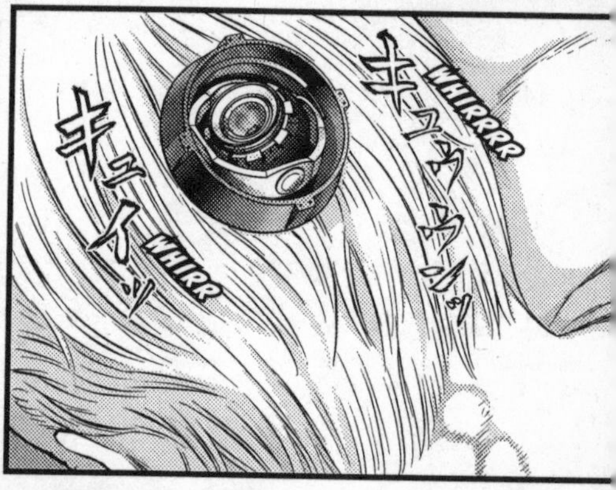
WHIRRRR
WHIRR

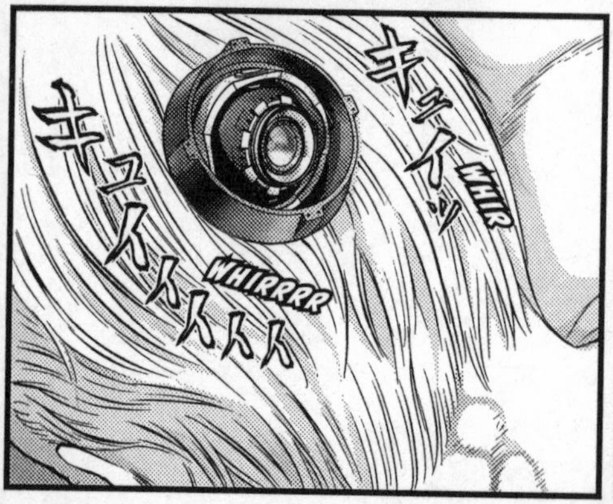
WHIR
WHIRRRR

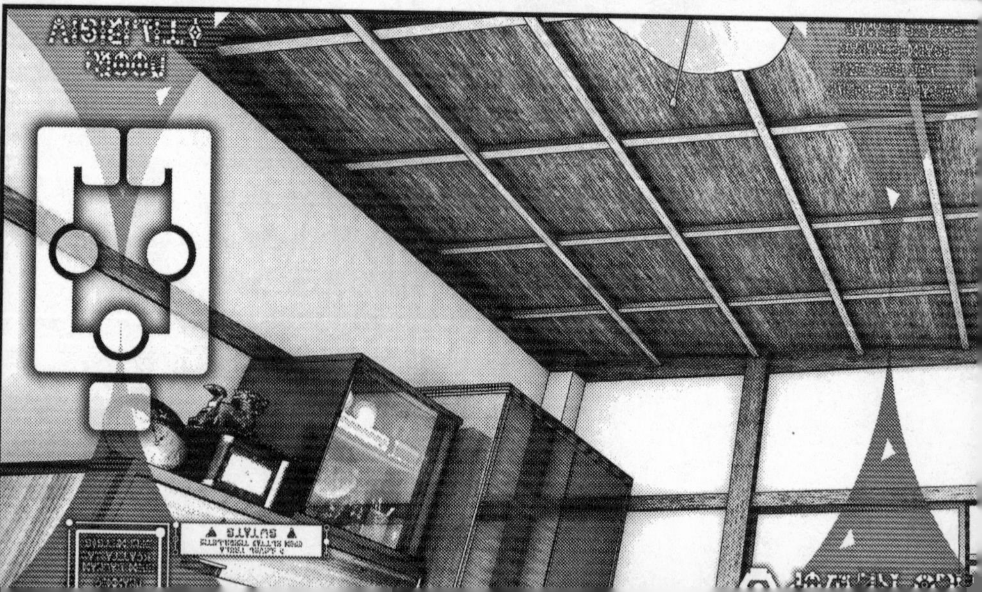

UH...
NG...

HUH?

OH...

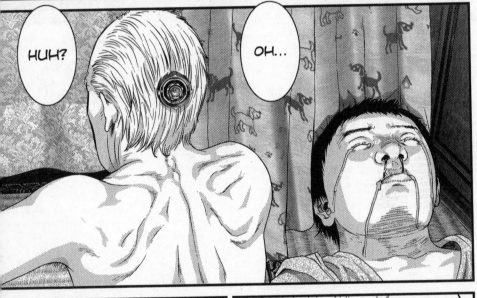

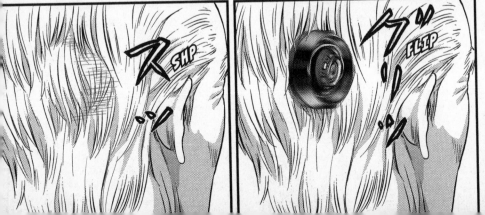

SHP

FLIP

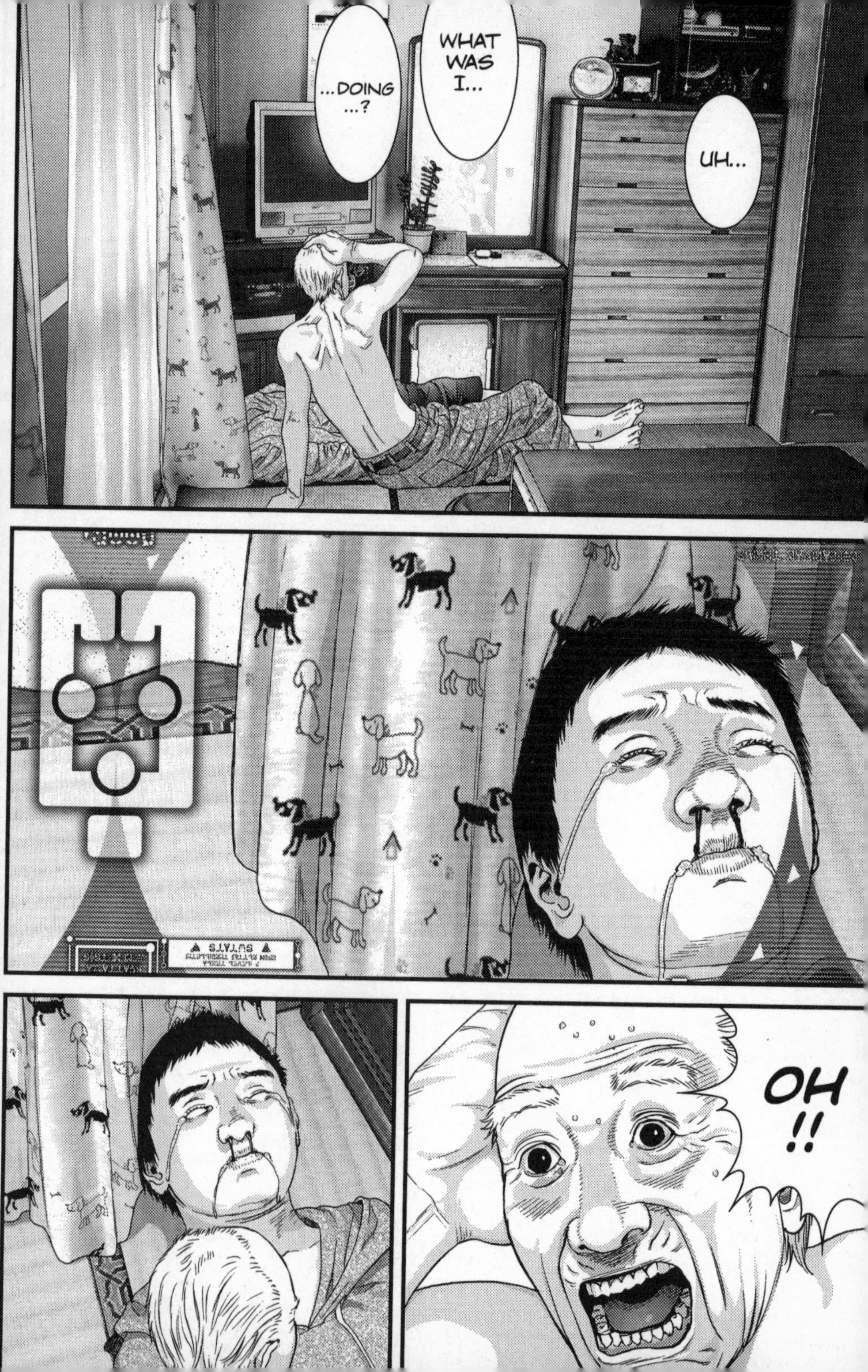
UH...
WHAT WAS I...
...DOING ...?
OH !!

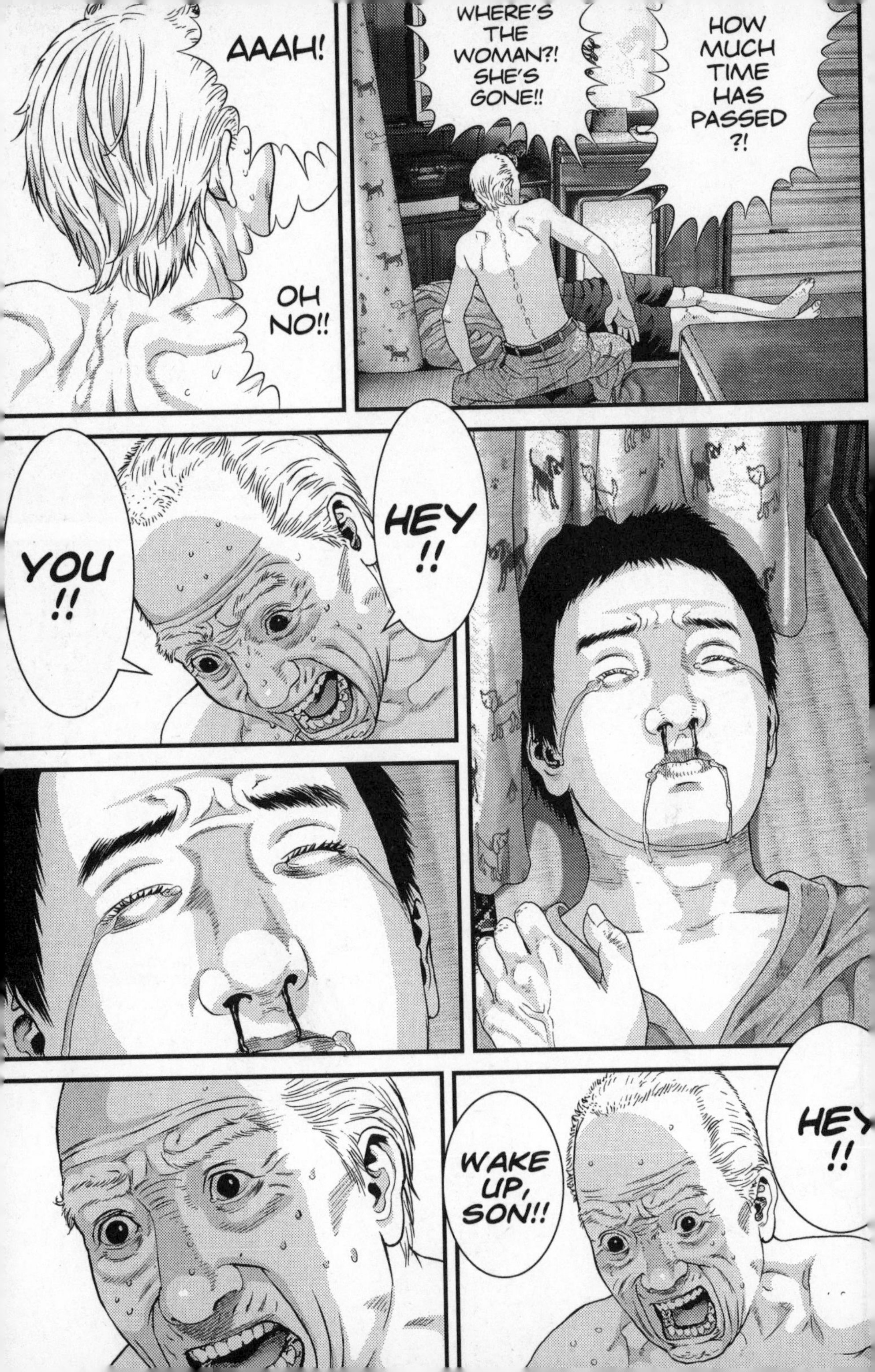
HOW MUCH TIME HAS PASSED?!
WHERE'S THE WOMAN?! SHE'S GONE!!
AAAH!
OH NO!!
HEY!!
YOU!!
HEY!!
WAKE UP, SON!!

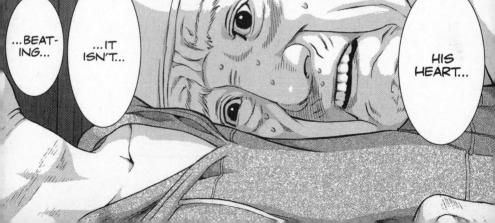

...BEAT-
ING...

...IT
ISN'T...

HIS
HEART...

HE'S DEAD...
HE'S DEAD...
OH, NO NO NO...
HE'S DEAD...

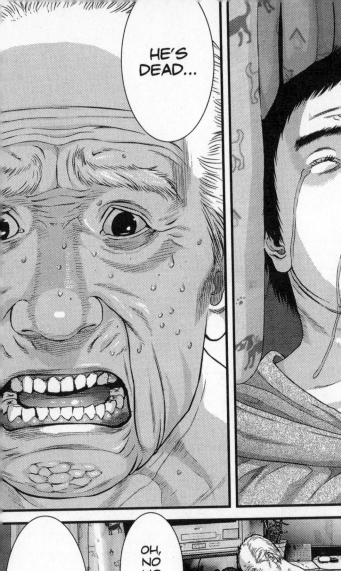

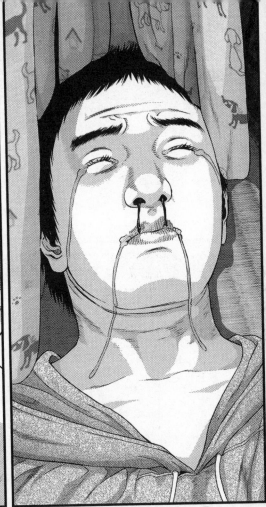

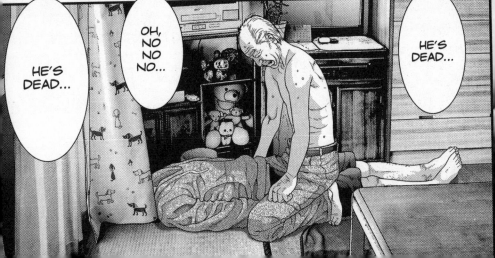

I CAN DO THIS!!
YES, THAT'S RIGHT!!

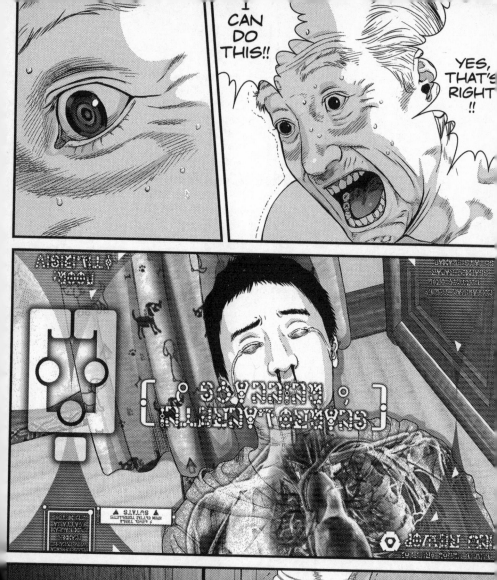

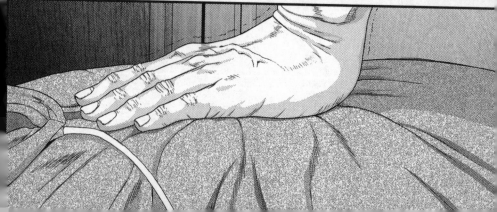

WHAT?

WHAT?

WHAT?

HUH? NOTHING'S HAPPENING.

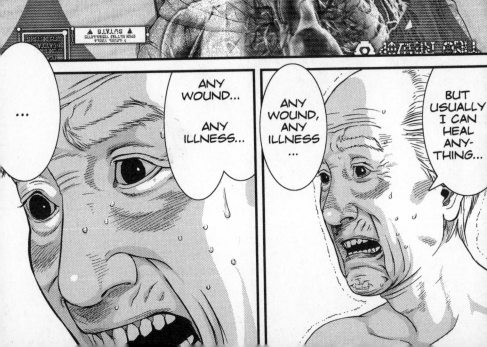

...

ANY WOUND...

ANY ILLNESS...

ANY WOUND, ANY ILLNESS...

BUT USUALLY I CAN HEAL ANYTHING...

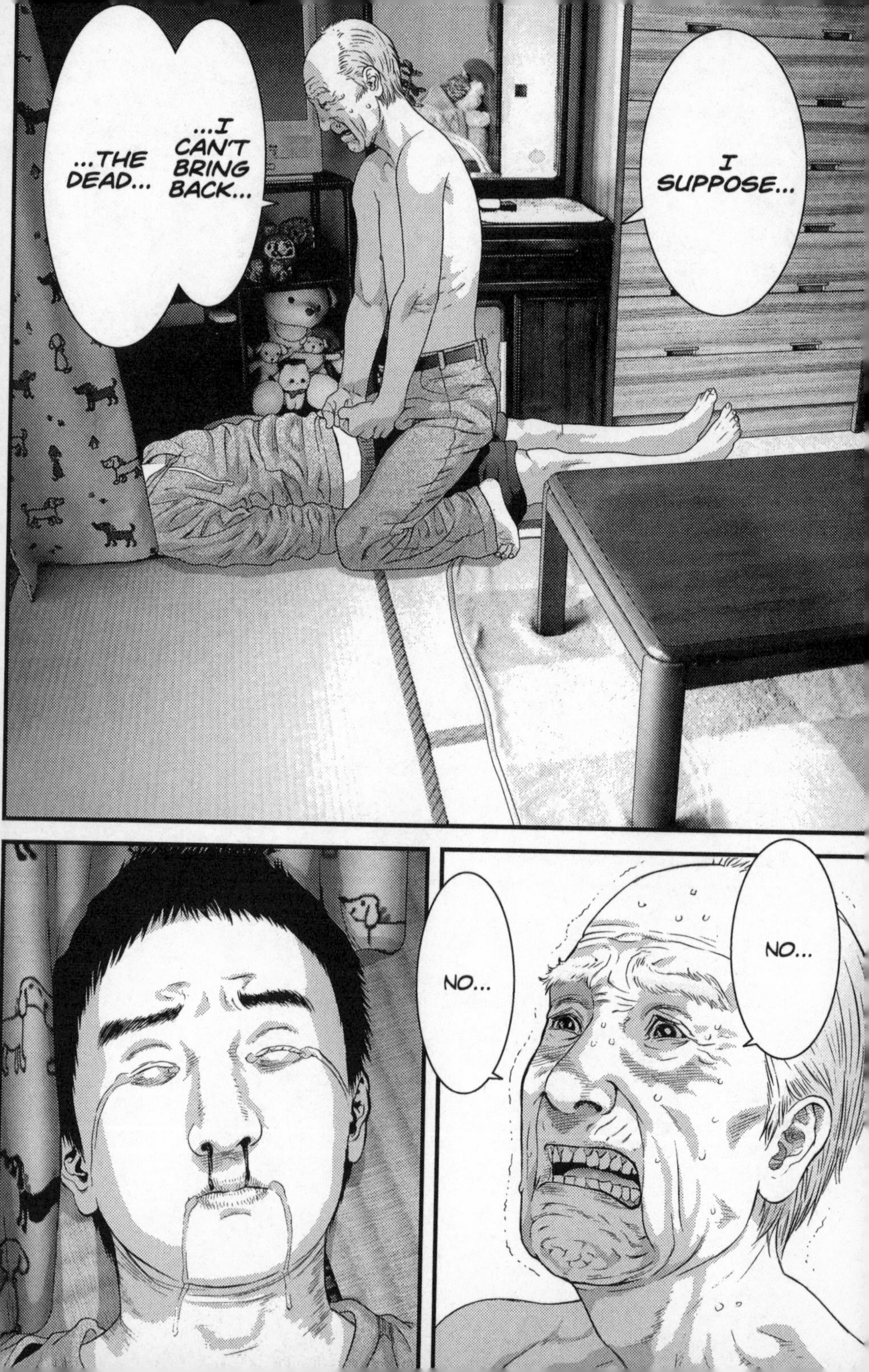
I SUPPOSE...
...I CAN'T BRING BACK...
...THE DEAD...
NO...
NO...

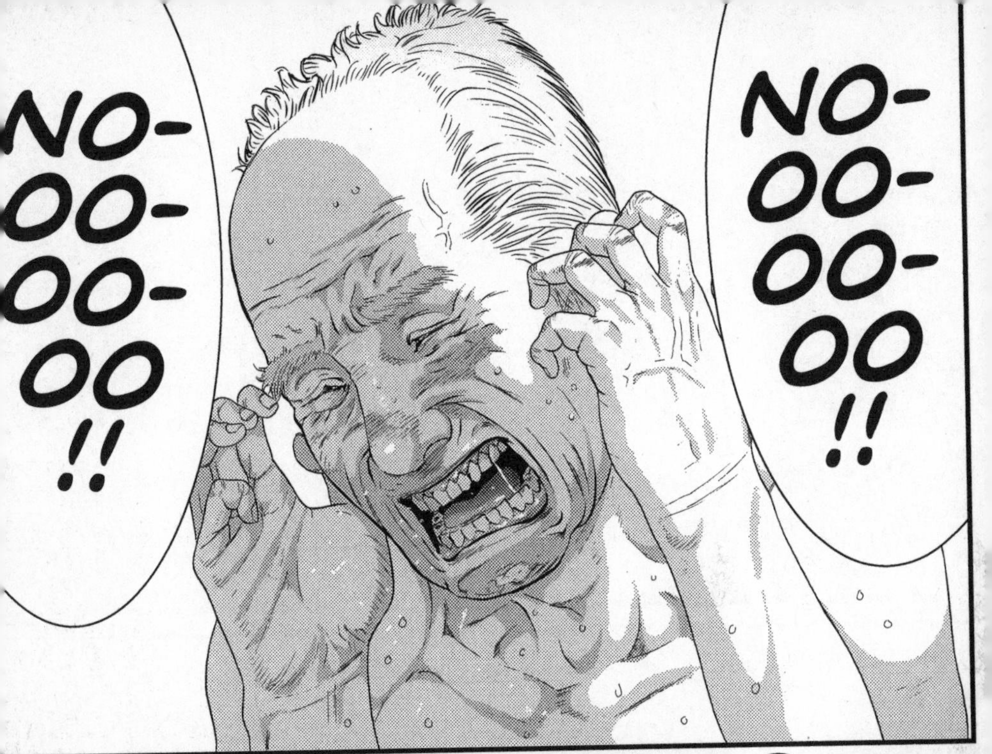
NO-OO-OO-OO!!
NO-OO-OO-OO!!
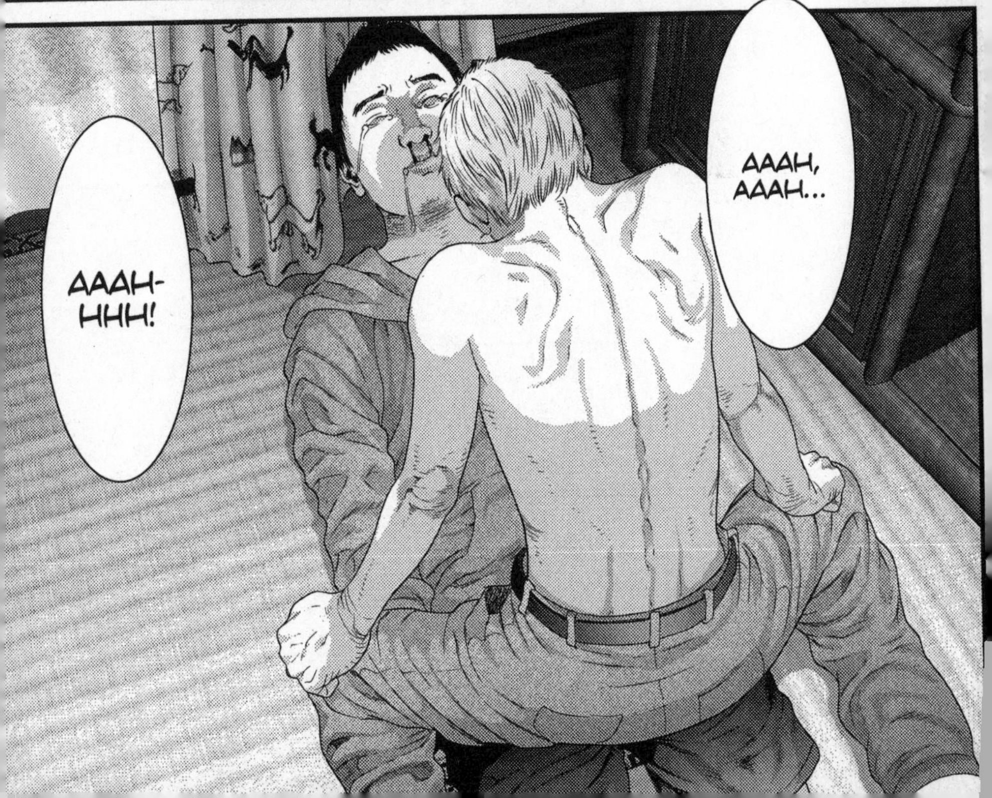
AAAH, AAAH...
AAAH-HHH!

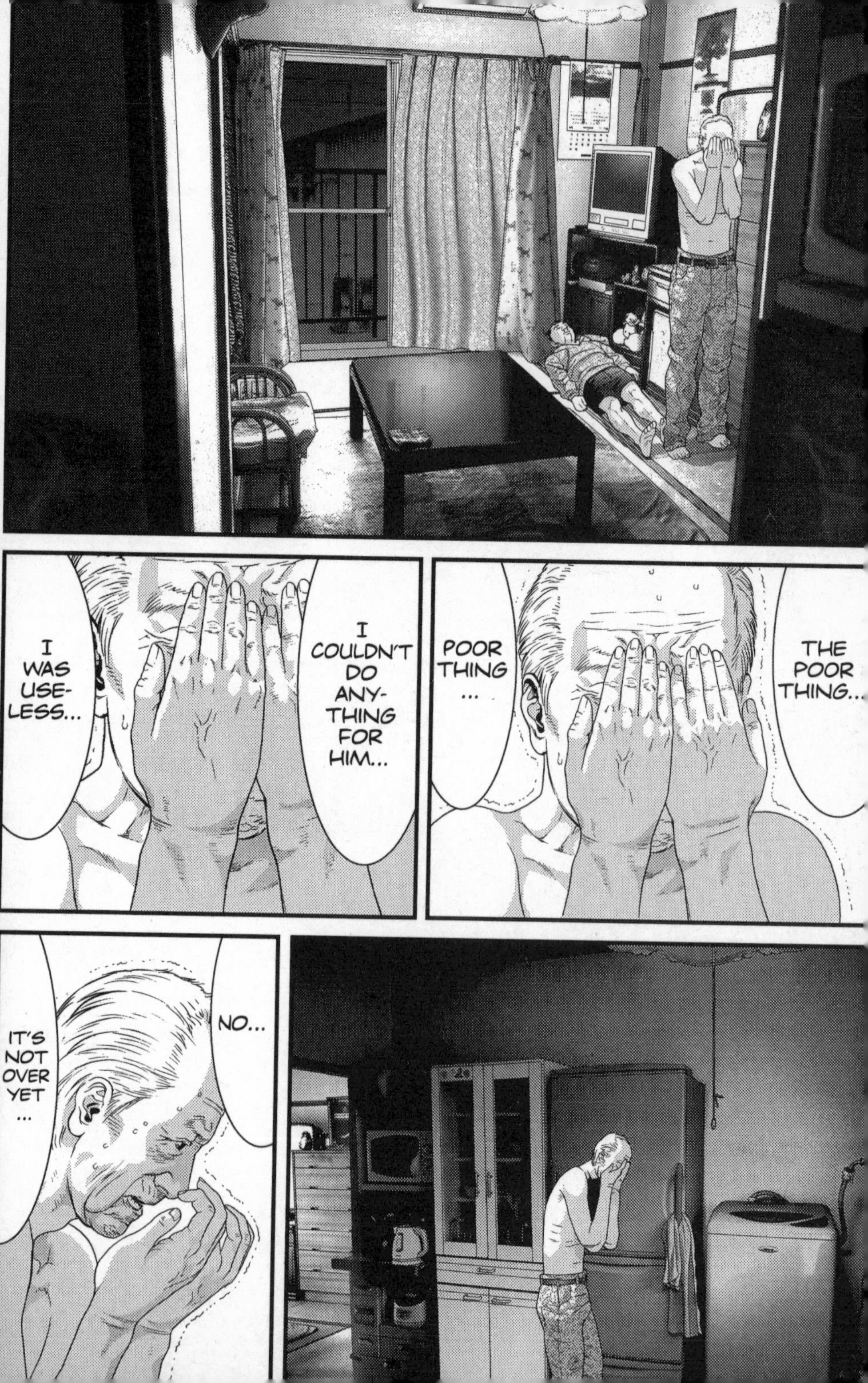
THE POOR THING...
POOR THING...
I COULDN'T DO ANY-THING FOR HIM...
I WAS USE-LESS...
NO...
IT'S NOT OVER YET...

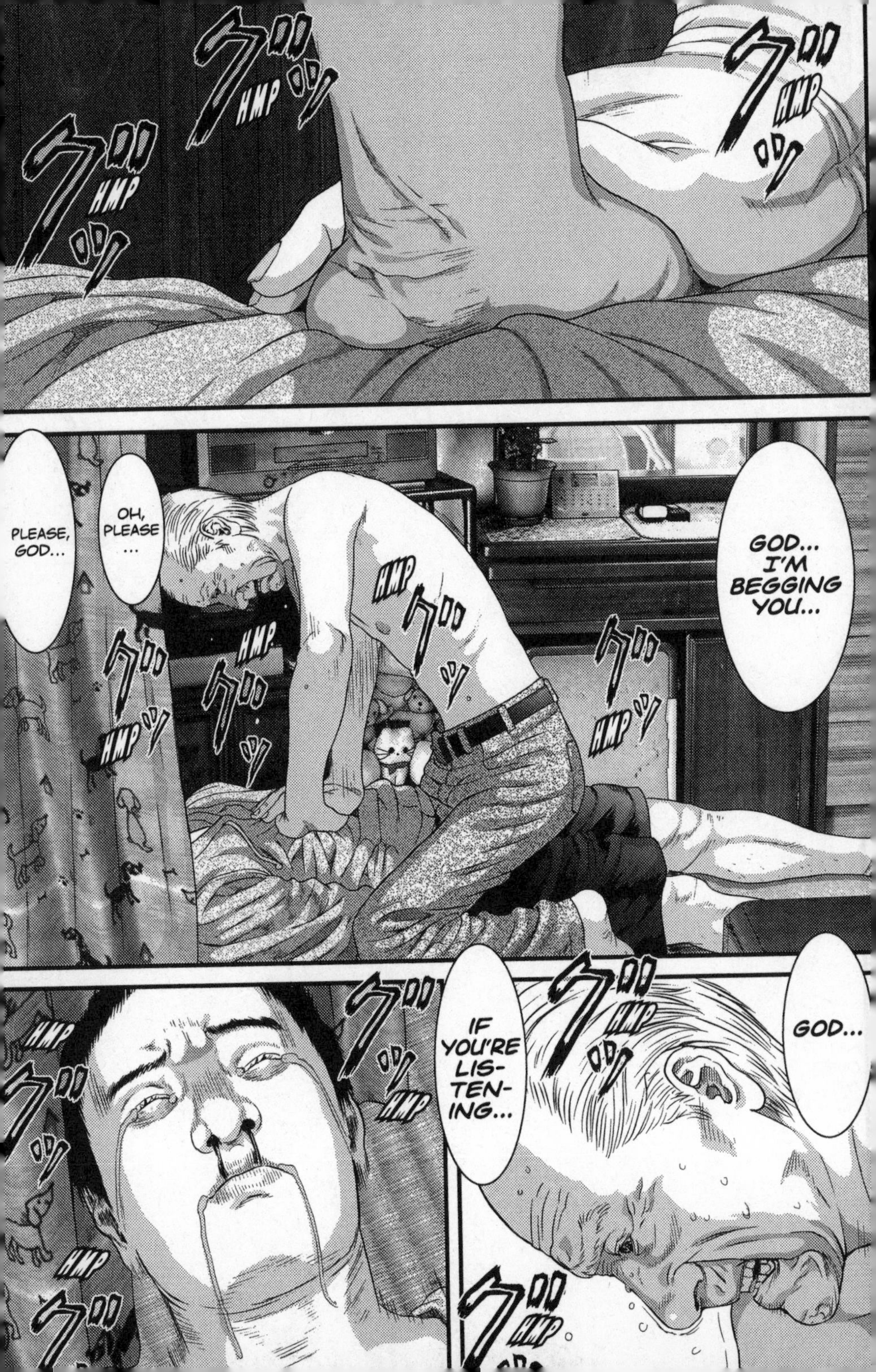
HMP
HMP
HMP
GOD... I'M BEGGING YOU...
HMP
HMP
HMP
HMP
OH, PLEASE ...
PLEASE, GOD...
GOD...
HMP
IF YOU'RE LIS- TEN- ING...
HMP
HMP
HMP
HMP

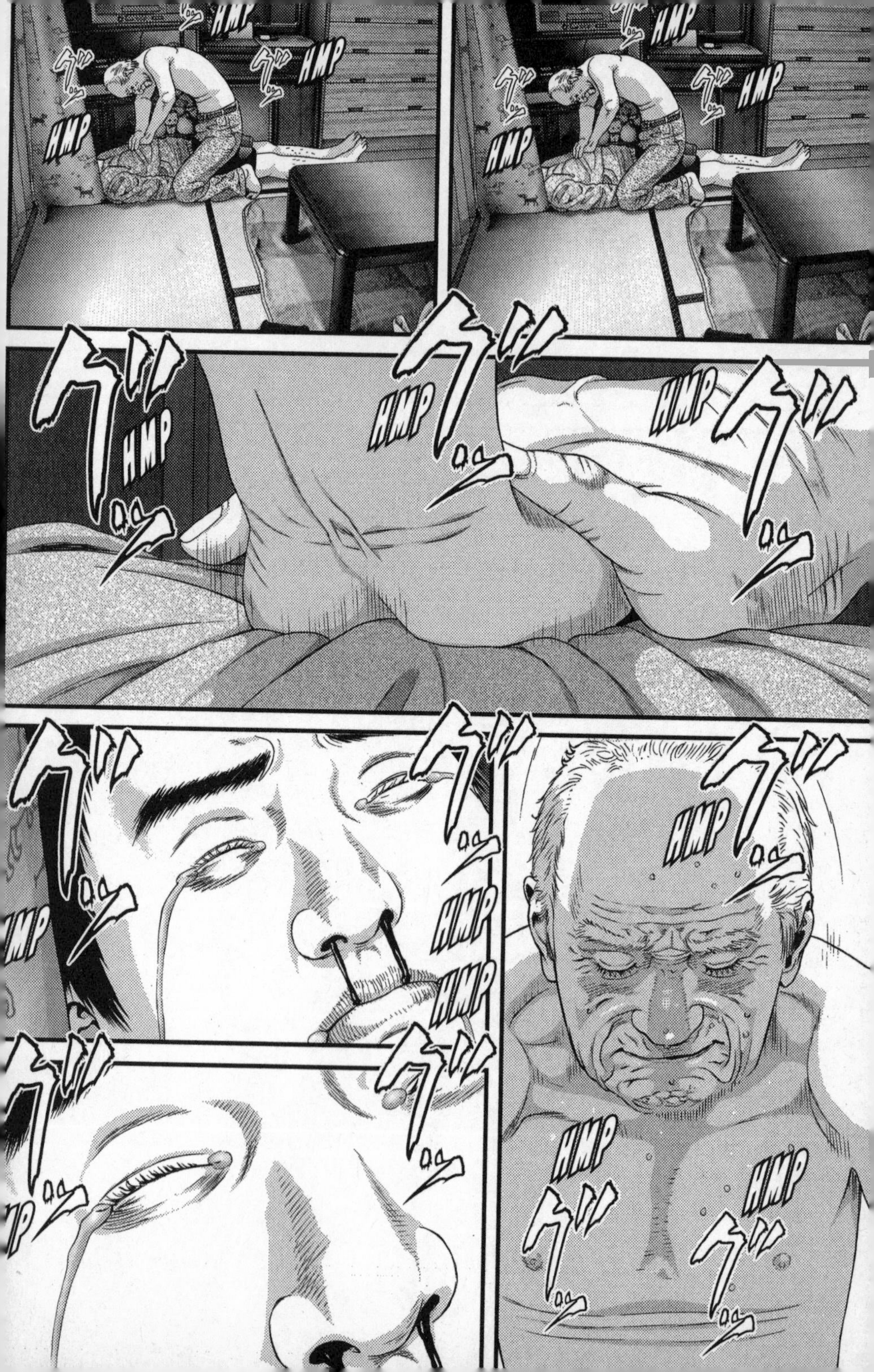

HMP
グッ
HMP
グッ
HMP
HMP
グッ
HMP
グッ
HMP
グッ
HMP
グッ
HMP
グッ
HMP
グッ
HMP
グッ
HMP
グッ
HMP
グッ
HMP
グッ
HMP
HMP
グッ
HMP
グッ
HMP
グッ

DON'T YOU WORRY... I'LL BE THERE...
...TO SAVE...
...YOUR GIRL-FRIEND, TOO!
JUST... COME BACK!
COME!
BACK!!
COME BACK !!
COME BACK !!

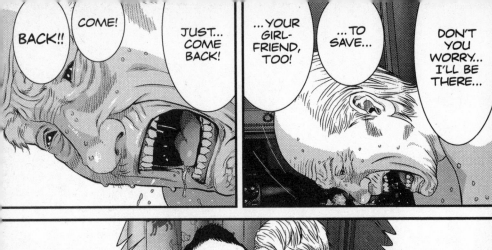

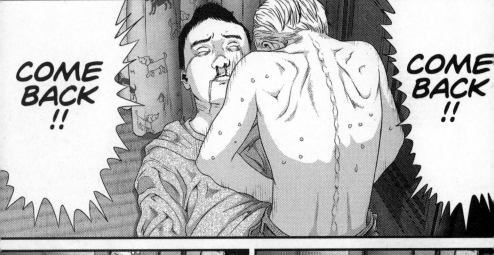

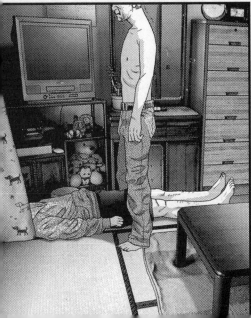

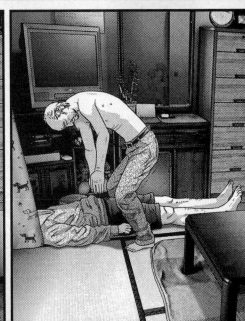

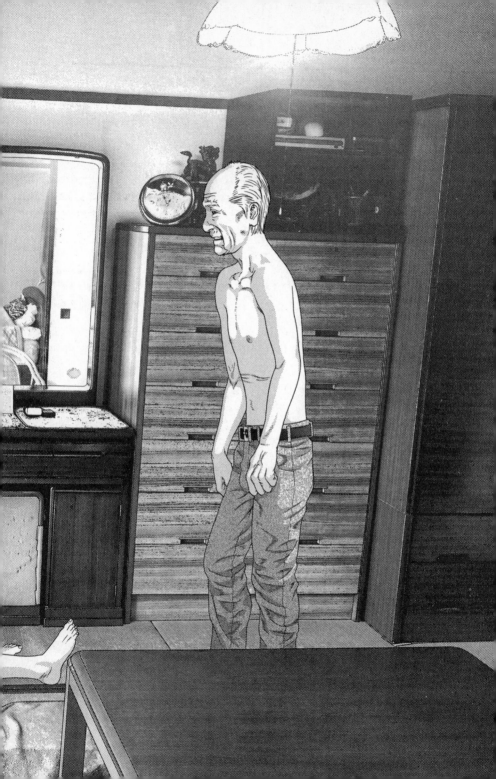

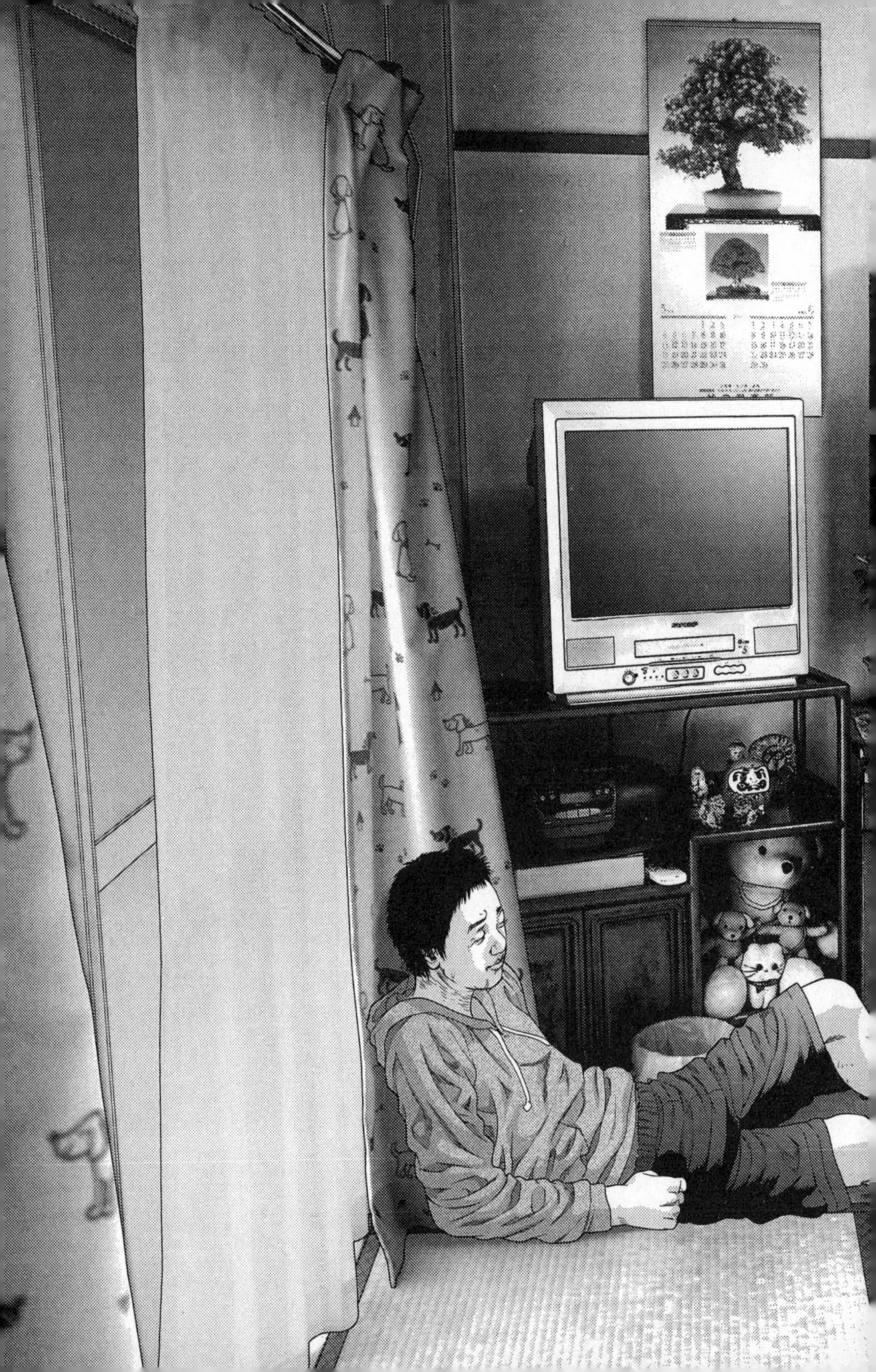

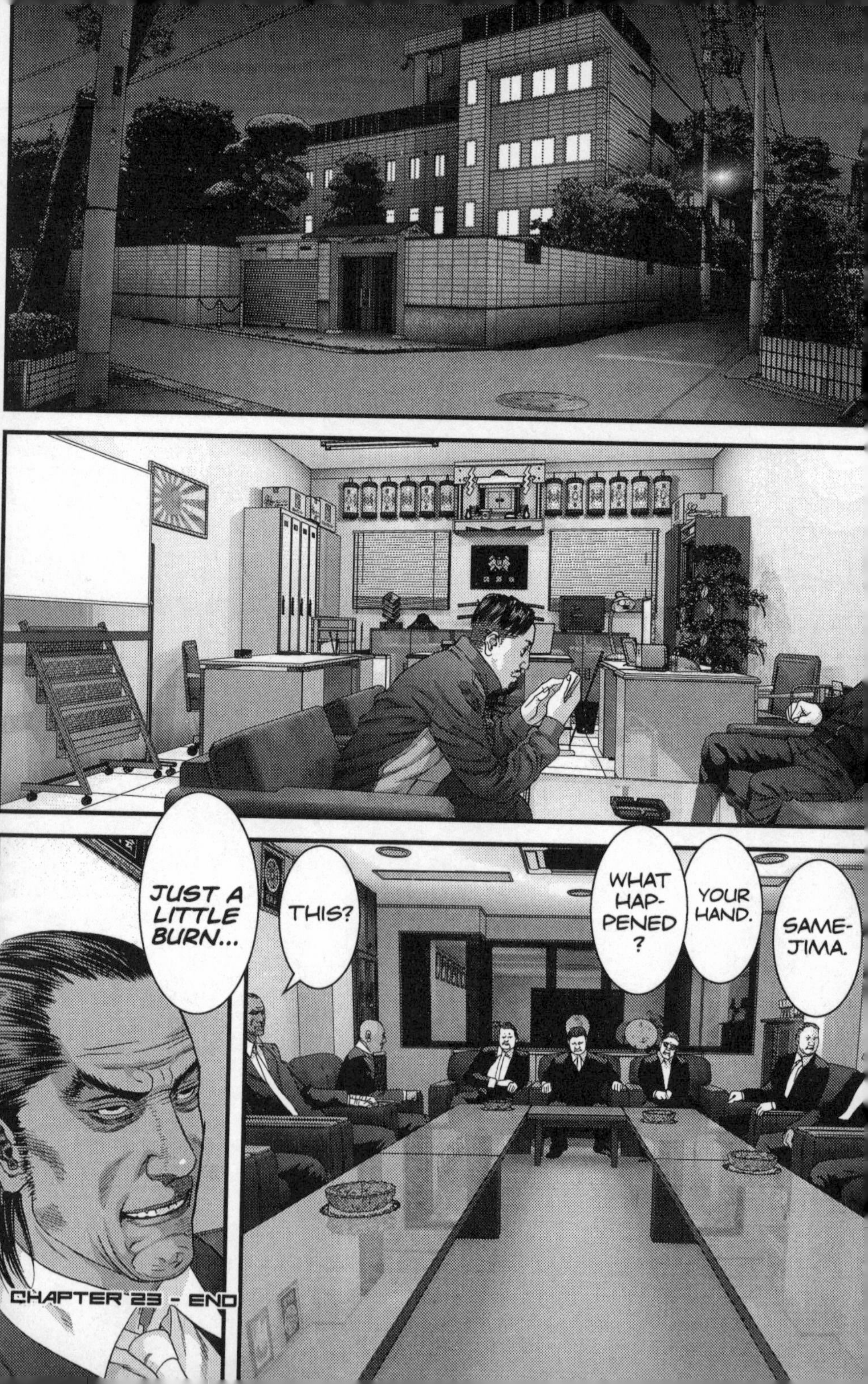
SAME-JIMA.
YOUR HAND.
WHAT HAP-PENED?
THIS?
JUST A LITTLE BURN...
CHAPTER 23 - END

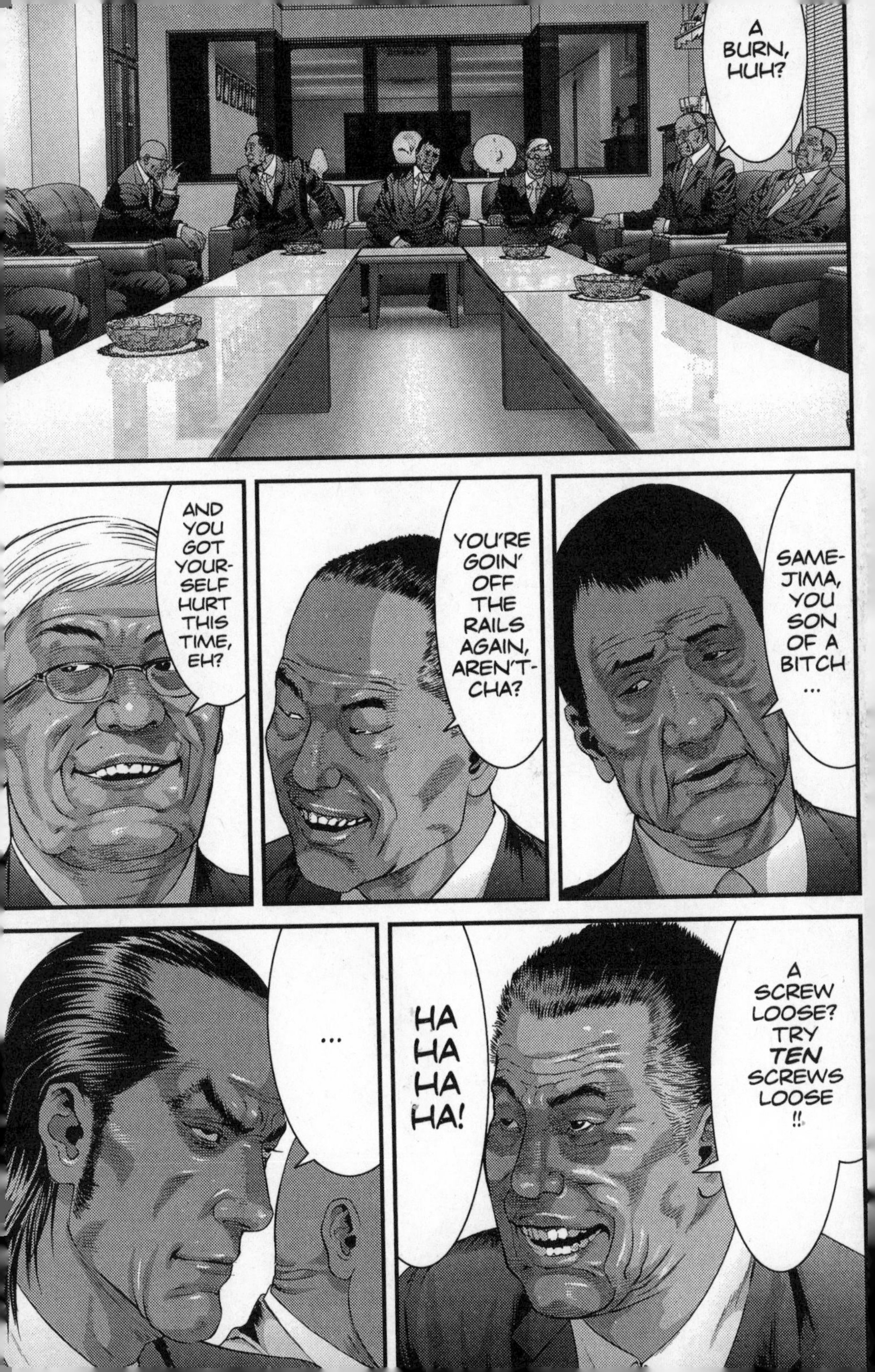
A BURN, HUH?
SAME-JIMA, YOU SON OF A BITCH ...
YOU'RE GOIN' OFF THE RAILS AGAIN, AREN'T-CHA?
AND YOU GOT YOUR-SELF HURT THIS TIME, EH?
A SCREW LOOSE? TRY TEN SCREWS LOOSE !!
HA HA HA HA!
...

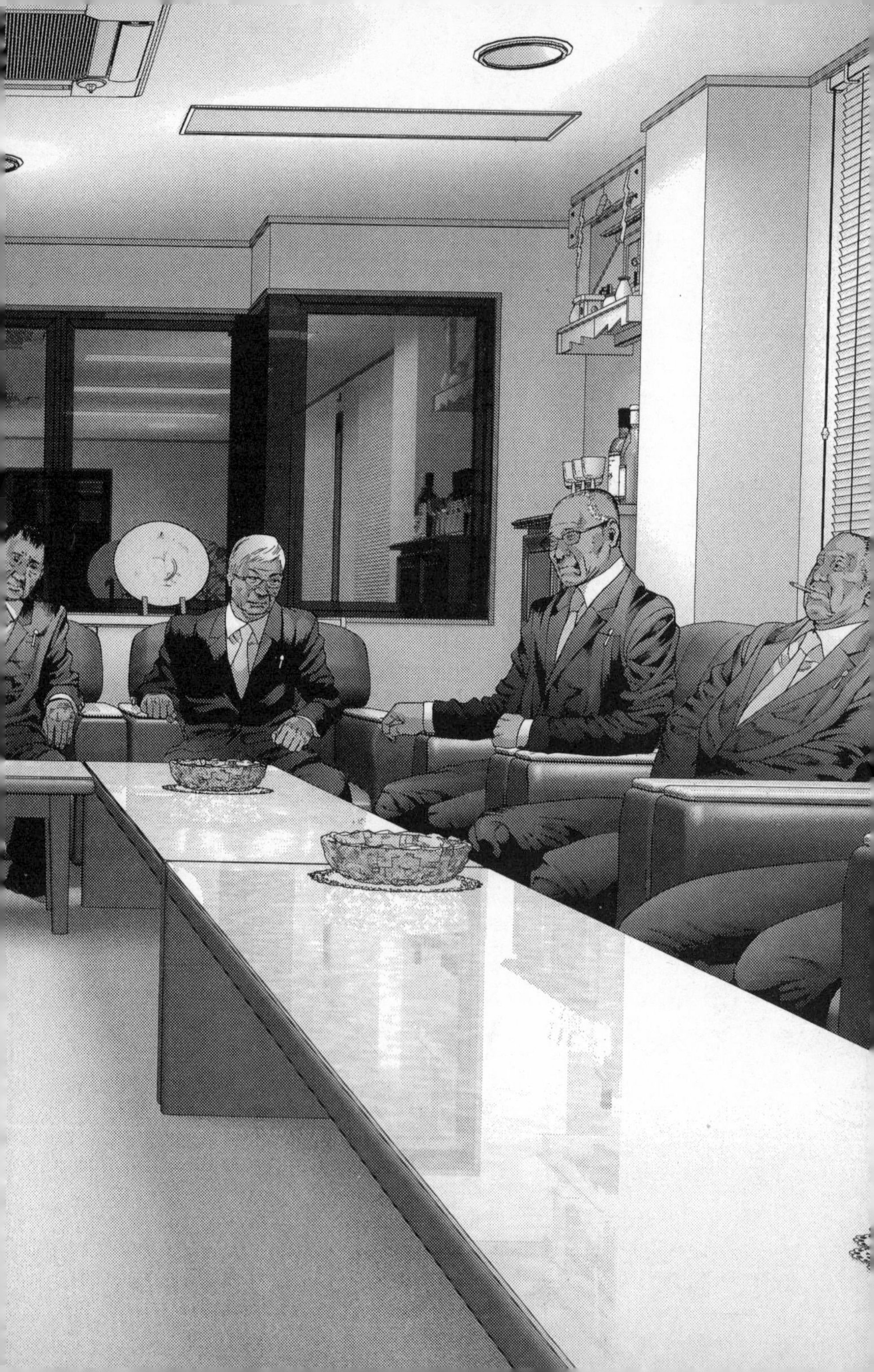

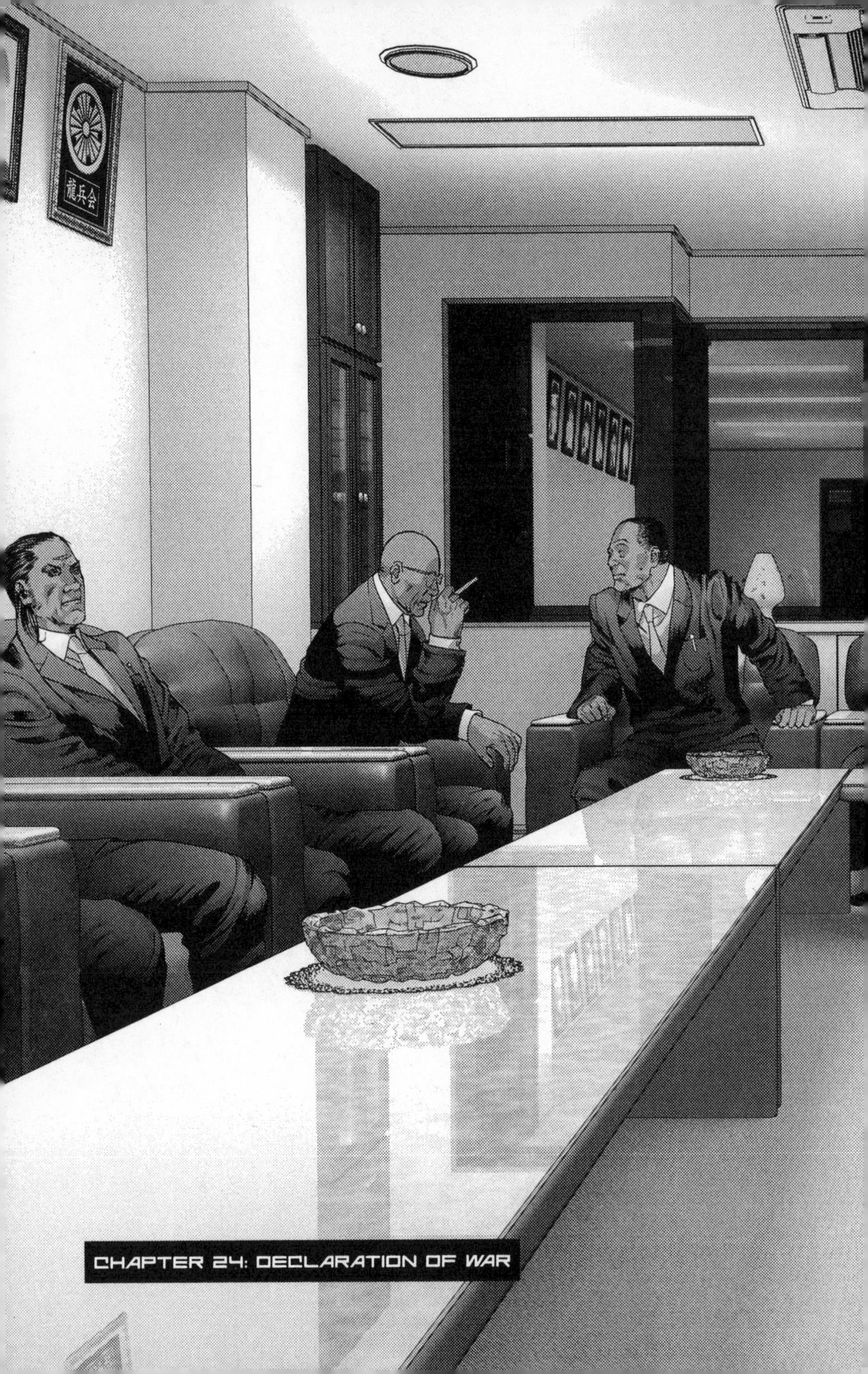
龍兵会
CHAPTER 24: DECLARATION OF WAR

THANK GOODNESS.

OHH...

THANK GOODNESS...

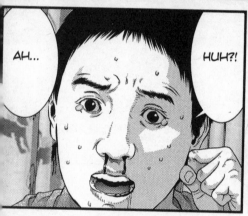

AH...

HUH?!

HUH? HUH?

HUH? I WAS...

WHERE'S FUMINO?!

WHERE'S FUMINO?!

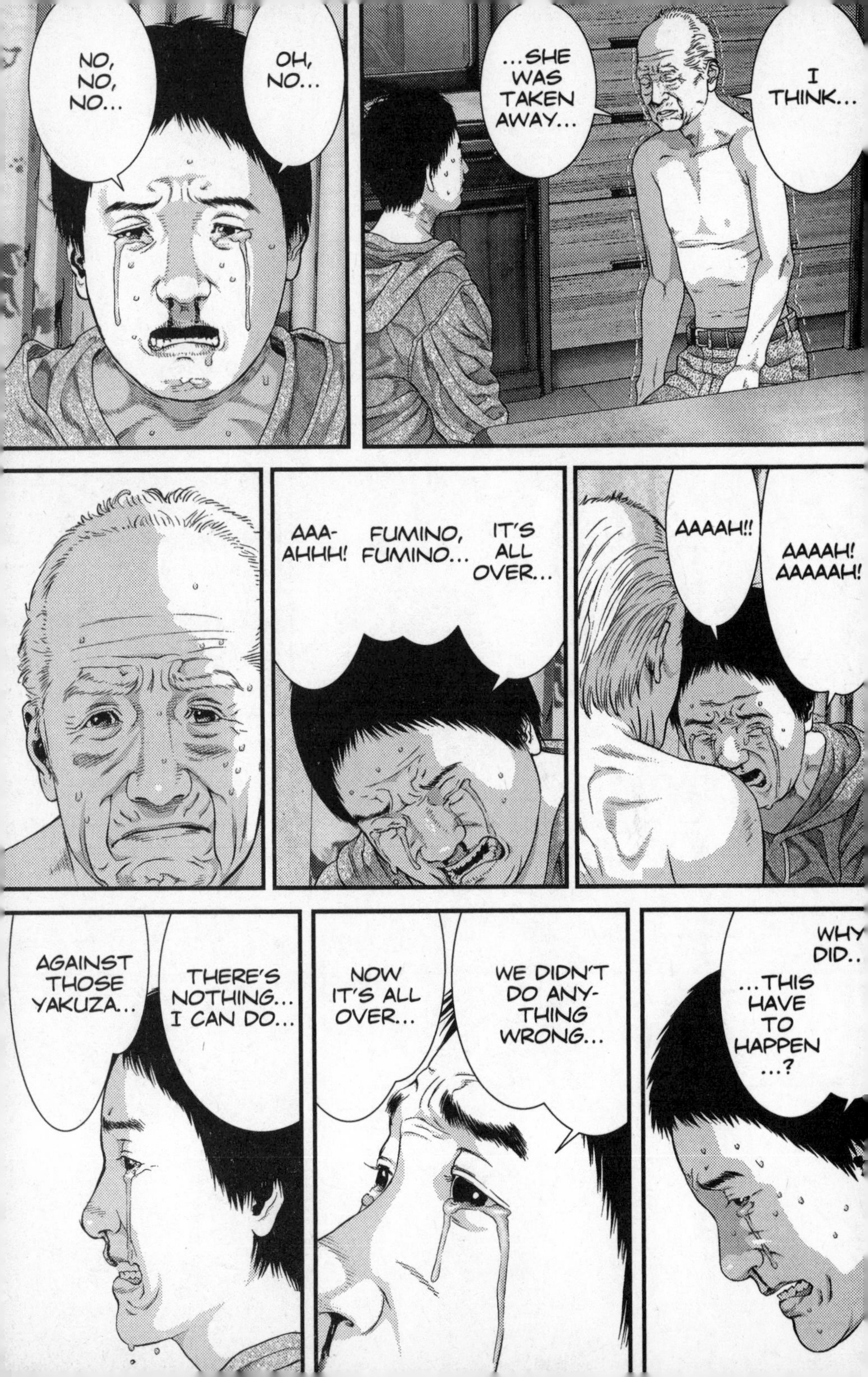
I THINK...
...SHE WAS TAKEN AWAY...
OH, NO...
NO, NO, NO...
AAAAH! AAAAAH!
AAAAH!!
IT'S ALL OVER...
FUMINO, FUMINO...
AAA-AHHH!
WHY DID.. ...THIS HAVE TO HAPPEN ...?
WE DIDN'T DO ANY-THING WRONG...
NOW IT'S ALL OVER...
THERE'S NOTHING... I CAN DO...
AGAINST THOSE YAKUZA...

ALL
MISSED
Fumino
iPhone
2014/05/14
Fumino
iPhone
2014/05/14
Fumino (2)
iPhone
2014/05/13
Serizawa-san
Cellular
2014/05/13
Sato-san (4)
Other
Fumino (2)
iPhone
Asai-san
Cell
Kojima-san
Cellular
BEEP
Fumino
iPhone
Fumino
iPhone
Fumino (2)
iPhone
Serizawa-san
Cellular
TRRRR
TRRRR
TRRR
TRRR
TRRR
...
?!
FUMINO
00:03
mute
keypad
speaker
add call
FaceTime
contacts
...WHO THE HELL IS THIS...?
WHO THE HELL... IS CALLING THIS NUMBER?

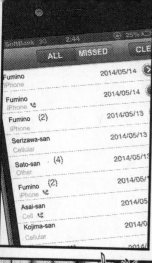

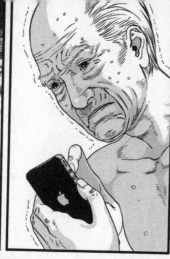

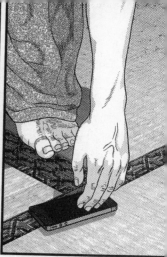

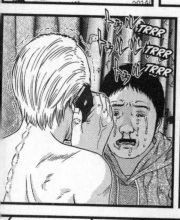

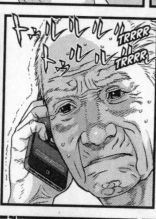

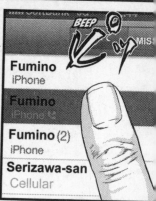

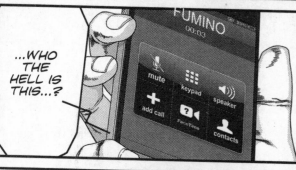

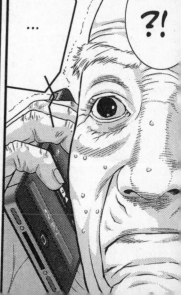

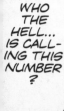

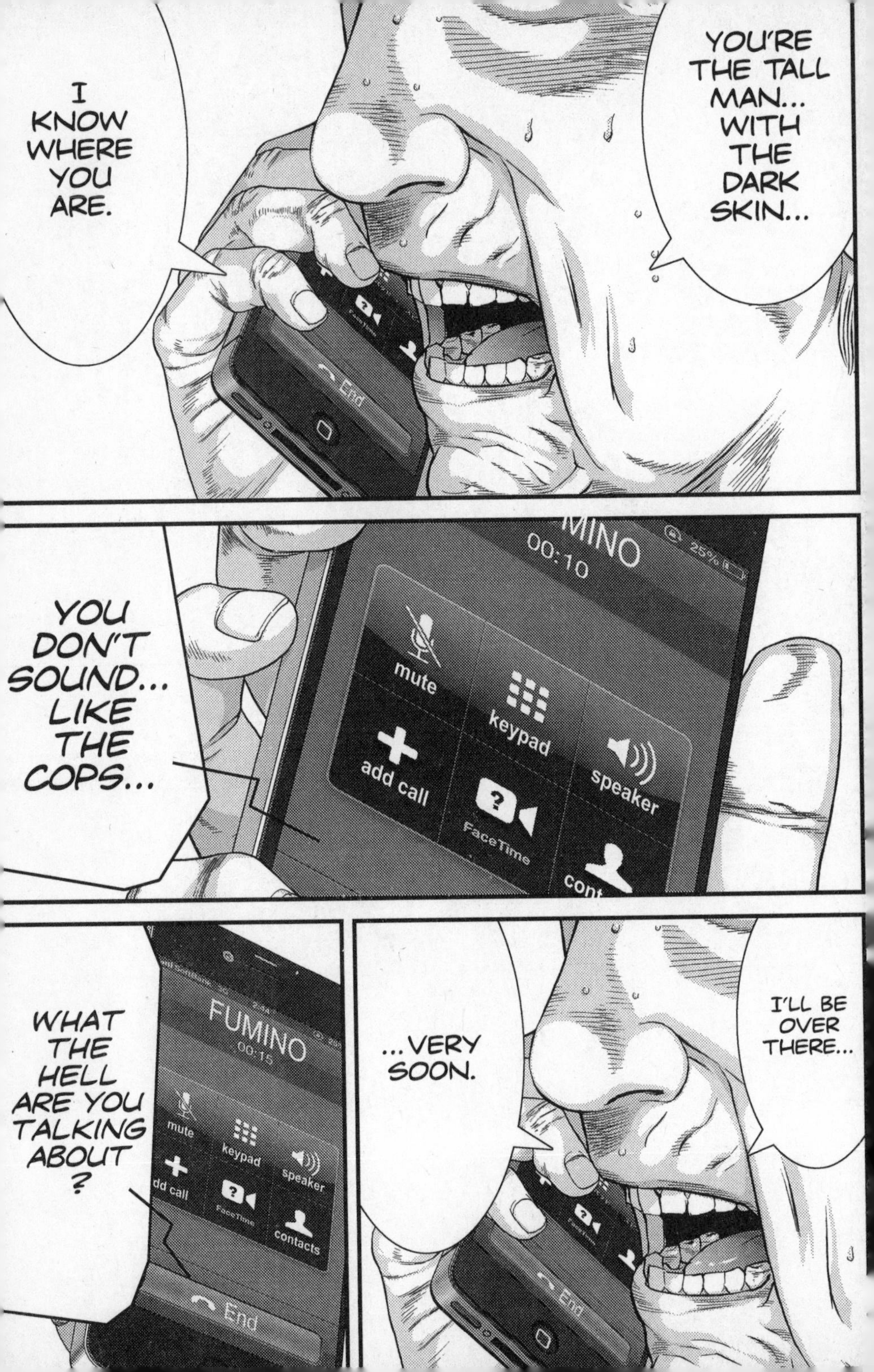
YOU'RE THE TALL MAN... WITH THE DARK SKIN...
I KNOW WHERE YOU ARE.
End
MINO
00:10
25%
mute
keypad
add call
speaker
FaceTime
YOU DON'T SOUND... LIKE THE COPS...
I'LL BE OVER THERE...
...VERY SOON.
End
FUMINO
00:15
mute
keypad
speaker
dd call
FaceTime
contacts
End
WHAT THE HELL ARE YOU TALKING ABOUT?

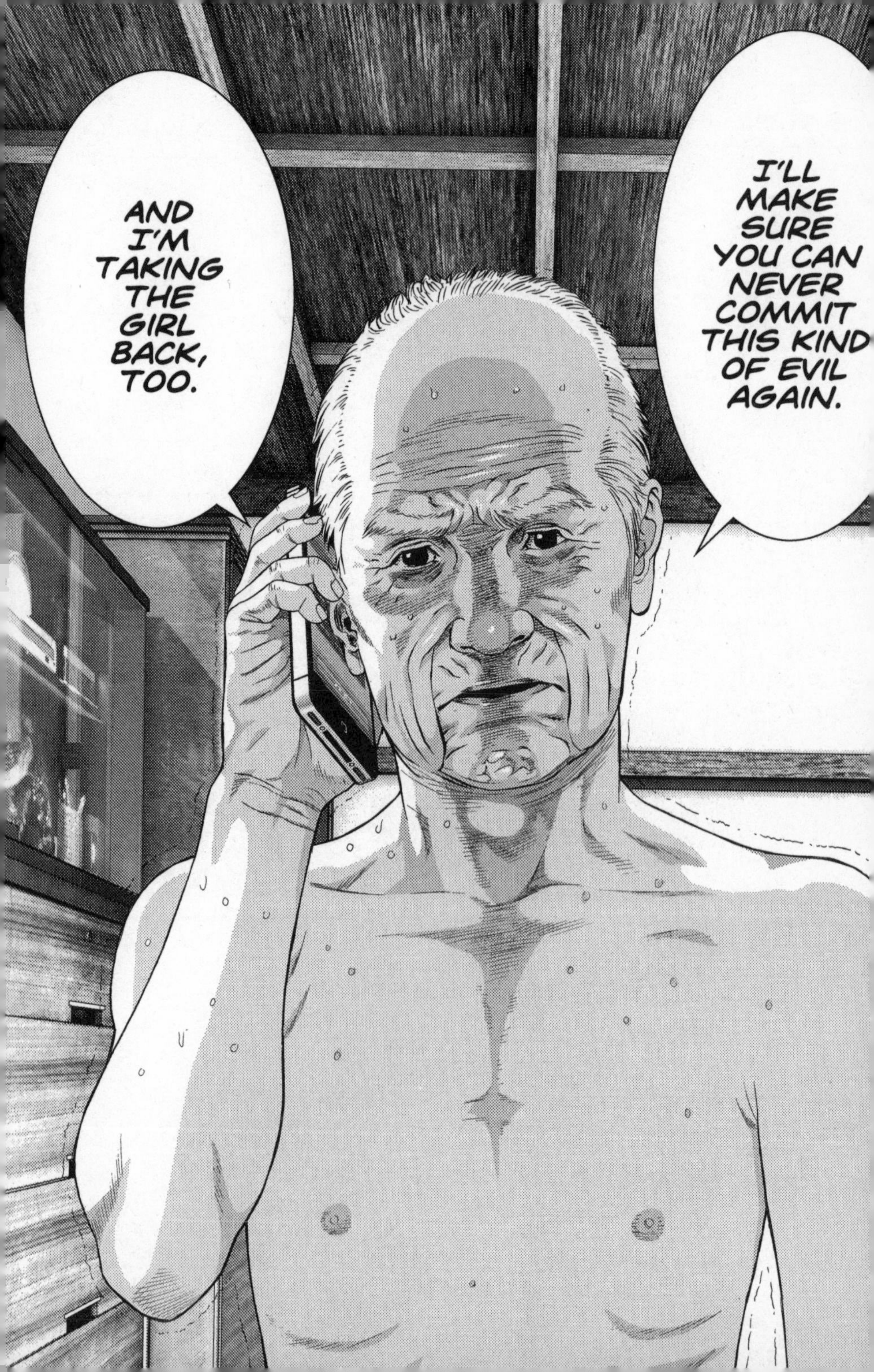
I'LL MAKE SURE YOU CAN NEVER COMMIT THIS KIND OF EVIL AGAIN.
AND I'M TAKING THE GIRL BACK, TOO.

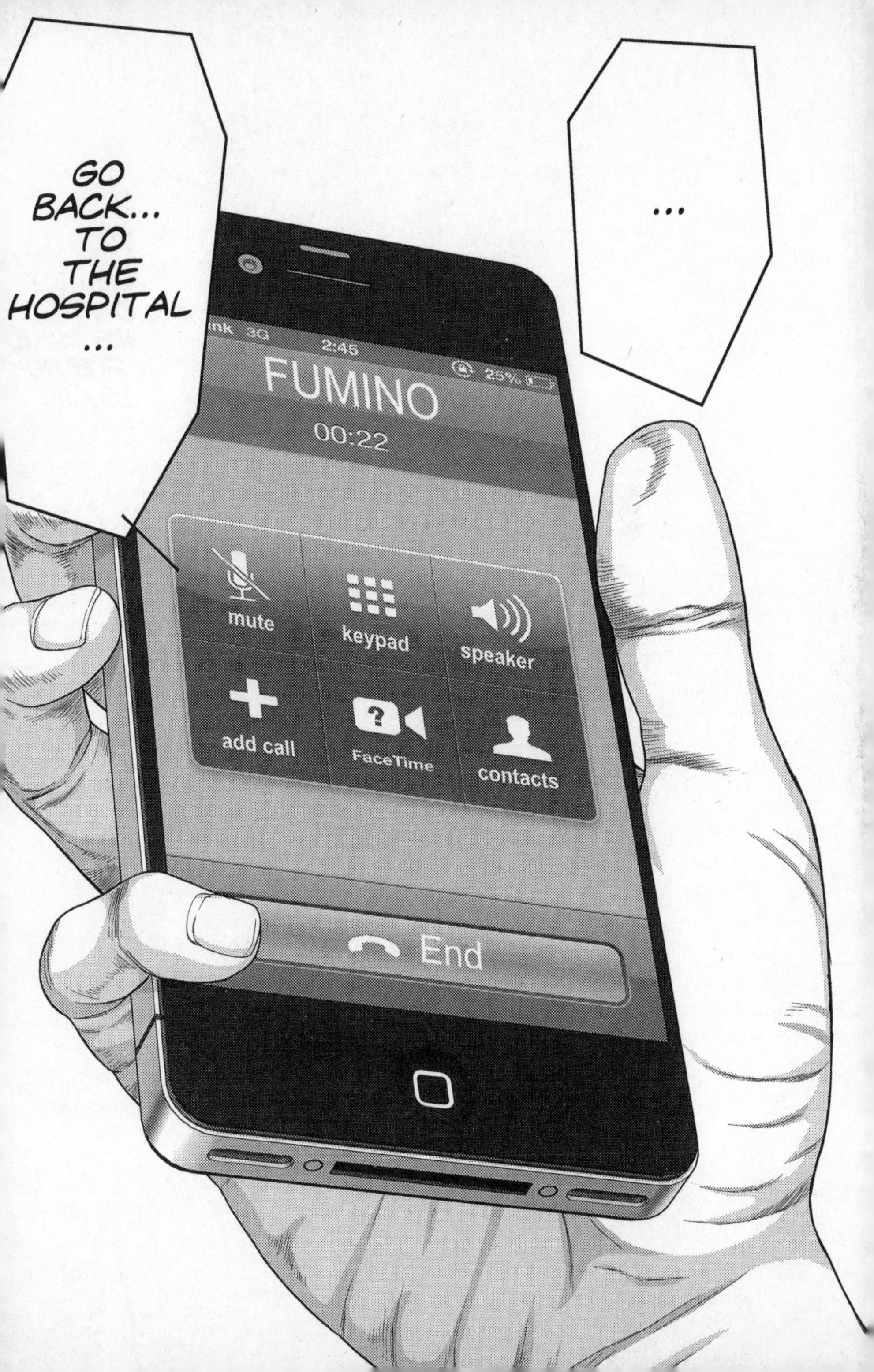
GO BACK... TO THE HOSPITAL ...
...
3G
2:45
25%
FUMINO
00:22
mute
keypad
speaker
add call
FaceTime
contacts
End

...WHO
...

...ARE
YOU?

JUST...

HEY,
MIS-
TER
...

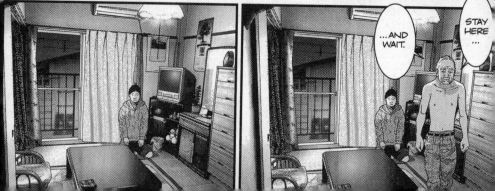

...AND
WAIT.

STAY
HERE
...

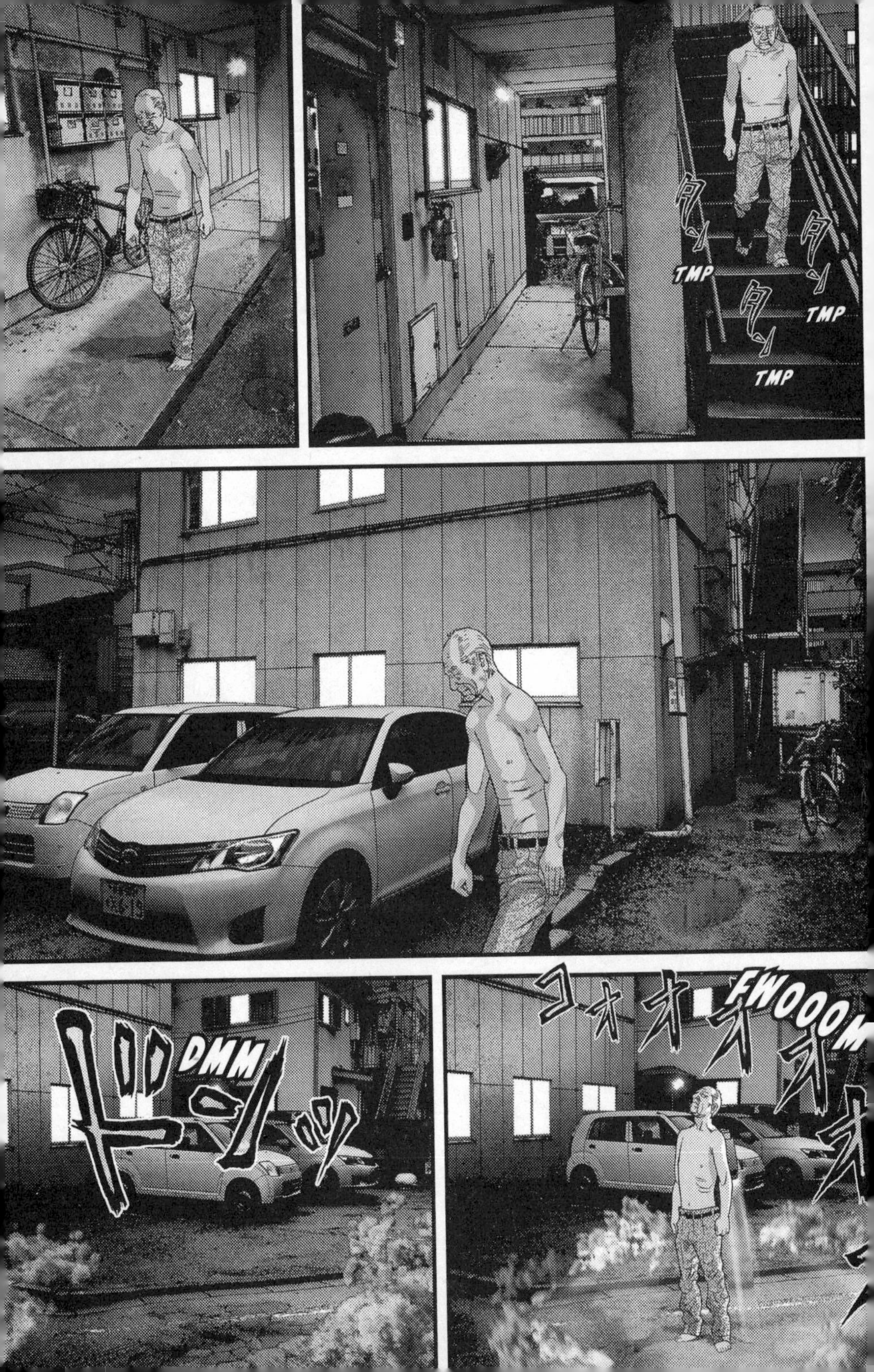
TMP
TMP
TMP
FWOOOM
DMM

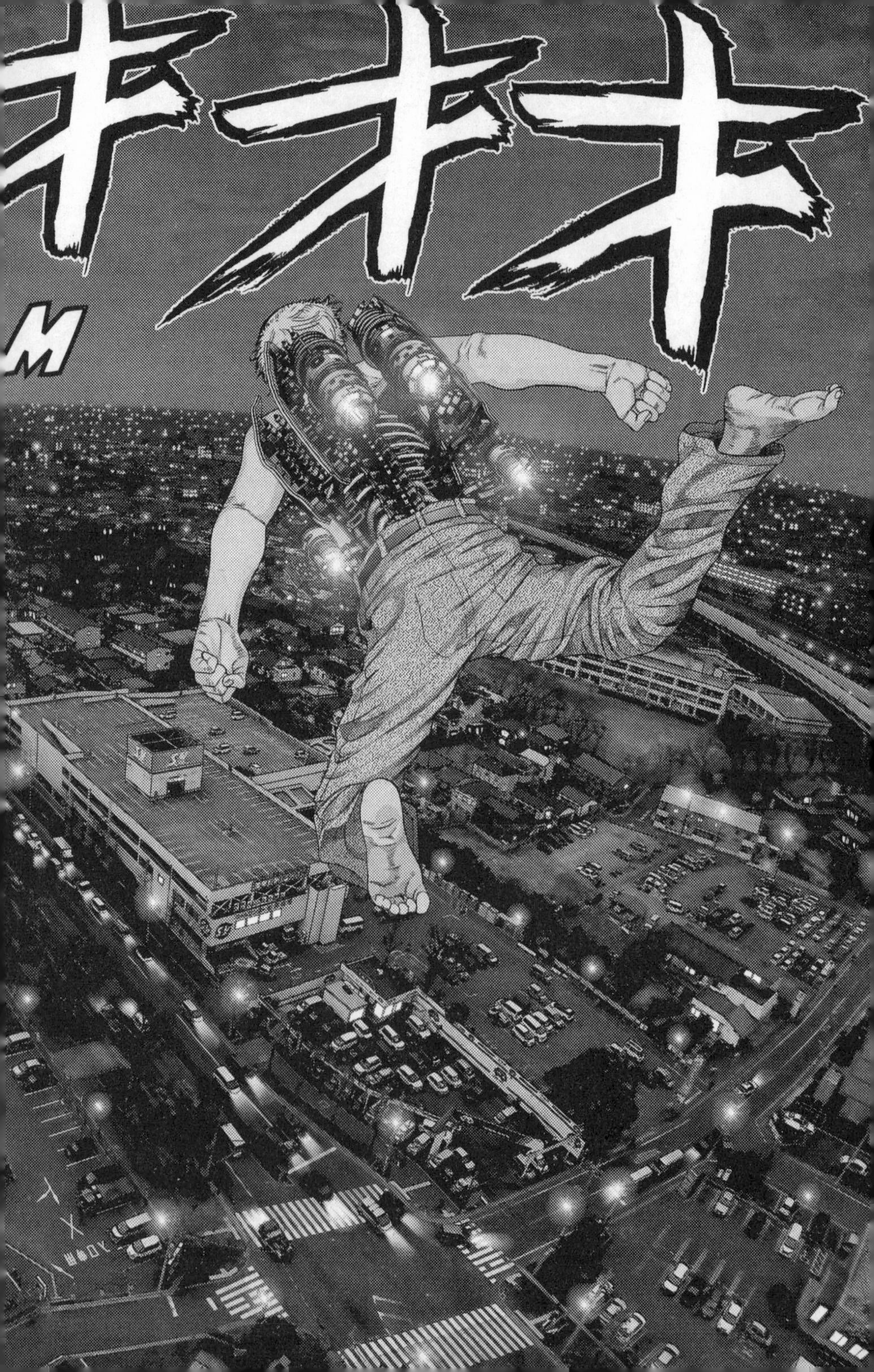

オオオ
M

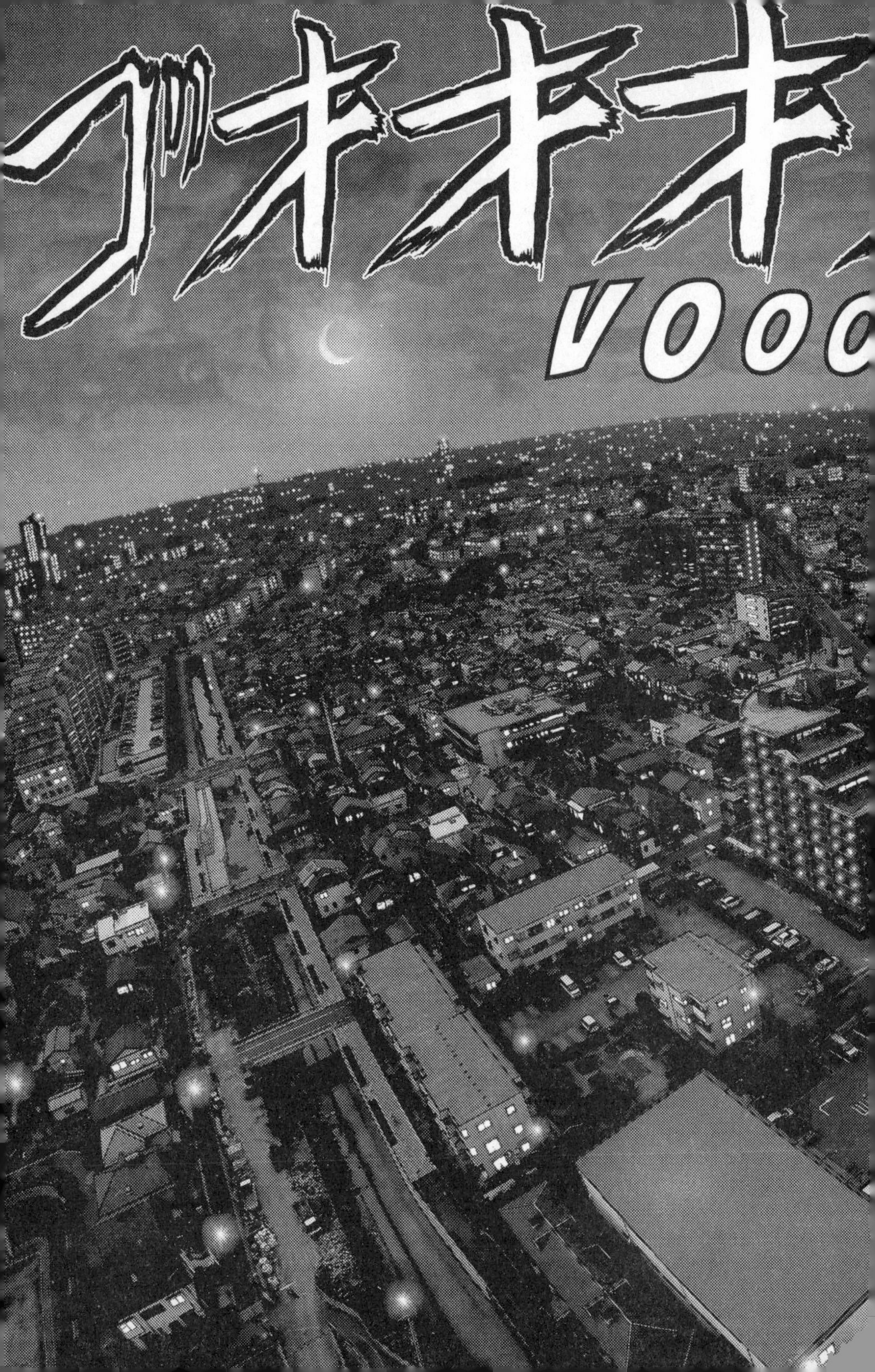
ゴオオオ
VOOO

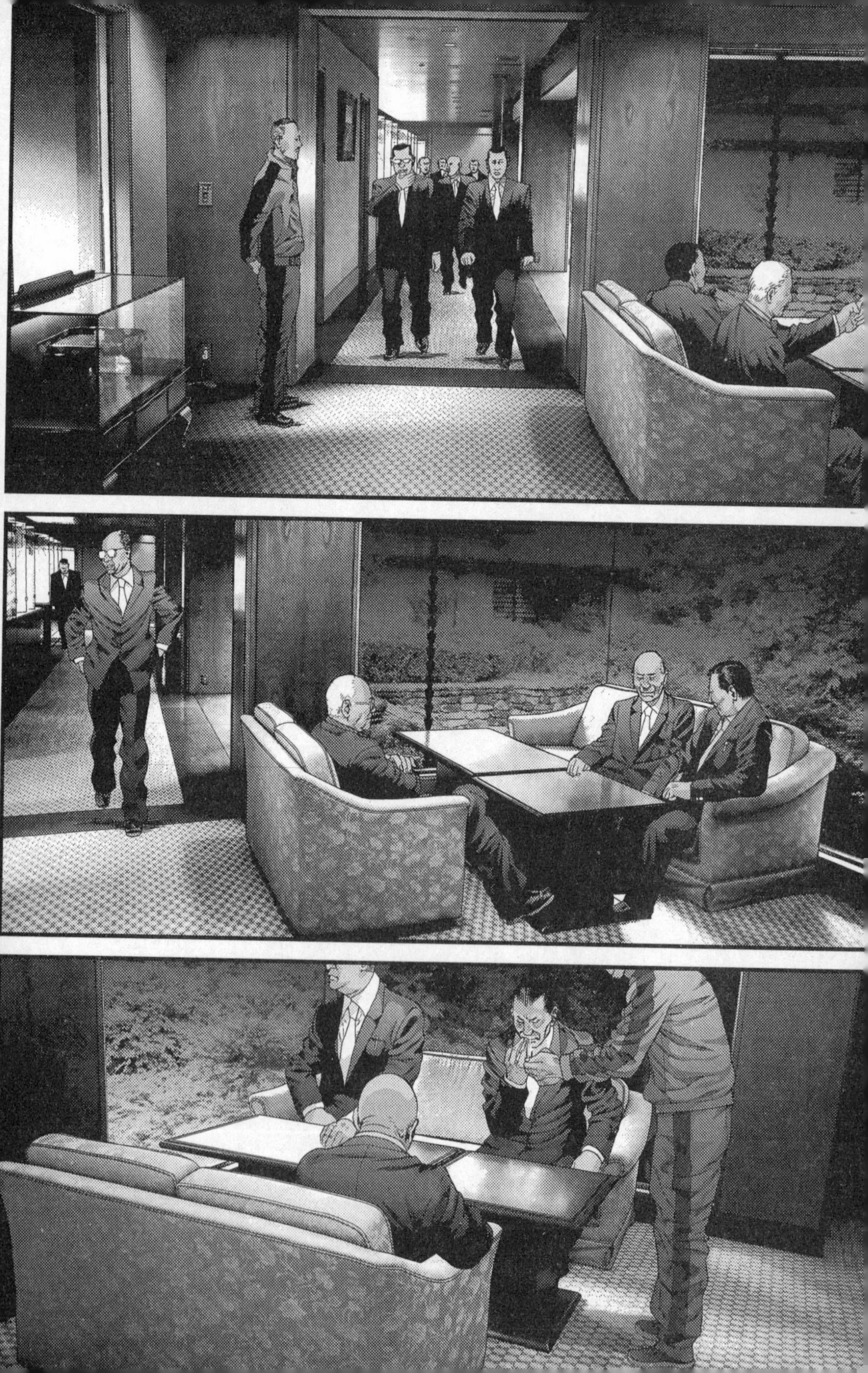

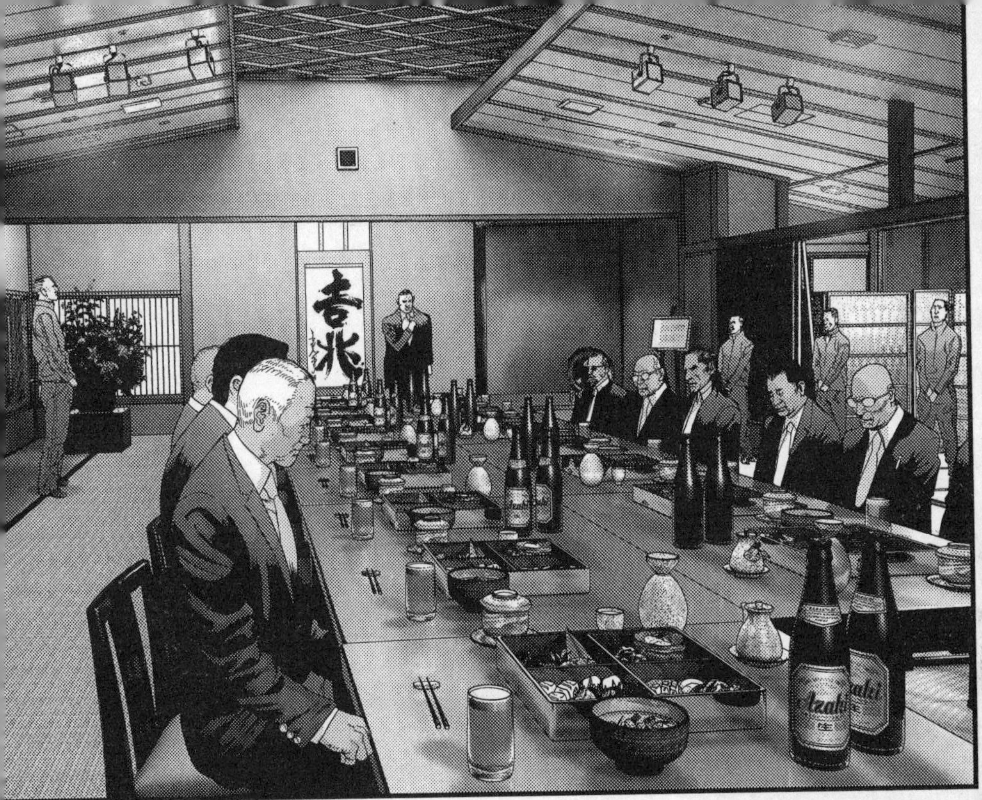
吉兆
WALL SCROLL: GOOD OMEN

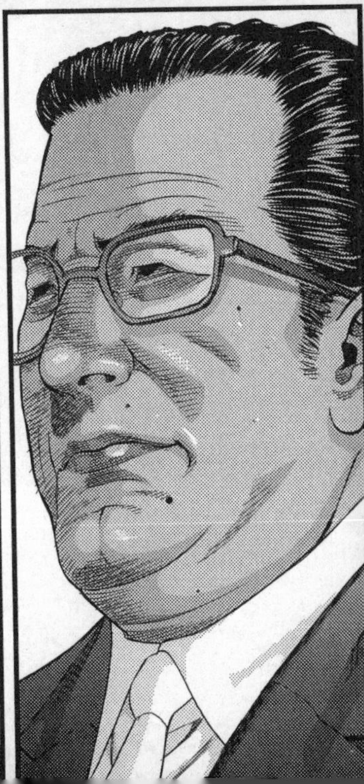

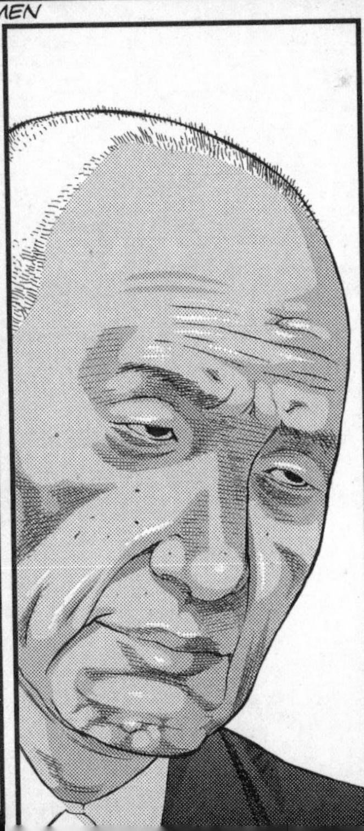

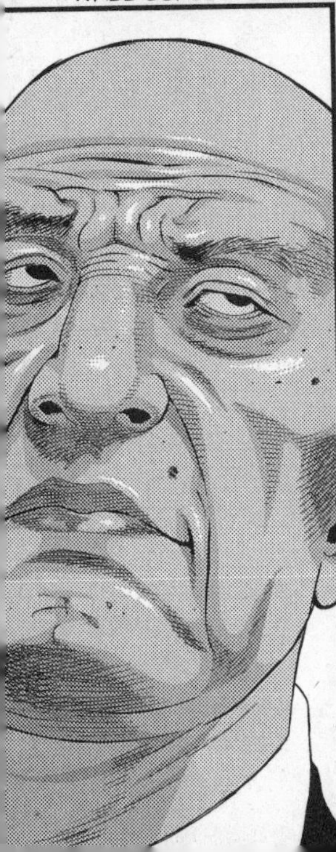

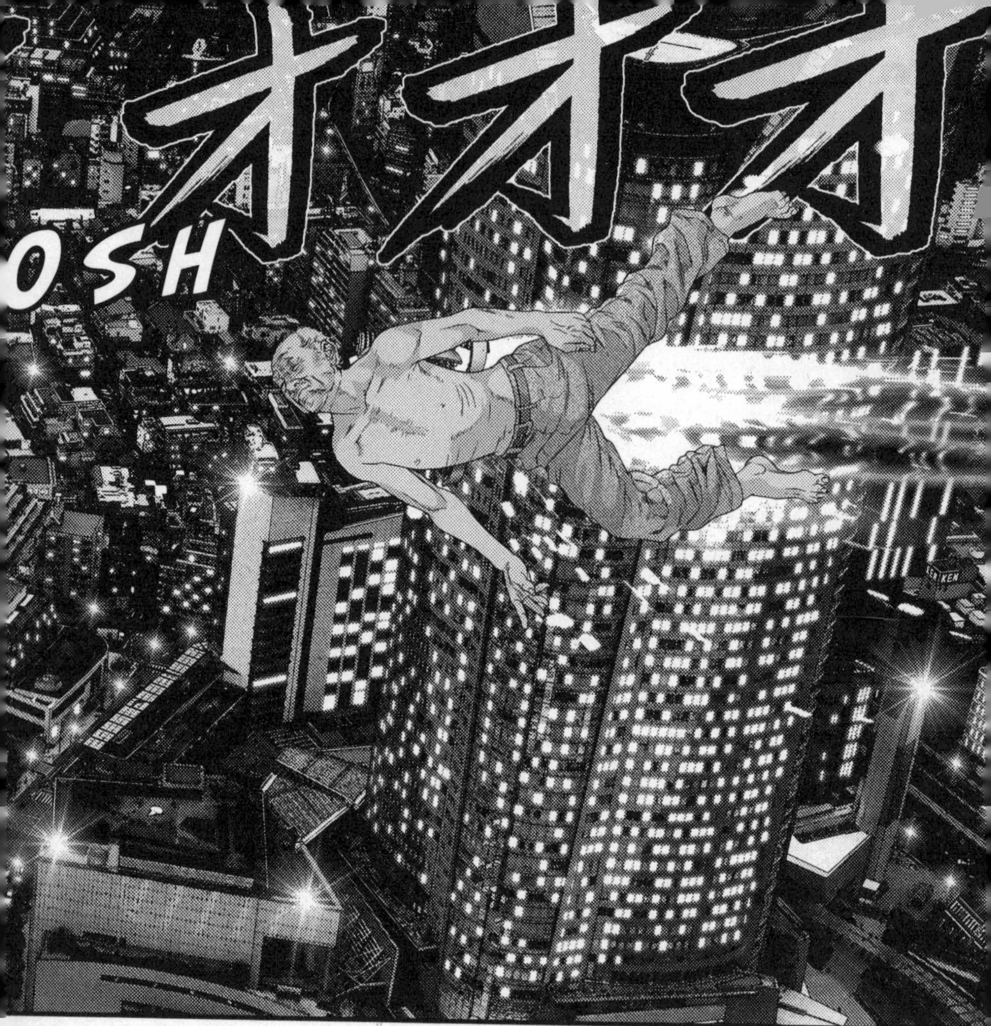
オオオ
OSH
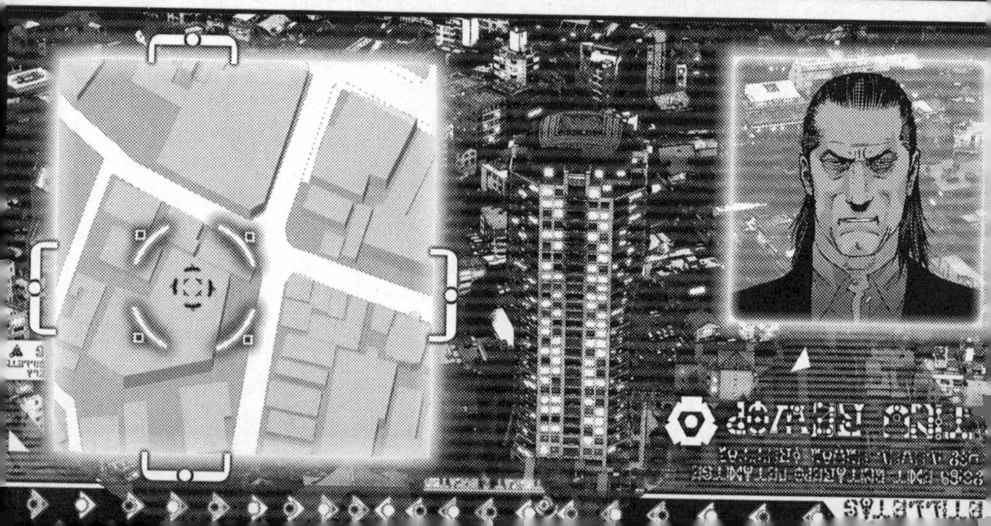

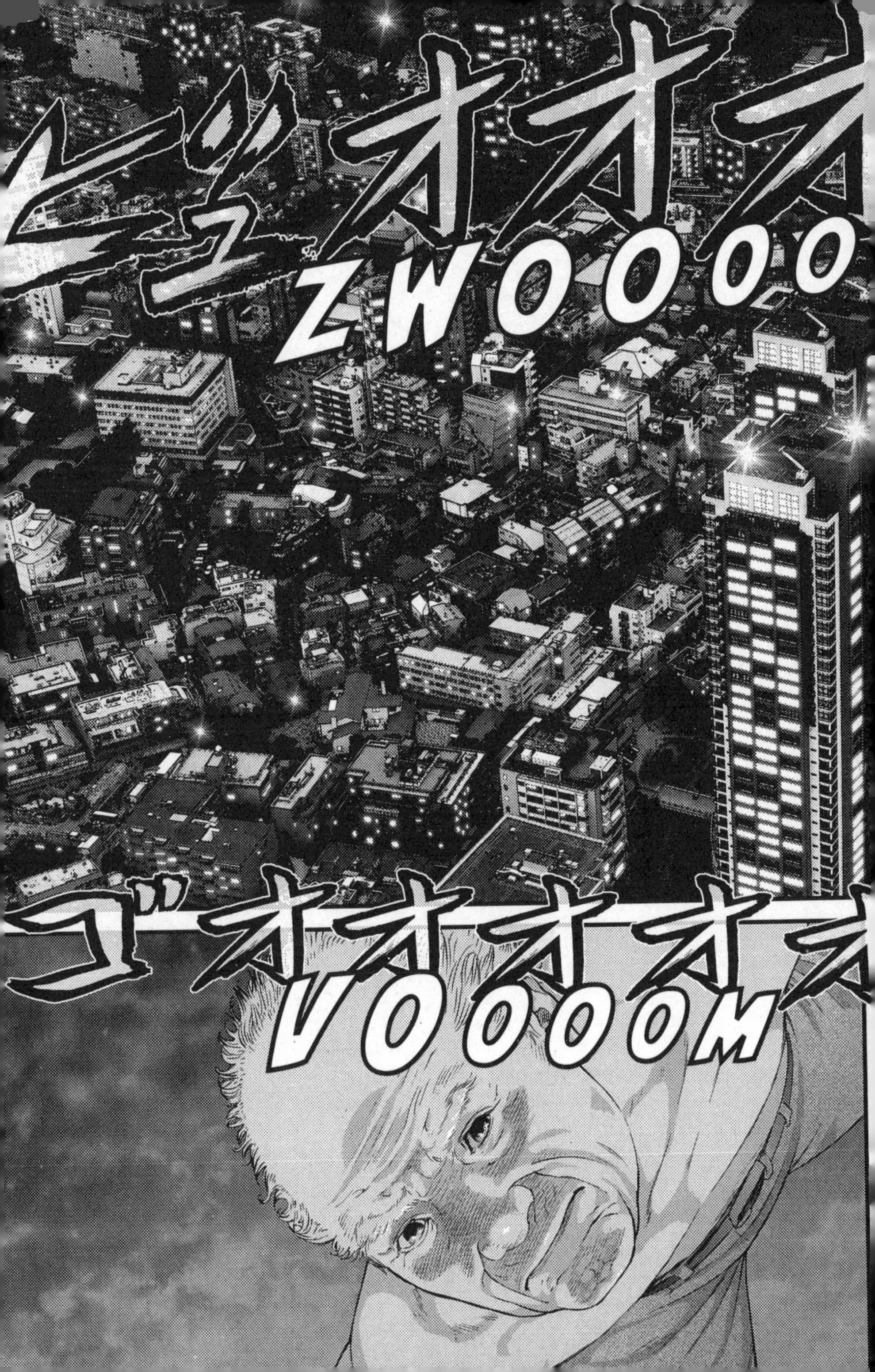
ZWOOOO
ゴオオオオ
VOOOOM

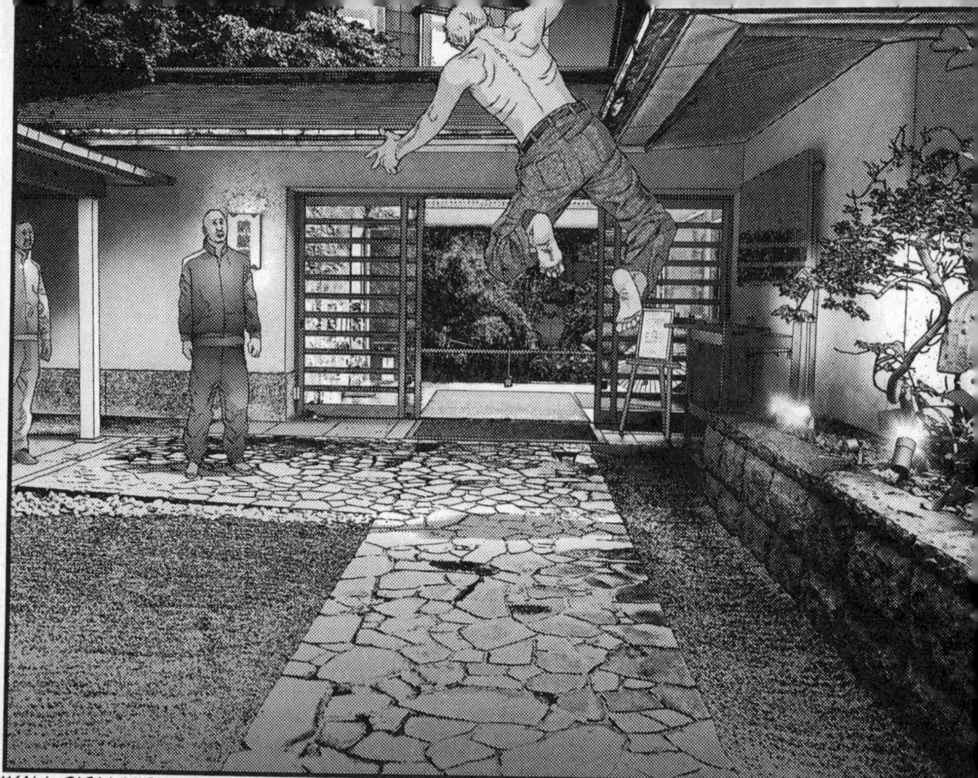

WALL SIGN: NISHIKORI-AN

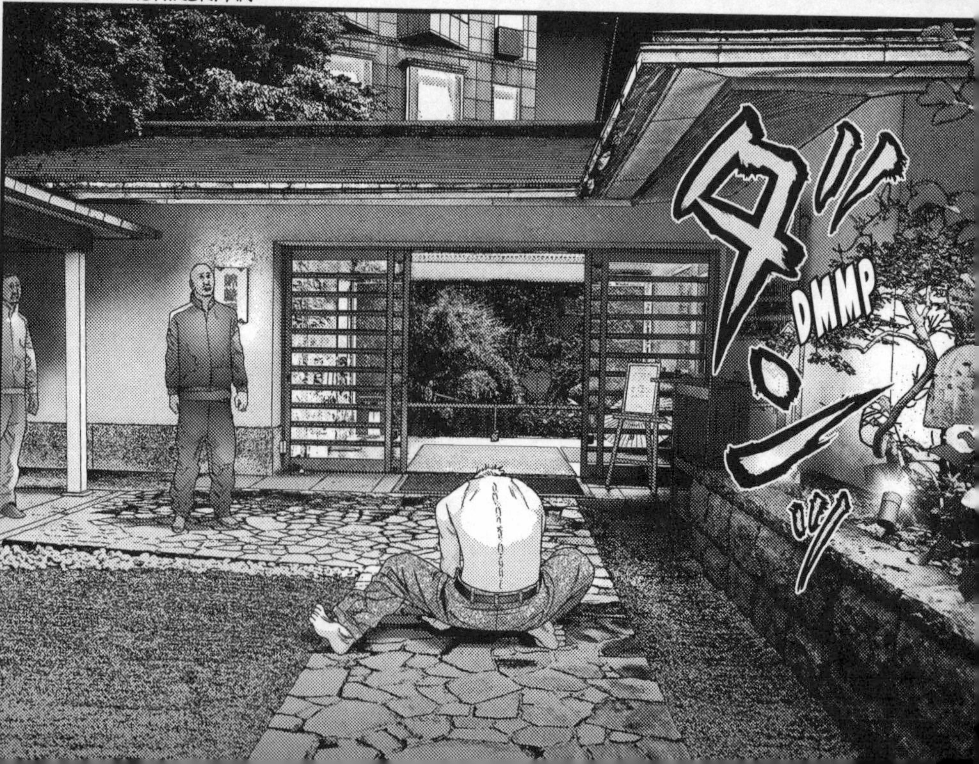
DMMP

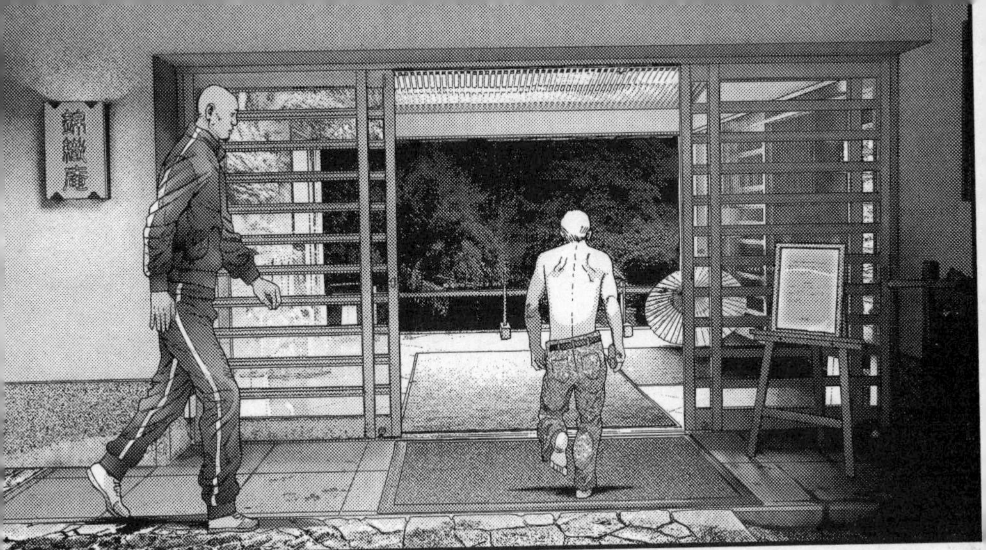
錦織庵
WALL SIGN: NISHIKORI-AN

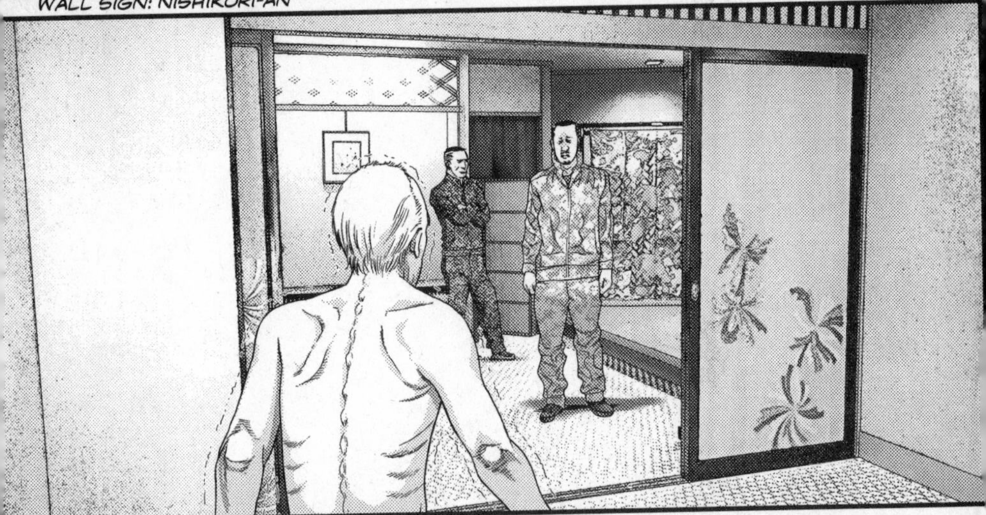

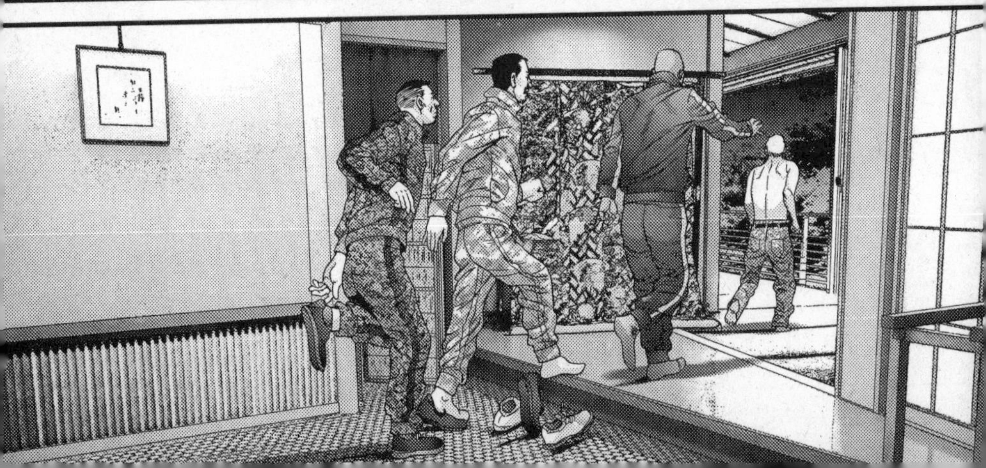

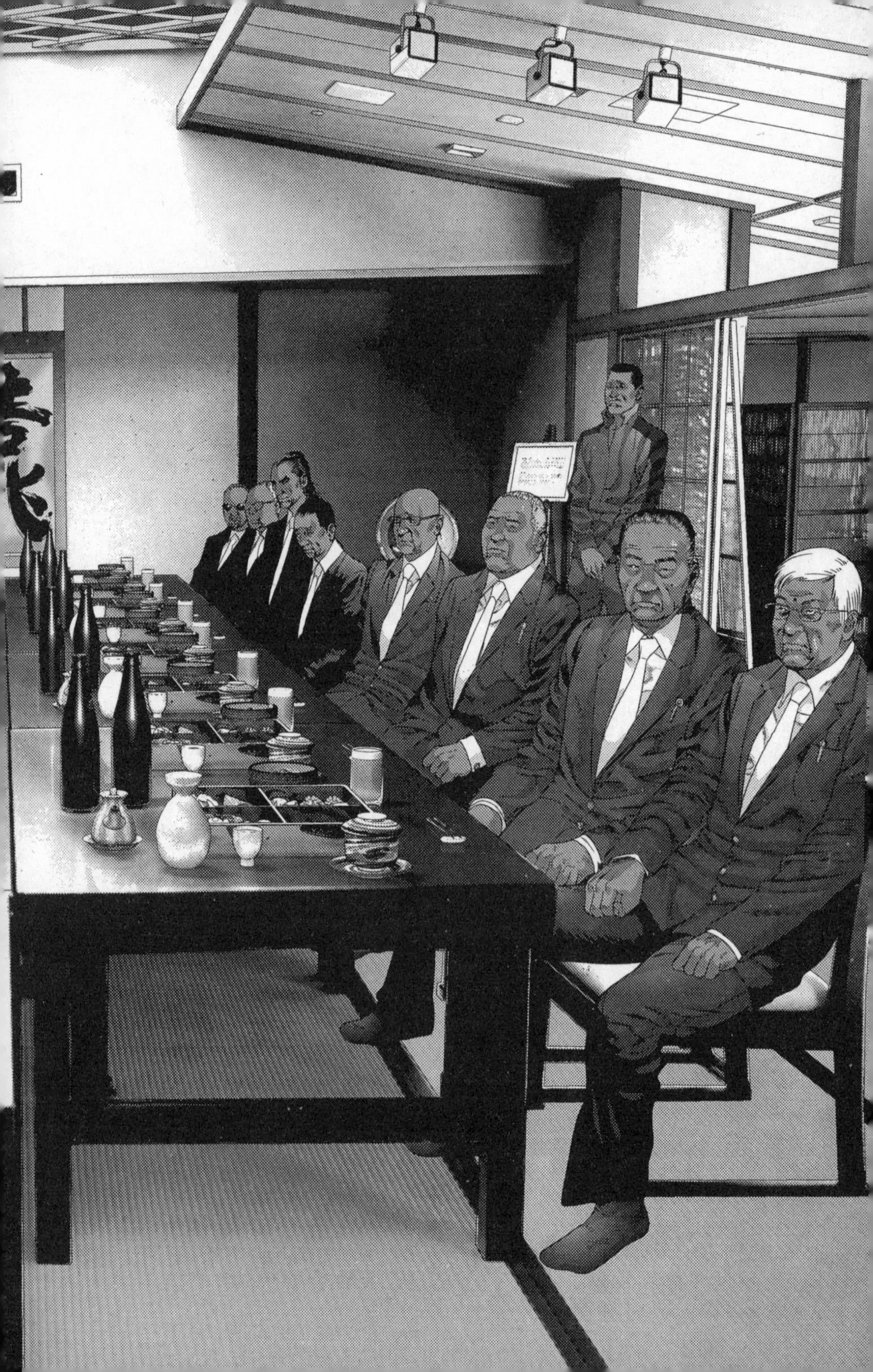

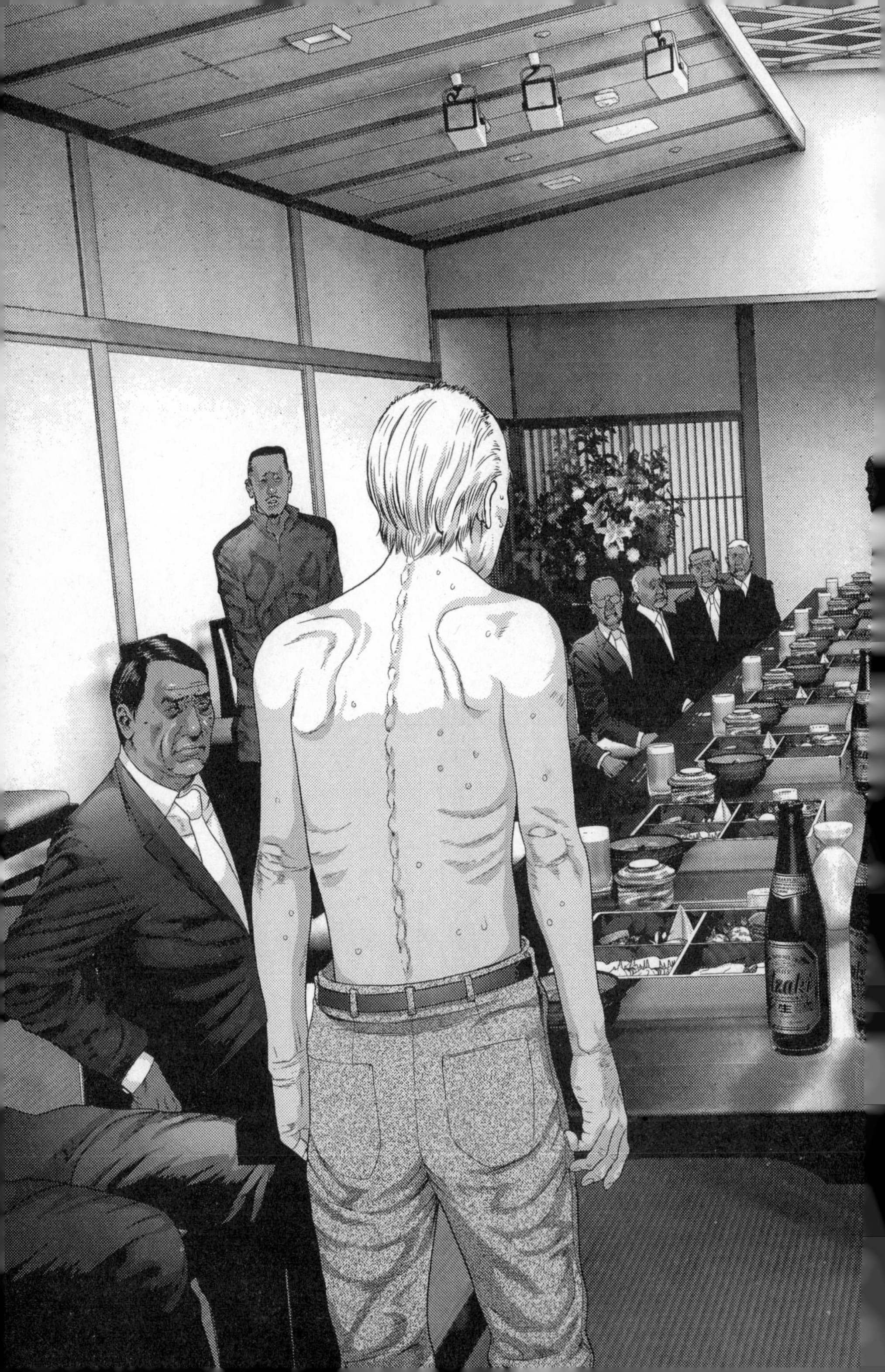

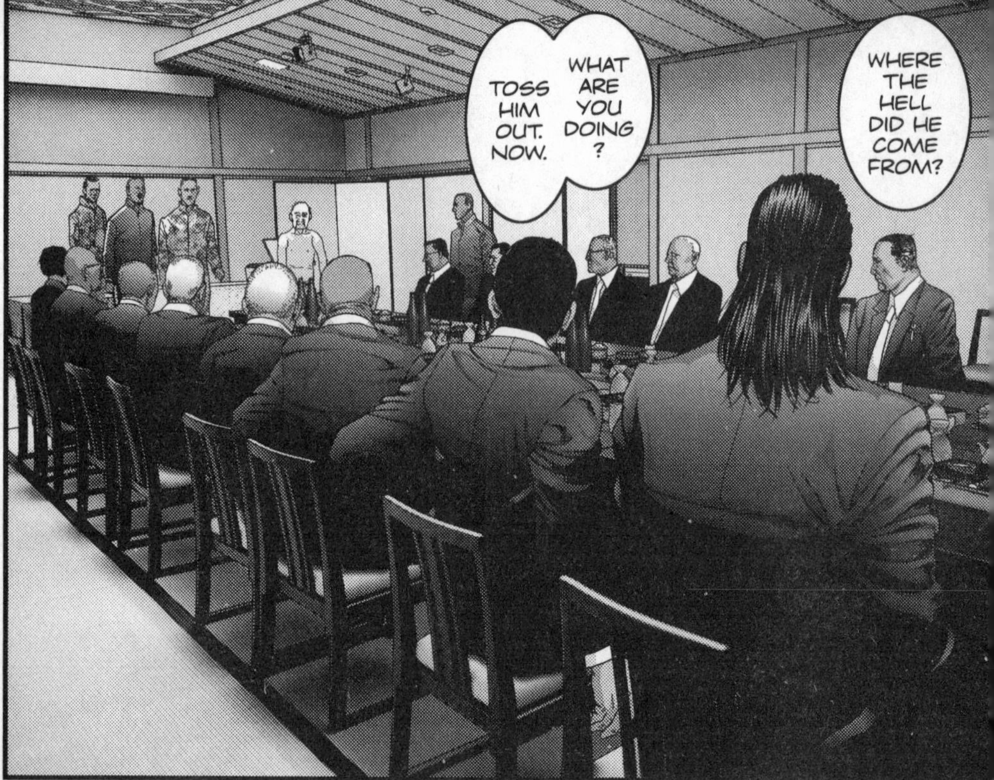
WHERE THE HELL DID HE COME FROM?
WHAT ARE YOU DOING?
TOSS HIM OUT. NOW.

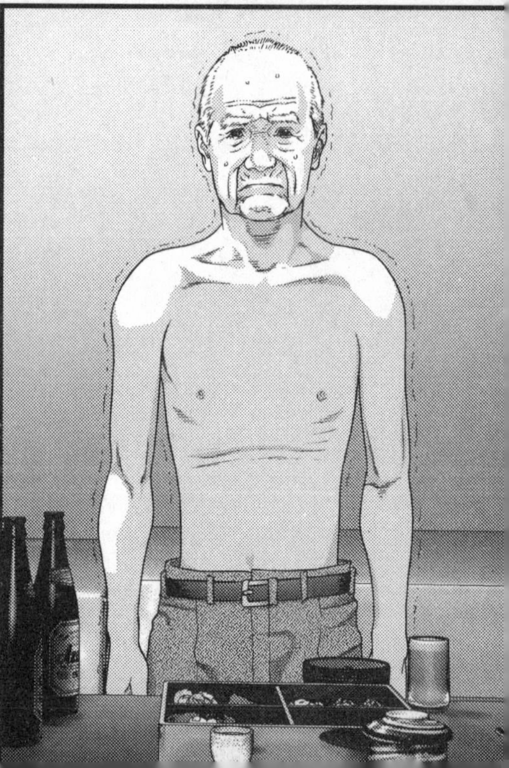

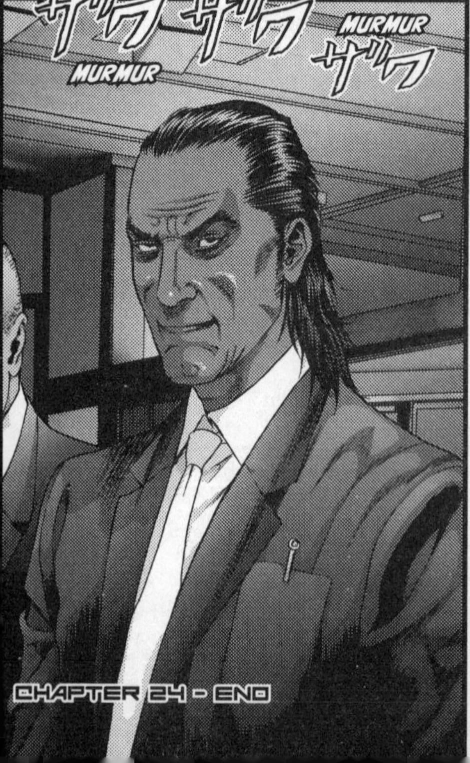
ザワ ザワ
MURMUR
ザワ
MURMUR
CHAPTER 24 - END

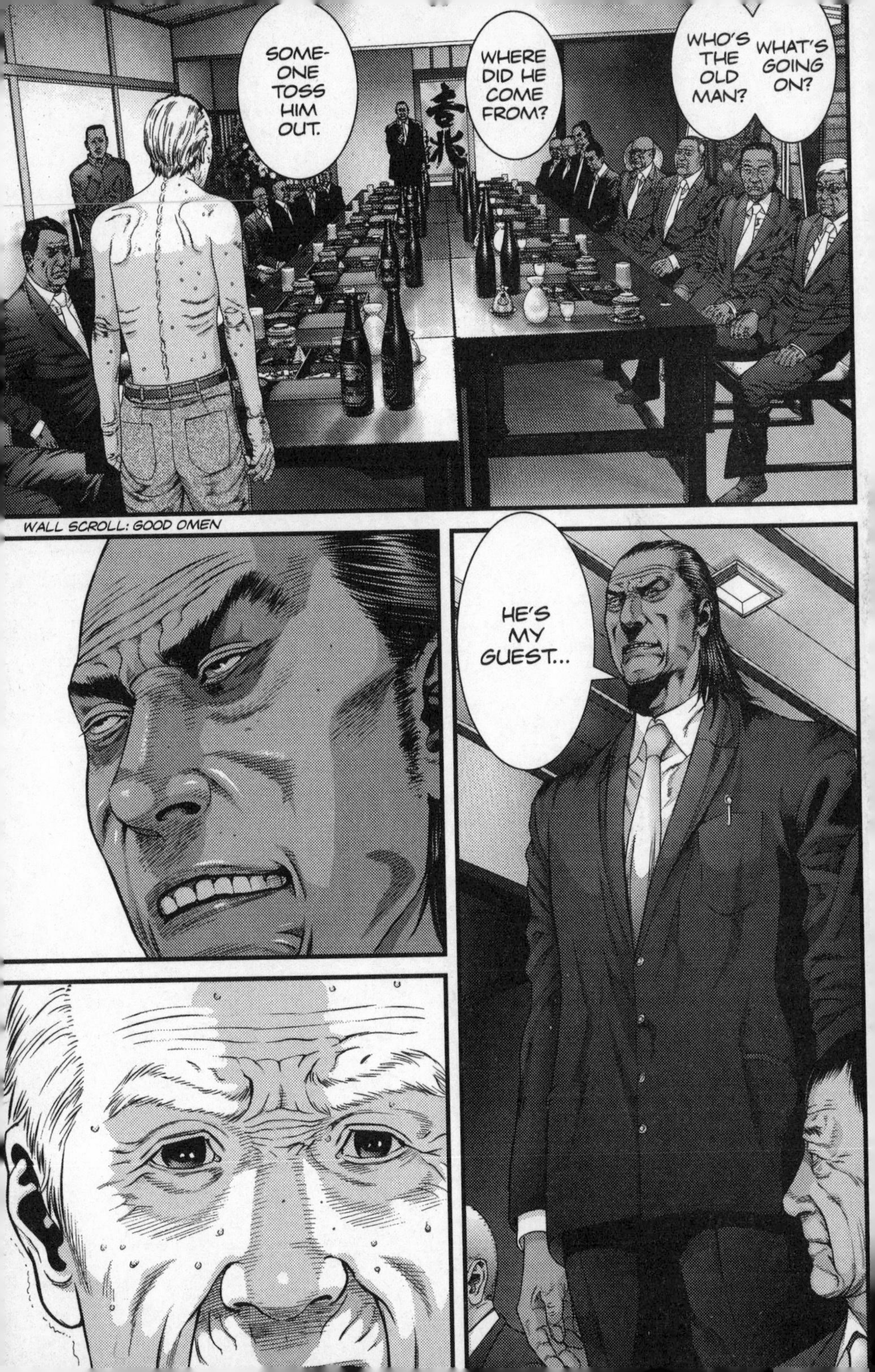
WHAT'S GOING ON?
WHO'S THE OLD MAN?
WHERE DID HE COME FROM?
SOME-ONE TOSS HIM OUT.
WALL SCROLL: GOOD OMEN
HE'S MY GUEST...

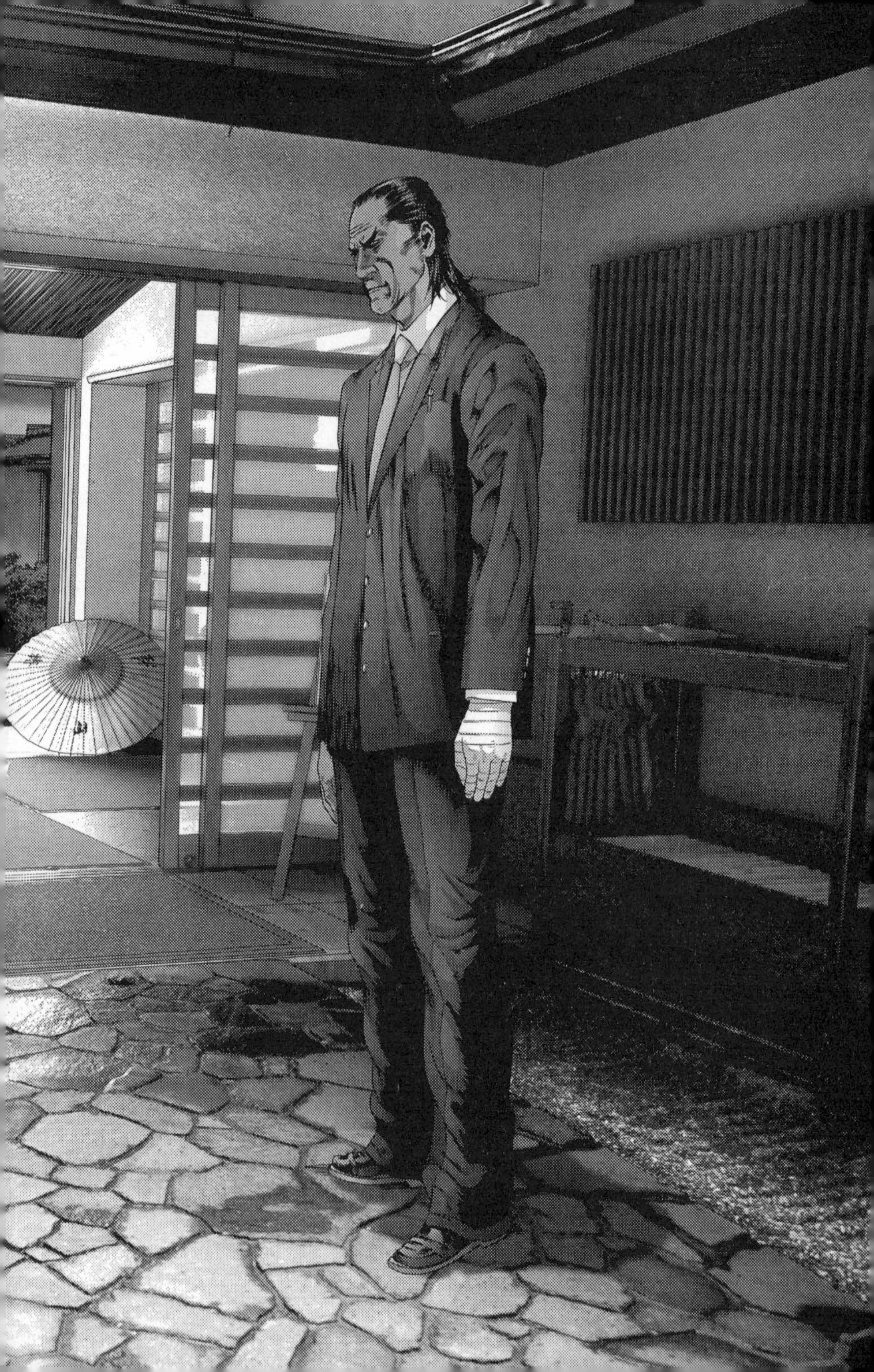

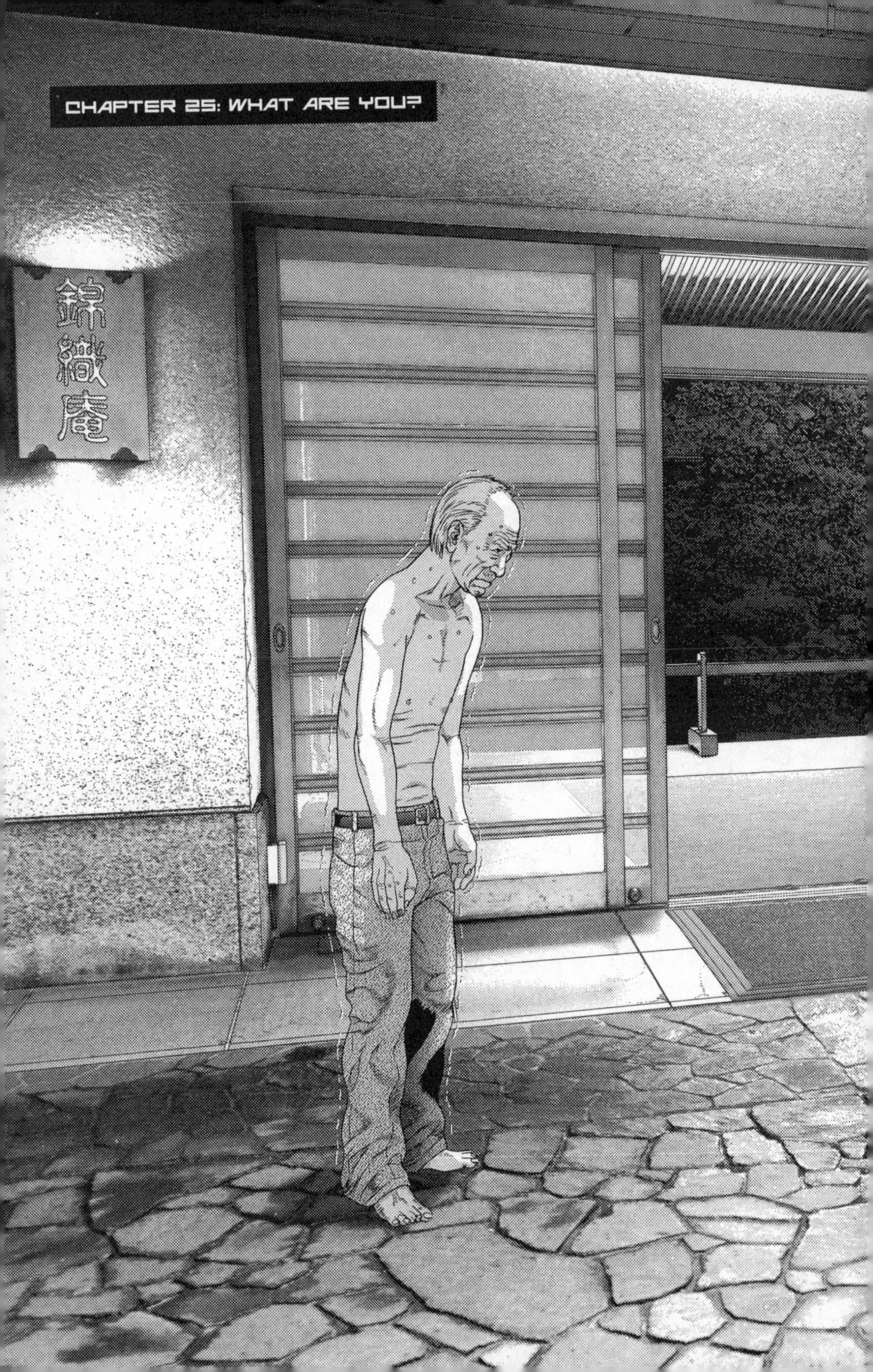
CHAPTER 25: WHAT ARE YOU?
錦織庵

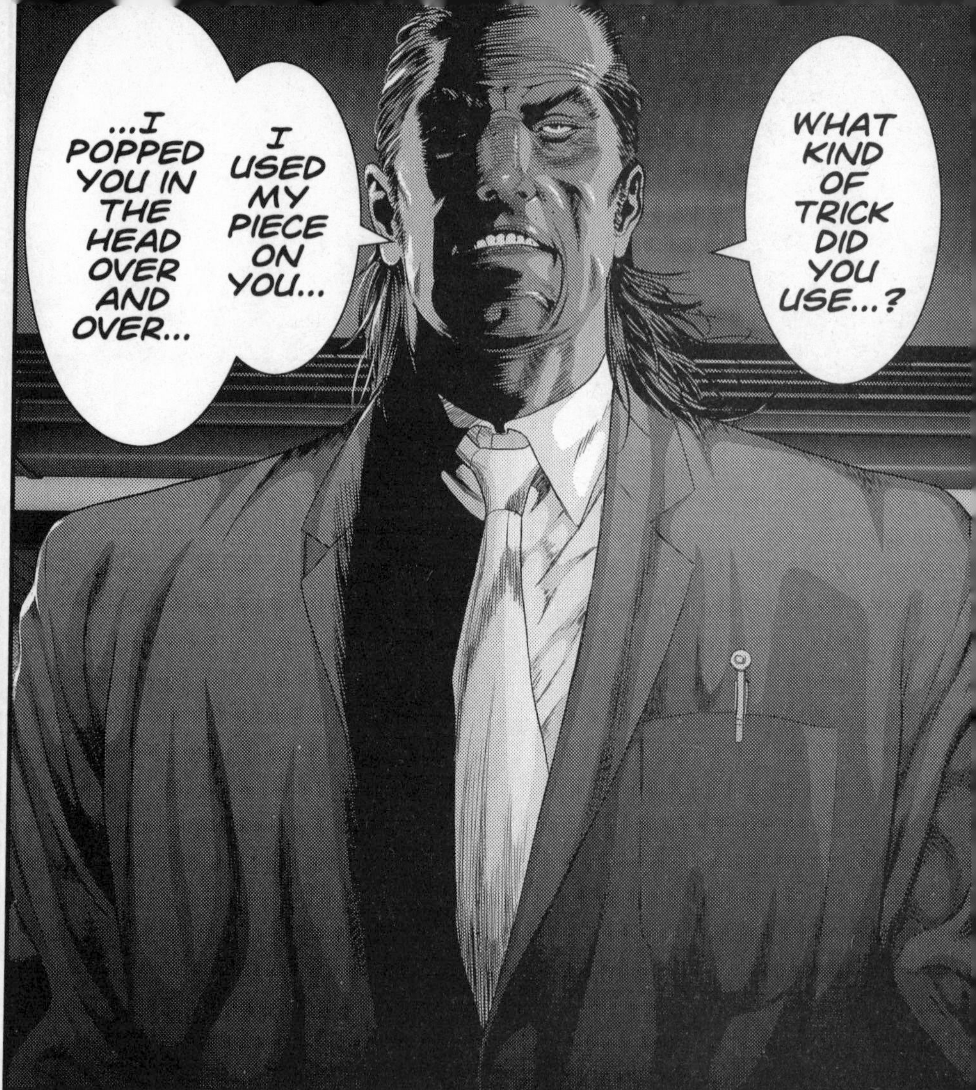
WHAT KIND OF TRICK DID YOU USE...?
I USED MY PIECE ON YOU...
...I POPPED YOU IN THE HEAD OVER AND OVER...
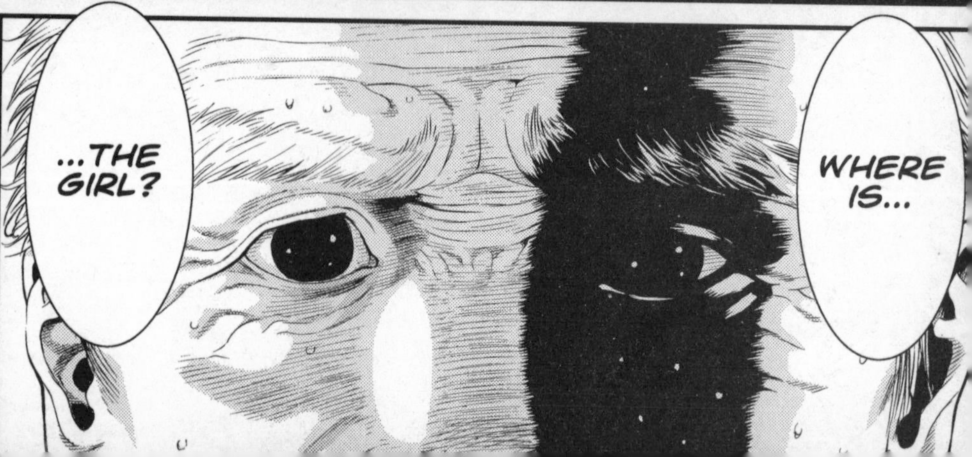
WHERE IS...
...THE GIRL?

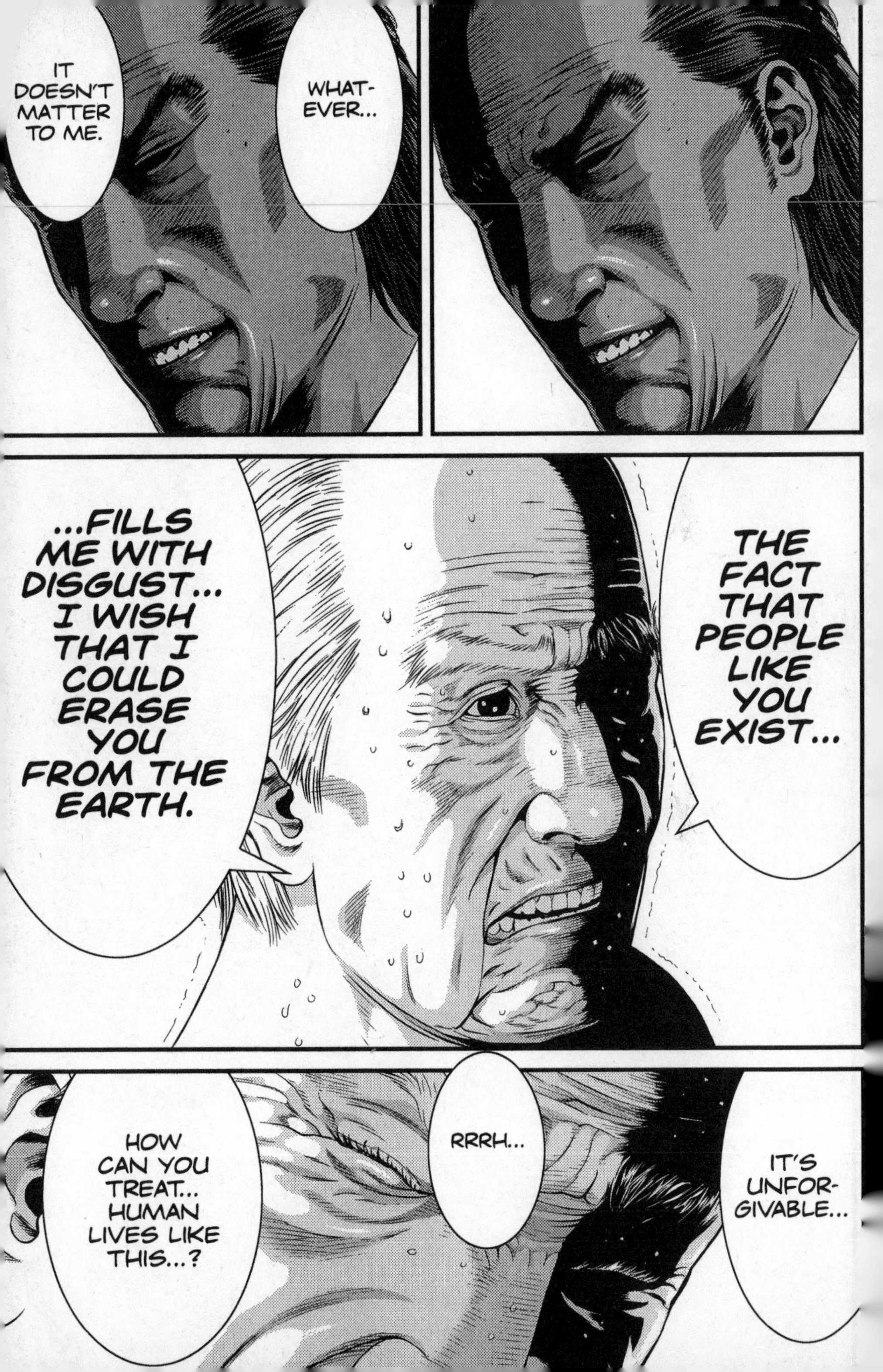
WHAT-EVER...
IT DOESN'T MATTER TO ME.
THE FACT THAT PEOPLE LIKE YOU EXIST...
...FILLS ME WITH DISGUST... I WISH THAT I COULD ERASE YOU FROM THE EARTH.
IT'S UNFORGIVABLE...
RRRH...
HOW CAN YOU TREAT... HUMAN LIVES LIKE THIS...?

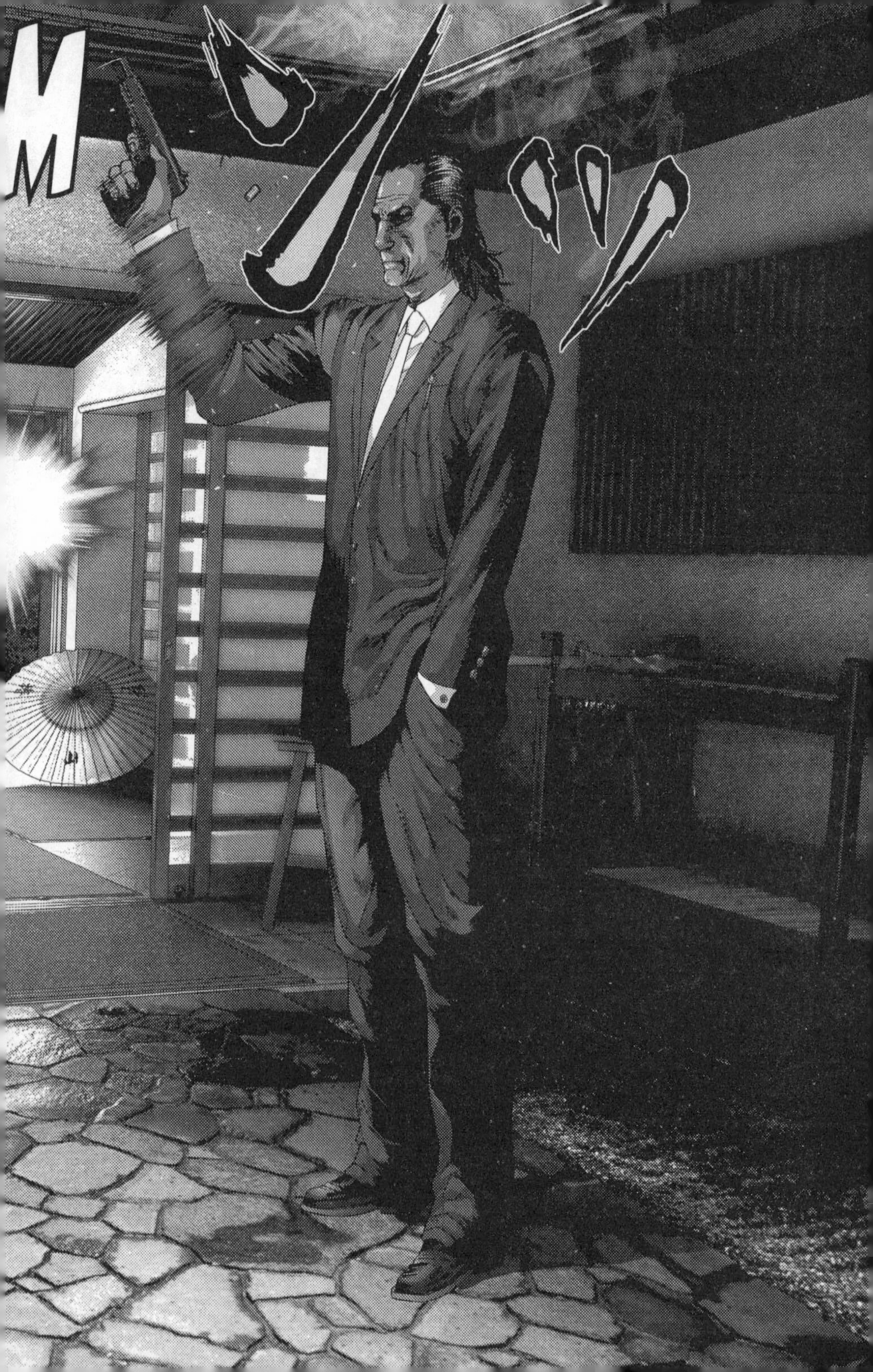
M
M

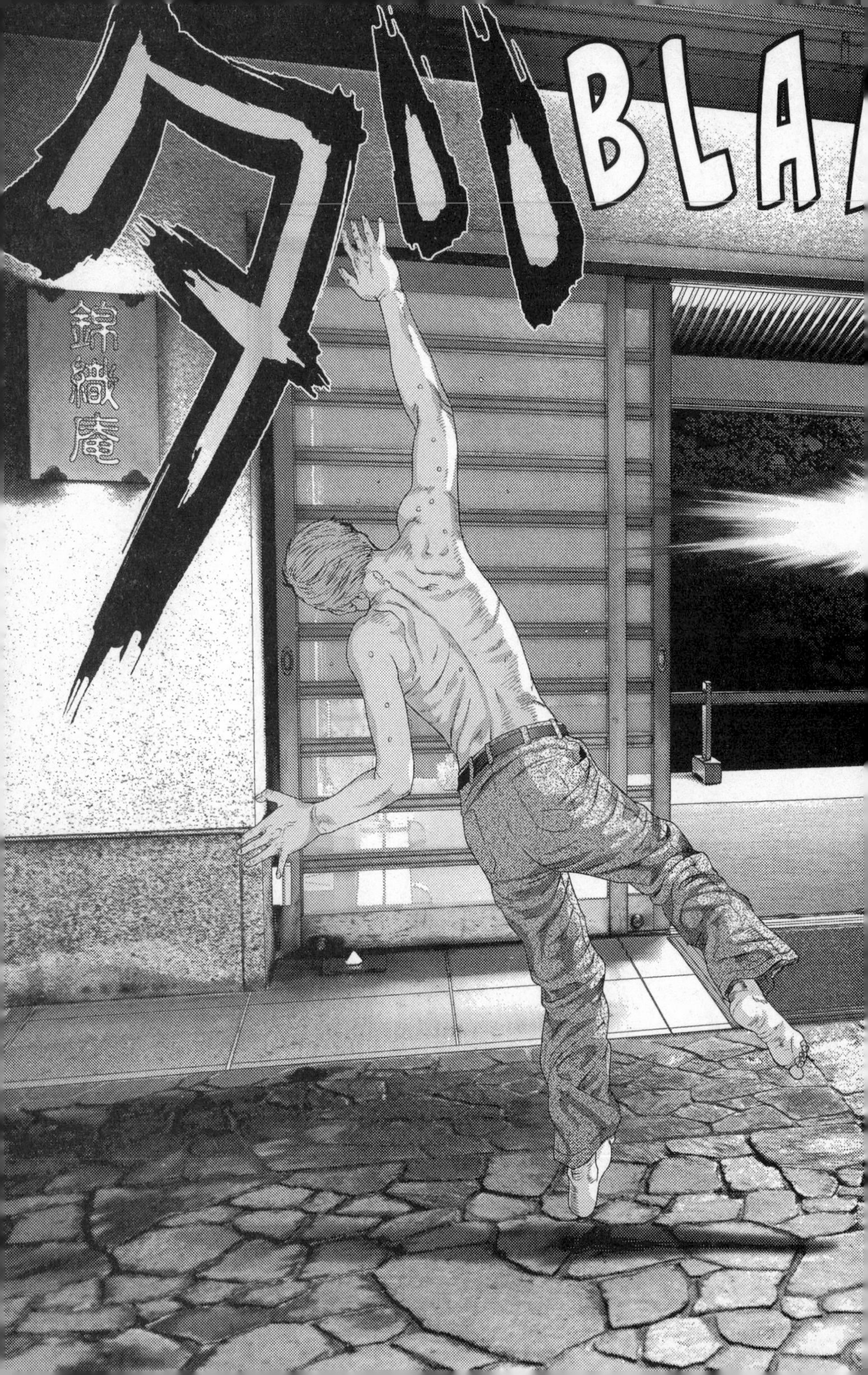
BLA
錦織庵

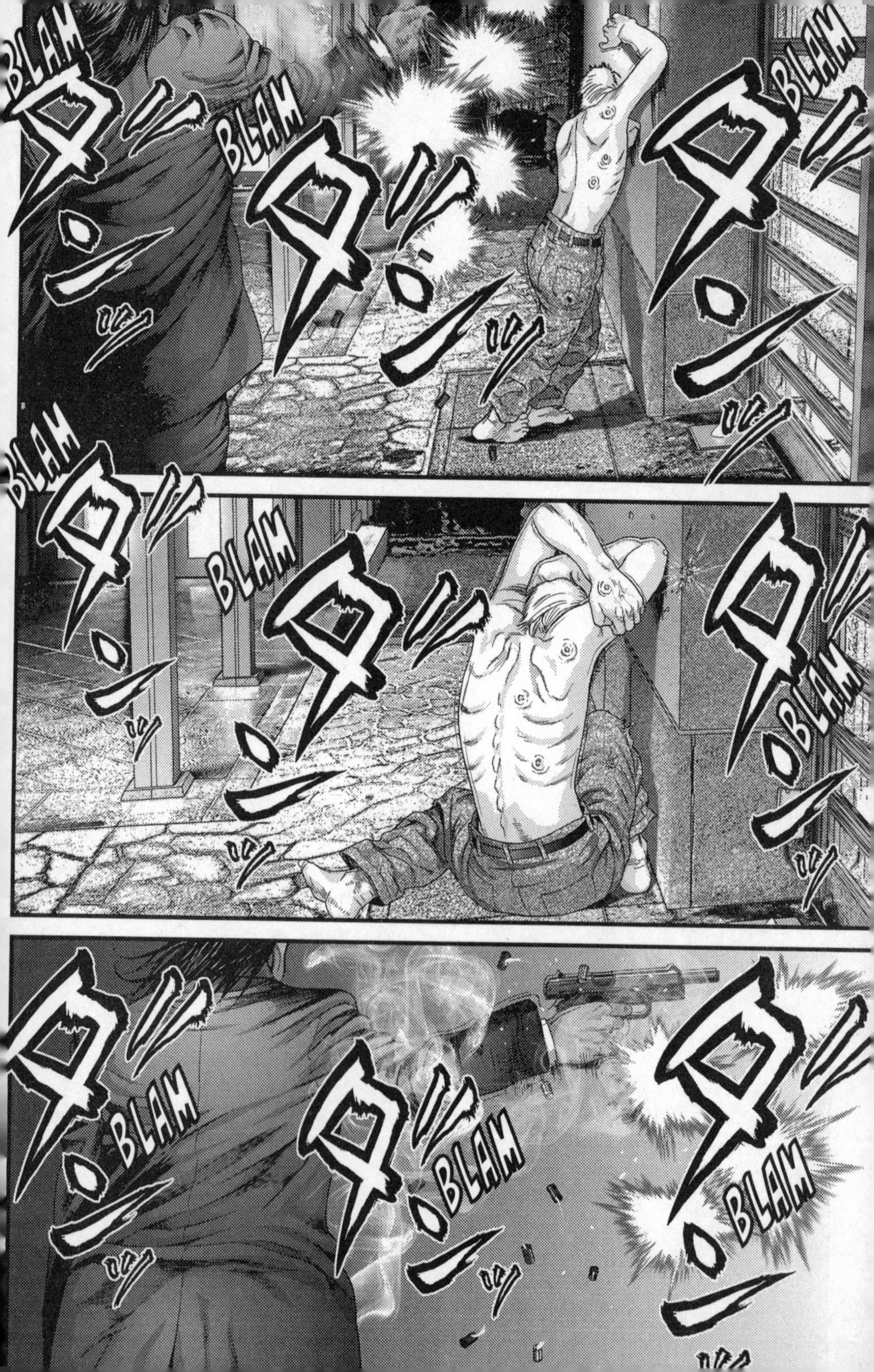
BLAM
BLAM
BLAM
BLAM
BLAM
BLAM
BLAM
BLAM
BLAM

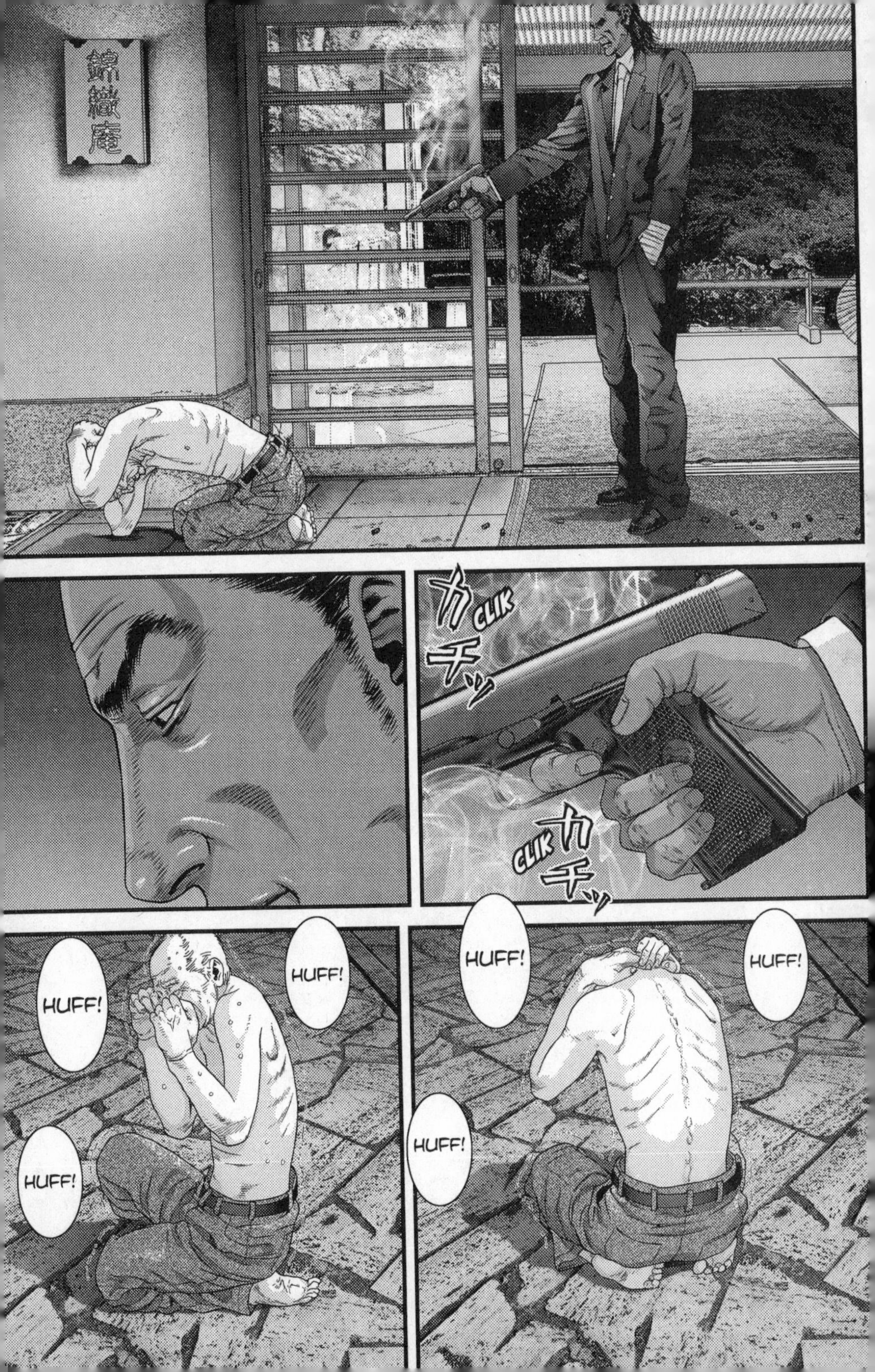
錦織庵
カチッ
CLIK
CLIK
カチッ
HUFF!
HUFF!
HUFF!
HUFF!
HUFF!
HUFF!

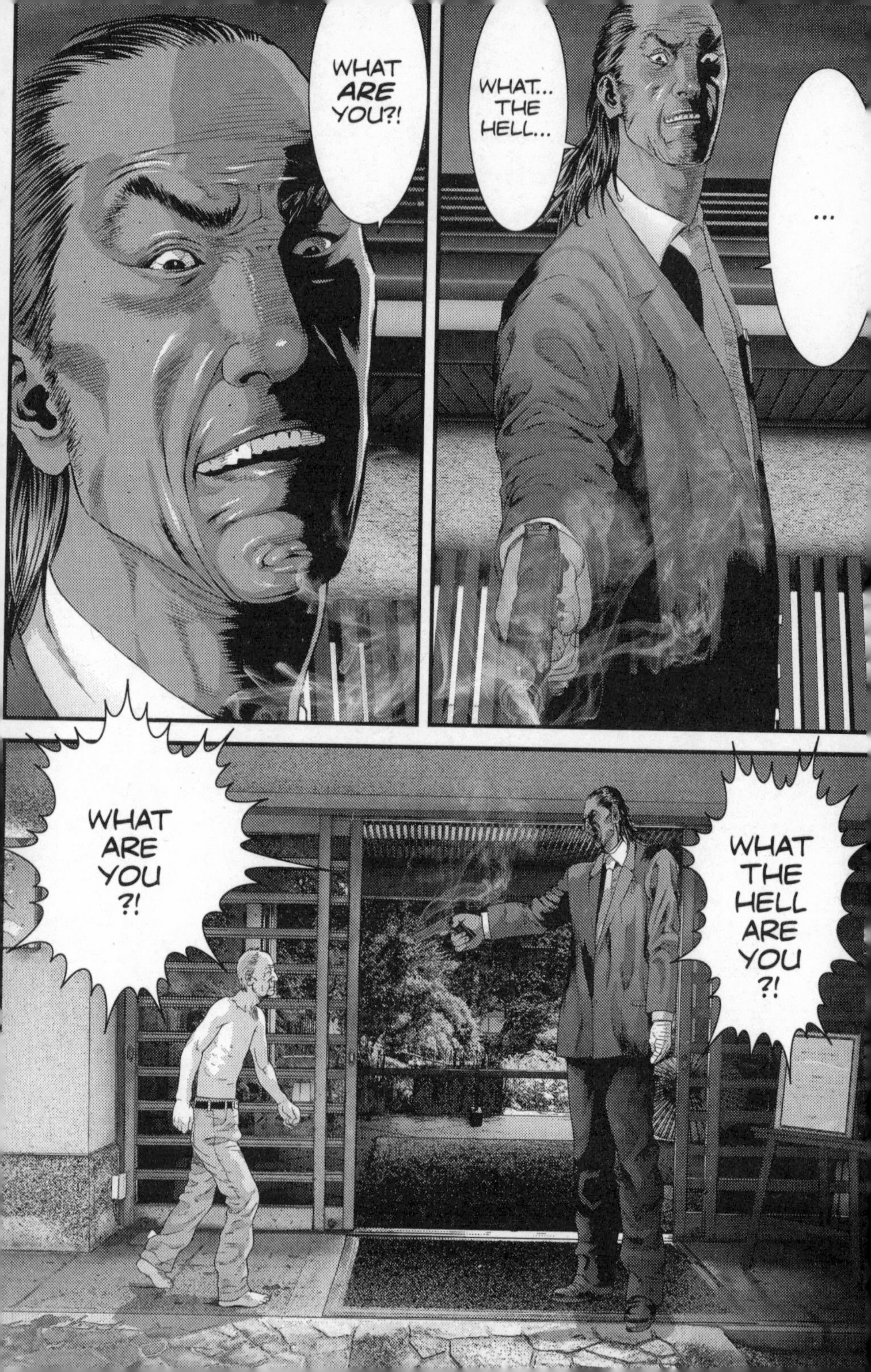
...
WHAT... THE HELL...
WHAT **ARE** YOU?!
WHAT THE HELL ARE YOU ?!
WHAT ARE YOU ?!

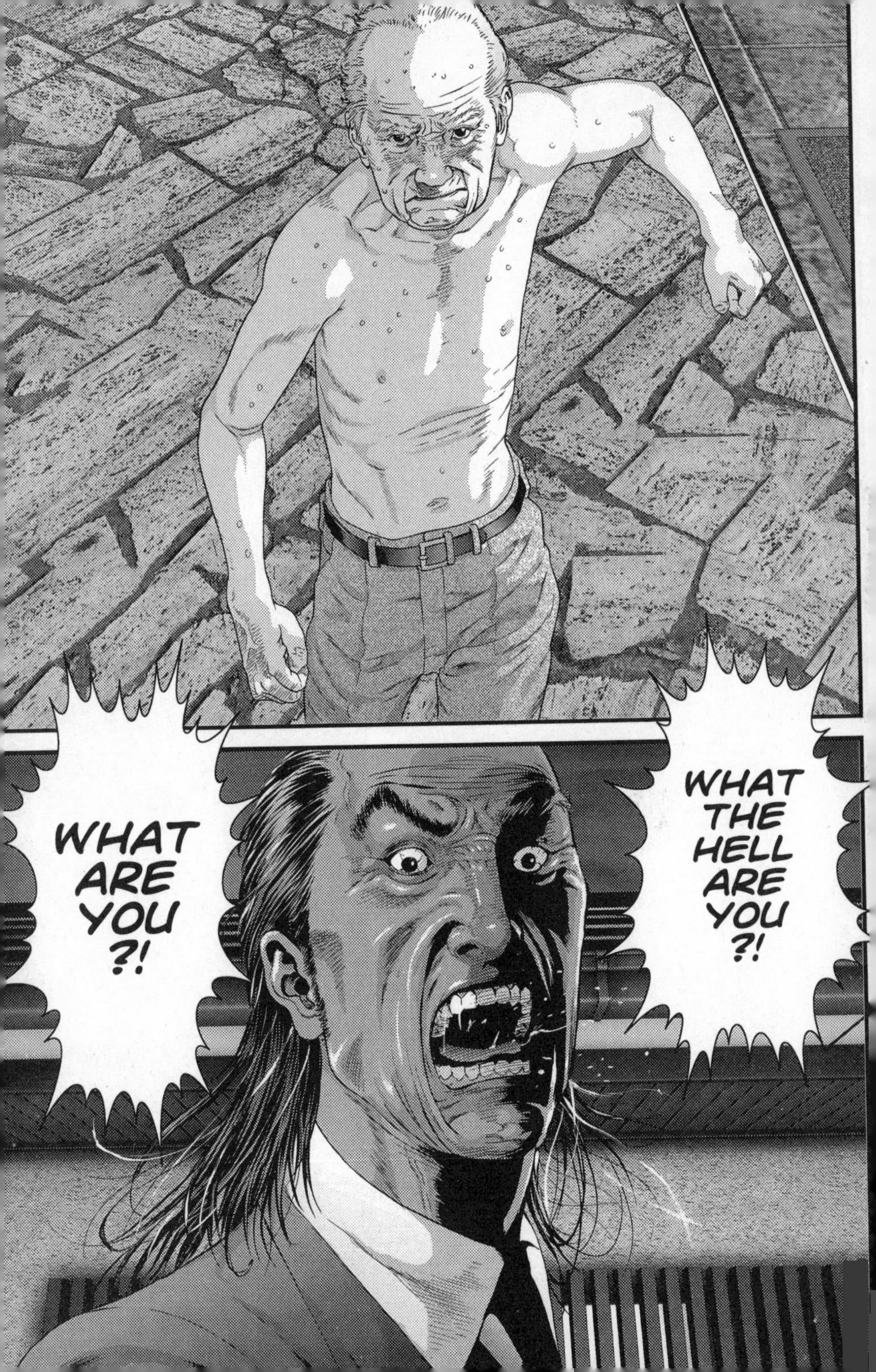
WHAT THE HELL ARE YOU ?!
WHAT ARE YOU ?!

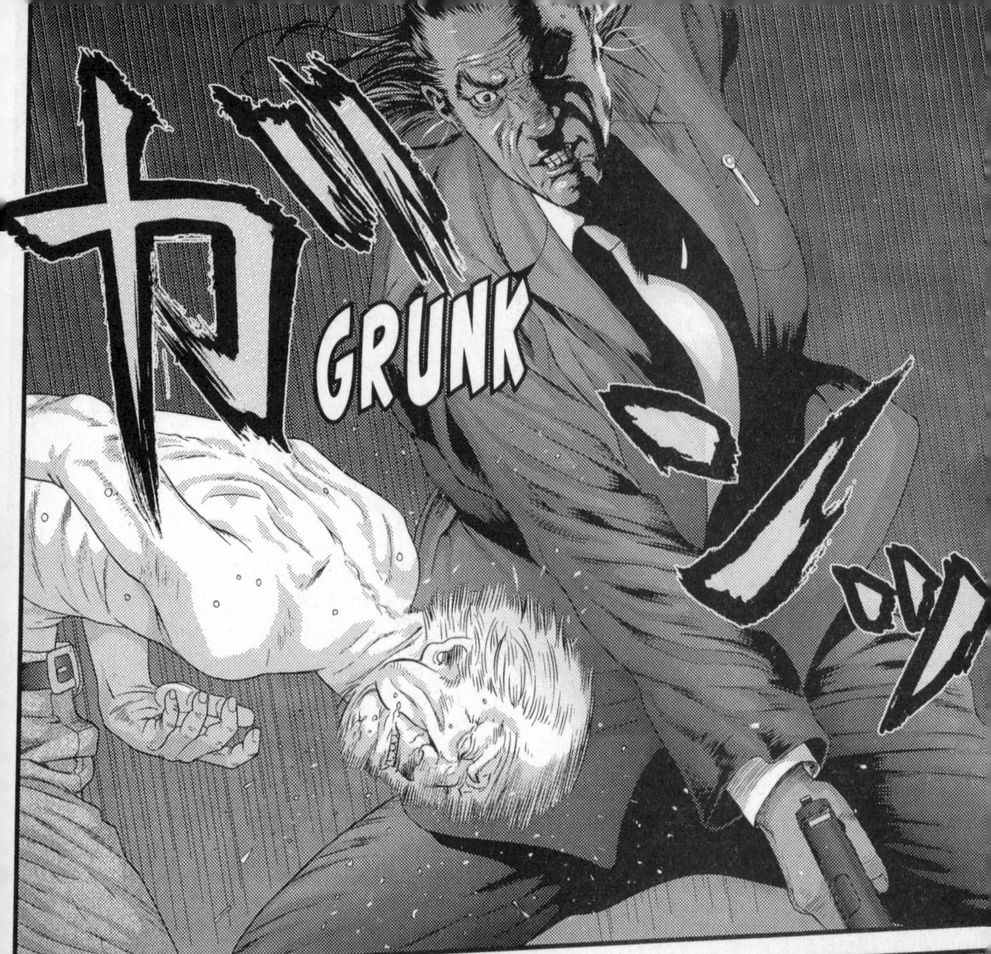
GRUNK
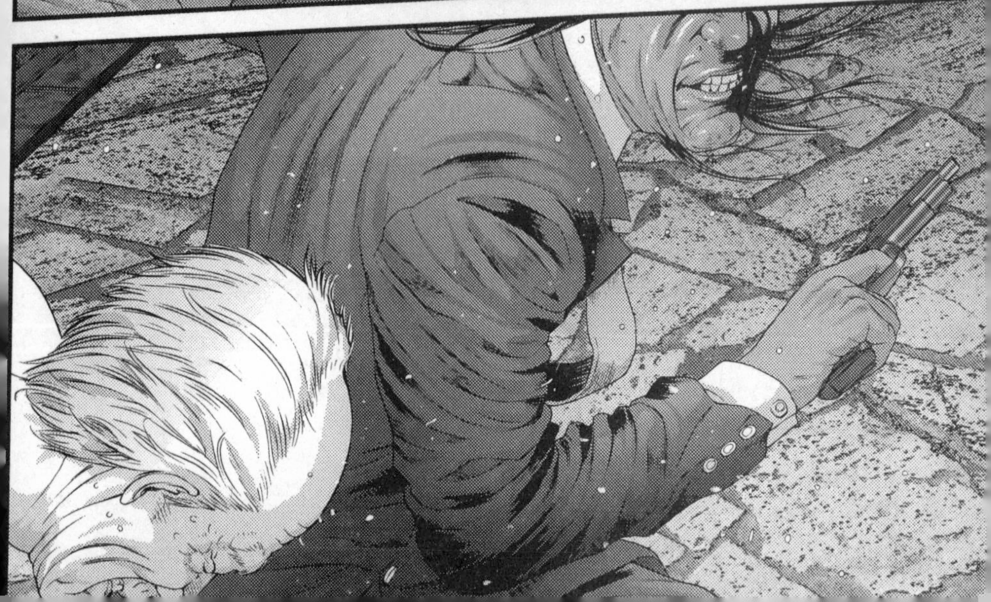

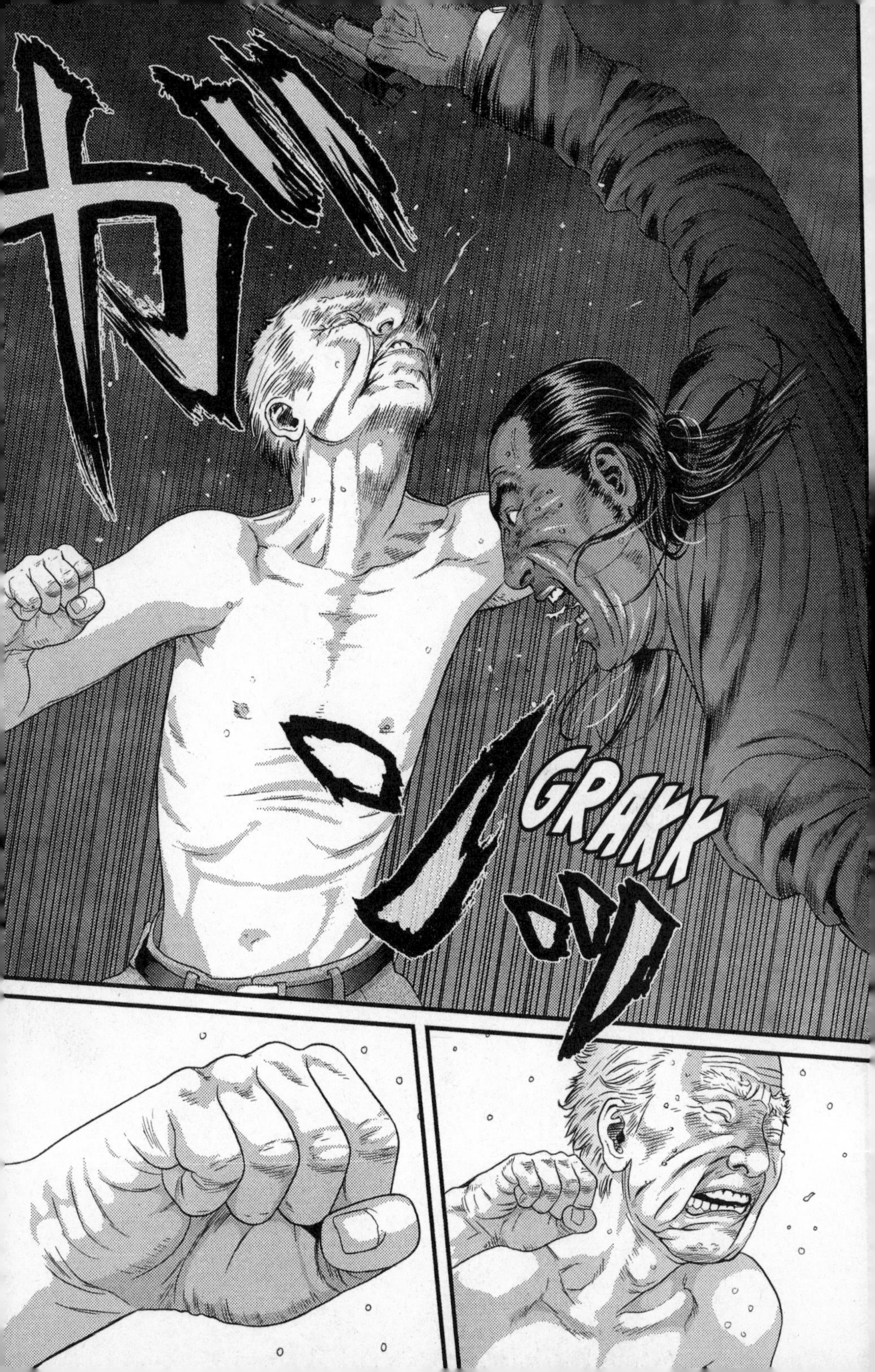
GRAKK

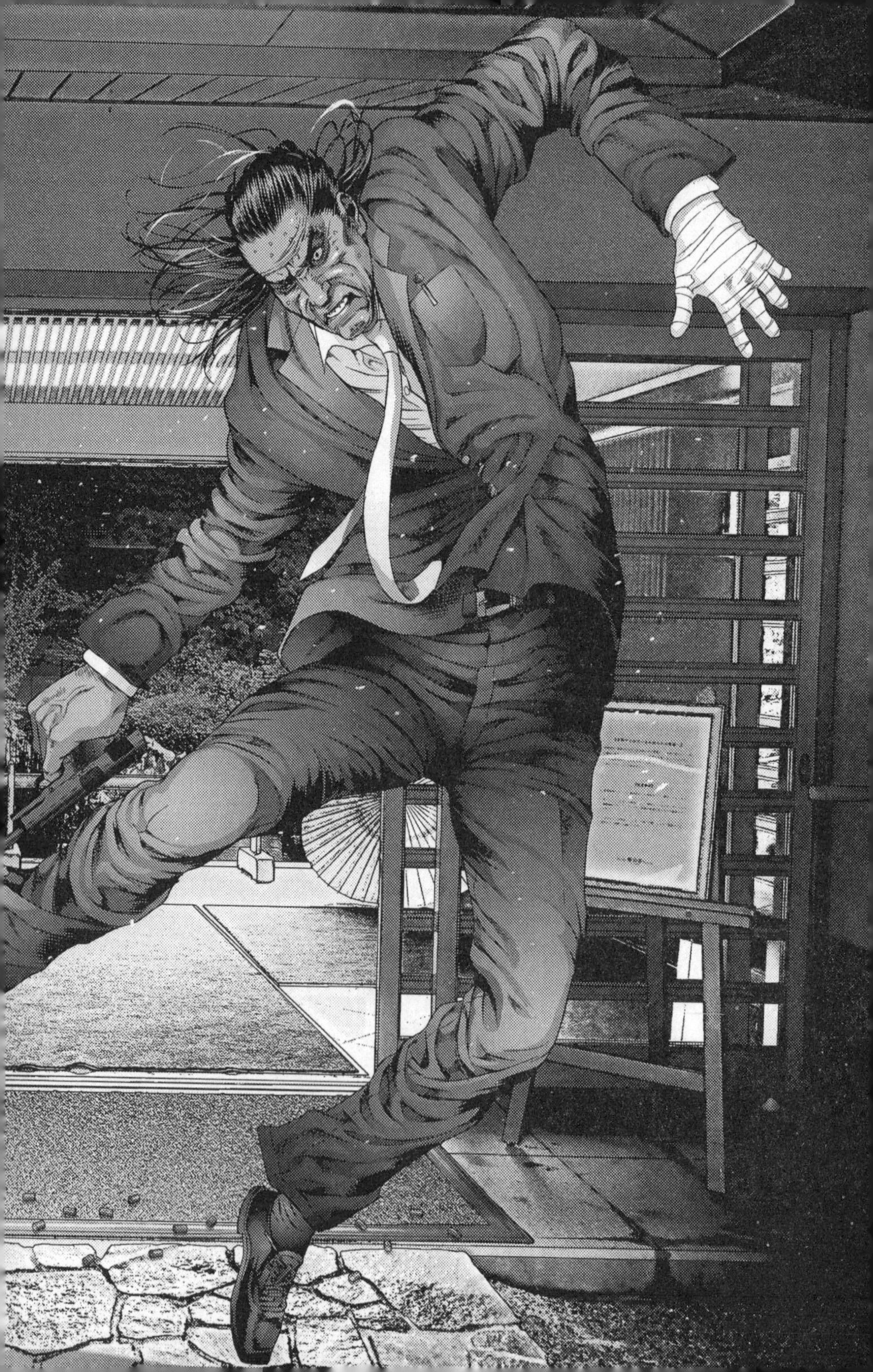

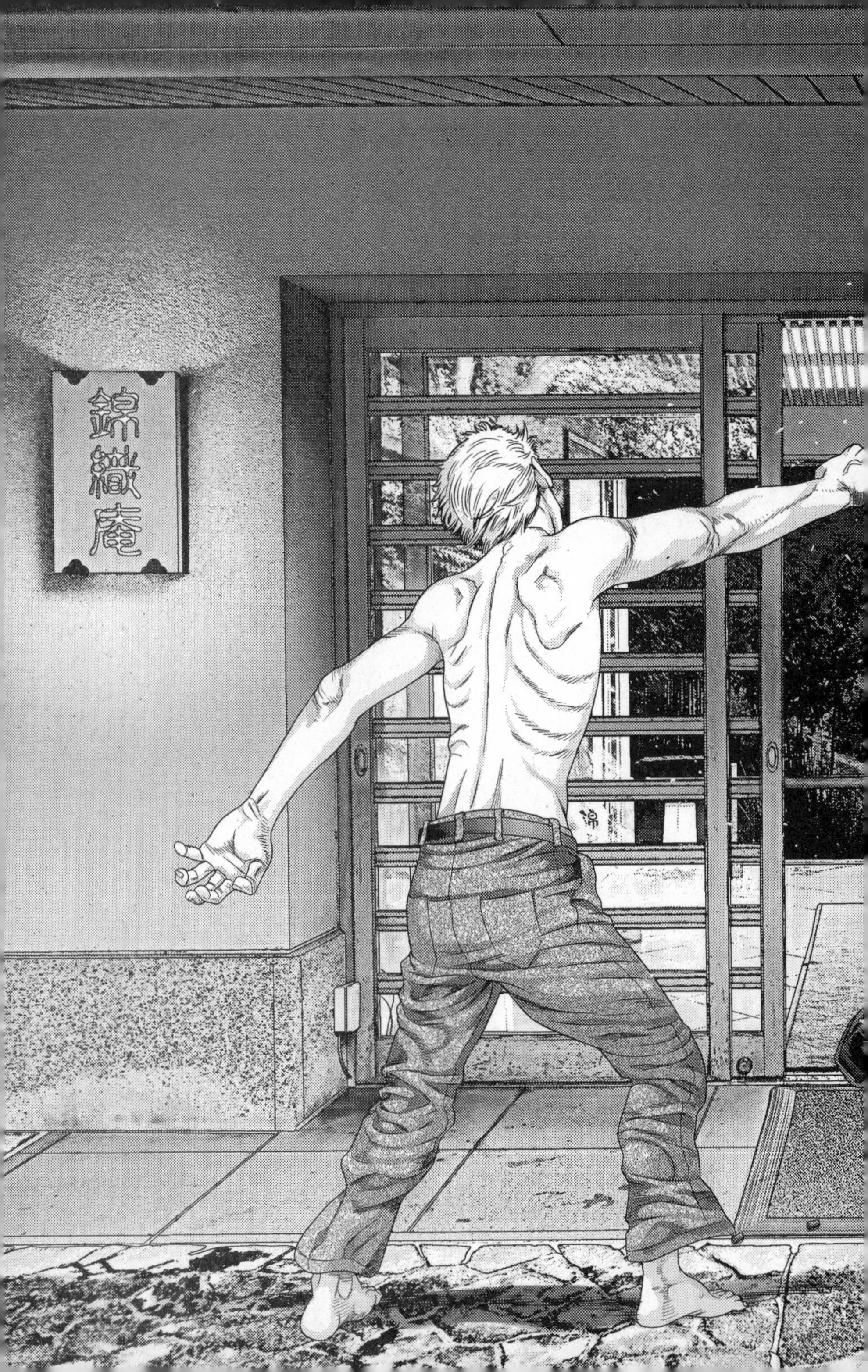
錦織庵

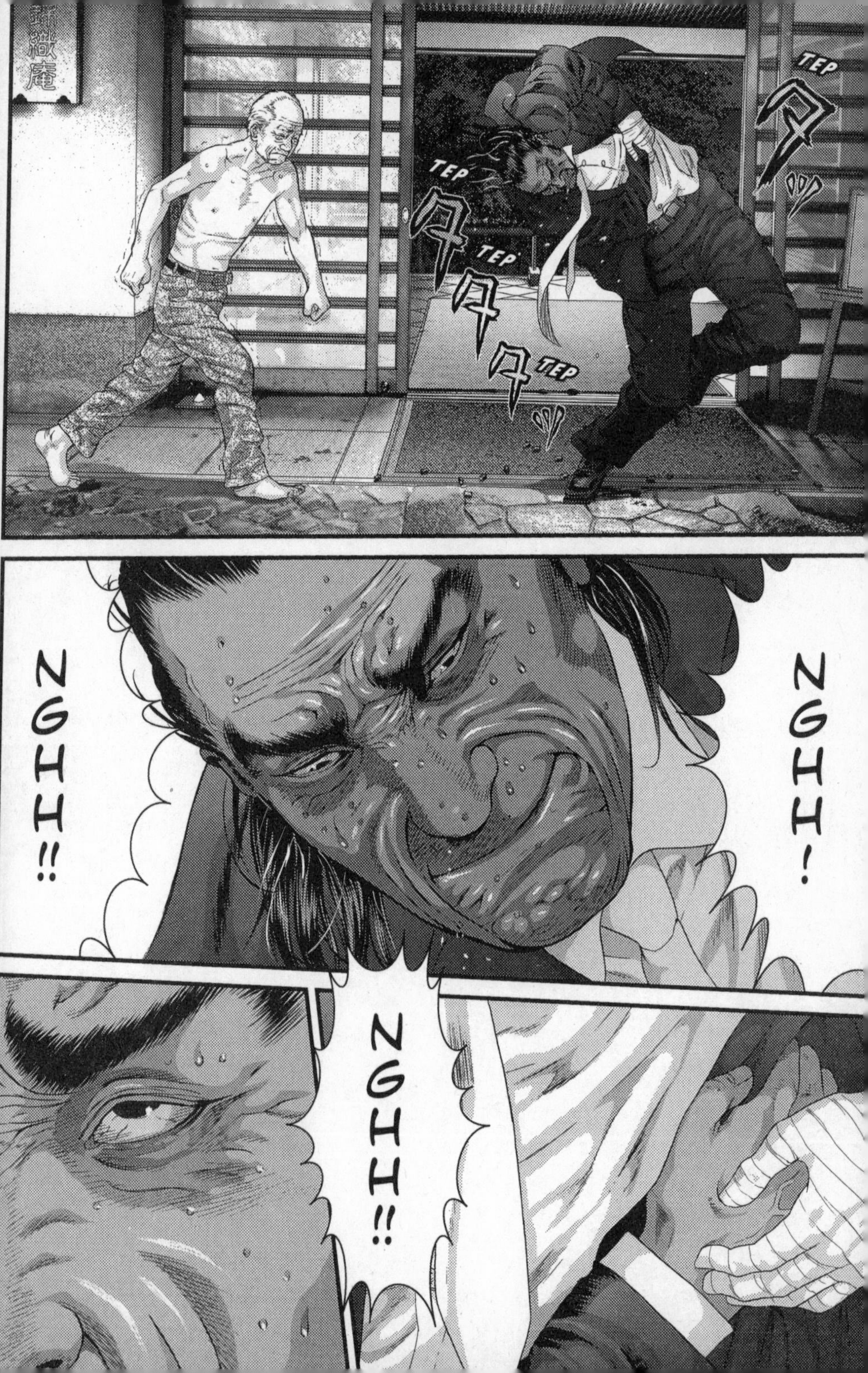

TEP
TEP
TEP
TEP
NGHH!
NGHH!!
NGHH!!

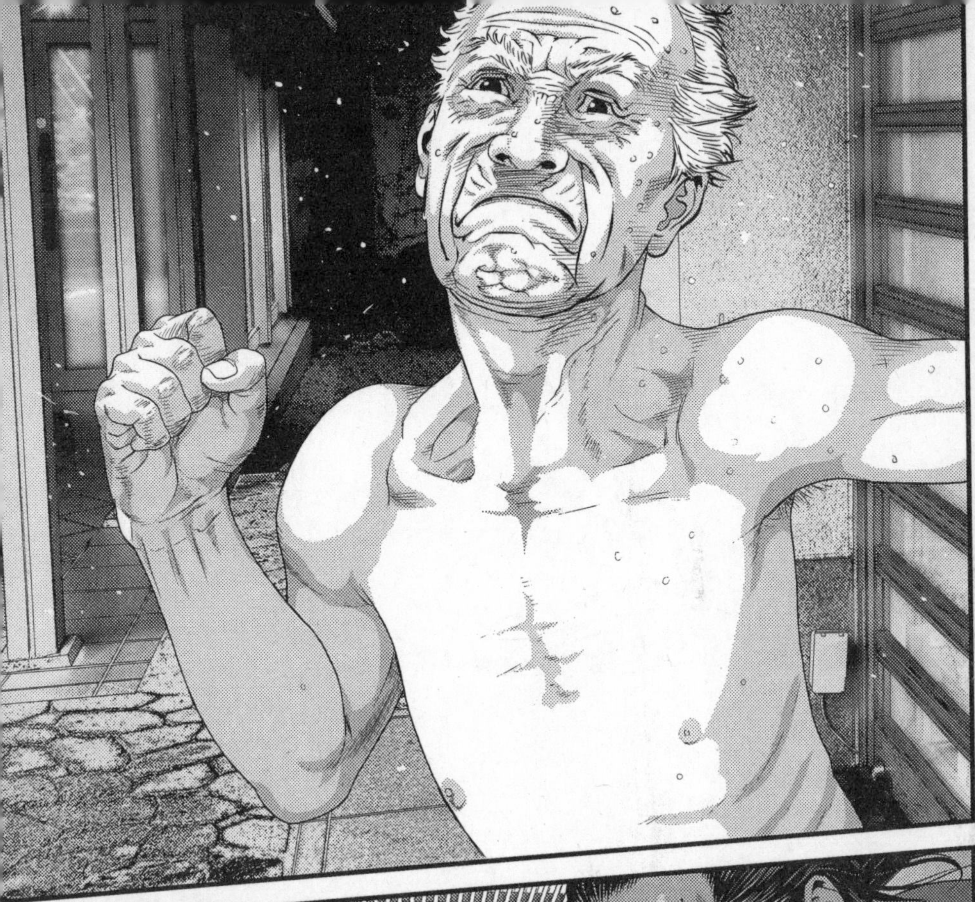
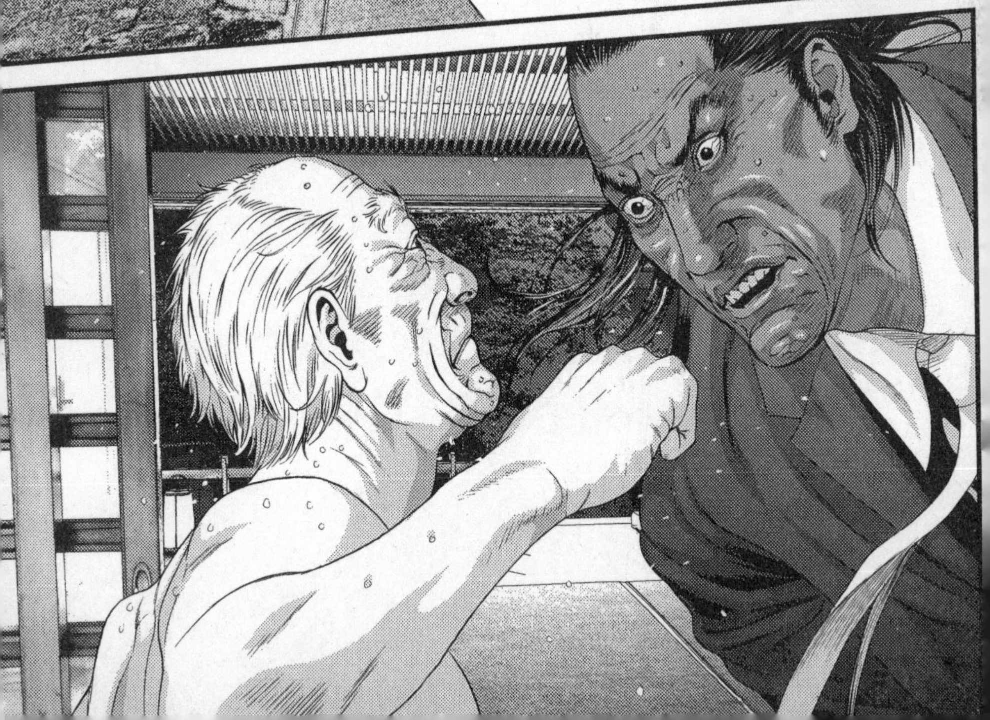

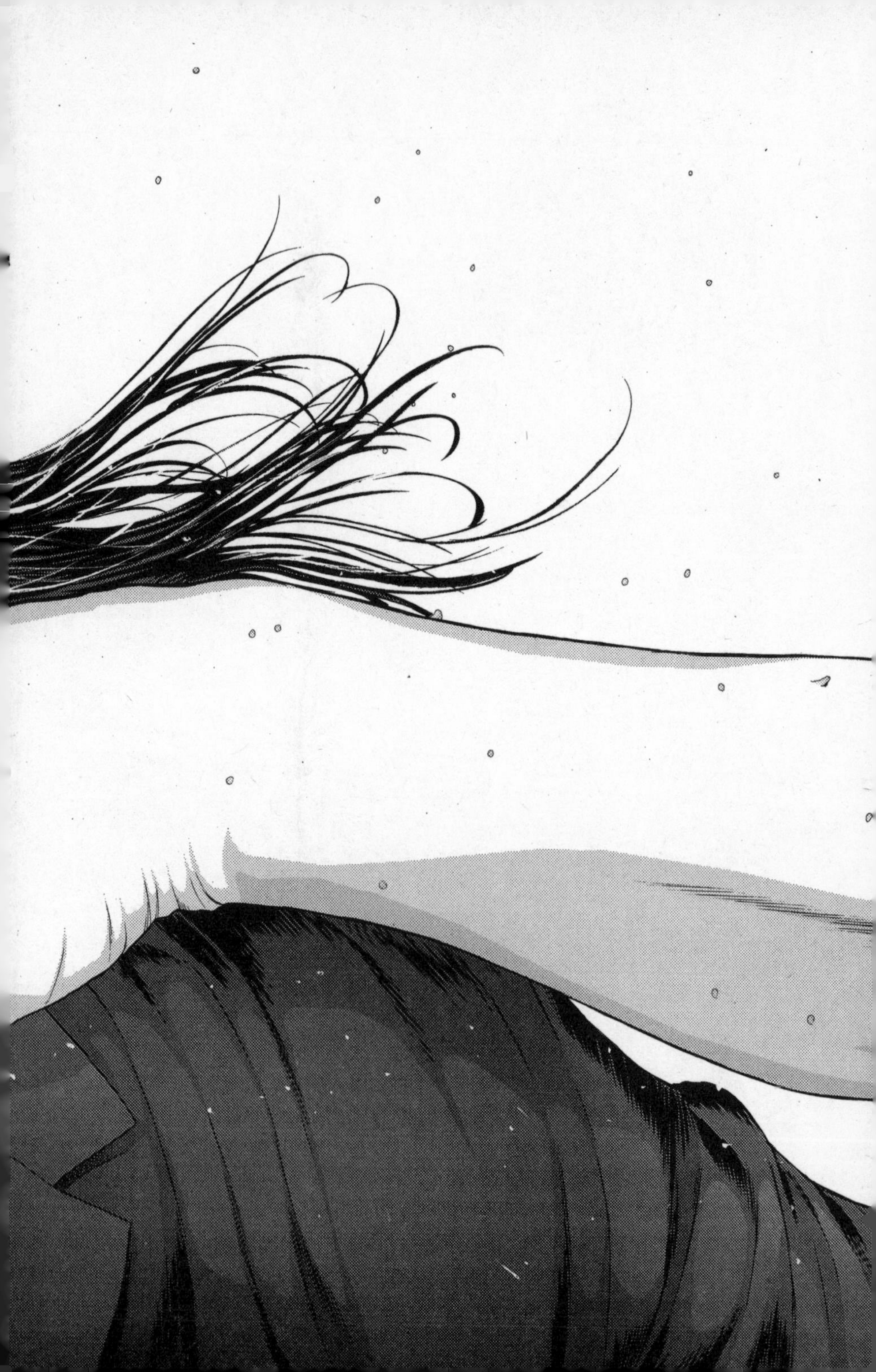

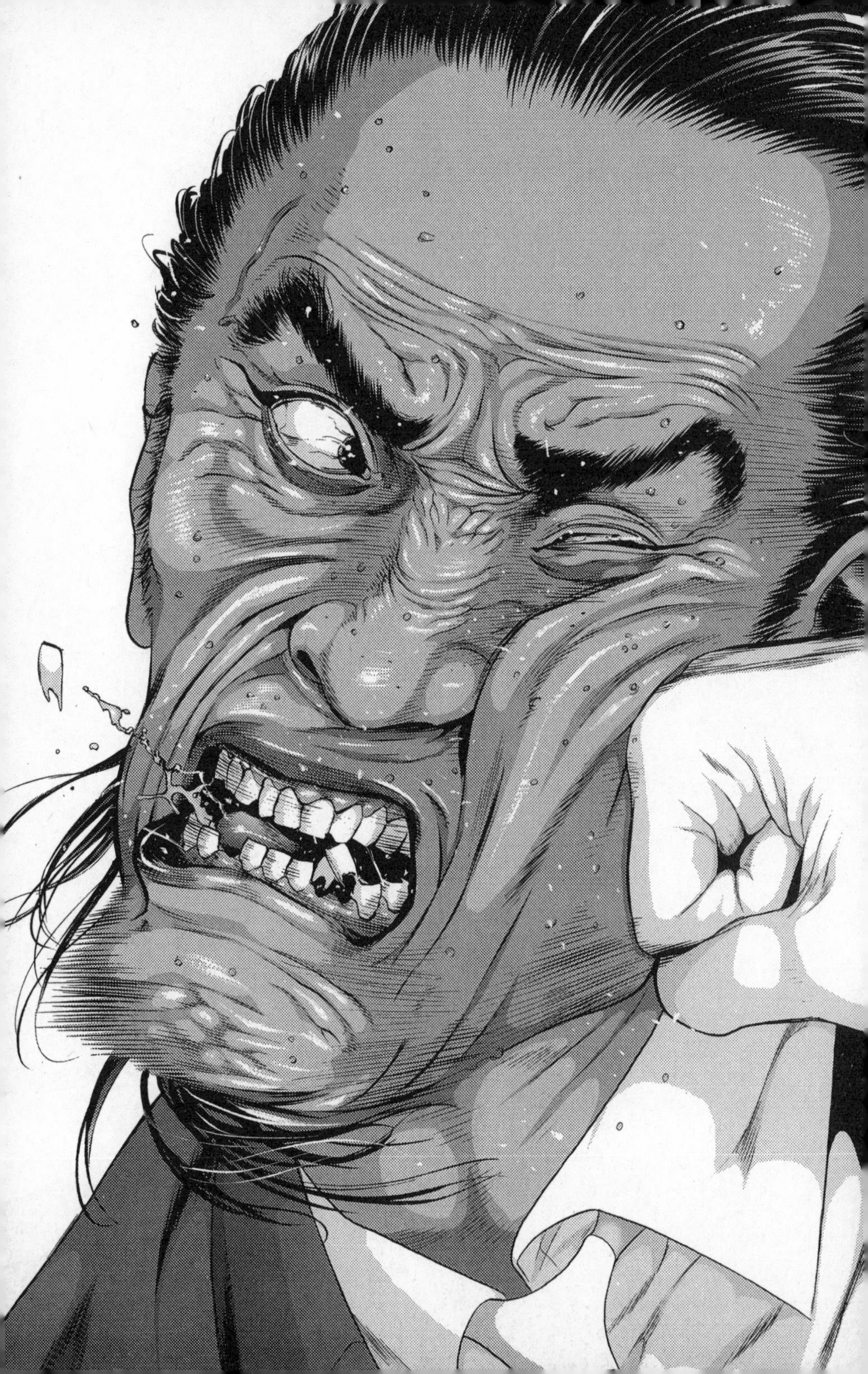

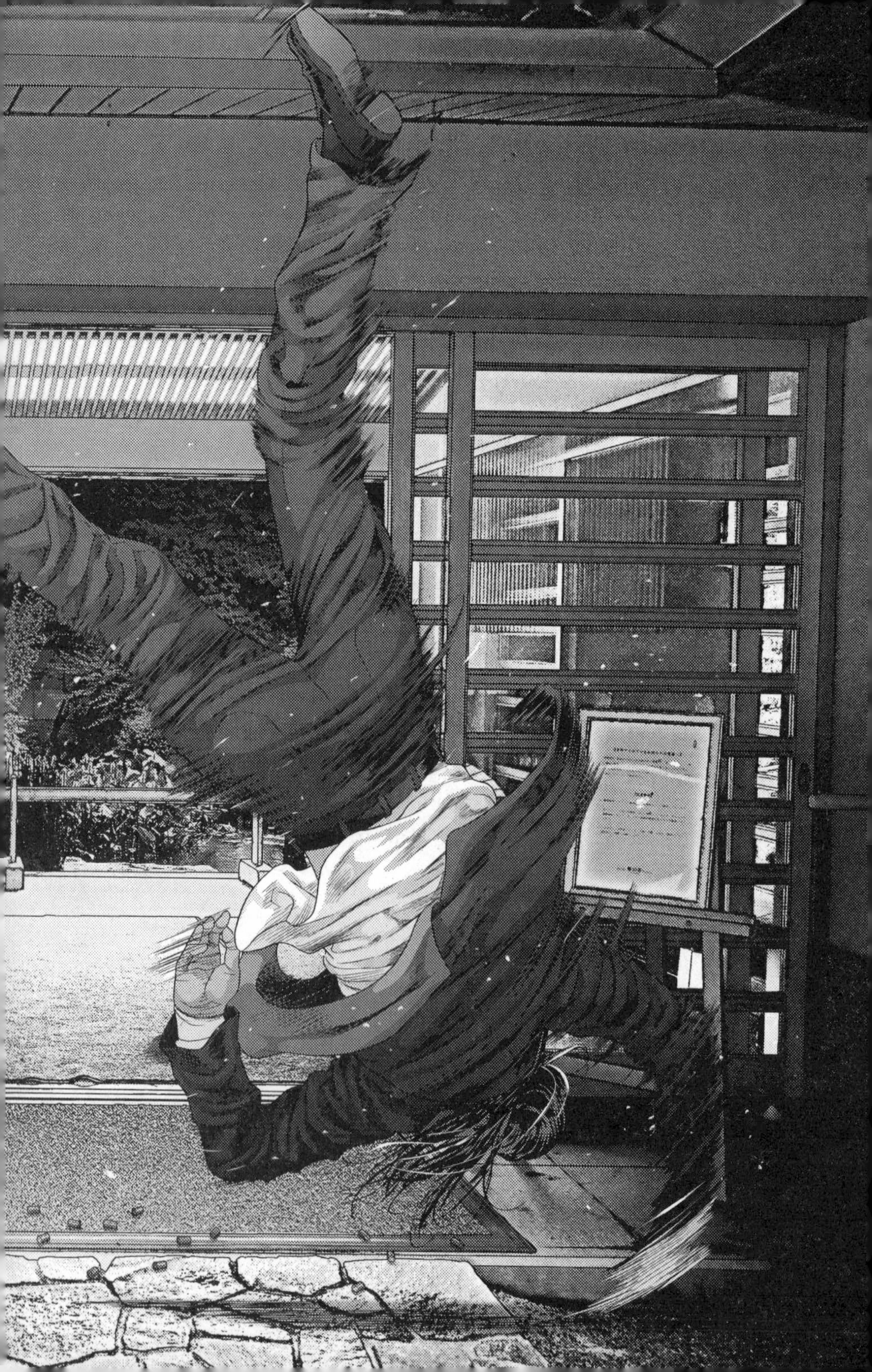

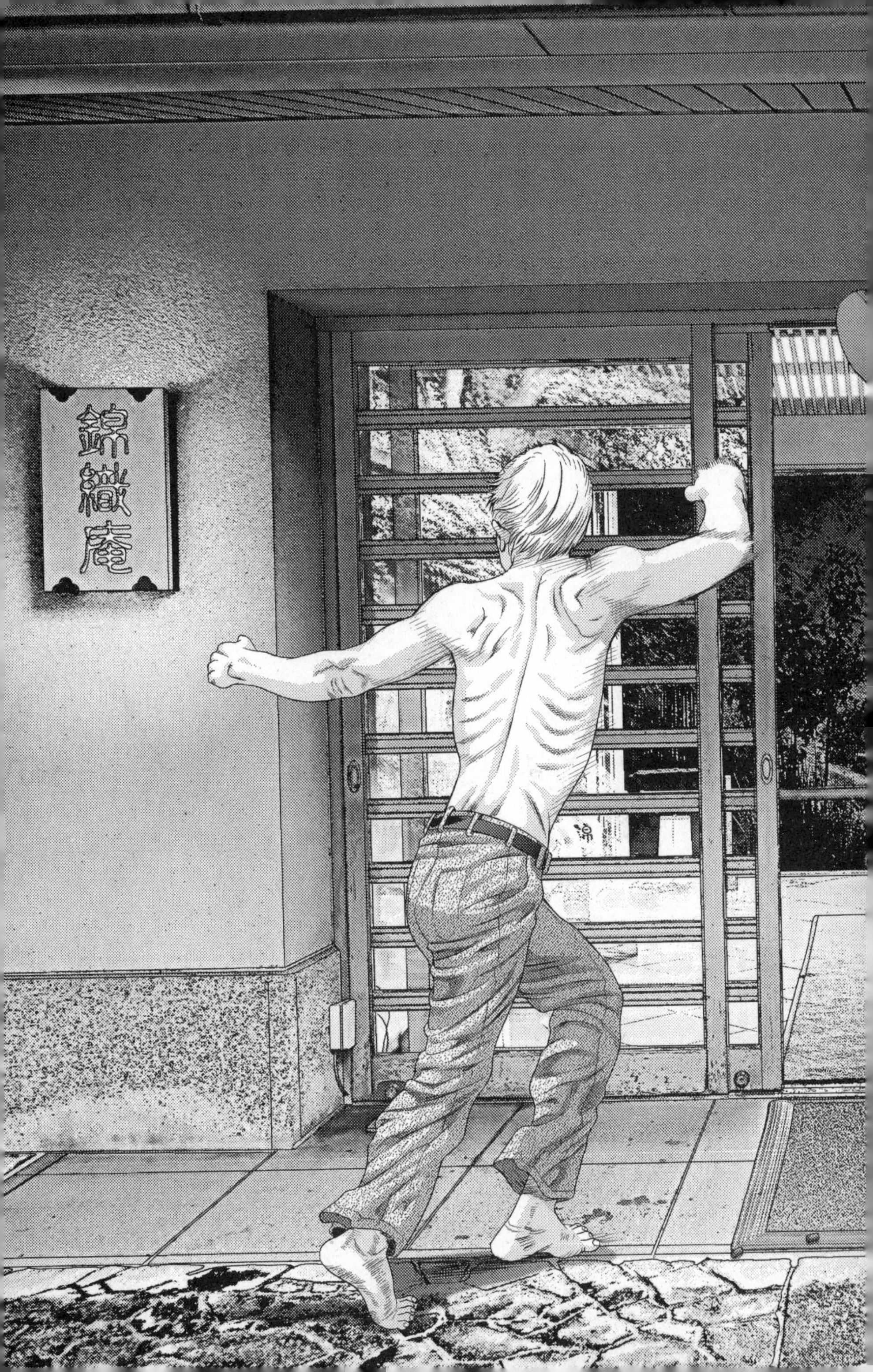
錦織庵

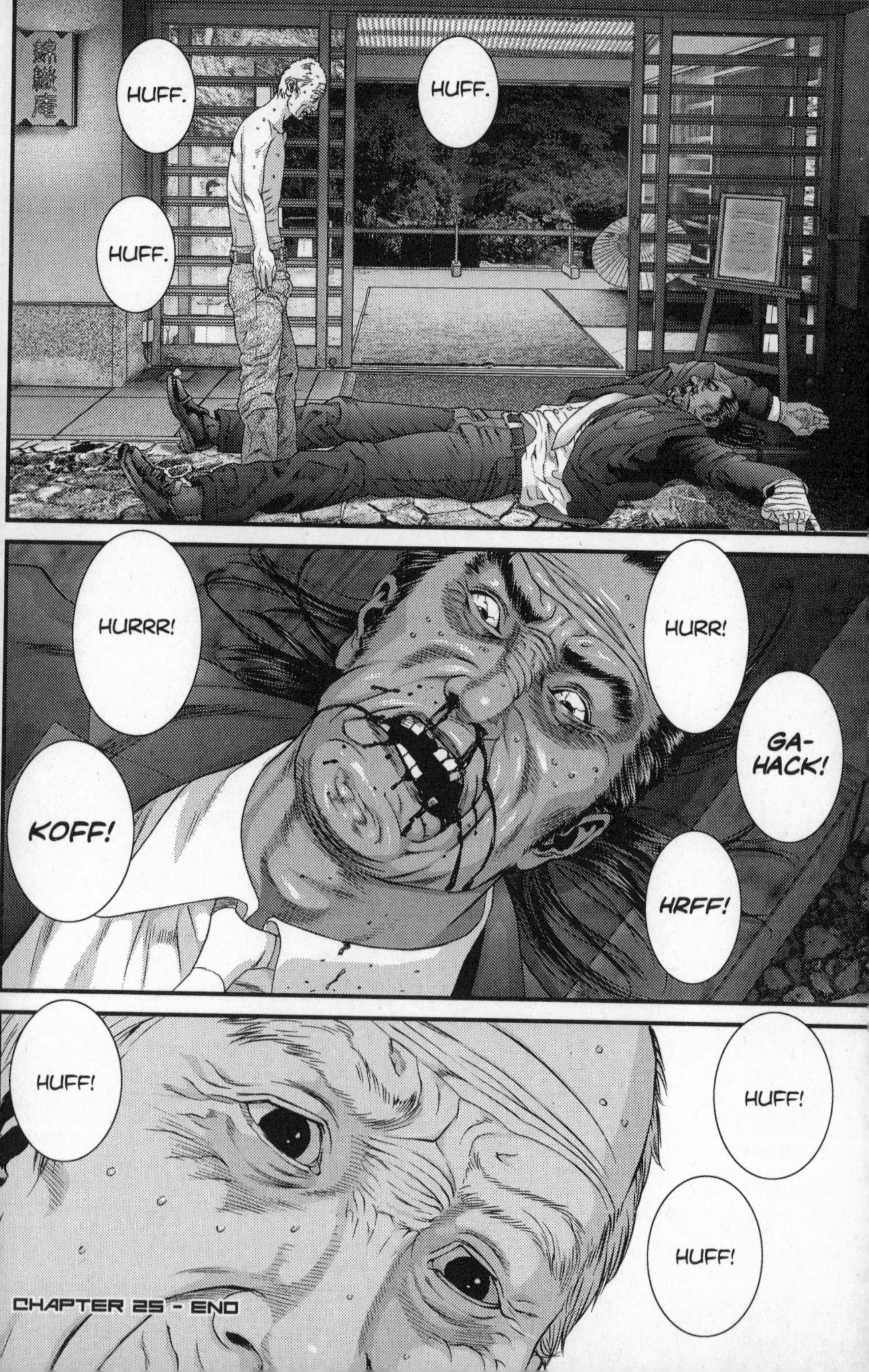
HUFF.
HUFF.
HUFF.
HURR!
HURRR!
GA-HACK!
KOFF!
HRFF!
HUFF!
HUFF!
HUFF!
CHAPTER 25 - END

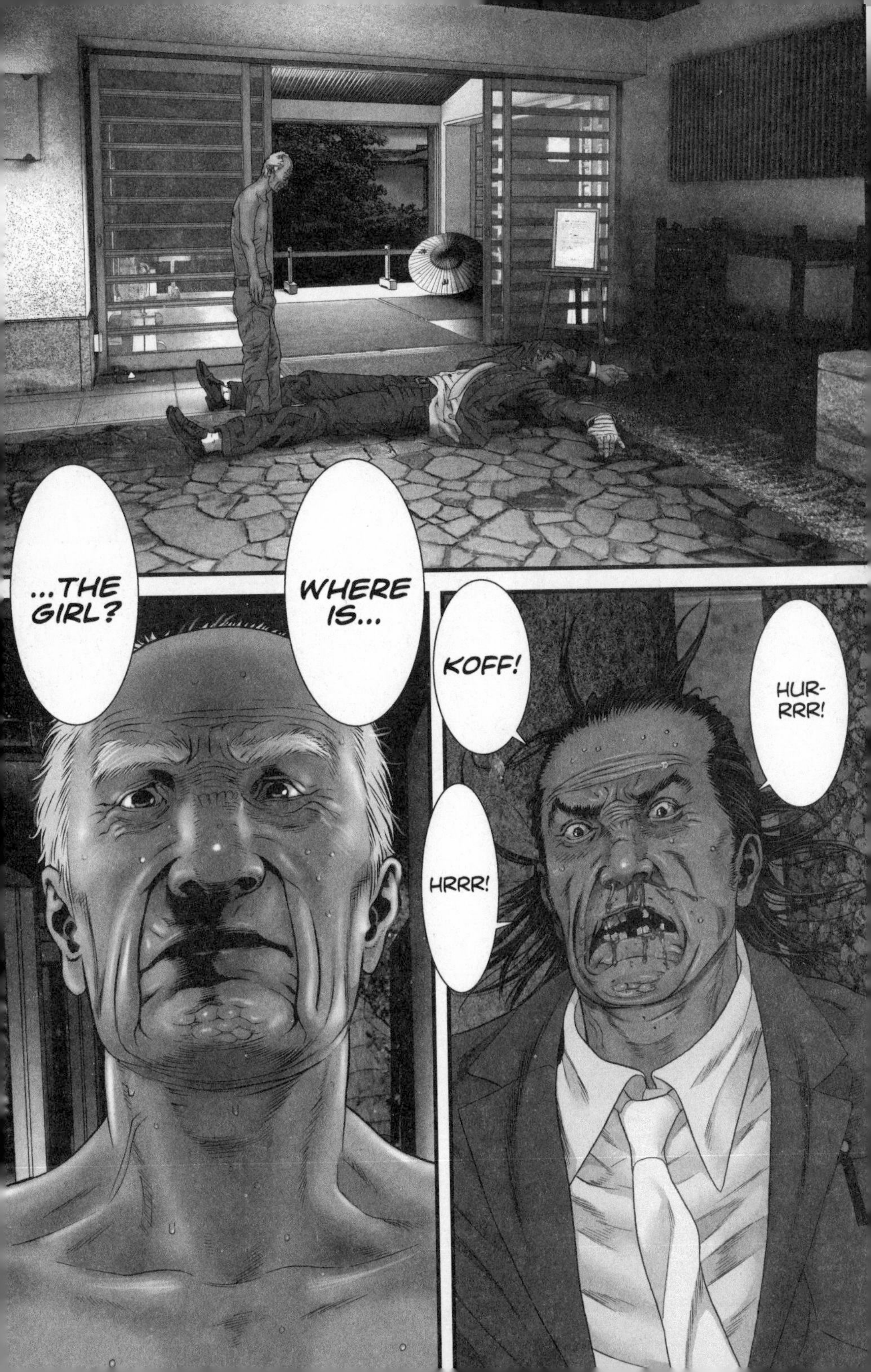
HUR-RRR!
KOFF!
HRRR!
WHERE IS...
...THE GIRL?

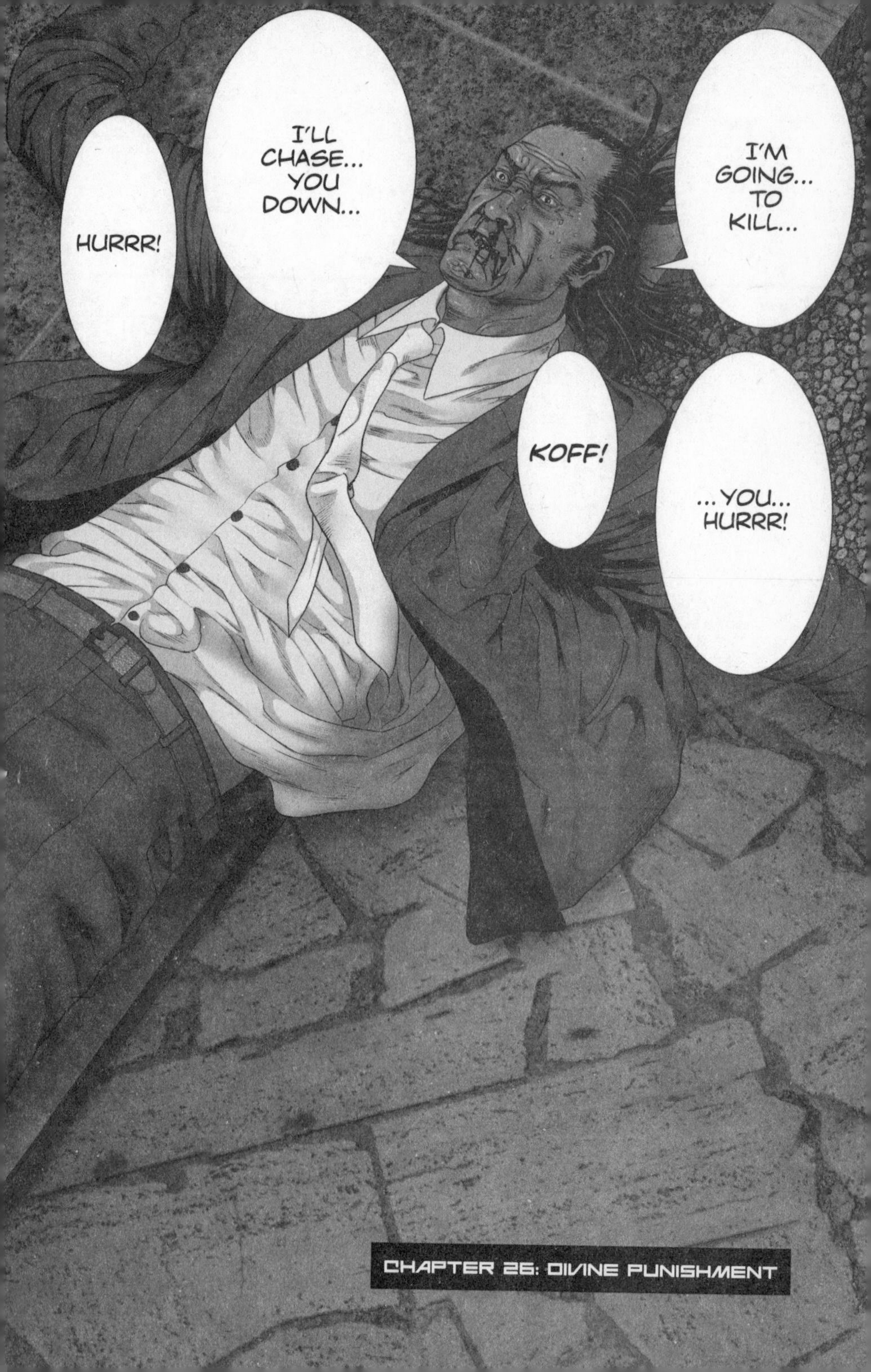
I'M GOING... TO KILL...
...YOU... HURRR!
KOFF!
I'LL CHASE... YOU DOWN...
HURRR!

CHAPTER 26: DIVINE PUNISHMENT

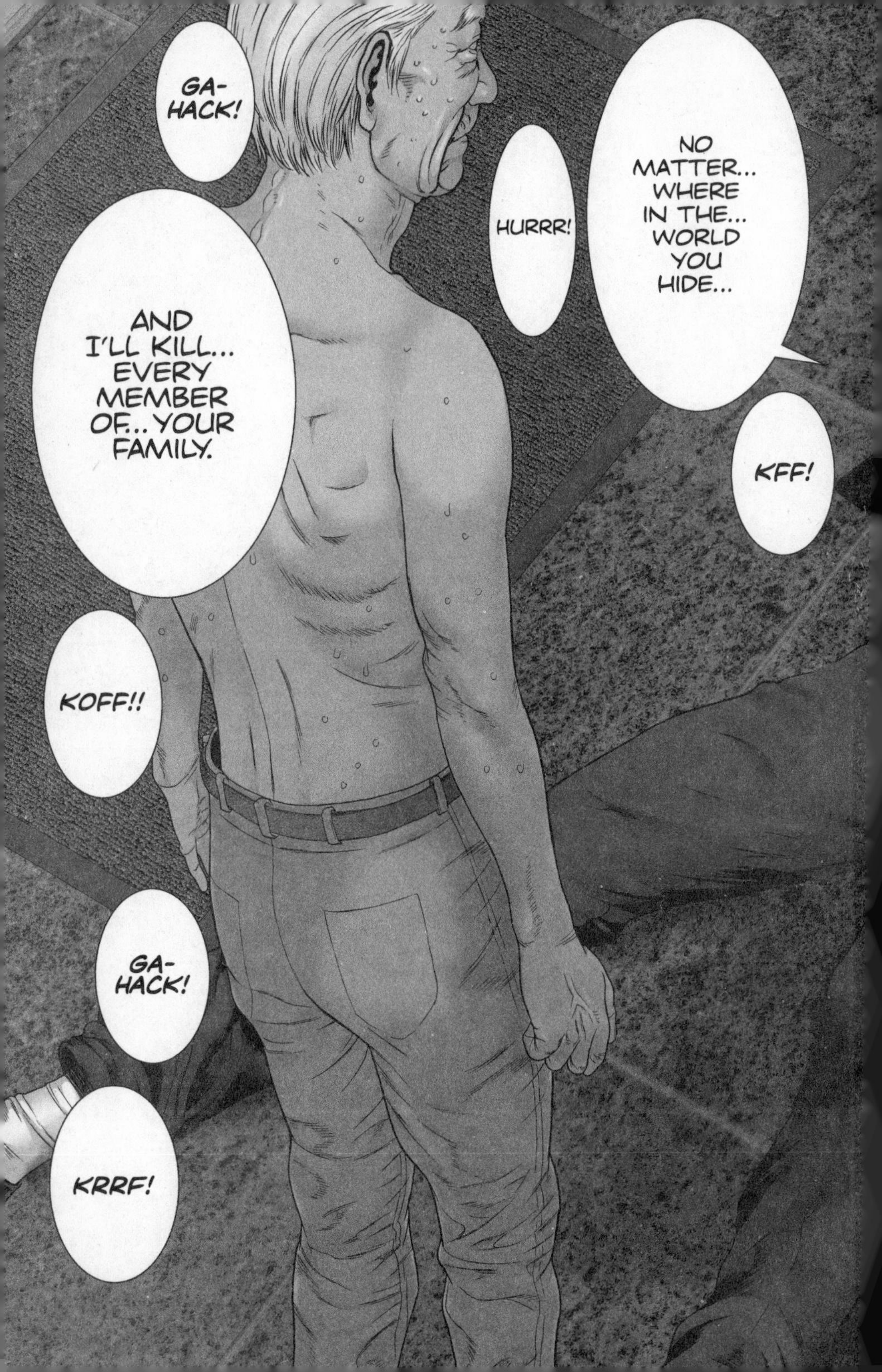
NO MATTER... WHERE IN THE... WORLD YOU HIDE...
HURRR!
GA-HACK!
KFF!
AND I'LL KILL... EVERY MEMBER OF... YOUR FAMILY.
KOFF!!
GA-HACK!
KRRF!

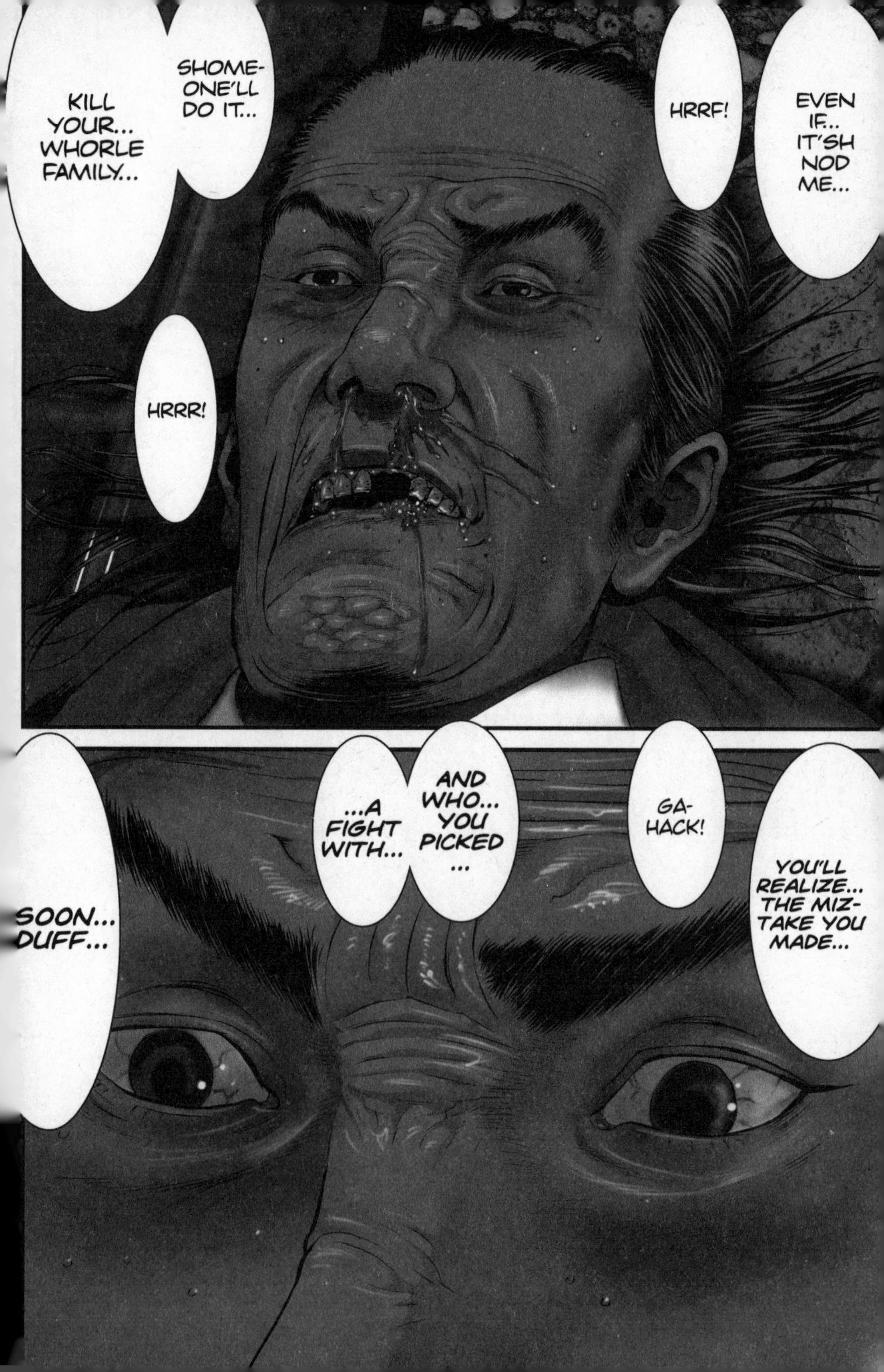
EVEN IF... IT'SH NOD ME...
HRRF!
SHOME-ONE'LL DO IT...
KILL YOUR... WHORLE FAMILY...
HRRR!
YOU'LL REALIZE... THE MIZ-TAKE YOU MADE...
GA-HACK!
AND WHO... YOU PICKED ...
...A FIGHT WITH...
SOON... DUFF...

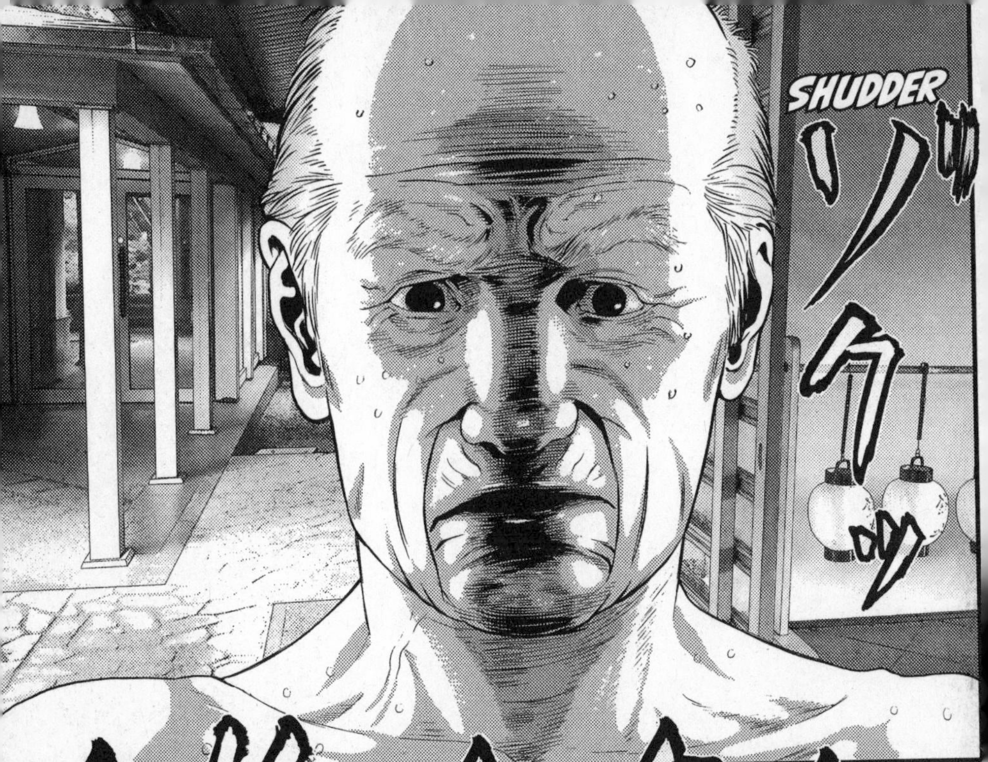
SHUDDER
ゾクッ

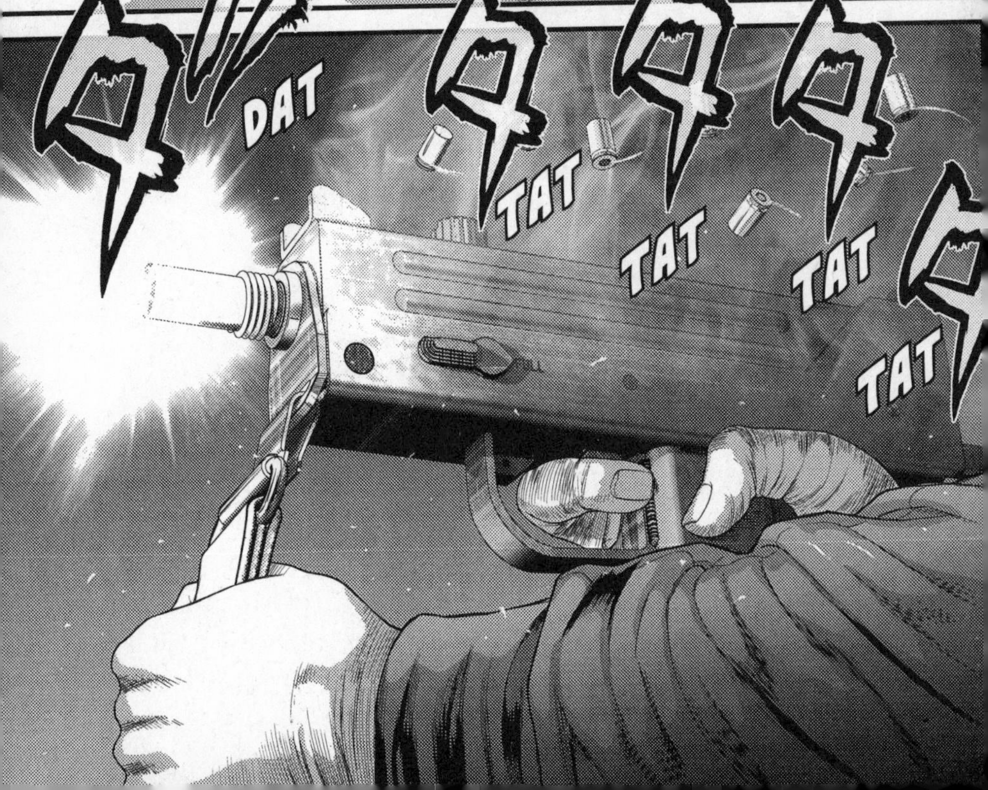
ダッ
DAT
タ
TAT
タ
TAT
タ
TAT
タ
TAT

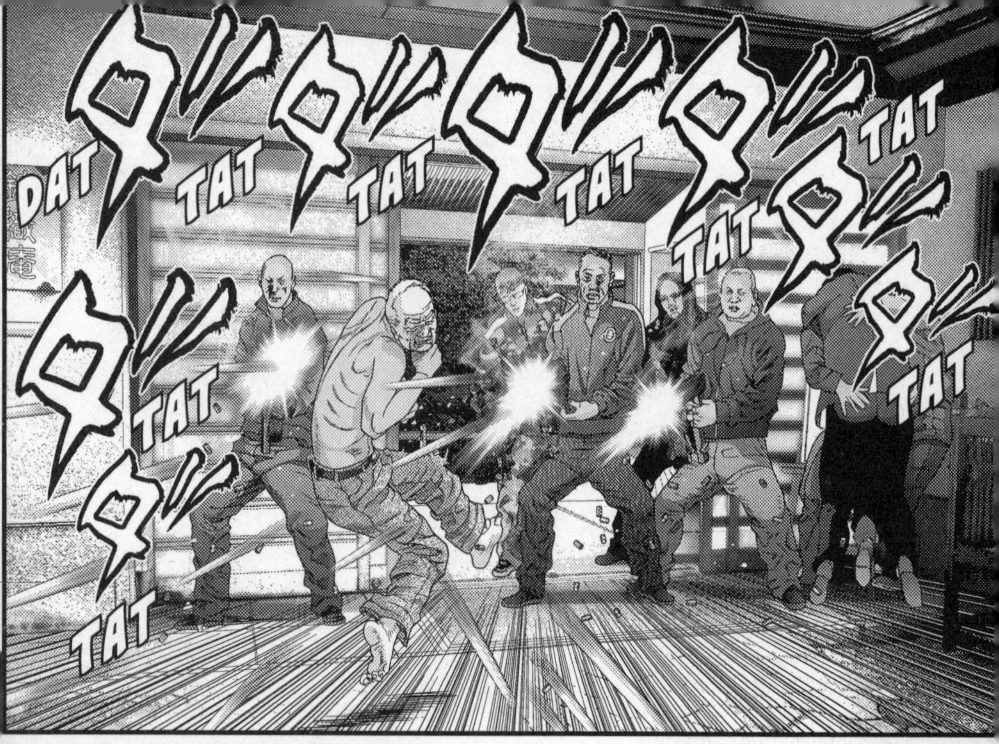
TAT
TAT
TAT
TAT
TAT
TAT
DAT
TAT
TAT
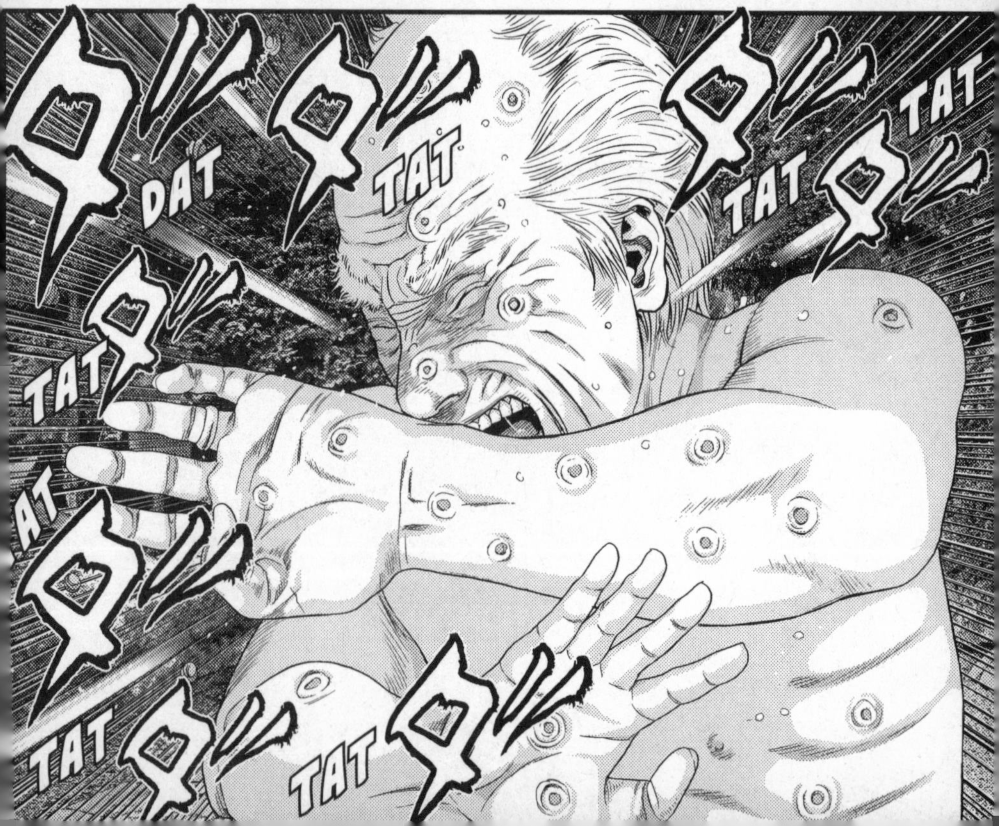
TAT
TAT
TAT
DAT
TAT
AT
TAT
TAT

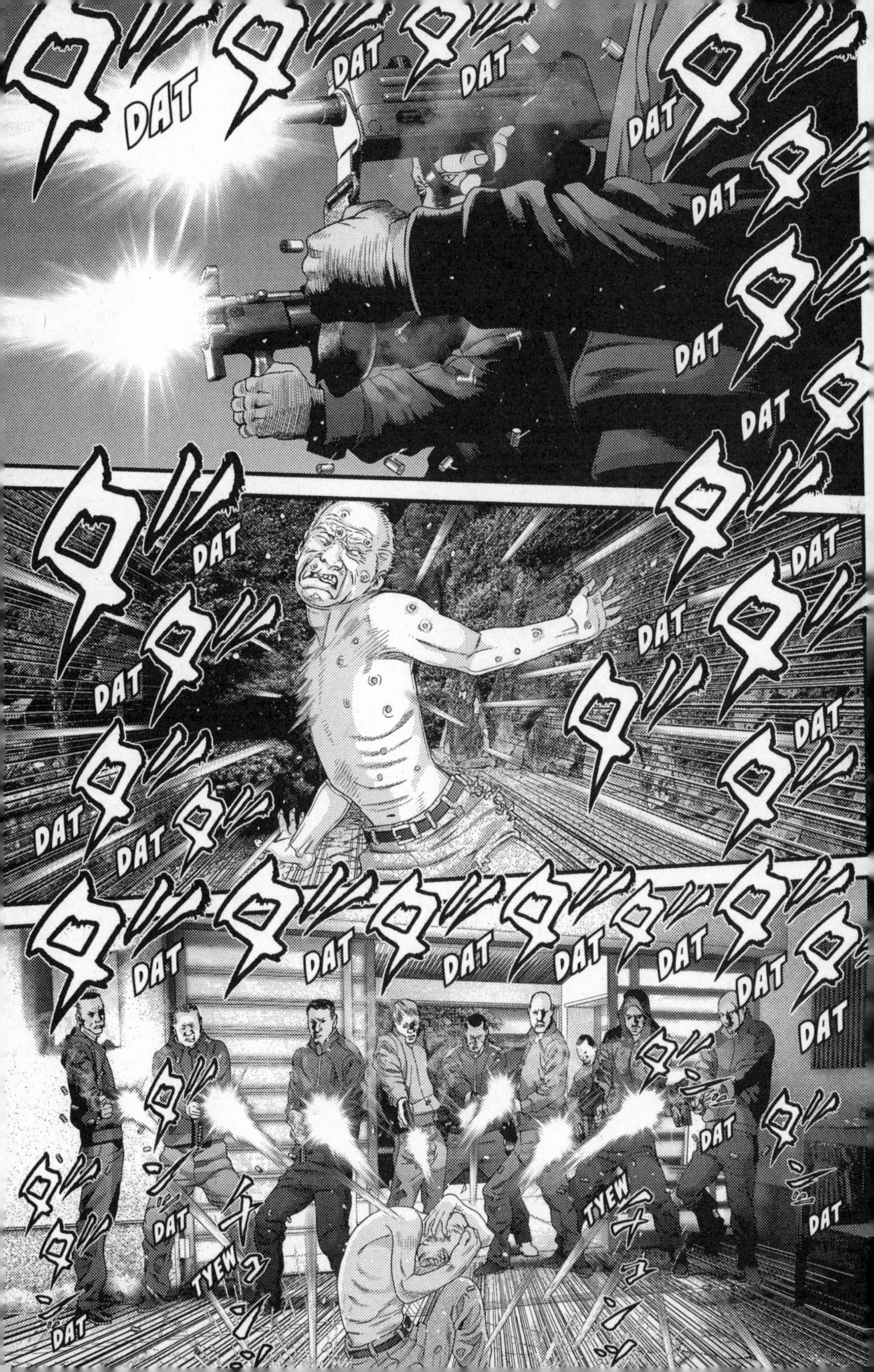
DAT
DAT
DAT
DAT
DAT
DAT
DAT
DAT
DAT
DAT
DAT
DAT
DAT
DAT
DAT
DAT
DAT
DAT
DAT
DAT
DAT
DAT
DAT
TYEW
DAT
DAT
TYEW
DAT

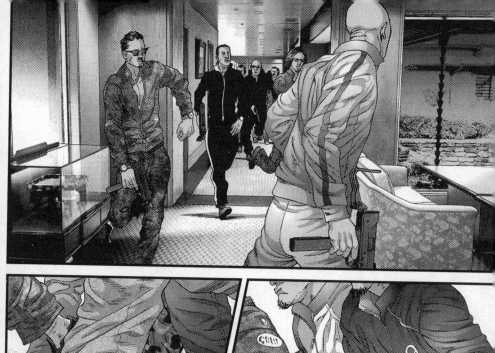

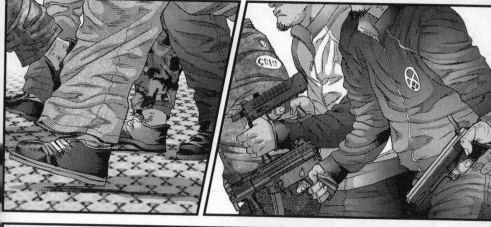

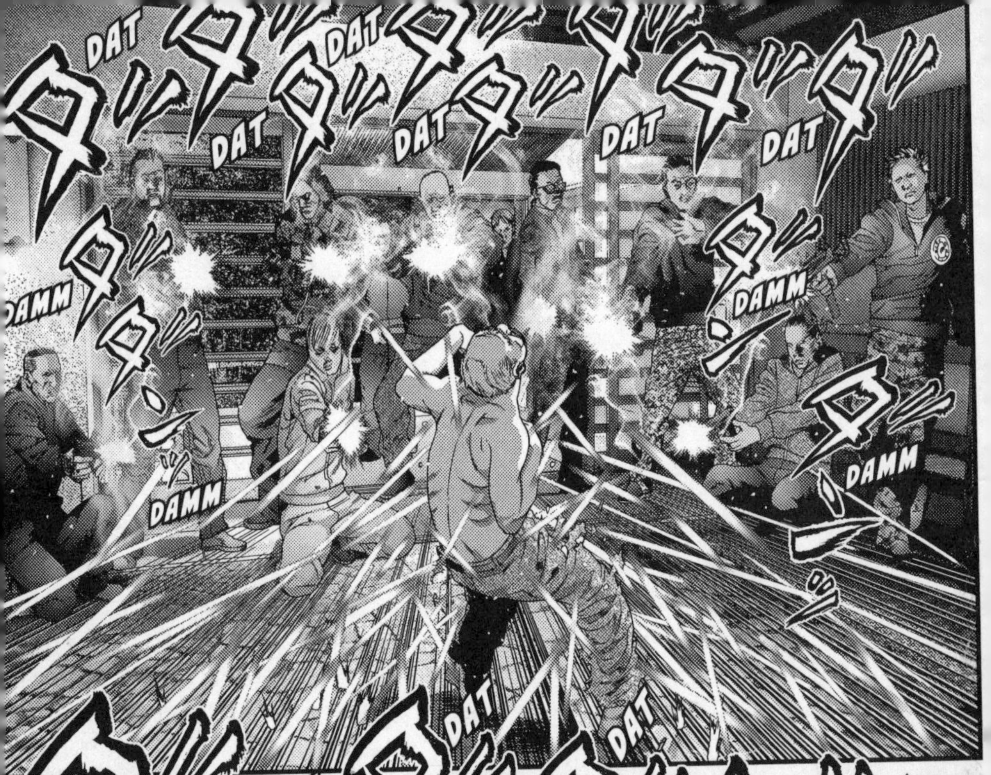
DAT
DAT
DAT
DAT
DAT
DAT
DAMM
DAMM
DAMM
DAMM
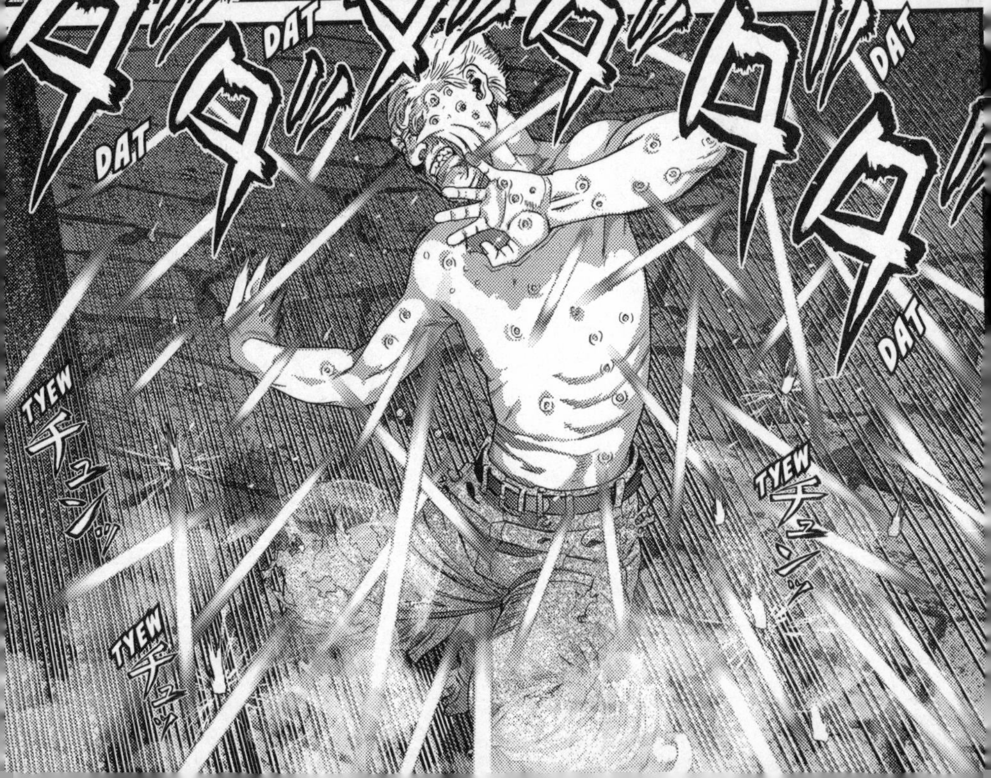
DAT
DAT
DAT
DAT
DAT
TYEW
チュンッ
TYEW
チュンッ
TYEW
チュンッ

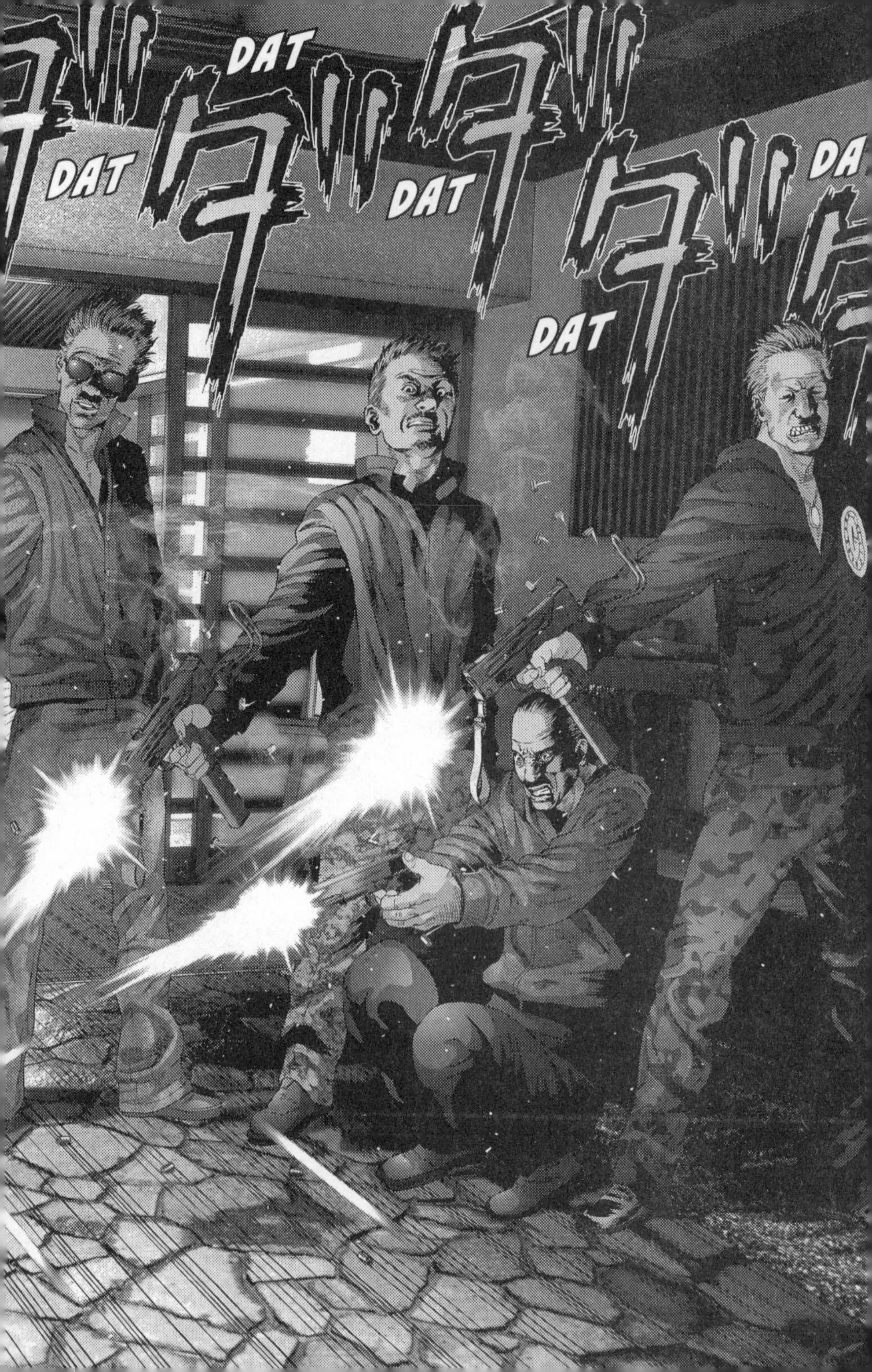
DA
DAT
DAT
DAT
DAT
DAT

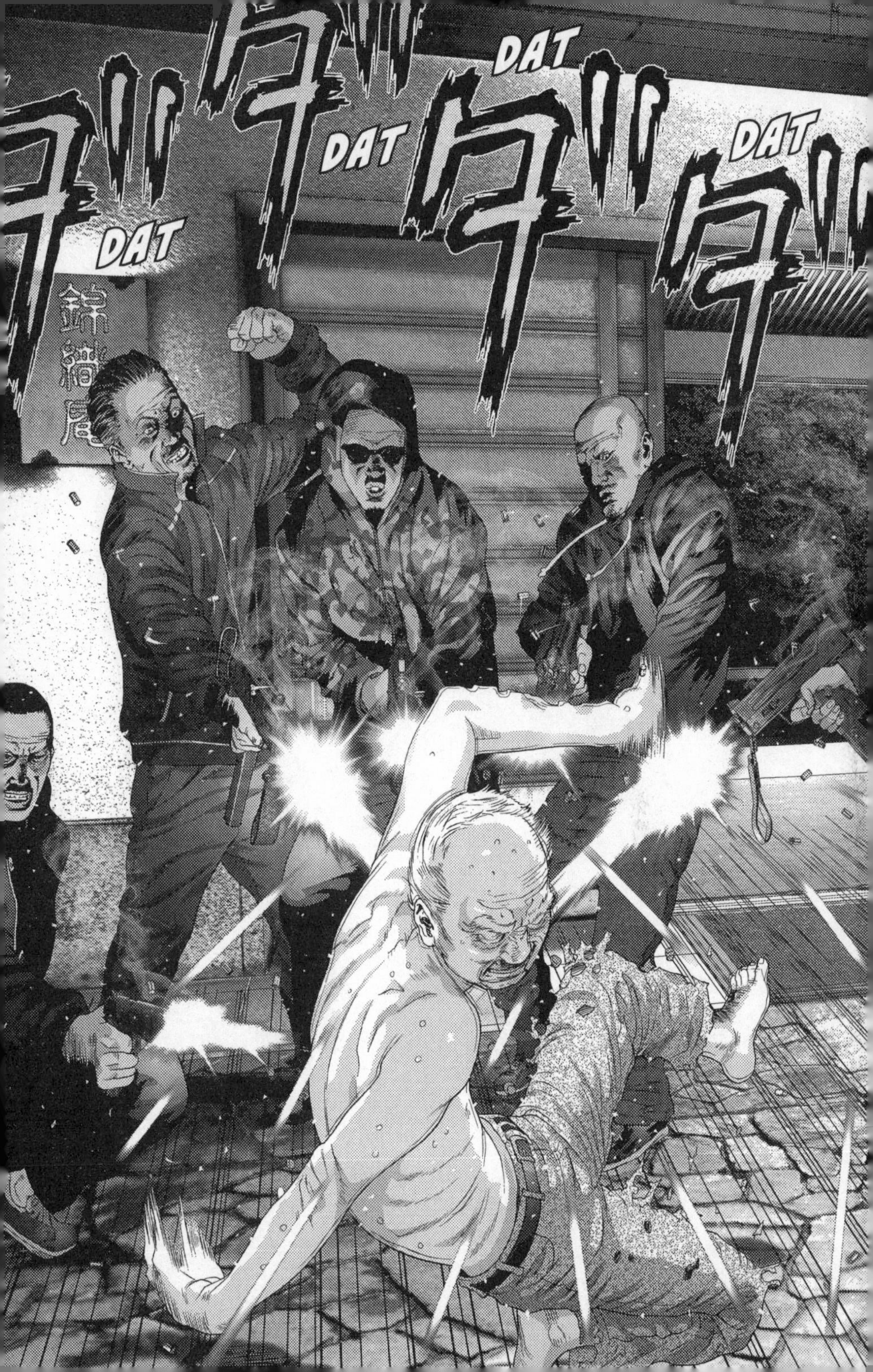
DAT
DAT
DAT
DAT

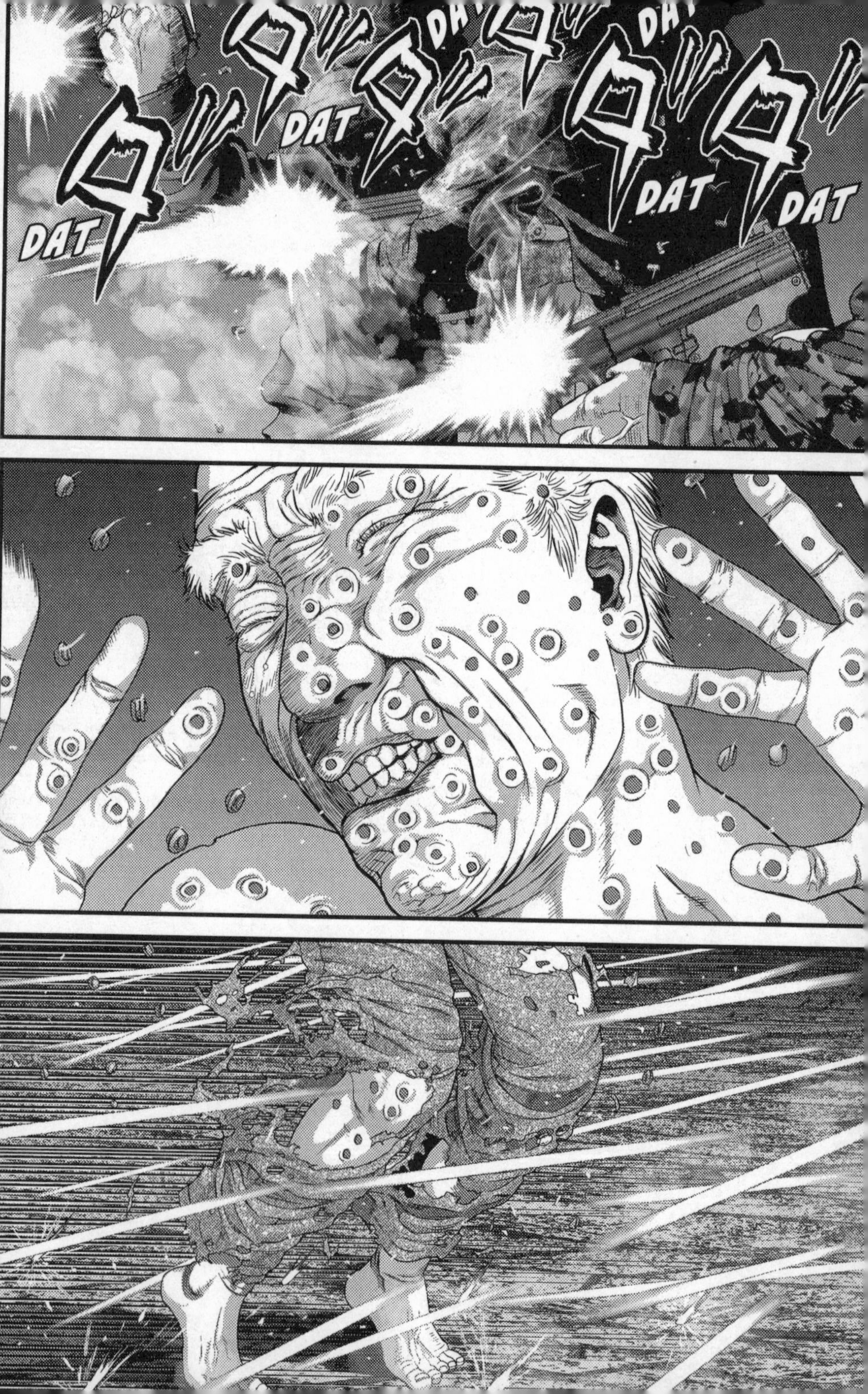
DAT
DA
DAT
DAT
DAT
DAT

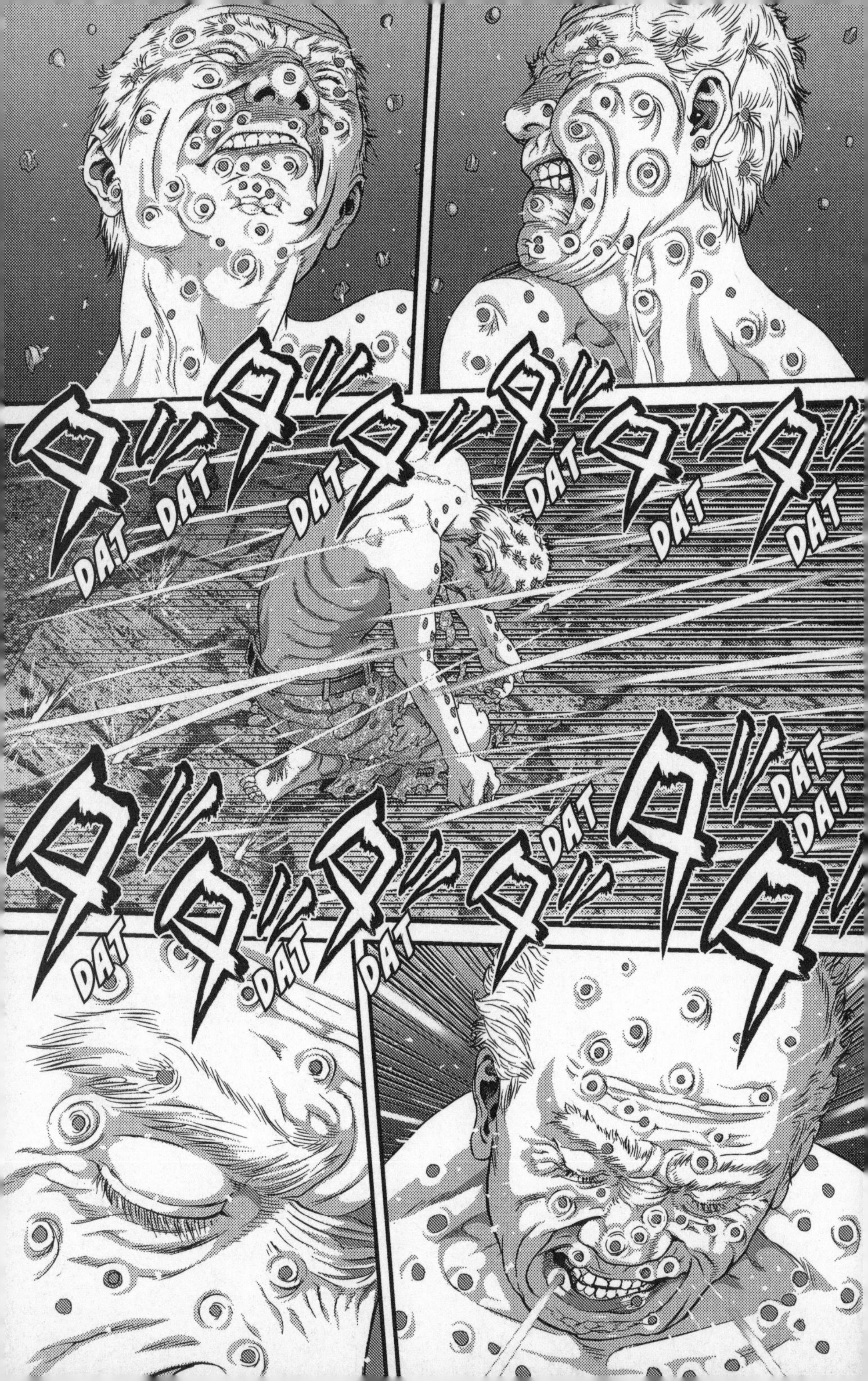
DAT
DAT
DAT
DAT
DAT
DAT
DAT
DAT
DAT
DAT
DAT
DAT

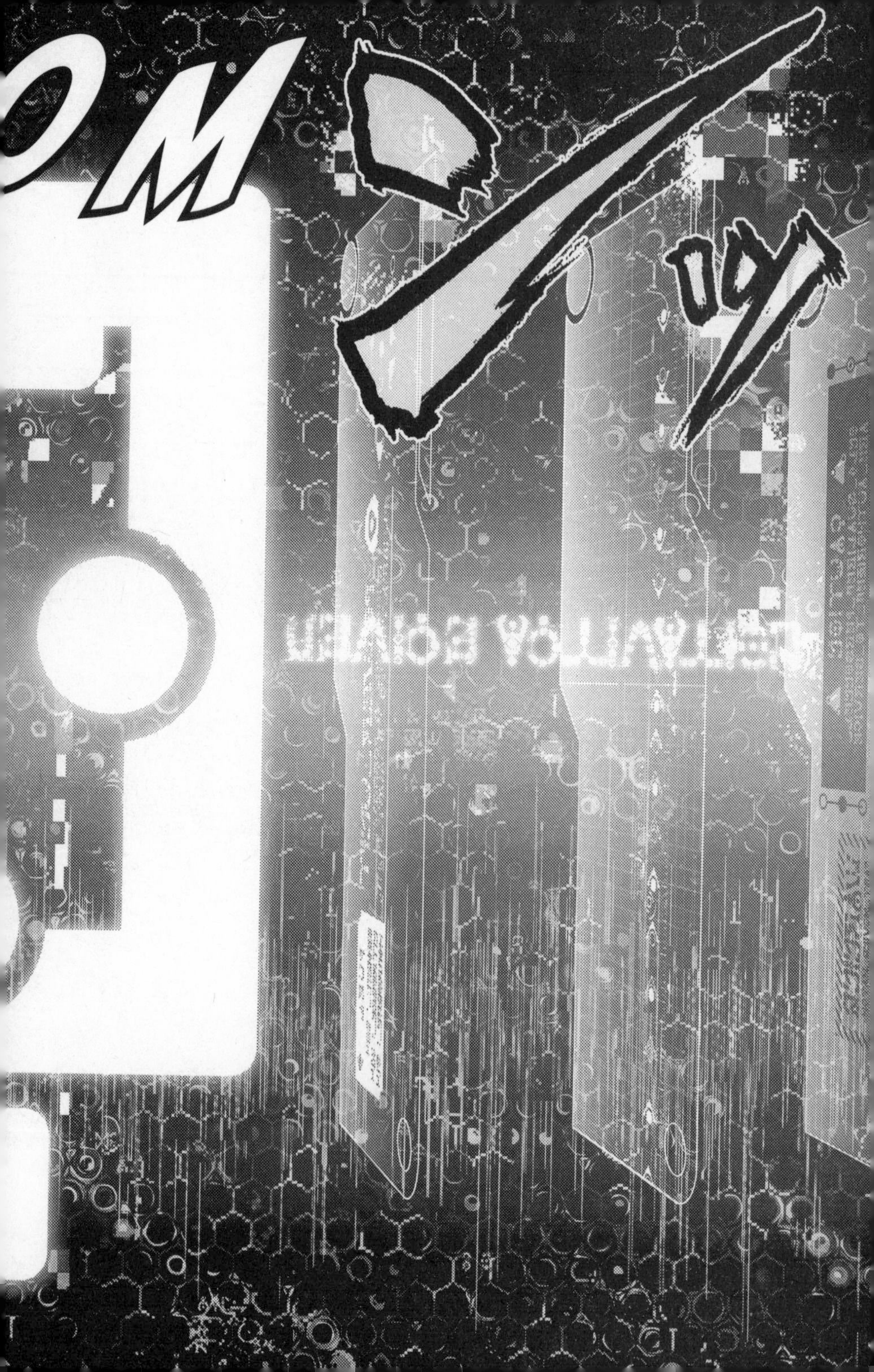
OM

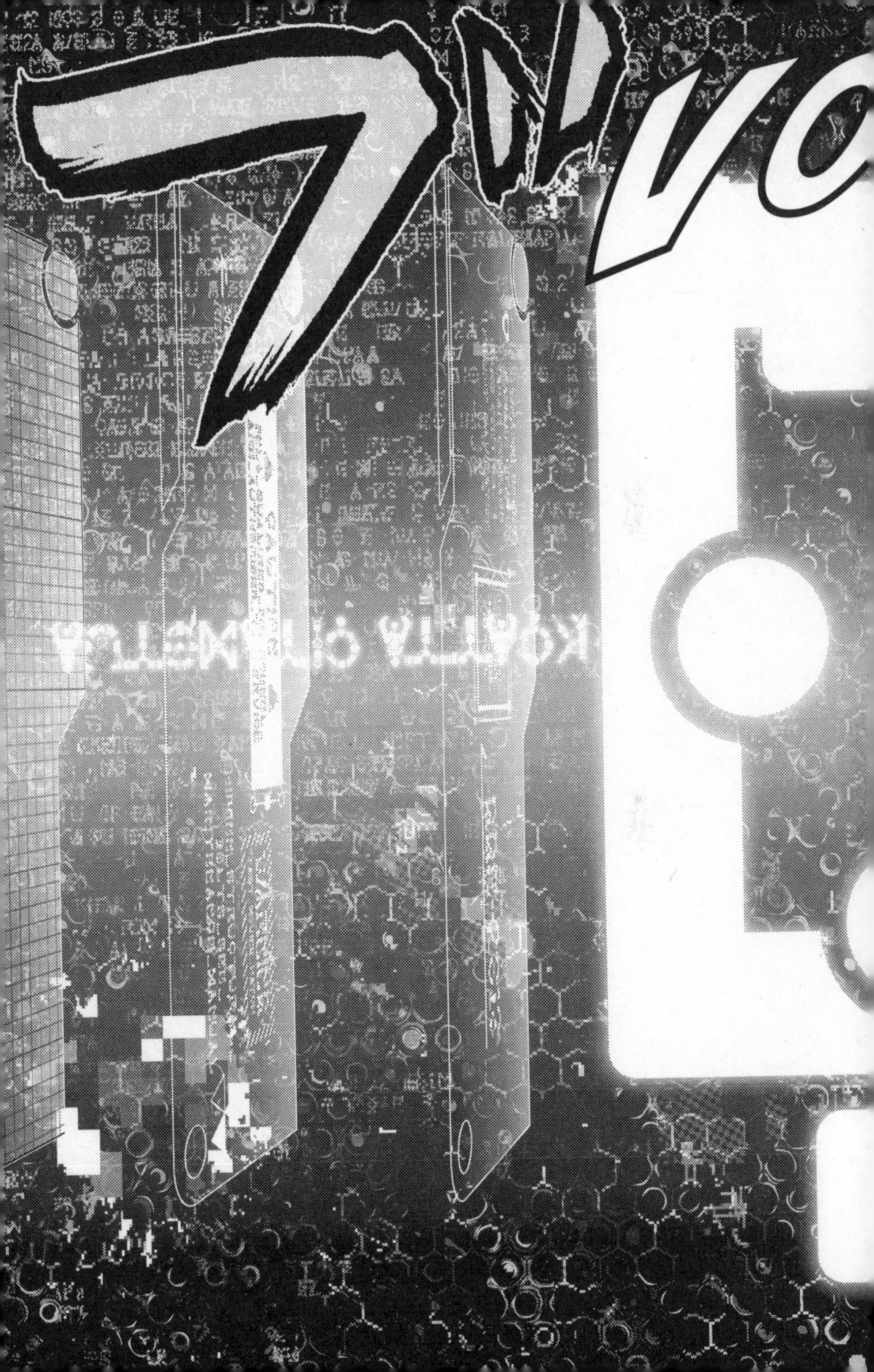

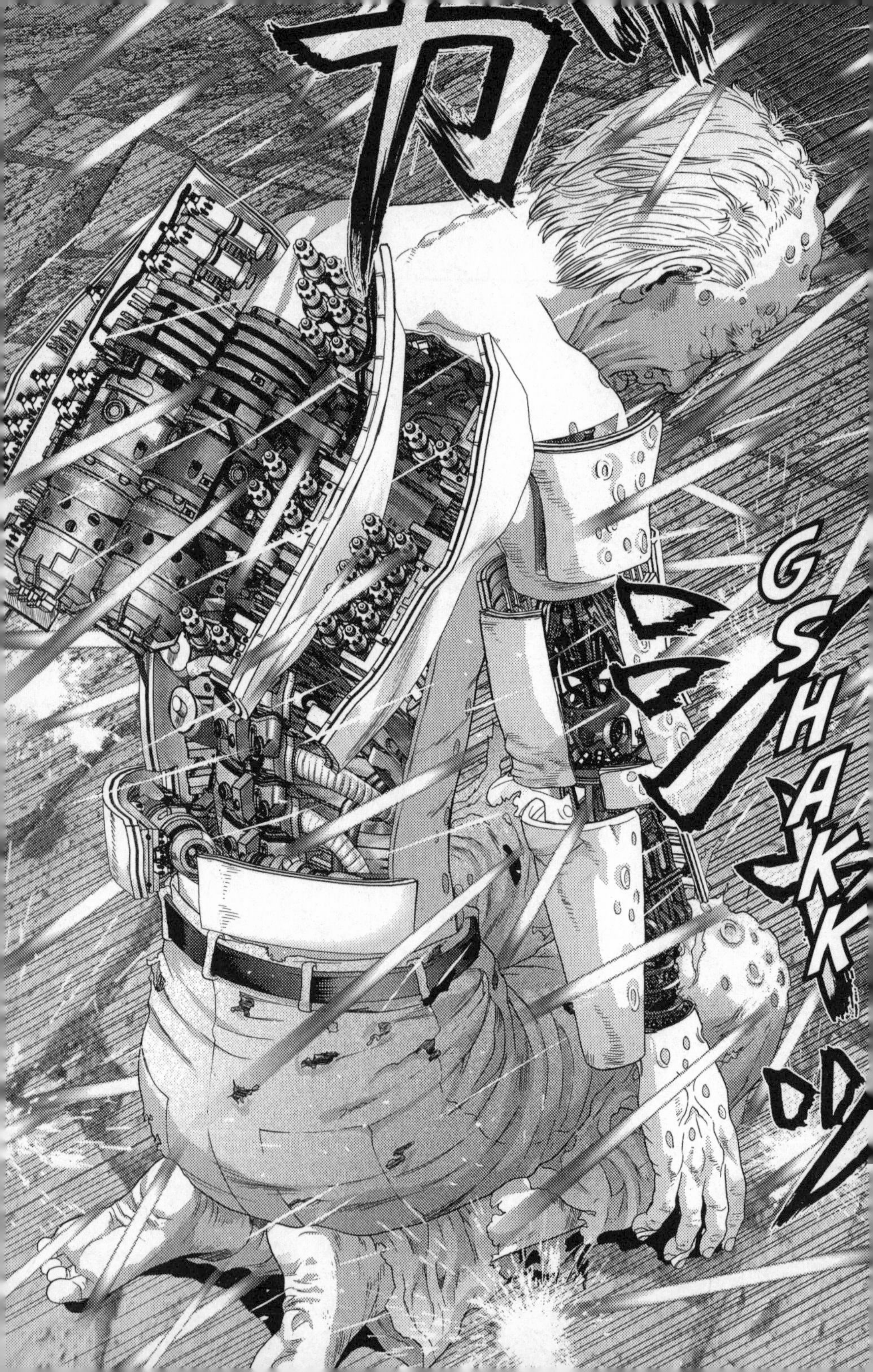
GSHAKK

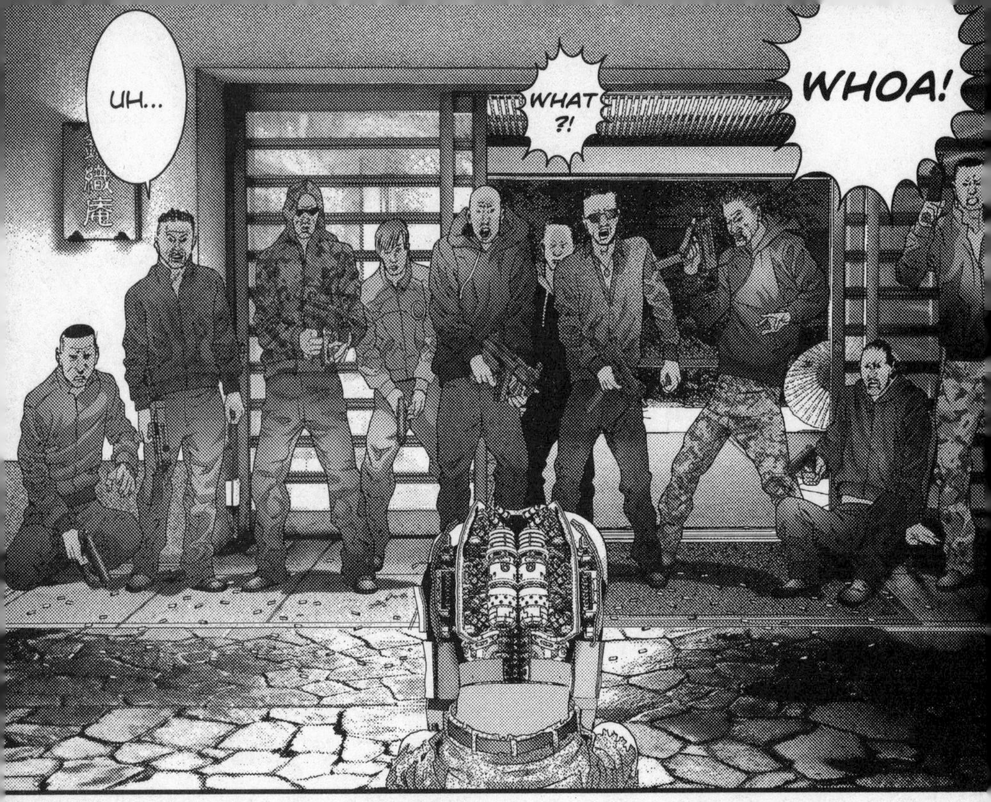
WHOA!
WHAT ?!
UH...
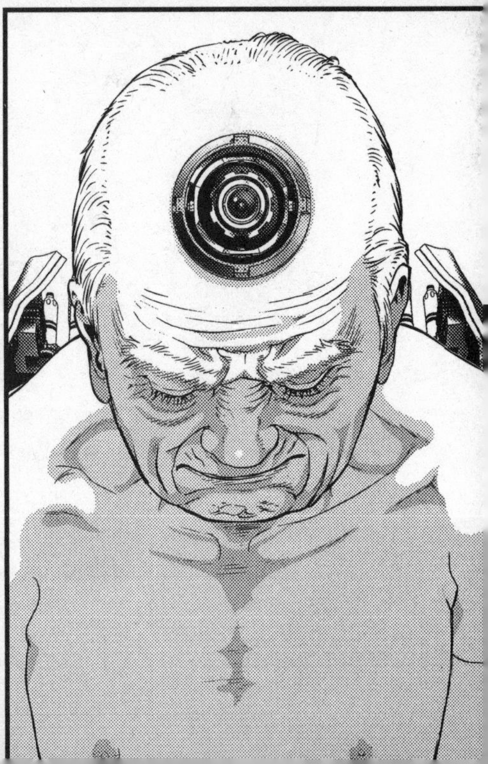
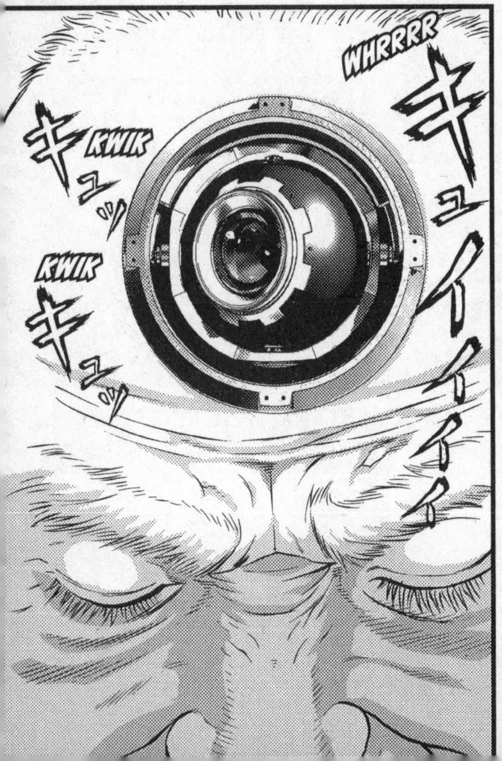
WHRRRR
キュイイイイイ
KWIK
キュッ
KWIK
キュッ

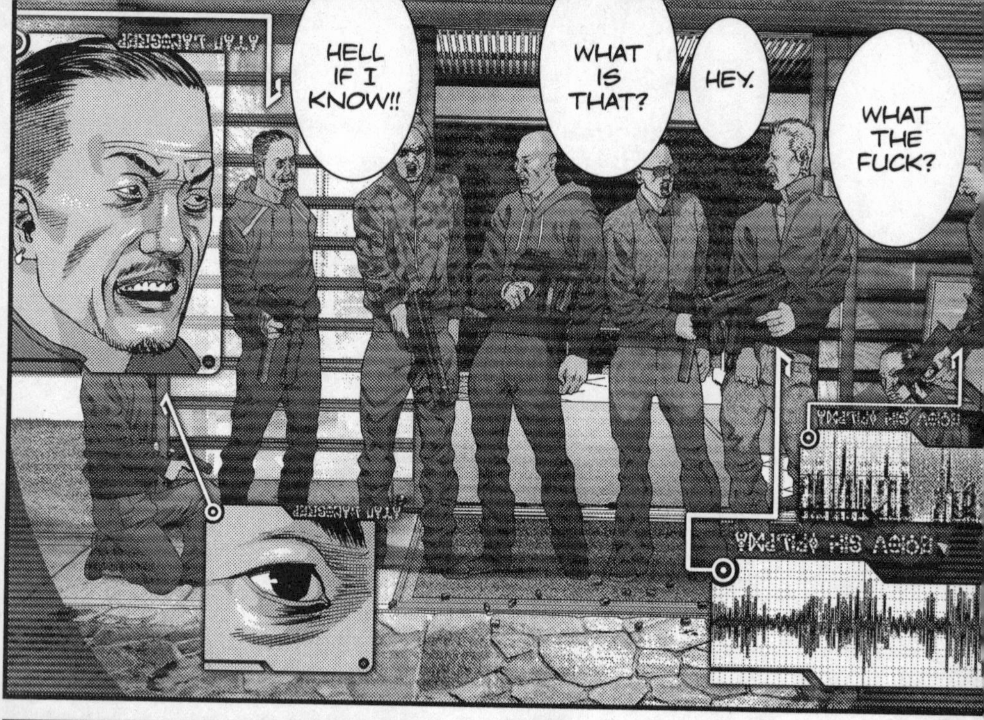
WHAT THE FUCK?
HEY.
WHAT IS THAT?
HELL IF I KNOW!!
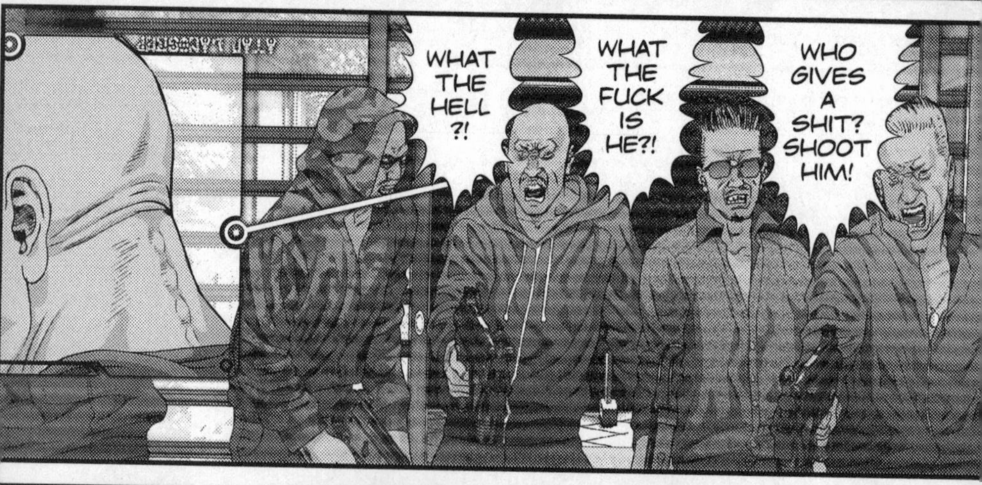
WHO GIVES A SHIT? SHOOT HIM!
WHAT THE FUCK IS HE?!
WHAT THE HELL ?!
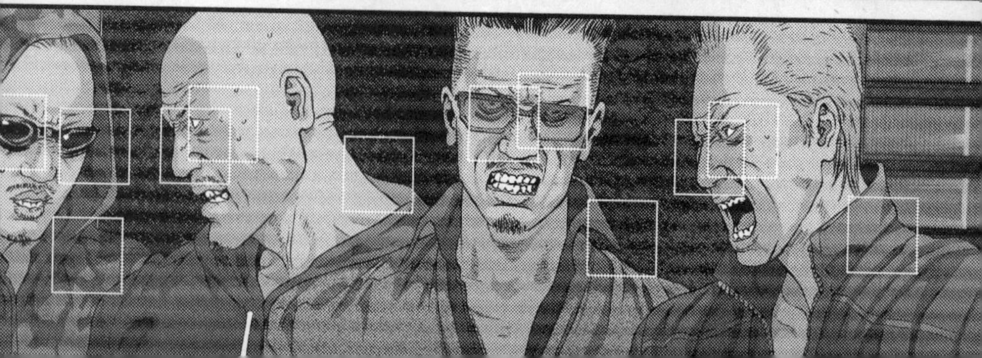

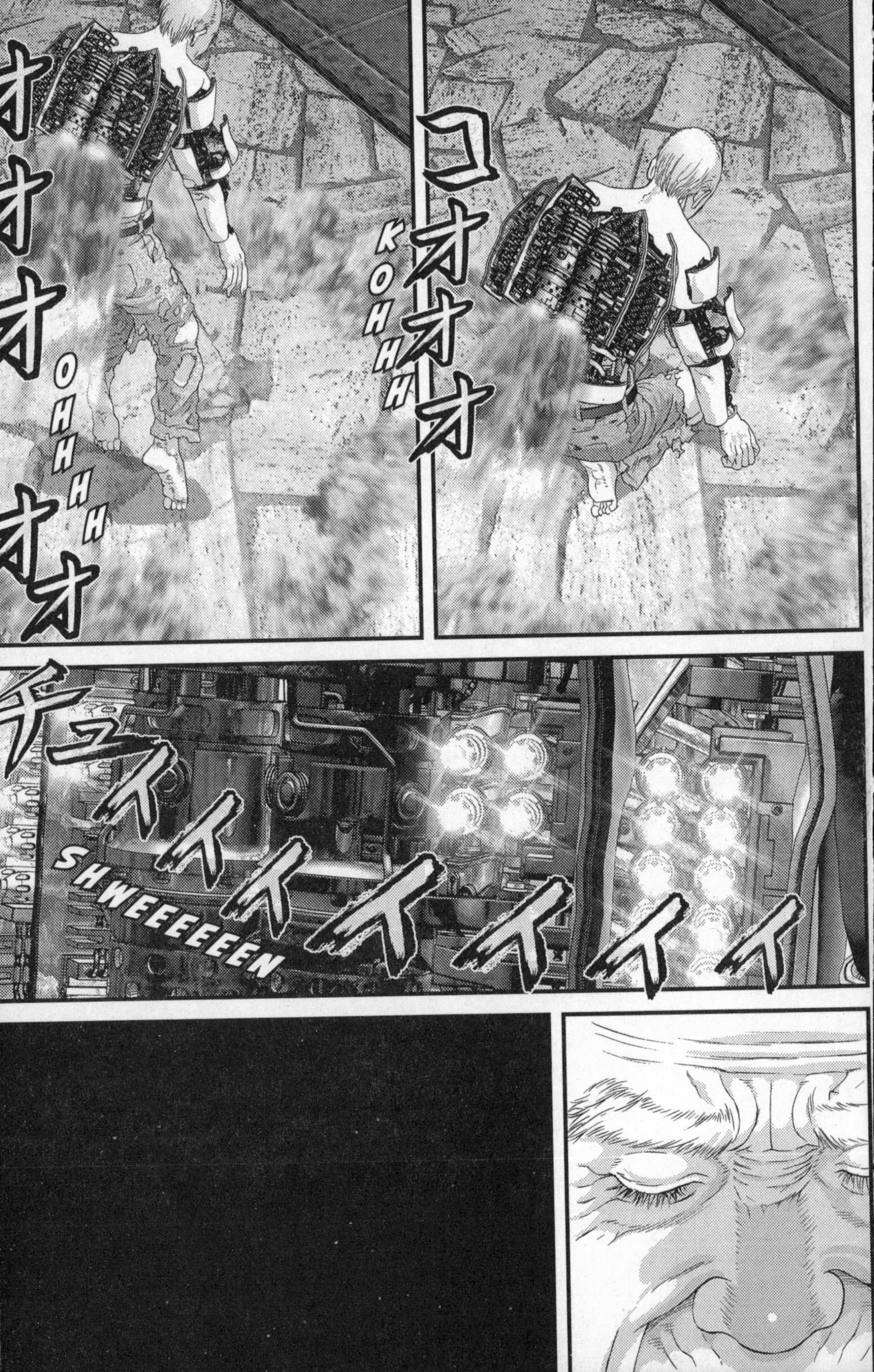
コオオオ
KOHHHH
オオオオ
OHHHHH
チュイイイイイ
SHWEEEEEEEN

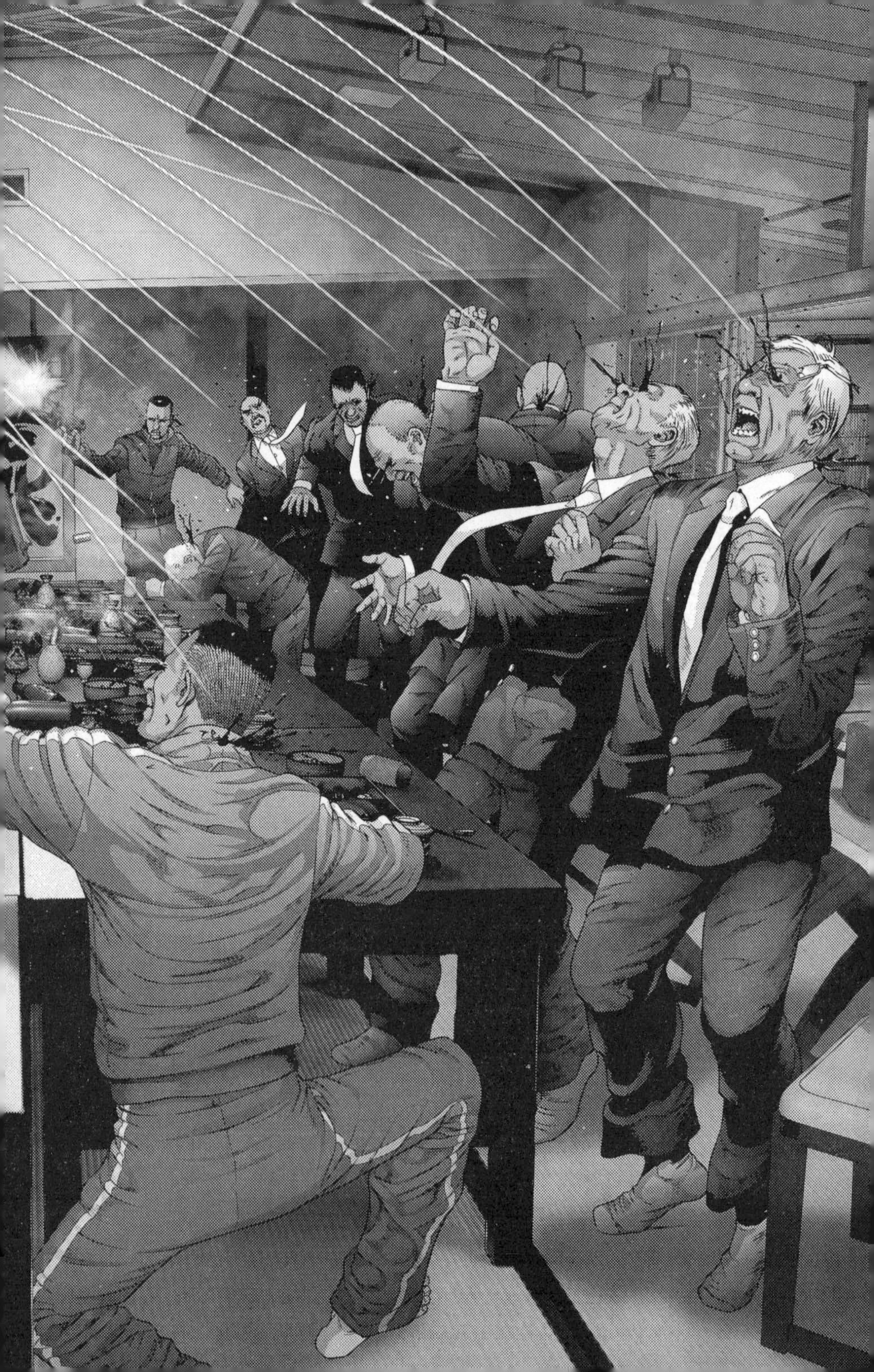

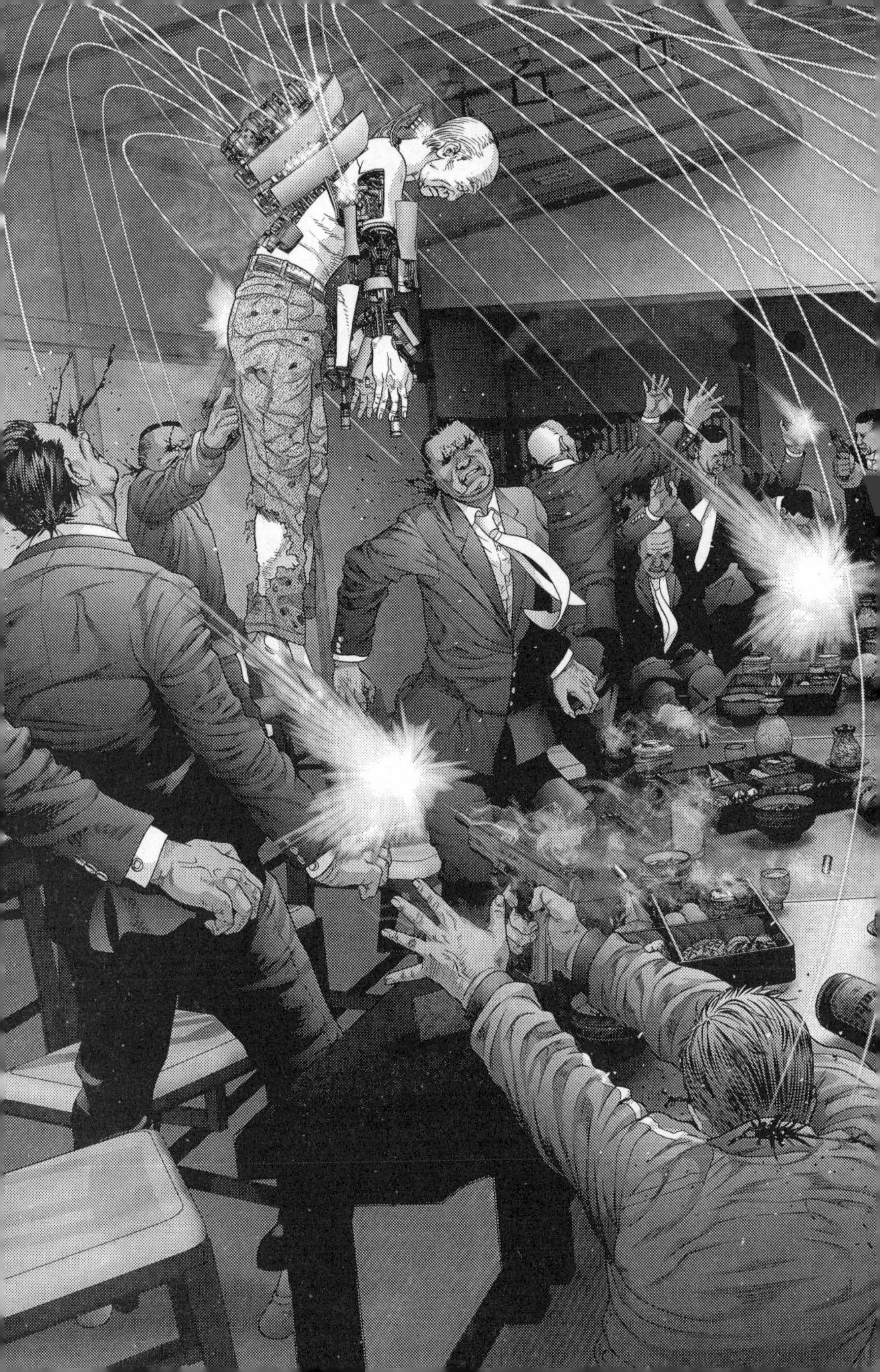

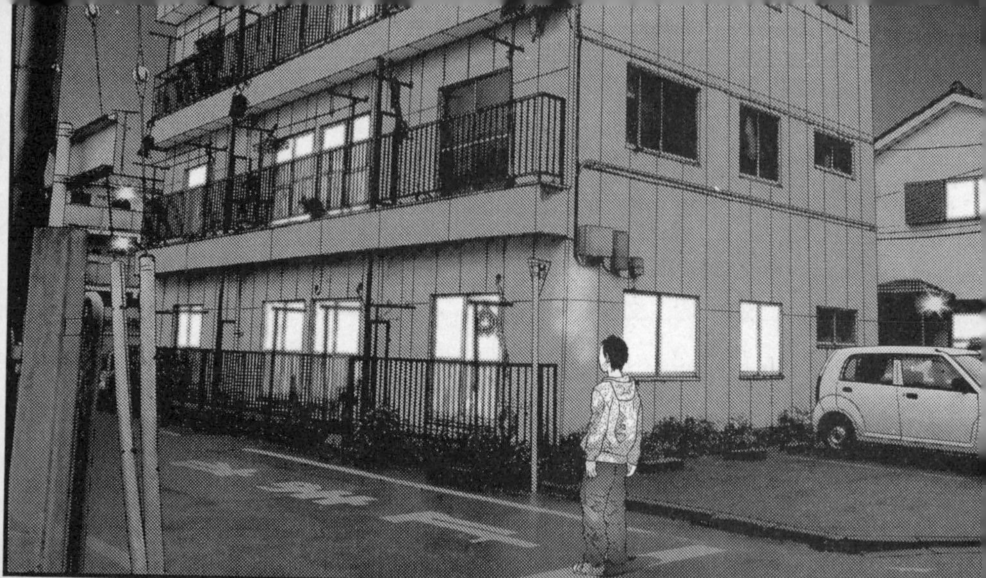
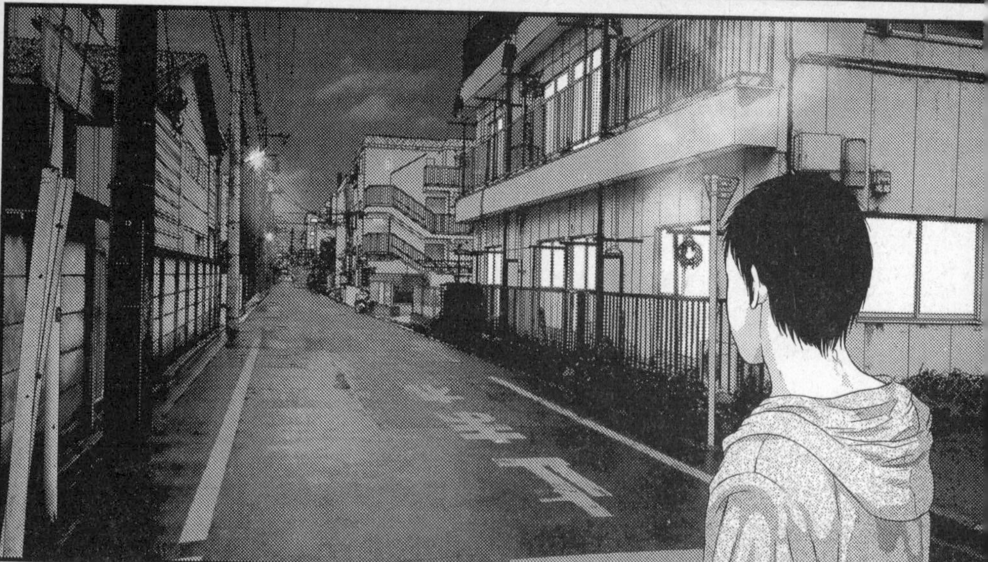
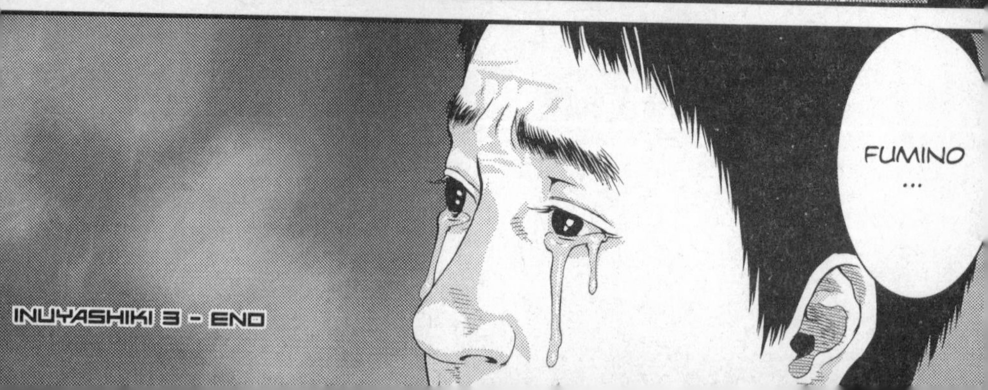
FUMINO
...
INUYASHIKI 3 - END

Translation Notes

Matsuko Deluxe, page 18

The TV appears to be showing a picture of celebrity figure Matsuko Deluxe, a very heavy-set crossdresser who is known for her sharp tongue and quick wit. Her ability to cut through BS and social niceties to get to “real talk” (a rarity in polite Japanese media) has made huge hits out of her shows like Ikari Shintô (New Anger Party), in which she and co-host Hiroiki Ariyoshi, a fellow acerbic critic, decide which suggestions from viewers about new social “rules” are fit to be implemented, and which should be mercilessly shredded.

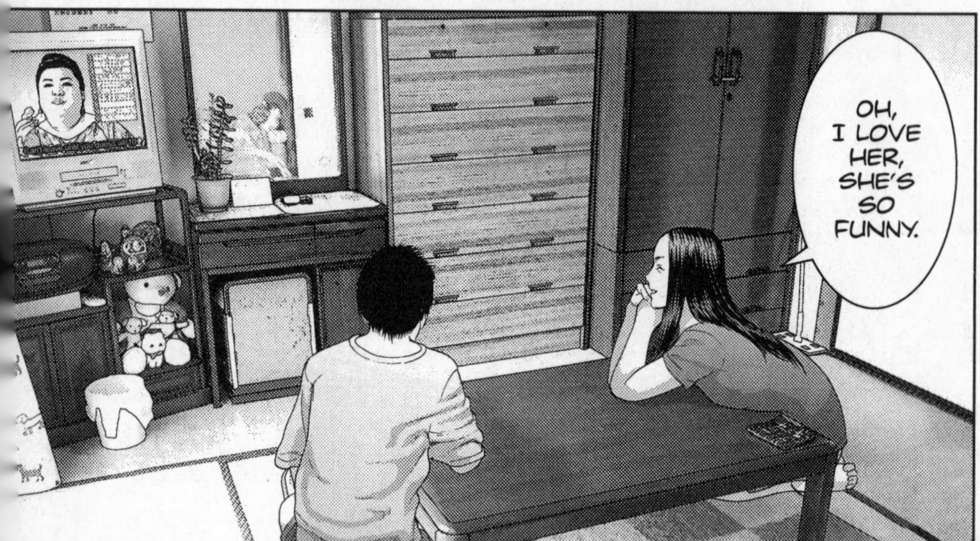
OH, I LOVE HER, SHE'S SO FUNNY.

Natsue Aran, page 23

parody of Namie Amuro, a megahit pop singer from Okinawa who first came into ominence in the mid-1990s and transitioned to more of an R&B style later in the 2000s. The -ballad compilation album being referenced in this advertisement is real, but titled *Ballada* ther than *Basket*.

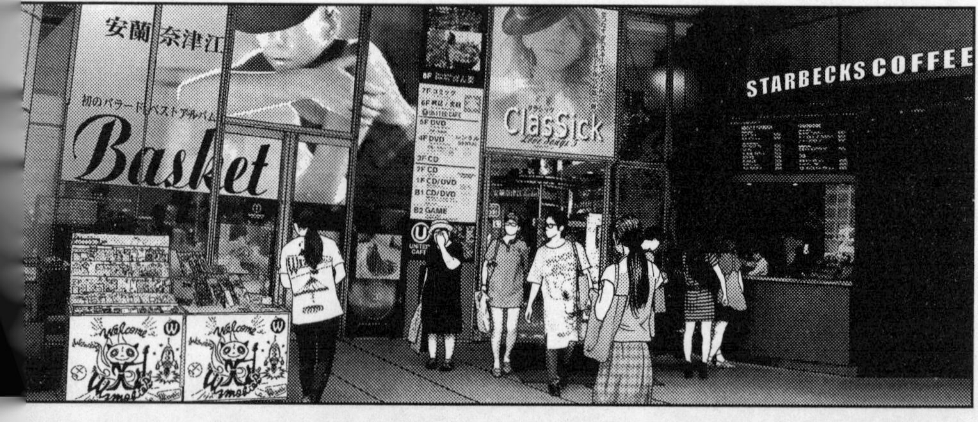
安蘭奈津江
Basket
ClasSick
STARBECKS COFFEE
5F DVD
4F DVD
3F CD
2F CD
1F CD/DVD
B1 CD/DVD
B2 GAME

Tsutaya, page 24-25

A major movie rental chain. While the rest of the developed world transitions to the convenience of streaming options like Netflix, the video rental business is still hanging on in Japan, though it too has declined significantly from its peak.

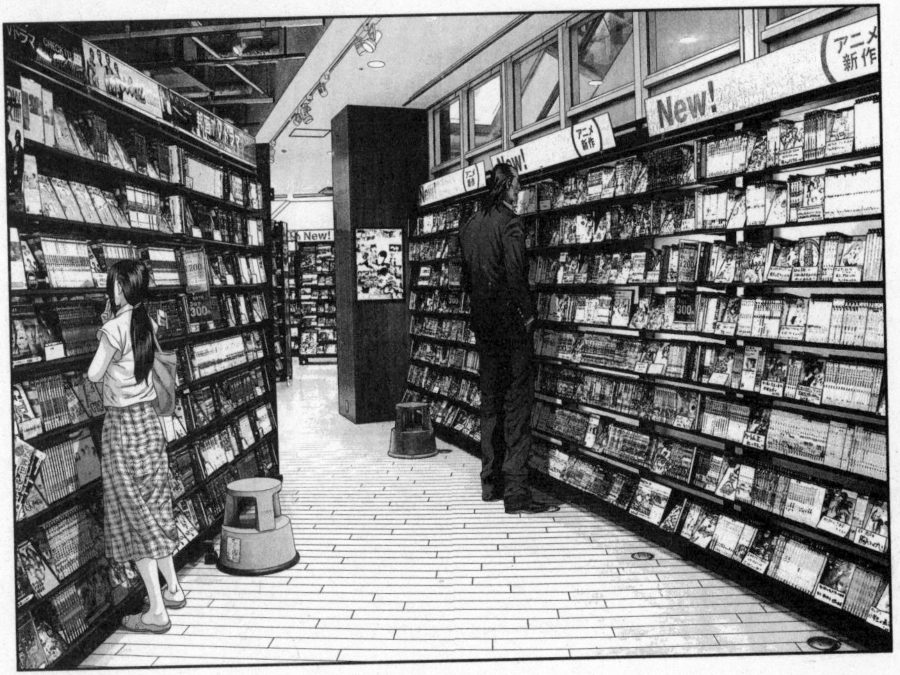
アニメ新作
New!
New!
アニメ新作
New!

Long-term fishing expedition, page 76

A long-term fishing expedition usually refers to deep-sea tuna fishing expeditions that typically last about one year. In the past, due to grueling conditions and the length of the expedition, the payout for the experience was running at about $100,000. Because of this above-average salary, this job was usually an option for those who racked up high debts fro loan sharks, but lately, due to cheaper labor costs, the pay has been almost halved, making i less appealing.

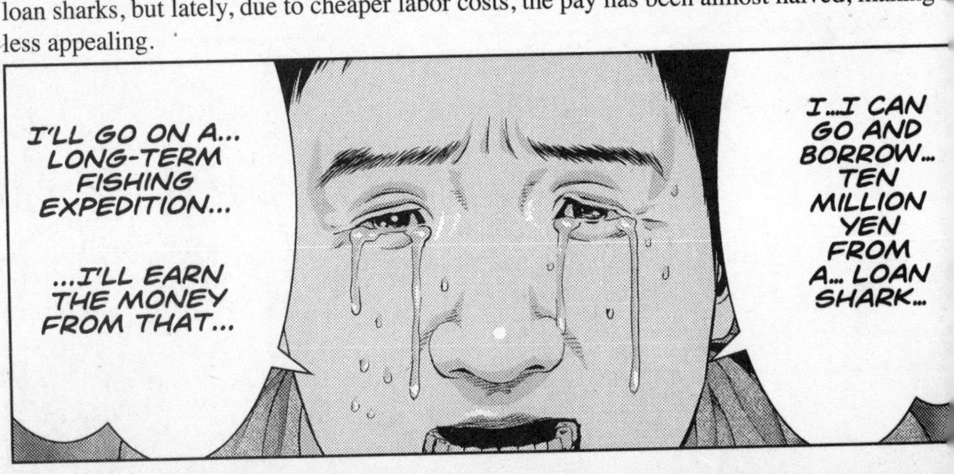
I...I CAN GO AND BORROW... TEN MILLION YEN FROM A... LOAN SHARK...
I'LL GO ON A... LONG-TERM FISHING EXPEDITION...
...I'LL EARN THE MONEY FROM THAT...

hRya

Inuyashiki volume 3 is a work of fiction. Names, characters, places, and incidents are the products of the author's imagination or are used fictitiously. Any resemblance to actual events, locales, or persons, living or dead, is entirely coincidental.

A Kodansha Comics Trade Paperback Original.

Published in the United States by Kodansha Comics, an imprint of Kodansha USA Publishing, LLC, New York.

Publication rights for this English edition arranged through Kodansha Ltd., Tokyo.

First published in Japan in 2015 by Kodansha Ltd., Tokyo, as *Inuyashiki* volume 3.

ISBN 978-1-63236-205-6

Printed in the United States of America.

www.kodanshacomics.com

9 8 7 6 5 4 3 2 1

Translation: Stephen Paul
Lettering: Scott Brown
Editing: Ajani Oloye
Kodansha Comics Edition Cover Design: Phil Balsman